German
vocabulary handbook

Joy Saunders

120th
anniversary
Berlitz

Berlitz Publishing Company, Inc.

Princeton   Mexico City   Dublin   Eschborn   Singapore

German Vocabulary Handbook

Published by Berlitz Publishing Company, Inc.
400 Alexander Park, Princeton, NJ 08540 USA
9-13 Grosvenor St., London W1X 9FB UK

Reprinted June 1998
Printed in Canada
ISBN 2-8315-6392-5

The Author:

Joy Saunders is an experienced teacher, schools inspector and educational consultant.

The Series Editor:

Christopher Wightwick was formerly principal inspector of Modern Languages for England and UK representative on the Council of Europe Modern Languages Project.

CONTENTS

How to use this Handbook

C   Subject Index   215

D   Vocabulary Index   246

How to use this Handbook

This Handbook is a carefully ordered work of reference covering all areas of German vocabulary and phrasing. It is based on the thesaurus structure of the Council of Europe's Threshold Level, and expanded to include other major topics, especially in the fields of business, information technology, and education. Unlike a dictionary, it brings together words and phrases in related groups. It also illustrates their usage with contextualized example sentences, often in dialogue form. This enables learners and users of the language to:

- refresh and expand their general knowledge of vocabulary;
- organize systematically revision for public examinations, using the word groups to test their knowledge from German to English and vice versa;
- extend their knowledge of authentically German ways of saying things by studying the example sentences;
- support their speaking and writing on a given topic, as the logical arrangement of the sections will often prompt new ideas as well as supplying the means of expressing them.

The structure of the Handbook

The Handbook is divided into three parts:

A Introduction

The introduction is a concise account of the ways in which German creates compound words and phrases in order to express more complex ideas. (For a more extensive treatment of this topic, see the Berlitz *German Grammar Handbook.*)

B Vocabulary topics

There are 27 major areas of experience. Vocabulary samples are divided into a number of sections, so that words and phrases are gathered together into closely related groups. Almost all sections contain example sentences showing the vocabulary in use. Wherever it makes sense to do so, these sentences are linked together to form short narratives or dialogues that help to fix them in the memory.

Lists of specific terms such as the names of countries or musical instruments. These would simply clutter up the main Vocabularies, but they are linked to them by clear cross-references. Each

Appendix is numbered according to the Vocabulary to which it most closely relates.

C The subject index

An alphabetical index of topics and themes enables you to locate quickly the area you are interested in.

Locating the right section

The Handbook can be approached in two main ways:

• If you are not sure which topic will be best suited to your needs, start with the *List of Contents* on page iii. This will give you a general picture of the areas covered. You can then browse through the sections until you find the one you want.

• Alternatively, if you have a specific topic in mind, look it up in the *Subject Index* at the end of the book. This will take you directly to the relevant vocabulary section or appendix. To help you find what you are looking for, topics are often listed more than once, under different headings. Within most sections, there are cross-references to other, related areas.

A
INTRODUCTION

Word formation in German

Conventions used in this Handbook

Word formation in German

One of the great strengths of German is its ability to combine or modify words so as to express new meanings. A knowledge of how this is done helps the learner to understand new language and to build up a wide vocabulary.

1 Nouns

1a Many nouns are formed from the stem of strong verbs, using:

(a) the stem of the infinitive: **der Fall** "fall", **der Schlaf** "sleep";

(b) dropping the **-n** of the infinitive: **die Bitte** "request", **die Hilfe** "help", **die Lüge** "lie";

(c) the simple past: **der Griff** "grip", **der Klang** "sound";

(d) another vowel, often **-u-**: **der Schuß** "shot", **der Fluß** "river".

Sometimes the connection is not very easy to see, but it is worth noting the link: **ankommen - die Ankunft** 'arrival', **ziehen - der Zug** 'train', 'draft', **gehen - der Gang** 'corridor', 'gait'.

1b Forming nouns with suffixes

Nouns are often formed by adding suffixes to other words. Note that suffixes may cause the preceding vowel to take an Umlaut, particularly if the suffix has a short **i** in it.

(i) Diminutives (with Umlaut):

-chen	**das Kätzchen**	kitten
-lein	**das Entlein**	duck

(ii) Other suffixes

-e	**die Größe** 'size', **die Ferne** 'distance'	
-ei	**die Metzgerei** 'butcher's shop', **die Angeberei** 'boasting'	
-er, ler	**der Bäcker** 'baker', **der Sportler** 'sportsman'	
-ie	**die Harmonie** 'harmony', **die Philosophie** 'philosophy'	
-in	*(female form)* **die Ärztin** 'woman doctor', **die Sportlerin** 'sportswoman'	

-nis	die **Finsternis** 'darkness', das **Verhältnis** 'relationship'
-schaft	die **Eigenschaft** 'quality', die **Gesellschaft** 'society'
-sal	das **Schicksal** 'fate'
-tum	der **Reichtum** 'wealth', das **Christentum** 'Christianity'
-ung	die **Hoffnung** 'hope', die **Begegnung** 'meeting'
-heit, -(ig)keit	die **Schönheit** 'beauty', die **Tapferkeit** 'bravery', die **Tätigkeit** 'activity'

1c Nouns formed with prefixes

Erz-	der **Erzbischof** 'archbishop'
Miß-	das **Mißverständnis** 'misunderstanding'
Un-	das **Unglück** 'misfortune'
Ur-	der **Urgroßvater** 'great-grandfather', der **Urwald** 'primeval forest'

1d Compound nouns

Many nouns are formed by combining two or more words. With very few exceptions, they take the gender of the final part.

noun + noun	das **Rathaus** 'town hall'
noun + **s** + noun	die **Landungsbrücke** 'landing stage'
noun + **(e)n** + noun	das **Studentenheim** 'student hostel'
adjective + noun	das **Schwarzbrot** 'black bread'
verb stem + noun	das **Schlafzimmer** 'bedroom'
particle + noun	die **Umwelt** 'environment', das **Abteil** 'compartment' (but der **Teil** 'part')

1e Adjectival nouns

Many adjectives and present and past participles can be used as nouns. They start with a capital letter, but otherwise behave just like adjectives:

der **Deutsche** 'the German', der **Verletzte** 'the injured man',
die **Fremde** 'the stranger' (female);
ein **Beamter** 'official' (male), eine **Auszubildende** 'trainee' (female);
Deutsche, 'Germans';
etwas **Interessantes** 'something interesting'.

1f Verbal nouns

The infinitive is often used as a noun, usually with a meaning similar to the English form in '-ing': das **Parken** 'parking', das **Schreiben** 'writing'.

INTRODUCTION

2   Genders & plurals

The gender and plural of a noun should be learned at the same time as the word.

The gender of nouns is shown in the word list by giving the definite article: **der** (masculine), **die** (feminine), or **das** (neuter). The article is given with most noun entries.

2a   There are four common plural endings: **-e**, **-er**, **-(e)n**, **-s**, but some words take no plural ending. Words with a stem vowel in **a**, **o**, or **u**, and no ending or **-e** in the plural, sometimes have an umlaut on the stem vowel. Those with a plural in **-er** always take an umlaut. The plural form is given with every noun entry.

2b   Other case endings are not shown, so remember to add:

(i) **-s** to the genitive singular of masculine and neuter nouns, e.g., **des Arms**;

(ii) **-(e)n** to the dative plural of all nouns not ending in **-n** or **-s**, e.g., **den Häusern**.

2c   Weak masculine nouns

A few nouns, usually ending in **-e** in the nominative singular, add **-n** or **-en** in every other case of the singular and in the plural: **der Junge, den Jungen, des Jungen, dem Jungen, die Jungen**, etc.

Note that:

(i) many of these nouns refer to people or animals;

(ii) a large number of foreign nouns ending in **-and, -ant, -arch, -at, -ent, -ist, -krat, -loge,** and **-nom** are also weak: **der Student, den Studenten; der Demokrat, den Demokraten;**

(iii) **Herr** takes **-n** in the singular and **-en** in the plural: **den Herrn, die Herren;**

(iv) a few masculine nouns ending in **-e** add **-n** in every case and also **-s** in the genitive singular: **der Gedanke, des Gedankens;** others include: **der Glaube, der Wille.** One neuter noun, **das Herz,** follows this pattern but has no ending in the accusative singular.

2d Useful short cuts

(i) many masculine nouns add **-e** or **-̈e: der Stuhl**, *pl* **Stühle**

(ii) many feminine nouns add **-(e)n: die Frau**, *pl* **Frauen**

(iii) many neuter nouns, mostly one-syllable, add **-̈er: das Haus**, *pl* **Häuser**.

(iv) masculine and neuter nouns ending in **-el**, **-en**, or **-er** add no ending (other than the dative plural **-n** after **-el** and **-er**), but may take an umlaut: **der Garten**, *pl* **Gärten**.

Some suffixes always take the same plural ending and are almost always linked to a particular gender:

Feminine:

(i) add **-en**: words ending in **-anz**, **-ei**, **-enz**, **-heit**, **-ie**, **-ik**, **-ion**, **-keit**, **-schaft**, **-tät**, **-ung**, **-ur**;

(ii) add **-nen**: words ending in **-in**.

Masculine:

(i) add no plural ending: words ending in **-ler**, **-ner**, **-er** (words formed from verbs);

(ii) add **-e**: words ending in **-an**, **-än**, **-är**, **-eur**, **-ich**, **-ig**, **-ling**, stressed **-or**;

(iii) add **-en**: words ending in **-and**, **-ant**, **-ent**, **-et**, **-graph**, **-ist**, **-krat**, **-logen**, **-nom**, unstressed **-or**;

(iv) words with the ending **-ismus** change it to **-ismen**.

Neuter:

(i) add no plural ending: words ending in **-chen**, **-lein**, **-sel**, **-tel**;

(ii) add **-̈er**: words ending in **-tum**;

(iii) add **-e**: words ending in **-at**, **-ett**, **-il**, **-ment**;

(iv) words with the ending **-um**: change **-um** to **-en** or **-a**.

3 Adjectives

3a Forming adjectives with suffixes

-bar '-able, -ible'

berechenbar predictable		**sichtbar**	visible

-en, -ern 'made of'

golden	golden	**hölzern**	wooden

-haft 'like a'

fehlerhaft	deficient	**vorteilhaft**	advantageous

-ig '-y'

staubig	dusty	**gütig**	kind

-isch '-ish',

identisch	identical	**kindisch**	childish

-lich '-ly, -able, -ish'

täglich	daily	**möglich**	possible
gelblich	yellowish		

-los '-less'

hilflos	helpless	**namenlos**	nameless
arbeitslos	unemployed		

-mäßig 'according to'

planmäßig	according to plan	**verhältnismäßig**	relatively

-sam 'having the quality of'

grausam	cruel	**ratsam**	advisable

-voll 'full'

sorgenvoll	anxious	**anspruchsvoll**	demanding
liebevoll	loving		

3b Adjectives formed with prefixes

The prefixes **un-** and **miß-** are used in the same way as with nouns:

unglücklich	unhappy	**mißverstanden**	misunderstood

3c Compound adjectives

Adjectives, like nouns, can be formed of two or more words. Only the last part adds endings:

blutarm	anaemic
wasserdicht	watertight
schwarzweiß	black and white

4 Formation of verbs

4a Verbs formed from nouns

-(e)n (often with Umlaut) **der Trost - trösten** 'comfort', **der Gruß - grüßen** 'greet'

-ieren (common with new verbs) **marschieren** 'march', **konkurrieren** 'compete'

4b Verb families formed with prefixes and verbal particles

German uses prefixes and particles to extend the meaning of basic verbs. For any one verb there may be an immense range of compound verbs, and of nouns and adjectives formed from these compounds. It is worth studying these word families to enlarge your vocabulary, e.g.:

er fällt	he falls	**er fällt hin**	he falls down
er überfällt	he attacks	**es verfällt**	it decays
der Fall	the fall		

Sometimes compounds develop figurative meanings or meanings only loosely linked with each other or the basic verb:

der Fall	case	**der Zufall**	chance
die Abfälle pl	rubbish	**es fällt ihm ein**	it occurs to him

These prefixes are always attached to the verb stem:

be-, ent-, er-, ge-, hinter-, miß-, ver-, zer-.

Particles are always placed in the final part of the sentence and are therefore often separated from the verb stem, e.g.:

particles from prepositions: **ab, an, aus, ein, mit, nach, vor, zu;**

compound particles: **hinunter, vorbei, durcheinander, davon;**

particles from other verbs, adverbs, adjectives or nouns: **stehen, spazieren, statt, fern.**

The following can be used either as prefixes or as particles:

durch-, über-, um-, unter-, wider-, wieder-.

5 English cognates

German is rich in words that have a similar origin to English, or have been borrowed from English or other languages. Understanding can often be greatly helped by referring to the English.

5a   Categories of words

(i) identical spelling and meaning: **die Hand, der Computer**

(ii) similar spelling, and identical meaning; note some common consonant changes:

offen	open	**helfen**	help
der Pfeffer	pepper	**das Pfund**	pound
lassen	let	**essen**	eat
sitzen	sit	**das Herz**	heart
gut	good	**tun**	do
dies	this	**der Bruder**	brother
machen	make	**suchen**	seek
kommen	to come	**der Keller**	cellar
leben	live	**lieben**	love
der Schnee	snow	**schlafen**	sleep
der Tag	day	**der Weg**	way

(iii) similar or identical spelling but a different meaning:

Lust haben	to want (to do something), but not in the sexual sense
aktuell	present, modern
das Gymnasium	Secondary School (US) or High School

(iv) loan translations from English or Latin stems:

der Buchmacher	bookmaker
das Mitleid	compassion
der Einfluß	influence

5b   Sometimes a word derived from an English or common international source exists alongside a word of German origin: **der Hörfunk, das Radio; der Fernsprecher, das Telefon; der Mittelpunkt, das Zentrum.** With recent introductions, particularly those relating to technology, the English/international form is usually preferred, especially in speech.

Conventions used in this Handbook

(i) Noun plurals

The plural of almost every word is indicated in brackets (except for adjectival nouns, where the plural depends on the presence of the article:

Entry	plural
Arm(e)	**Arme**
Hand(⁻e)	**Hände**
Haus(⁻er)	**Häuser**
Garage(n)	**Garagen**
Auto(s)	**Autos**
Wagen(-)	**Wagen**
Garten(⁻)	**Gärten**
Fluß (⁻sse)	**Flüsse**
Zentrum (-en)	**Zentren**
Praktikum (-a)	**Praktika**
Ministerium (-ien)	**Ministerien**

For some nouns the plural is shown in full in the bracket:

Firma (Firmen)

(ii) Feminine forms

Feminine forms ending in **-in** are not given in full. They are freely formed, and where they are in normal use they are indicated after the masculine form by **[-in]**:
der Lehrer(-) [-in] = **der Lehrer**, *pl* **die Lehrer** male teacher, **die Lehrerin**, *pl* **die Lehrerinnen** female teacher.
Masculine nouns ending in **-e** drop this before adding **-in**:
der Zeuge, die Zeugin.

(iii) Cases

The cases taken by a preposition or verb are only indicated where there might be confusion.

(iv) Verbs

Verbs are given in the first or occasionally the third person in the word lists, so that the particle is always placed after the stem.
To avoid confusion, the particle is marked with an asterisk, e.g., **ich komme an*** 'I arrive'. To check the verb in a dictionary you need to find the infinitive, which will start with the particle, e.g., **ankommen**.

Where a verb is shown in the third person singular and there is a vowel change, the infinitive, without the particle, is shown in brackets, e.g., **es gibt** *(geben).*

Abbreviations

acc	accusative
adj	adjective
adj/n	adjectival noun (plurals in **-e** or **-en**)
adv	adverb
conj	conjunction
dat	dative
etw.	**etwas**
fam	familiar form
gen	genitive
inf	infinitive
invar	invariable
jdn.	**jemanden** (accusative)
jdm.	**jemandem** (dative)
n	noun
pl	plural
pol	polite form
pop	popular form
sing	singular
sth	something
wk	weak masculine noun

Symbols

-	no ending: **Wagen(-)** = plural **Wagen**
( )	plural ending or a part of a word which is optional: **ich (ver)traue**
( )	the infinitive, where the third person singular entry shows a vowel change: **es gibt** *(geben)*
*	the particle is separable: **ich komme an***, infinitive **ankommen**
/	a) alternatives in adjective endings: **dieser/e/es = dieser, diese, dieses**, **mein/e/- = mein, meine, mein**
	b) alternative word: **erst als/wenn** = **erst als** or **erst wenn**
,	an alternative translation
➤	a cross-reference to a vocabulary topic or chapter

B
VOCABULARY TOPICS

1 Functional words

Personal pronouns

	Nom	Acc	Gen	Dat
I	ich	mich	meiner	mir
you (fam)	du	dich	deiner	dir
he, it	er	ihn	seiner	ihm
she, it	sie	sie	ihrer	ihr
it	es	es	seiner	ihm
we	wir	uns	unser	uns
you (fam pl)	ihr	euch	euer	euch
you (pol)	Sie	Sie	Ihrer	Ihnen
they	sie	sie	ihrer	ihnen
one	man	einen	seiner	einem

Reflexive pronouns

	Acc	Dat
myself	mich	mir
yourself (fam)	dich	dir
himself	sich	sich
herself	sich	sich
itself	sich	sich
ourselves	uns	uns
yourselves (fam)	euch	euch
yourself/ves (pol)	sich	sich
themselves	sich	sich
oneself	sich	sich
each other	sich	sich

Interrogative pronouns

	Nom	Acc	Gen	Dat
who?	wer	wen	wessen	wem
which one?	welcher/e/es			
what?	was			

what sort of? *(sing)* **was für einer/e/es?**

what sort of? *(pl)* **was für welche?**

Relative pronouns who, that, which

	Masc	Fem	Neut	Plur
Nom	der	die	das	die
Acc	den	die	das	die
Gen	dessen	der	dessen	deren
Dat	dem	der	dem	denen

what you say is true **das, was du sagst, stimmt**

Demonstrative pronouns

Demonstrative adjective/pronouns *this, this one, that one* :

	Masc	Fem	Neut	Plur
Nom	dieser	diese	dieses	diese
Acc	diesen	diese	dieses	diese
Gen	dieses	dieser	dieses	dieser
Dat	diesem	dieser	diesem	diesen

this **dies** *(invar)*

this **dieser/e/es**

this **der/die/das** *(stressed)*

this one **der/die/das** *(declined like relative pronoun)*

this one **dieser/e/es**

these (ones) **diese**

that **das (hier)** *(invar)*

that **jener/e/es**

those (ones) **jene**

that one **der/die/das, derjenige/diejenige/dasjenige** *(both parts decline)*

the one, which **der(jenige), der**

the same one **derselbe, dieselbe, dasselbe** *(both parts decline)*

the red one **der/die/das Rote**

such a one   **solch/so einer**
ones like that   **solche**

Indefinite pronouns

anybody   **irgendeiner**
both (people)   **beide**
both (things)   **beides**
each one   **jeder/e/es**
everyone   **jeder/e/es**
everything   **alles**
everyone   **alle**
one   **einer/e/es**
one like that   **so einer**
one which   **einer, der**
none, not any   **keiner/e/es**
nobody   **keiner**
no-one   **niemand, keiner/e/es**
not a single one   **kein einziger**
nothing   **nichts** *(invar)*
a lot   **vieles**
quite a lot   **manches**
not much   **weniges**
someone/body   **jemand**
something   **etwas** *(invar)*
something else   **etwas anderes**
something good   **etwas Gutes**
some things   **einiges**

Stressed pronouns

it's me   **ich bin es, ich bin's**
it's us   **wir sind es, wir sind's, etc.**
it's he who   **er ist derjenige, der**
it's she who   **sie ist diejenige, die, etc.**

*Possessive pronouns (declined like **dieser**)*

mine   **meiner/e/es**
yours *(fam)*   **deiner/e/es**
his   **seiner/e/es**
hers   **ihrer/e/es**
its   **seiner/e/es**
ours   **unserer/e/es**
yours *(fam)*   **eu(e)rer/e/es**
yours *(pol)*   **Ihrer/e/es**
theirs   **ihrer/e/es**
ones   **seiner/e/es**

this is mine   **das ist meiner/meine/mein(e)s**
mine is better   **meiner/meine/meines ist besser**

*Possessive adjectives (declined like **ein**)*

my   **mein/e/-**
your *fam*   **dein/e/-**
his/its   **sein/e/-**
her/its   **ihr/e**
its   **sein/e/-**
our   **unser/e/-**
your *fam*   **euer/eu(e)re/euer**
your *pol*   **Ihr/e/-**
their   **ihr/e/-**
one's   **sein/e/-**

Determiners

DEFINITE ARTICLE *the*

	Masc	Fem	Neut	Plur
Nom	der	die	das	die
Acc	den	die	das	die
Gen	des	der	des	der
Dat	dem	der	dem	den

INDEFINITE ARTICLE *a(n)*, **kein** *not any*

	Masc	Fem	Neut	Plur
Nom	ein	eine	ein	keine
Acc	einen	eine	ein	keine
Gen	eines	einer	eines	keiner
Dat	einem	einer	einem	keinen

DEMONSTRATIVES

this, that   **der/die/das**
this   **dieser/e/es**
that   **jener/e/es**
that   **derjenige/diejenige/ dasjenige**
the same   **derselbe, dieselbe, dasselbe**
such a   **solcher/e/es, solch ein/e/-**

*Indefinite determiners (declined like **ein** or **dieser**)*

a few   **wenige**
a couple/few   **ein paar** *(invar)*
a little   **ein bißchen, ein wenig** *(invar)*
all (of them)   **alle**

all kinds of **allerlei, allerhand** (*invar*)
all sorts of **vielerlei** (*invar*)
all the same **einerlei** (*invar*)
any **irgendein/e/-**
any **irgendwelcher/e/es**
both **beide**
both (of them) **die beiden**
each **jeder/e (der beiden)**
every **jeder/e/es**
every child **alle Kinder**
many **viele**
many a **mancher/e/es, manch
ein/e/-**
no **kein/e/-**
not any **kein/e/-**
several **mehrere**
some (of them) **einige**
two kinds of **zweierlei, usw.** (*invar*)

Question forms

how many **wie viele?**
how **wie?**
how much **wieviel?**
how many **wie viele?**
what **was?**
what kind of **was für ein/e/-?**
when **wann?**
where **wo?**
which (one) **welcher/e/es?**
who **wer?**
whom **wen?**
to whom **wem?**
whose **wessen?**
why **warum?**

Logical relations

COORDINATING CONJUNCTIONS
as well as **sowie**
or **oder**
and **und**
both ... and **sowohl ... als/wie**
but **aber**
either ... or **entweder ... oder**
for (because) **denn**
neither ... nor **weder ... noch**
not only ... but also **nicht (nur) ...
sondern (auch)**

or alternatively **beziehungsweise**

SUBORDINATING CONJUNCTIONS
although **obgleich**
as **wie, da**
before **bevor, ehe**
after **nachdem**
especially as **zumal**
although **obwohl**
even though **trotzdem**
in case, if **falls**
unless **es sei denn, (daß)**
whenever **wenn**
as if **als ob**
as soon as **sobald**
as long as **solange**
as well as **sowohl**
as (since) **da**
as soon as **sobald**
because **weil**
even though **auch wenn**
if **wenn, ob**
in order that **damit**
not until **erst als/wenn**
provided that **wenn nur**
since (time) **seit(dem)**
since (as) **da**
so that **so daß, damit**
that **daß**
unless **wenn nicht**
until **bis**
when **als, wenn, wann**
whether **ob**
while/whereas **während**

(in order) to **um ... zu** +inf
instead of (doing) **(an)statt ... zu** +inf
without (doing) **ohne ... zu** +inf
apart from (doing) **außer ... zu** +inf

Adverbial expressions

about **etwa, ungefähr**
admittedly **allerdings**
again **wieder**
allegedly **angeblich**
almost **fast, beinahe**
also **auch**
by chance **zufällig**

certainly **bestimmt, doch**
entirely **ganz**
equally **gleich**
exactly **genau**
extremely **äußerst, höchst**
for that reason **darum, deshalb**
hardly **kaum**
hopefully **hoffentlich**
however **aber, jedoch**
in fact **zwar, tatsächlich**
in those days **damals**
just **eben, mal**
like **ähnlich**
merely **bloß**
naturally **natürlich**
naturally **selbstverständlich**
no longer **nicht mehr**
not at all **keineswegs**
not at all **gar nicht**
not either **auch nicht**
not even **nicht einmal**
not **nicht**
only **nur, erst**
perhaps **vielleicht**
possibly **möglicherweise**
probably **wohl, wahrscheinlich**
quite **ganz**
rather **lieber**
really **ja, recht**
relatively **verhältnismäßig**
so **so**
then **denn, dann**
therefore, consequently **deshalb**
to be sure **zwar**
too **auch**
totally **durchaus**
very **sehr**

Prepositions

WITH ACCUSATIVE
against **gegen**
along **entlang**
at about **gegen**
by *(time)* **schon um, bis**
for **für**
round **um**

through **durch**
until **bis**
without **ohne**

WITH DATIVE
according to **nach**
after **nach**
ago **vor**
along **an ... entlang**
at the house of **bei**
beside **außer**
except for **außer**
from **von**
opposite **gegenüber**
out of **aus**
since (time) **seit**
to **zu, nach**
towards **nach, entgegen**
with **mit**

WITH DATIVE OR ACCUSATIVE
across **über**
apart from **neben**
at **an**
behind **hinter**
between **zwischen**
in **in**
in front of **vor**
next to **neben**
on **auf**
over **über**
to **an**
under **unter**

WITH GENITIVE
above **oberhalb**
because of **wegen**
below **unterhalb**
during **während**
in spite of **trotz**
inside **innerhalb**
instead of **anstatt**
not far from **unweit**
on both sides of **beiderseits**
outside **außerhalb**
this side of **diesseits**

2 Where? – position & movement

2a Position

about **ungefähr, circa**
above **über** +acc/dat
  above *(adv)* **oben, nach oben**
across **über** +acc/dat
  across there **da drüben**
after **nach** +dat
against **gegen** +acc
ahead *(adv)* **vorne, nach vorne**
ahead of **vor** +acc/dat
along **entlang** +acc, **an** +dat
among **unter** +acc/dat
anywhere **irgendwo**
around **um** +acc
  around the tree **um den Baum herum**
around *(adv)* **umher/herum**
  around in the garden **im Garten umher**
as far as **bis zu** +dat
at **an** +acc/dat
  at home **zu Hause**
  at school **in der Schule**
  at work **bei der Arbeit**
back **die hintere Seite(n)**
  at the back *(adv)* **hinten**
  at the back of **hinter** +acc/dat
  to the back **nach hinten**
backward **rückwärts, nach hinten**
before **vor** +acc/dat
  before *(adv)* **vorher**
behind **hinter** +acc/dat
  behind *(adv)* **hinten**
below **unter** +acc/dat
  below **unterhalb** +gen
  below *(adv)* **unten, (nach) unten**
beside **neben** +acc/dat
between **zwischen** +acc/dat
beyond **jenseits** +gen
bottom **der Grund, der Boden,**

der Fuß
  at the bottom (of) **unten (in** +dat)
center **die Mitte(n), das Zentrum (-en)**
  in the center **in der Mitte, mitten in** +acc/dat
direction **die Richtung(en)**
  in the direction of Bonn **Richtung Bonn**
distance **die Entfernung(en)**
  in the distance **in der Ferne**
distant **fern**
down **hinab, hinunter** +acc
  down there **dort unten**
  downstairs **(nach) unten**
edge **der Rand(-̈er)**
  at the edge **am Rande**
end **das Ende(n)**
  I end **ich beende**
  at the end **am Schluß**
everywhere **überall**
far **weit, fern**
  far away (from) **weit weg/entfernt (von** +dat)
first **erst**
  first (of all) **zuerst**
  I am first **ich komme als Erste(r)**
for **für** +acc
forward **vorwärts**
from **von** +dat
front **der vordere Teil(e)**
  at the front **vorn(e)**
  I am in front **ich stehe an der Spitze**
  in front of **vor** +acc/dat
  to the front **nach vorn**
here **hier**
  here and there **hier und da**

in **in** +acc/dat
  in there **da drinnen**
inside *(adv)* **drinnen**
  inside **innerhalb** +gen
into **in** +acc
last *(adj)* **der/die/das letzte**
  last of all **der/die/das allerletzte**
  last of all *(adv)* **zu allerletzt**
  I am last **ich stehe hinten**
left *(adj)* **der/die/das linke**
  the left **die linke Seite**
  on the left **links**
  to the left **nach links**
middle **die Mitte(n)**
  in the middle (of) **mitten (in**
  +acc/dat**)**
I move **ich bewege mich**
movement **die Bewegung(en)**
near **neben** +acc/dat
near(by) **in der Nähe, nebenbei**
neighborhood **die Nachbarschaft**
  in the neighborhood of **in der**
  Nähe von +dat
next *(adj)* **der/die/das nächste**
  next *(adv)* **daneben, zunächst,**
  dann
  next to **neben** +acc/dat, **dicht**
  bei +dat
nowhere **nirgendwo**
on **auf** +acc/dat
onto **auf** +acc
opposite **gegenüber** +dat
out of **aus** +dat
  out there **dort draußen**
outside *(adv)* **draußen**

outside **außerhalb** +gen
over **über** +acc/dat
  over there **dort drüben**
  over where **da drüben, wo**
past **an** +dat **vorbei**
right *(adj)* **der/die/das rechte**
  the right **die rechte Seite**
  on the right **rechts**
  to the right **nach rechts**
side **die Seite(n)**
  at the side **an der Seite**
  at both sides of **beiderseits**
  +gen/**von** +dat
I am situated **ich befinde mich**
somewhere **irgendwo**
there **dort, da**
  there, where **dort, wo**
to **zu** +dat, **an** +acc, **nach** +dat
top **die Spitze(n)**
  top *(of mountain)* **der Gipfel(-)**
  at the top **oben auf der**
  Spitze/dem Gipfel
  on top *(adv)* **oben**
  to the top **nach oben**
toward **nach** +dat, **auf** +acc, **zu**
  +dat
under **unter** +acc/dat
up **hinauf** +acc
  up here/there **hier/dort oben**
upstairs *(adv)* **(nach) oben**
where? **wo?**
where from? **woher?**
where to? **wohin?**
with **mit** +dat

We are going to London.	**Wir fahren nach London.**
He is going to work.	**Er geht zur Arbeit.**
We fly to the States.	**Wir fliegen in die USA.**
He walked to the front.	**Er ging nach vorne.**
She goes to school every day.	**Sie geht jeden Tag in die Schule.**
He went to the door.	**Er ging an die Tür.**
I am going home.	**Ich fahre nach Hause.**

2b Directions & location

Directions

atlas   **der Atlas(se/Atlanten)**
compass   **der Kompaß (-sse)**
on the corner   **an der Ecke**
east   **der Osten**
   east *(adj)*   **Ost-, östlich**
   in the east   **im Osten**
   to the east   **nach Osten**
   east of   **östlich von**
first left   **die erste links**
first right   **die erste rechts**
floor   **die Etage(n)**
   on the first floor   **in der ersten Etage**
the furthest *(adj)*   **der/die/das weitentfernteste**
at the junction   **an der Kreuzung**
Keep left   **Links halten!**
Keep right   **Rechts halten!**
latitude   **die Breite(n)**
location   **die Lage(n), die Positionsbestimmung(en)**
longitude   **die Länge(n)**

map   **die Karte(n)**
two miles from here   **zwei Meilen von hier**
the nearest *(adj)*   **die nahegelegendste/nächste**
north   **der Norden**
   north *(adj)*   **Nord-, nördlich**
   in the north   **im Norden**
   to the north   **nach Norden**
northeast   **der Nordosten**
   northeast *(adj)* **nordöstlich**
northnortheast   **der Nordnordosten**
northwest   **der Nordwesten**
northnorthwest   **der Nordnordwesten**
point of the compass   **die Himmelsrichtung(en)**
second right   **die zweite rechts**
south   **der Süden**
   south *(adj)*   **Süd-, südlich**
   in the south   **im Süden**
   to the south   **nach Süden**

Bonn is approximately 100 km north of here.

Bonn ist ungefähr 100 km nördlich von hier.

To the south of the woods you can see the church spire.

Südlich vom Wald sehen Sie den Kirchturm.

– Are you lost?

– Haben Sie sich verlaufen?

– Yes, I'm looking for the tourist office. Is it nearby?

– Ja, ich suche das Touristenbüro. Ist es hier in der Nähe?

Do you know your way around in the center of town?

Kennen Sie sich in der Stadtmitte aus?

Can you find your way?

Können Sie sich zurechtfinden?

southeast **der Südosten**
southsoutheast **der Südsüdosten**
southwest **der Südwesten**
southsouthwest **der Südsüdwesten**
straight ahead **gerade (da)vor, geradeaus**
third left **die dritte links**
this way **hier entlang**
west **der Westen**
   west *(adj)* **West-, westlich**
   in the west **im Westen**
   to the west **nach Westen**

Location & existence

I am **ich bin**

there is **es gibt** *(geben)* +acc
there isn't (any) **es gibt** *(geben)* **keinen/-e/-**
I become **ich werde**
I have got/I have **ich habe, ich besitze**
I exist **ich existiere, ich bestehe**
existence **die Existenz, das Dasein**
I possess **ich besitze**
possession **der Besitz** *(no pl)*, **das Besitztum(¨er)**
present **anwesend**
   I am present **ich bin da/zugegen**
   I am present at **ich bin bei** +dat

Some contracted forms

at the **an das → ans**
at/by the **an dem → am**
by the **bei dem → beim**
from the **von dem → vom**

in the **in dem → im**
into the **in das → ins**
onto the **auf das → aus**
to the **zu der → zur**
to the **zu dem → zum**

The river is not very far from our house.

Der Fluß ist nicht sehr weit von unserem Haus.

Opposite the houses is the church and next to it are the shops/stores.

Den Häusern gegenüber befindet sich die Kirche und daneben sind die Geschäfte.

– Who's there? – It's me.

– Wer ist da? – Ich bin es/bin's.

My sister has five children.

Meine Schwester hat fünf Kinder.

Is there any cake? Are there still any biscuits/cookies?

Gibt's Kuchen? Sind noch Plätzchen da?

To get to the train station, you have to take the third left and then just go straight ahead.

Um zum Bahnhof zu gelangen, müssen Sie die dritte Straße links gehen und dann immer geradeaus.

2c Movement

I arrive **ich komme an***
I bring **ich bringe (mit*)**
by car **mit dem Auto**
I carry **ich trage**
I climb *(intr)* **ich steige, ich klettere**
 I climb *(tr)* **ich besteige**
I come **ich komme**
 I come along **ich komme mit***
I creep **ich krieche**
I drive **ich fahre**
 I drive on the right **ich fahre rechts**
I fall **ich falle, ich stürze**
 I fall down **ich falle um***
I follow **ich folge** +dat
I go **ich gehe**
 I go along **ich gehe mit***
 I go for a walk **ich gehe spazieren***
I go (by vehicle) **ich fahre**
I hike **ich wandere**
I hurry **ich eile**
 I hurry up **ich beeile mich**
I jump **ich springe**
I leave **ich fahre ab***
 I leave sth **ich verlasse etw.**
I march **ich marschiere**
I move **ich bewege mich**
on foot **zu Fuß**

I pass **ich gehe an** +dat **vorbei**
 I pass *(in car)* **ich überhole**
I pull **ich ziehe**
I push **ich stoße, schiebe**
I put (flat) **ich lege**
 I put (into) **ich tue, ich stecke**
 I put (onto) **ich setze**
 I put (upright) **ich stelle**
I ride **ich fahre**
 I ride *(a horse)* **ich reite**
I run **ich laufe**
 I run away **ich laufe weg***
I rush **ich stürze (mich)**
I sit up **ich setze mich aufrecht**
I slip **ich rutsche aus***
I stand **ich stehe**
 I stand still **ich bleibe stehen***
I step/come/go **ich trete**
I stop **ich halte, ich bleibe stehen***
straight **gerade**
 straight ahead **geradeaus**
I stroll **ich schlendere, ich bummele**
I take **ich nehme, ich bringe**
I turn **ich biege (ein*)**
 I turn left **ich biege nach links**
 I turn off **ich biege ab***
 I turn around **ich drehe mich um***
 I turn to so **ich wende mich an** +acc

Frank and I are going to the movies by car, but Susanne is walking to the theater.

Frank und ich fahren mit dem Auto zum Kino, aber Susanne geht zu Fuß.

Yesterday Annette's husband slipped on the ice in front of our house.

Gestern ist Annettes Mann auf dem Eis vor unserem Haus ausgerutscht.

We have to go down the hill, then along the river, and turn left by the inn.

Wir müssen den Berg hinunter gehen, dann am Fluß entlang und am Gasthof links abbiegen.

walk **der Gang(¨e), der Spaziergang(¨e)**
I walk **ich gehe**
I wander **ich wandere**
way **der Weg(e)**

Here & there

Come here! **Komm her!***
I go there **ich gehe hin***
I rush there **ich stürze hin***
I travel there **ich fahre hin***

In & out

Come in! **Herein!**
I come in **ich komme herein***
I come here **ich komme (hier)her***
I come out **ich komme heraus***
I go in **ich gehe hinein***
I go into the house **ich gehe in das Haus (hinein)***
I go into the room **ich betrete das Zimmer**
I come in (to the room) **ich trete ein***
I get in **ich steige ein***
I get out *(of vehicle)* **ich steige aus***
Get out! **Raus!**
I go out **ich gehe hinaus***
Go out! **Gehen Sie hinaus*!**
I go out of the room **ich gehe aus dem Zimmer (hinaus*)**

I go out (on an outing) **ich gehe aus***
I get out (of vehicle) **ich steige aus***

Up & down

I climb the mountain **ich besteige den Berg**
I climb up the mountain **ich klettere auf den Berg (hinauf*)**
I climb the stairs **ich steige die Treppe hinauf***
I climb the wall **ich steige auf die Mauer**
I come down **ich komme herunter***
I come up **ich komme herauf***
I fall down **ich falle/stürze hin***
I get up **ich stehe auf***
I go down the path **ich gehe den Weg hinab*/hinunter***
I go up **ich gehe hinauf***
I lie down **ich lege mich hin**
Stand up! **Stehen Sie auf*!**
Do sit down! **Setzen Sie sich hin*!**

Around

I go around the town **ich gehe um die Stadt (herum*)**
I run around in the garden **ich laufe im Garten umher***
I run around **ich laufe umher/herum***

– Where are you going? – To town. Are you coming? – No, I am going to my mother's.

Every evening our neighbors take a long walk.

Please go into the room. Mr. Schmidt will be here shortly.

– Wo gehen Sie hin? – In die Stadt. Kommen Sie mit? – Nein, ich gehe zu meiner Mutter.

Jeden Abend machen unsere Nachbarn einen langen Spaziergang.

Gehen Sie bitte in das Zimmer hinein. Herr Schmidt kommt gleich.

Note use of **hin** (movement away from the speaker) and **her** (movement toward the speaker) to make compound verbs expressing movement.

③ When? – expressions of time

3a Past, present, & future

about **gegen** +acc
after **nach** +dat
  after *(conj)* **nachdem**
  afterward **nachher, danach, hinterher**
again **nochmals, wieder**
  again and again **immer wieder**
ago **her** *(adv)*, **vor** +dat *(prep)*
  a short time ago **vor kurzem**
already **schon**
always **immer**
anniversary **der Jahrestag(e), der Hochzeitstag(e)**
annual **jährlich**
annually **jedes Jahr, jährlich**
as long as *(conj)* **solange**
as soon as *(conj)* **sobald**
at once **sofort, gerade, gleich**
before *(adj)* **vor** +acc/dat
  before *(conj)* **bevor, ehe**
  before, beforehand **vorher, davor**
I begin **ich beginne, ich fange an***
  it begins **es geht los***
beginning **der Anfang(ꞓe)**
birthday **der Geburtstag(e)**
brief *(adj)* **kurz**
briefly **vorübergehend**
by (next month) **bis (nächsten Monat)**
calendar **der Kalender(-)**
centenary **der hunderste Geburtstag(e)**
century **das Jahrhundert(e)**
  in the twentieth century **im zwanzigsten Jahrhundert**
continuous(ly) **dauernd, ständig**
daily **täglich**
date **das Datum (-en)**
  date **der Termin(e)**

dawn **der Tagesanbruch(ꞓe)**
  at dawn **bei Tagesanbruch**
day **der Tag(e)**
  by day **bei Tag**
  every day **jeden Tag**
decade **das Jahrzehnt(e)**
delay **die Verspätung(en)**
  delayed **verspätet**
during **während** +dat/gen
early **früh**
  I am early **ich bin früh dran**
  I am early **ich komme zu früh**
end **das Ende(n)**
  I end *(sth)* **ich beende etw.**
  it ends **es endet, es ist aus**
ever **je**
every **jeder/-e/-es**
  every time **jedesmal**
  every day **jeden Tag**
exactly **genau, punkt**
fast **schnell**
  my watch is fast **meine Uhr geht vor***
finally **schließlich**
I finish (reading) **ich (lese) zu Ende**
first *(adj)* **der/die/das erste**
  at first **zuerst**
firstly **erstens**
for **seit** +dat, **für** +acc, **auf** +acc
  for a day *(duration)* **einen Tag (lang)**
  (past continuous/progressive) **seit einem Tag**
  (future) **auf/für einen Tag**
for good/ever **auf immer**
formerly **früher**
fortnight/two weeks **vierzehn Tage**
frequent **häufig**
frequently **häufig, öfters**

from **von** +dat
   as from (today) **ab (heute)**
   from now on **von nun an, von jetzt ab**
I go on (reading) **ich (lese) weiter**
half **die Hälfte(n)**
   half *(adj)* **der/die/das halbe**
   one and a half **anderthalb, eineinhalb** *(invar)*
   two and a half **zweieinhalb** *(invar)*
it happens **es ereignet sich**
holiday/vacation **der Feiertag(e)**
I hurry up **ich beeile mich, ich mache schnell**
   hurry **die Eile**
   I am in a hurry **ich habe es eilig**
instant **der Moment(e)**
just **gerade**
   just now **gerade jetzt**
last *(final) (adj)* **der/die/das letzte**
   last night **gestern in der Nacht**
   last *(previous) (adj)* **der/die/das vorige/vergangene**
   it lasts a long time **es dauert lange**

last a short time **es dauert kurze Zeit**
late **spät**
   I am late **ich komme zu spät**
   lately **neulich**
   later (on) **später**
long **lang**
   long term **langfristig**
   in the long term **langfristig gesehen**
many **viele**
   many times **vielmals**
meanwhile **unterdessen**
   in the meanwhile **inzwischen**
middle **die Mitte(n)**
moment **der Augenblick(e)**
moment **der Moment(e)**
   at the moment **im Moment**
   at this moment **in diesem Augenblick**
   at this moment *(right now)* **zur Zeit**
   in a moment **in einem Augenblick**
month **der Monat(e)**
   monthly **monatlich, jeden Monat**
much **viel**

The train from Frankfurt was delayed, and my girlfriend didn't arrive until eleven o'clock.

Der Zug aus Frankfurt hatte Verspätung, und meine Freundin ist erst um elf Uhr angekommen.

– Can you please tell me how often a bus goes to Würzburg?

– Können Sie mir bitte sagen, wie häufig ein Bus nach Würzburg fährt?

– From eight a.m. to five p.m., there's a bus every half hour. Every morning at dawn Stefan's mother takes her dog for a walk.

– Von acht bis siebzehn Uhr geht jede halbe Stunde ein Bus. Stefans Mutter führt jeden Morgen bei Tagesanbruch ihren Hund spazieren.

Jochen and Angelika recently celebrated their second anniversary.

Jochen und Angelika haben vor kurzem ihren zweiten Hochzeitstag gefeiert.

never **nie**
next *(adj)* **nächst-, kommend-, folgend-**
next *(adv)* **dann**
not till/until **erst (um)**
not before **erst**
not always **nicht immer**
now **jetzt**
now *(next)* **nun**
nowadays **heutzutage**
occasionally **zufällig**
it occurs **es ereignet sich**
often **oft**
on and off **ab und zu**
once **einmal, mal**
once upon a time **einmal**
once in a while **ab und zu**
once a day **einmal am Tag**
one day (when) **eines Tages (als/wo)**
only **nur**
only when **erst als/wenn**
past **die Vergangenheit**
past **nach** +dat
per (day) **pro (Tag)**
present **die Gegenwart**
present *(adj)* **gegenwärtig**
presently **bald**
at present **zur Zeit**

previous(ly) **früher**
prompt **pünktlich**
promptly (at two) **punkt (zwei Uhr)**
rare(ly) **selten**
recent **neu**
recently **kürzlich, neulich**
regular(ly) **regelmäßig**
I remain **ich bleibe**
right away **sofort**
Saint's day **der Namenstag(e)**
school term/semester **das Trimester(-), das Semester(-)**
season **die Jahreszeite(n)**
seldom **selten**
several **mehrere**
several times **mehrmals**
short **kurz**
short term **kurzfristig**
in the short term **kurzfristig gesehen**
shortly **in kurzem**
since *(conj)* **seit** +dat
slow **langsam**
my watch is slow **meine Uhr geht nach**
some **einige**
sometime **irgendwann**
sometimes **manchmal**

– When are you going on vacation?
– Next month. We're staying in France for three weeks.

– Wann fahren Sie in Urlaub?
– **Nächsten Monat. Wir bleiben drei Wochen in Frankreich.**

My boss often makes short business trips to London.

Mein Chef macht oft kurzfristige Geschäftsreisen nach London.

This morning Peter and his colleague arrived in the office at the same time.

Heute morgen sind Peter und sein Kollege gleichzeitig im Büro angekommen.

– How often do you see your parents?
– If possible, every weekend.

– **Wie oft siehst du deine Eltern?**
– **Wenn möglich, jedes Wochenende.**

soon **bald**
  sooner or later **früher oder später**
  the sooner the better **je eher desto besser**
I stay **ich bleibe**
still **noch**
I stop (doing) **ich höre auf* (zu ... tun)**
suddenly **plötzlich, auf einmal**
sunrise **der Sonnenaufgang(ˉe)**
  at sunrise **bei Sonnenaufgang**
sunset **der Sonnenuntergang(ˉe)**
  at sunset **bei Sonnenuntergang**
I take (an hour) **ich brauche (eine Stunde)**
  it takes (an hour) **es dauert (eine Stunde)**
then (next) **dann**
  then (at that time) **da, damals, dann**
thousand years **das Jahrtausend(e)**
till **bis** +acc
time (in general) **die Zeit(en)**
time (occasion) **das Mal(e)**
  at any time **jederzeit**
  at other times **zu anderen Zeiten**
at the same time **gleichzeitig**
from time to time **von Zeit zu Zeit**
for a long time **lange, lange Zeit**
in good time **rechtzeitig**
a long time ago **längst**
the whole time **immer, die ganze Zeit**
time zone **die Zeitzone(n)**
twice **zweimal**
until **bis** +acc
  until **bis zu** +dat
usually **meistens**
I wait **ich warte auf** +acc
week **die Woche(n)**
  this week **diese Woche**
  weekly **jede Woche**
  weekday **der Werktag(e), der Wochentag(e)**
  weekend **das Wochenende(n)**
when **wann, wenn, als**
whenever **wenn**
while (conj) **während**
year **das Jahr(e)**
  yearly **jährlich, jedes Jahr**
yet **schon**
  not yet **noch nicht**

– I'll call you as soon as we get there.

– Ich werde dich anrufen, sobald wir ankommen.

– Hello Peter, John Brown here. I have been working on the project for a few days. We have to meet. What about tomorrow?

– Hallo Peter, John Brown hier. Ich arbeite seit einigen Tagen an dem Projekt. Wir müssen uns unbedingt treffen. Wie wäre es mit morgen?

– From time to time I get a letter from an old school friend.

Von Zeit zu Zeit bekomme einen Brief von einer alten Schulfreundin.

3b Time, days, & date

Time of day

a.m.   **vormittags**
morning   **der Morgen(-), der**
 Vormittag(e)
 in the morning   **morgen früh**
 in the mornings   **vormittags**
 early in the morning
 frühmorgens
 this morning   **heute morgen**
noon   **der Mittag(e)**
at noon   **zu Mittag**
afternoon   **der Nachmittag(e)**
 in the afternoon   **am**
 Nachmittag
 in the afternoons   **nachmittags**
 this afternoon   **heute**
 nachmittag
p.m.   **nachmittags**
evening   **der Abend(e)**
 in the evening   **am Abend**
 in the evenings   **abends**
 this evening   **heute abend**
night   **die Nacht(-e)**
 at night   **nachts**
midnight   **die Mitternacht(-e)**
 at midnight   **um Mitternacht**
today   **heute**
 a week from today   **heute in**
 einer Woche
tomorrow   **morgen**
 tomorrow morning   **morgen früh**
 tomorrow afternoon   **morgen**
 nachmittag
 tomorrow evening   **morgen**
 abend
 the day after tomorrow
 übermorgen
tonight   **heute abend/nacht**
yesterday   **gestern**
 yesterday afternoon   **gestern**
 nachmittag
 yesterday morning   **gestern**
 vormittag
 yesterday evening   **gestern**

 abend
 the day before yesterday
 vorgestern

Telling the time

second   **die Sekunde(n)**
minute   **die Minute(n)**
hour   **die Stunde (n)**
 half an hour   **die halbe**
 Stunde(n)
 in an hour's time   **in einer**
 Stunde
 hourly   **jede Stunde**
quarter   **das Viertel(-)**
 quarter of an hour   **die**
 Viertelstunde(n)
 three quarters of an hour   **drei**
 Viertelstunden
 quarter past/after (two)   **Viertel**
 nach (zwei)
 quarter to/of (two)   **Viertel vor**
 (zwei)
half past (two)   **halb (drei)**
17:45   **siebzehn Uhr**
 fünfundvierzig
five past/after six   **fünf nach sechs**
five to/of six   **fünf vor sechs**
twenty five to/of six
 fünfundzwanzig (Minuten) vor
 sechs
twenty five to/of six   **fünf nach halb**
 sechs
twenty five past/after five
 fünfundzwanzig (Minuten) nach
 fünf
twenty five past/after five   **fünf vor**
 halb sechs
two a.m.   **zwei Uhr nachts**
eight a.m.   **acht Uhr vormittags**
two p.m.   **zwei Uhr nachmittags**
eight p.m.   **acht Uhr abends**
12:00 noon   **zwölf Uhr mittags**
12:00 midnight   **zwölf Uhr nachts**

The days of the week

Monday   **der Montag(e)**
Tuesday   **der Dienstag(e)**
Wednesday   **der Mittwoch(e)**
Thursday   **der Donnerstag(e)**
Friday   **der Freitag(e)**
Saturday   **der Samstag(e),**
   Sonnabend(e)
Sunday   **der Sonntag(e)**

The months

January   **der Januar(e)**
February   **der Februar(e)**
March   **der März(e)**
April   **der April(-)**
May   **der Mai(e)**
June   **der Juni(s)**
July   **der Juli(s)**
August   **der August(e)**
September   **der September(-)**
October   **der Oktober(-)**
November   **der November(-)**
December   **der Dezember(-)**

The seasons

spring   **der Frühling(e)**
summer   **der Sommer(-)**

autumn/fall   **der Herbst(e)**
winter   **der Winter(-)**

The date

last Friday   **letzten Freitag**
on Tuesday   **am Dienstag**
on Tuesdays   **dienstags**
by Friday   **bis Freitag**
the first of January   **der erste**
   Januar
on the third of January   **am dritten**
   Januar
in (the year) 2000   **2000, im Jahre**
   2000
1st January/January 1st, 1994   **den**
   ersten Januar 1994
1/1/1994   **1.1.1994**
at the end of 1999   **Ende 1999**
by the end of 1999   **bis Ende 1999**
at the beginning (of July)   **Anfang**
   (Juli)
by the beginning (of July)   **bis**
   Anfang (Juli)
in December   **im Dezember**
in mid/the middle of January   **Mitte**
   Januar
at the end of March   **Ende März**
in spring   **im Frühling**

– I'm going shopping tomorrow morning. Would you like to come along?
– Yes, but I'd prefer to go in the afternoon. I always have a lot to do on Monday mornings.

– Okay. Let's meet at two thirty.

– What time does the movie start this evening?
– At 19:00 hours.
– And how long is it?
– One and a half hours. It will be over at 20:30 hours.

– **Ich gehe morgen früh ein-kaufen. Möchtest du mitkommen?**
– **Ja, aber ich würde lieber nach-mittags gehen. Ich habe montags morgen immer viel zu tun.**

– **In Ordnung. Treffen wir uns um halb drei.**

– **Wann beginnt der Film heute abend?**
– **Um neunzehn Uhr.**
– **Und wie lange dauert er?**
– **Anderthalb Stunden. Er ist um zwanzig Uhr dreißig zu Ende.**

➤ NUMBERS 4c

4 How much? – expressions of quantity

4a Length and shape

angle **der Winkel(-)**	perpendicular **senkrecht**
area **die Fläche(n)**	point **der Punkt(e)**
big **groß**	room **der Platz(-̈e)**
center **die Mitte(n)**	round **rund**
concave **konkav**	ruler **das Lineal(e)**
convex **konvex**	shape **die Form(en)**
curved **gebogen**	short **kurz**
deep **tief**	size **die Größe(n)**
degree **der Grad** *(no pl)*	small **klein**
depth **die Tiefe(n)**	space **der Raum(-̈e)**
diagonal **schräg**	straight **gerade**
distance **die Entfernung(en)**	tall **groß, hoch**
I draw **ich zeichne**	thick **dick**
hectare **das Hektar(e)**	thin **dünn**
height **die Höhe(n)**	wide **breit, weit**
high **hoch, hoh-**	width **die Breite(n)**
horizontal **waagerecht**	
large **breit**	*Shapes*
length **die Länge(n)**	circle **der Kreis(e)**
line **die Linie(n)**	circular **kreisförmig**
long **lang**	cube **der Würfel(-)**
low **niedrig**	cubic **Kubik-**
it measures **es beträgt**	cylinder **der Zylinder(-)**
narrow **eng**	pyramid **die Pyramide(n)**
parallel **parallel**	rectangle **das Rechteck(e)**

You need a straight ruler and pencil.	**Sie brauchen ein gerades Lineal und einen Bleistift.**
Measure the space and then draw a plan.	**Messen Sie den Raum and machen Sie dann einen Entwurf.**
The driveway is too narrow for Alfred's new car.	**Die Einfahrt ist zu eng für Alfreds neuen Wagen.**
Leave room for some vegetables.	**Lassen Sie Platz für das Gemüse.**
The distance from the house to the fence is 12 meters.	**Die Entfernung vom Haus bis zum Zaun beträgt 12 Meter.**

rectangular **rechteckig**
sphere **die Kugel(n)**
  spherical **kugelförmig**
square **das Quadrat(e)**
  square **Quadrat-**
  square **quadratisch, viereckig**
triangle **das Dreieck(e)**
triangular **dreieckig**

Units of length

centimeter **der Zentimeter(-), cm**
foot **der Fuß** *(no pl)*
inch **der Zoll** *(no pl)*
kilometer **der Kilometer(-), km**
meter **der Meter(-), m**
mile **die Meile(n)**
millimeter **der Millimeter(-), mm**
yard **das Yard(s)**

Expressions of quantity

about **etwa, ungefähr**
almost **fast, beinahe**
approximate **ungefähr**
approximately **circa**
as much as **soviel**
at least **mindestens**
capacity **der Inhalt(e)**
  it contains **es enthält**
  (enthalten)
cubic capacity **das**
  Fassungsvermögen(-)
it decreases **es geht zurück***

difference **der Unterschied(e)**
empty **leer**
I empty **ich leere**
enough **genug**
it is enough **es reicht**
I fill **ich fülle**
full **voll**
full of **voll von** +dat, **voller** *(invar)*
I grow **ich wachse**
  growth **das Wachstum** *(no pl)*
hardly **kaum**
increase **die Vergrößerung(en)**
it increases **es nimmt zu***, es
  vermehrt sich
little **wenig** *(invar)*, **klein**
  a little **ein wenig, ein bißchen**
a lot (of) **viel**
I measure **ich messe**
  measuring tape **das Bandmaß(e)**
more **mehr** *(invar)*
nearly **fast**
number **die Zahl(en)**
part **der Teil(e)**
quantity **die Menge(n)**
rarely **selten**
it suffices **es genügt**
sufficient **genügend**
too much **zuviel**
volume **das Volumen**
whole **ganz**
whole **das Ganze**

The garden is not wide enough for a pool.

Der Garten ist nicht breit genug für ein Schwimmbecken.

– How high is the tree? – About five meters.

– Wie groß ist der Baum? – Ungefähr fünf Meter.

The shed will be at an angle of about 40 degrees to the house.

Der Schuppen wird in einem Winkel von 40 Grad zum Haus stehen.

The area of our garden/yard is 100 square meters.

Unser Garten mißt 100 Quadratmeter.

4b Measuring

Expressions of volume

bag	**die Tüte(n)**
bar	**die Tafel(n)**
bottle	**die Flasche(n)**
box	**das Etui(s), die Dose(n)**
container	**der Behälter(-)**
cup	**die Tasse(n)**
gallon	**die Gallone(n)**
glass	**das Glas(⁻er)**
liter	**der/das Liter**
centiliter	**der/das Zentiliter**
milliliter	**der/das Milliliter**
pack	**die Packung(en)**
packet	**das Paket(e)**
packet *(small)*	**die Schachtel(n)**
pair	**das Paar(e)**

piece **das Stück(e)**
  a piece of cake **ein Stück Kuchen**
pint **das Pint(s), das halbe Liter(-)**
portion **die Portion(en)**
pot **das Glas(⁻er)**
sack **der Sack(⁻e)**
tube **die Tube(n)**

Temperature

it boils **es kocht**
I chill **ich kühle, ich stelle kalt**
cold **kalt**
  cold **die Kälte**
cool **kühl**
  I cool down **ich kühle mich ab**

Do you have this soda in liter bottles?

Haben Sie diesen Sprudel in Literflaschen?

– How many cubic meters of concrete do you need? – About two.

– Wieviel Kubikmeter Beton brauchen Sie? – Ungefähr zwei.

– Would you like a cup of tea?
– No, I would prefer a glass of water.

– Möchten Sie eine Tasse Tee?
– Nein, ich möchte lieber ein Glas Wasser.

– How much wood do you want?
– Enough for the whole fence. Give me a bag of cement too, please.

– Wieviel Holz brauchen Sie?
– Genug für den ganzen Zaun. Geben Sie mir bitte auch einen Sack Zement.

I need about a cup of flour, a quarter pound of butter and three eggs for this recipe.

Ich brauche ungefähr eine Tasse Mehl, ein viertel Pfund Butter und drei Eier für dieses Rezept.

You have to chill the cake for three hours before cutting it.

Sie müssen den Kuchen drei Stunden kaltstellen, bevor Sie ihn schneiden.

degree **der Grad** *(no pl)*
I freeze **ich friere**
heat **die Hitze**
  I heat **ich erhitze**
  I heat *(the house)* **ich heize**
hot **heiß**
temperature **die Temperatur(en)**
I warm (up) **ich wärme auf***
  warmth **die Wärme**

Weight & density

dense **dicht**
density **die Dichte(n)**

gram **das Gramm** *(no pl)*
heavy **schwer**
kilo **das Kilo(gramm)** *(no pl)*
light **leicht**
mass **die Masse(n)**
ounce **die Unze(n)**
pound (lb) **das Pfund** *(no pl)*
scales/balance **die Waage(n)**
ton(*ne*) **die Tonne(n)**
I weigh **ich wiege**
weight **das Gewicht(e)**

It's so hot! The temperature must be 30 degrees.

Es ist so heiß! Die Temperatur muß 30 Grad sein.

It's very hot today, and Michael just jumped into the pool to cool off.

Es ist heute sehr heiß, und Michael ist gerade ins Schwimmbecken gesprungen, um sich abzukühlen.

The fall and winter were very cold last year. We already had to put the heating on in September.

Der Herbst und Winter waren letztes Jahr sehr kalt. Wir mußten schon im September heizen.

If the temperature goes down further, we'll have to bring in our plants from the balcony.

Wenn die Temperatur noch weiter fällt, müssen wir unsere Pflanzen vom Balkon hereinbringen.

Would you please put the frozen vegetables into the boiling water?

Würdest du bitte das gefrorene Gemüse ins kochende Wasser tun?

Can you weigh the ingredients?

Können Sie die Zutaten wiegen?

How many grams of sugar do we need?

Wieviel Gramm Zucker brauchen wir?

The pizza can be warmed up in the oven.

Die Pizza kann im Ofen aufgewärmt werden.

➤ WEATHER 24d

HOW MUCH? — EXPRESSIONS OF QUANTITY

4c Numbers

Cardinal numbers

zero	**null**
one	**eins, einer/e/-**
two	**zwei**
two *(telephone)*	**zwo**
three	**drei**
four	**vier**
five	**fünf**
six	**sechs**
seven	**sieben**
eight	**acht**
nine	**neun**
ten	**zehn**
eleven	**elf**
twelve	**zwölf**
thirteen	**dreizehn**
fourteen	**vierzehn**
fifteen	**fünfzehn**
sixteen	**sechzehn**
seventeen	**siebzehn**
eighteen	**achtzehn**
nineteen	**neunzehn**
twenty	**zwanzig**
twenty-one	**einundzwanzig**
twenty-two	**zweiundzwanzig**
twenty-nine	**neunundzwanzig**
thirty	**dreißig**
thirty-one	**einunddreißig**
forty	**vierzig**
fifty	**fünfzig**
sixty	**sechzig**
seventy	**siebzig**

eighty	**achtzig**
ninety	**neunzig**
a hundred	**hundert**
a hundred and one	**hunderteins**
two hundred	**zweihundert**
a thousand	**(ein)tausend**
two thousand	**zweitausend**
million	**eine Million**
two million	**zwei Millionen**
milliard/billion *(U.S.)*	**die Milliarde(n)**

Ordinal numbers

first	**der/die/das erste**
second	**der/die/das zweite**
third	**der/die/das dritte**
fourth	**der/die/das vierte**
nineteenth	**der/die/das neunzehnte**
twentieth	**der/die/das zwanzigste**
twenty-first	**der/die/das einunzwanzigste**
hundredth	**der/die/das hundertste**

Nouns

zero	**die Null(en)**
one	**die Eins(en)**
unit	**der Einer(-)**
ten	**die Zehn, der Zehner(-)**
dozen	**das Dutzend(e)**
hundred	**das Hundert(e)**
hundreds of	**Hunderte von**
million	**die Million(en)**

Half of the house belongs to my brother.	**Die Hälfte des Hauses gehört meinem Bruder.**
– You cannot all have a bar of chocolate. There is only enough for a quarter each.	**– Ihr könnt nicht alle eine Tafel Schokolade haben. Es reicht nur für ein Viertel für jeden.**
– I don't want a quarter, I want a half.	**– Ich will kein Viertel haben, ich möchte die Hälfte.**

Writing numerals

1,000	**1.000**
1,500	**1.500**
1,000,000	**1 000 000**
1st	**1.**
2nd	**2.**
1.56	**1,56 (eins Komma fünf sechs)**
.05	**0,05 (null Komma null fünf)**

Fractions

half **die Hälfte(n)**
  a half **der/die/das halbe**
  one and a half **eineinhalb**
  (invar)

two and a half **zweieinhalb**
  (invar)
quarter **das Viertel(-)**
  a quarter **ein Viertel-**
  two and a quarter **zwei einviertel**
third **das Drittel(-)**
fifth **das Fünftel(-)**
five and five sixths **fünf fünf Sechstel**
tenth **das Zehntel(-)**
sixth **das Sechstel(-)**
hundredth **das Hundertstel(-)**

---

double the price **das Doppelte**
twice as much **das Doppelte**
second best **der/die/das zweitbeste**
third from last **der/die/das drittletzte**
fourfold **vierfach**
four times as much **das Vierfache**

1,800,265 **eine Million achthunderttausendzwei-hundertfünfundsechzig**
1995 **im Jahre neunzehn-hundertfünfundneunzig**

telephone number 360542
  Telefon sechsunddreißig, null fünf, zwoundvierzig
area code 0482 **Vorwahl null vier acht zwo**

It was A1 **Es war eins A**
the 100 (bus) **der Hunderter**
the ten-mark note/ten Pfennig coin
  der Zehner(-)
The Big Four **die Vier**
We went in fours **Wir sind zu viert (vieren) gefahren**
We make a foursome **Wir haben einen Vierer**

Only a few people can remember the twenties.

Nur wenige Leute erinnern sich an die zwanziger Jahre.

Yesterday we celebrated Jörg's nineteenth birthday.

Wir haben gestern Jörgs neunzehnten geburtstag gefeiert.

HOW MUCH? – EXPRESSIONS OF QUANTITY

4d Calculations

addition **die Addition(en)**
  I add **ich addiere, rechne zusammen***
  plus **plus, und**
  two plus two **zwei und/plus zwei**
average **der Durchschnitt(e)**
  I average out **ich nehme den Durchschnitt**
  on average **im Durchschnitt**
I calculate **ich berechne**
  calculation **die Berechnung(en)**
  calculator **der Taschenrechner(-)**
correct **richtig**
I count **ich zähle**
data **die Daten** *(pl)*
  piece of data **das Datum (-a/-en)**
decimal **die Dezimalzahl(en)**
  decimal point **das Komma(s)**
diameter **der Durchmesser(-)**
digit **die Ziffer(n)**

two digit **zweistellig**
I double **ich verdopple**
division **die Division(en)**
  I divide by **ich teile durch** +acc
  six divided by two **sechs geteilt durch zwei**
it equals **es gleicht**
equation **das Gleichnis(se)**
it is equivalent to **ist gleich**
I estimate **ich schätze**
even **gerade**
figure **die Ziffer(n)**
graph **der Graph(en), die Grafik(en)**
is greater than **ist größer als**
is less than **ist weniger als**
maximum **das Maximum(-a)**
  maximum **maximal, Maximal-**
  a maximum of **ein Maximum an** +dat
  up to a maximum of **bis zu maximal**

An inch is the same as 2.54 cm, and there are twelve inches in a foot, 36 in a yard. A mile is 1760 yards. A kilometre/kilometer is 1000 metres.

Ein Zoll ist gleich 2,54 Zentimeter, und es gibt 12 Zoll in einem Fuß, 36 in einem Yard. Eine Meile ist 1760 Yards. Ein Kilometer ist 1.000 Meter.

What is 14 plus 8? It equals 22. Did you get the right result?

Was macht 14 und 8? 14 plus 8 (ist) gleich 22. Hast du das richtige Ergebnis?

20 minus 5 is 15, 20 divided by 5 equals 4.

20 weniger 5 gleich 15, 20 geteilt durch 5 gleich 4.

Work out 12 times 22. That is an easy sum.

Rechnet 12 mal 22. Das ist eine leichte Aufgabe.

2 to the power of 3 is 8. Three squared equals 9.

Zwei hoch drei macht 8. Drei hoch zwei macht neun.

medium   **die Mitte(n)**
  medium   **Mittel-, mittler-**
minimum   **das Minimum(-a)**
  minimum   **Mindest-**
minus   **minus**
mistake/error   **der Fehler(-)**
multiplication   **die Multiplikation(en)**
  I multiply   **ich multipliziere**
  three times two   **drei mal zwei**
negative   **negativ**
number   **die Zahl(en)**
numeral   **die Ziffer(n)**
odd   **ungerade**
percent   **das Prozent(en)**
  by 10%   **um 10%**
  percentage   **der Prozentsatz(-̈e)**
positive   **positiv**
power   **die Potenz(en)**
  to the power of   **hoch**
  to the fifth   **hoch fünf**
problem   **die Aufgabe(n)**
quantity   **die Menge(n)**
ratio   **das Verhältnis(se)**

a ratio of 100:1   **im Verhältnis 100 zu 1**
result   **das Ergebnis(se)**
similar   **ähnlich**
solution   **die Lösung(en)**
  I solve   **ich löse**
square   **die Quadratzahl(en)**
square root   **die zweite Wurzel(n)**
  three squared   **drei hoch zwei, zum Quadrat**
statistic   **die Statistik**
statistics   **die Statistik(en)**
statistical   **statistisch**
sum   **die Rechenaufgabe(n)**
subtraction   **die Subtraktion(en)**
  I subtract   **ich ziehe ab***
symbol   **das Symbol(e)**
take away   **weniger**
total   **die Endsumme(n), Gesamtzahl(en)**
  in total   **insgesamt**
I treble   **ich verdreifache**
triple   **dreifach**
I work out   **ich rechne aus***
wrong   **falsch**

Two negatives make a positive.   **Zweimal minus gibt plus.**

You have made a mistake there.   **Da hast du einen Fehler gemacht.**

– I estimate that we have about 500 visitors a year.   **– Ich schätze, wir haben etwa 500 Gäste im Jahr.**
– What percentage of visitors are local? – 20% (percent).   **– Welcher Prozentsatz kommt aus der Gegend? – 20 Prozent.**
– Have you got any statistics about it?   **– Haben Sie eine Statistik darüber?**

A snail travels at an average speed of 0.04 miles per hour.   **Eine Schnecke bewegt sich mit einer Durchschnittsgeschwindigkeit von 0,06 Stundenkilometern.**

Can you do me a graph?   **Wollen Sie mir bitte eine Grafik zeichnen?**

⑤ What sort of? – descriptions & judgments

5a Describing people

appearance	**das Aussehen**
attractive	**attraktiv**
average	**mittel, mittelmäßig**
he is bald	**er hat eine Glatze**
beard	**der Bart("-e)**
bearded	**bärtig**
beautiful	**schön**
beauty	**die Schönheit(en)**
blond	**blond**
broad	**breit**
build	**der Körperbau** *(no pl)*
chic	**schick**
clean shaven	**glattrasiert**
clumsy	**ungeschickt**
complexion	**die Gesichtsfarbe(n)**
curly	**lockig**
dark	**dunkel**
I describe	**ich beschreibe**
description	**die Beschreibung(en)**
different (from)	**anders (als)**
elegant	**elegant**
energy	**die Energie(n)**
expression	**der Gesichtsausdruck("-e)**
far-sighted	**weitsichtig**
fat	**dick**
feature	**der Gesichtszug("-e)**
female/feminine	**weiblich**

figure	**die Figur(en)**
fit	**fit**
I frown	**ich runzele die Stirn**
glasses	**die Brille**
good-looking	**gutaussehend**
I grow	**ich wachse**
hair	**das Haar, die Haare**
hairstyle	**die Frisur(en)**
handsome	**gutaussehend**
heavy	**schwer**
height	**die Größe(n)**
homosexual	**homosexuell**
large	**breit, groß**
I laugh	**ich lache**
laugh	**das Lachen**
I am left-handed	**ich bin Linkshänder [-in]**
light	**leicht**
I look like	**ich sehe aus* wie**
I look well	**ich sehe gut aus***
male	**männlich**
masculine	**männlich**
moustache	**der Schnurrbart("-e)**
near-sighted	**kurzsichtig**
neat	**ordentlich**
neatness	**die Sauberkeit**
obese	**fettleibig**
overweight	**übergewichtig, pulent**

adolescence	**die Pubertät**
adolescent	**der/die Jugendliche** *(adj/n)*
age	**das Alter**
elderly	**ältlich, älter**
grown up	**der/die Erwachsene** *(adj/n)*
grown up *(adj)*	**erwachsen**
middle-aged	**in den mittleren Jahren**

old	**alt**
older/elder	**älter**
teenager	**der Teenager(-)**
young	**jung**
young person	**der/die Jugendliche** *(adj/n)*
young people	**junge Leute**
youth	**die Jugend**
youthful	**jugendlich**

part of body **der Körperteil(e)**	spot **der Pickel(-)**
paunch **der Bauch(-̈e)**	spotty **pickelig**
physical **körperlich**	stocky **stämmig**
plump **fett, pummelig**	strength **die Kraft(-̈e)**
pretty **hübsch**	striking **auffallend**
red-haired **rothaarig**	strong **stark**
I am right-handed **ich bin**	tall **groß, lang**
Rechtshänder [-in]	thin **mager, dünn**
I scowl **ich sehe jdn. finster an***	tiny **winzig**
sex/gender **das Geschlecht(er)**	trendy **schick**
short **kurz, klein**	ugliness **die Häßlichkeit**
similar (to) **ähnlich** +dat	ugly **häßlich**
similarity **die Ähnlichkeit(en)**	walk **der Gang**
size **die Größe(n)**	wavy **gewellt**
slim/slender **schlank**	I weigh **ich wiege**
small **klein**	weight **das Gewicht(e)**
I smile **ich lächele**	
smile **das Lächeln**	

– What a wonderful family photo! And that must be your uncle. You described him so well to me.

– Was für ein schönes Familienfoto! Und das muß dein Onkel sein. Du hast ihn mir ja so gut beschrieben.

– He looks a lot like my father, but he wears glasses and has darker hair than him.

– Er sieht meinem Vater sehr ähnlich, aber er trägt eine Brille und hat dunkleres Haar als er.

– Say, who's that tall, slim man over there?

– Sag mal, wer ist der große, schlanke Mann dort drüben?

– That's Beate's husband. He's a real exercise fanatic.

– Das ist Beates Mann. Er ist ein echter Trimm-Dich-Fanatiker.

I almost didn't recognize my girlfriend's niece. She used to be a little plump, and had short, dark hair. Now she's very slim and her hair is long, wavy and blond.

Ich habe die Nichte meiner Freundin fast nicht erkannt. Sie war immer ein bißchen pummelig und hatte kurzes, dunkles Haar. Jetzt ist sie sehr schlank und ihr Haar ist lang, gewellt und blond.

– Little Ben has dark hair and is about one meter tall. He looks healthy, but he's very thin. He only weighs 16 kilos.

– Der kleine Ben hat dunkles Haar und ist ungefähr ein Meter groß. Er sieht gesund aus, aber er ist sehr mager. Er wiegt nur 16 Kilo.

5b The senses

bitter **bitter**
bright **hell**
bright *(harsh)* **grell**
cold **kalt**
   cold **die Kälte**
colorful **bunt**
dark **dunkel**
darkness **das Dunkel, die Dunkelheit**
delicious **lecker**
disgusting **ekelhaft**
dull **matt**
ear **das Ohr(en)**
eye **das Auge(n)**
face **das Gesicht(er)**
I feel ... **ich fühle mich, mir ist ...**
   it feels **es fühlt sich an***
I feel very cold **Mir ist sehr kalt**
hand **die Hand(¨e)**
I hear **ich höre**
hot **heiß**
light *(color)* **hell**
I listen **ich höre** +dat **zu***
I look **ich blicke**

I look at sth **ich sehe etw. an***
loud **laut**
mouth **der Mund(¨er)**
noise **der Lärm** *(no pl)*, **das Geräusch(e)**
noisy **laut, lärmend**
nose **die Nase(n)**
odor **der Geruch(¨e)**
opaque **trüb, undurchsichtig**
perfume **das Parfüm(s)**
perfumed **parfümiert**
quiet **ruhig**
rough **rauh**
salty **salzig**
I see **ich sehe**
sense **der Sinn(e)**
silence **die Stille**
silent **schweigend, still**
   I am silent **ich schweige**
smell **der Geruch(¨e)**
   I smell **ich rieche**
   it smells (of) **es riecht nach** +dat
smelly **stinkend**

– What kind of coat did you buy yesterday?

— **Was für einen Mantel hast du gestern gekauft?**

– A very chic, red woolcoat.

– **Einen sehr schicken, roten Wollmantel.**

– Dark or light red?
– It's dark red, but actually more of a maroon than a true red.

– **Dunkel- oder hellrot?**
– **Er ist dunkelrot, aber eigentlich mehr rötlichbraun als ein echtes Rot.**

The garage in our new house absolutely has to be painted. It's an ugly green now, and the floor has stains and smells of oil.

Die Garage in unserem neuen Haus muß unbedingt gestrichen werden. Sie ist jetzt in einem häßlichen Grün, und der Boden hat Flecken und riecht nach Öl.

The jam tastes of fruit but is very bitter.

Die Marmelade schmeckt nach Obst, aber sie ist sehr bitter.

soft *(sound)* **sanft, leise**
  soft *(texture)* **weich**
sound **der Klang(⁻e), das**
  Geräusch(e)
it sounds **es klingt**
  it sounds like **es hört sich an***
sour **sauer**
sticky **klebrig, schmutzig**
  it is sticky **es klebt**
stomach **der Magen(-)**
sweet **süß**

taste **der Geschmack**
I taste **ich schmecke**
it tastes (of) **es schmeckt nach**
  +dat
tepid **lauwarm**
tooth **der Zahn(⁻e)**
I touch **ich berühre**
transparent **durchsichtig**
visible (in-) **sichtbar (un-)**
warm **warm**
warmth **die Wärme**

Colors

beige **beige** *(invar)*
black **schwarz**
blue **blau**
brown **braun**
brownish **bräunlich**
cream *(color)* **die Creme**
  cream *(adj)* **cremefarben**
gold **Gold-, golden**
green **grün**
grey/gray **grau**
maroon **rötlichbraun**
orange *(color)* **das Orange**

orange *(adj)* **Orangen-,**
  orangenfarbig
pink **rosa** *(invar)* **, rosarot**
purple **violett**
red **rot**
scarlet **hochrot, knallrot**
silver **Silber-, silbern**
turquoise *(color)* **das Türkis**
  turquoise *(adj)* **türkisfarben**
violet **lila** *(invar)*
white **weiß**
yellow **gelb**

– Please wash your hands before dinner. They're all sticky and dirty from playing.

– Our secretary has a terrible toothache. She can't eat anything, because she doesn't want anything to touch her tooth.

– I am very cold today, and it feels as if we're going to get snow.

– Bitte wasch dir die Hände vor dem Essen. Sie sind ganz klebrig und schmutzig vom Spielen.

– Unsere Sekretärin hat fürchterliche Zahnschmerzen. Sie kann nichts essen, weil sie nicht will, daß etwas ihren Zahn berührt.

– Mir ist heute sehr kalt, und ich habe das Gefühl, als ob wir Schnee bekommen.

NOTE: most colors can be used as neuter nouns, e.g., **das Blau**.

5c Describing things

big **groß**	flat **flach**
broad **breit**	flexible **flexibel**
broken **kaputt, gebrochen**	fresh **frisch**
appearance **die Erscheinung(en), das Aussehen**	full (of) **voll (von +dat), voller** *(invar)*
clean **sauber**	genuine/real **echt**
closed **zu, geschlossen**	hard **hart**
color **die Farbe(n)**	hardness **die Härte**
colorful **bunt**	height **die Größe(n)**
colored **farbig**	high **hoch**
damp **feucht**	kind **die Art(en)**
deep **tief**	large **groß**
depth **die Tiefe(n)**	liquid **flüssig**
dirt **der Schmutz**	little **klein**
dirty **schmutzig**	long **lang**
dry **trocken**	it looks like **es sieht aus* wie**
empty **leer**	low **niedrig**
enormous **ungeheuer**	main **Haupt-**
fashionable **modisch**	material **der Stoff(e)**
fat **dick**	it matches **es passt zu** +dat
firm **fest**	matter **der Stoff(e)**

– What's that over there?
– That thing? It's a new kind of bottle opener.
– Does it work?
–Yes indeed. It's the best there is.

– Was ist das da drüben?
– **Das Ding dort? Es ist eine neue Art Flaschenöffner.**
– **Funktioniert er?**
– **Selbstverständlich. Das ist der beste, den es gibt.**

– I'm looking for something big to stand on.
– Does it matter what?
– Well, it must be something solid.

– **Ich suche etwas Großes, worauf ich stehen kann.**
– **Ist es egal, was?**
– **Na, es muß etwas Solides sein.**

– What about this chair?

– **Wie wäre es mit diesem Stuhl da?**

– That's too low. Is there nothing bigger?

– **Der ist zu niedrig. Gibt es nichts Größeres?**

I can't believe it. The refrigerator is empty again.

Es ist nicht zu glauben. Der Kühlschrank ist schon wieder leer.

moist **feucht**
moldy **modrig**
narrow **eng**
natural **natürlich**
new **neu**
open **auf, offen**
painted **bemalt**
pale **blaß**
pattern **das Muster(-)**
plump **rundlich**
resistant **dicht**
rotten **morsch**
shade **der Farbton(-̈e)**
shallow **flach, seicht**
shiny **glänzend**
short **kurz**
shut **zu, geschlossen**
small **klein**
smooth **glatt**
soft *(texture)* **weich**
softness **die Weichheit**
solid **solid**

soluble **wasserlöslich**
sort **die Sorte(n)**
spot **der Punkt(-̈e)**
spotted **getupft**
stain **der Fleck(en)**
stained **fleckig**
stripe **der Streifen(-)**
striped **gestreift**
subsidiary **Neben-**
substance **die Substanz(en)**
synthetic **Kunst-, künstlich**
thick **dick**
thing **das Ding(e)**
thingamyjig **das Ding, das Dingsbums**
tint **der Ton(-̈e)**
varied **variiert**
waterproof **wasserdicht, wasserfest**
wet **naß**
wide **weit, breit**
width **die Weite**

Ten questions

What's that? **Was ist das?**
What's it for? **Wozu dient es?**
What do you use it for? **Wozu braucht man es?**
Can you see it? **Kannst du es sehen?**
What's it like? **Wie ist es?**
What does it look like? **Wie sieht es aus?**

What does it sound like? **Wie klingt es?**
What does it smell of? **Wonach riecht es?**
What color is it? **Welche Farbe hat es?**
What kind of thing is it? **Was für eine Sache ist das?**

– I am looking for a striped scarf, that matches my coat.

– This is a genuine natural material, soft and thick. That is a synthetic material, it feels smooth but the colors are harsh.

– **Ich suche einen gestreiften Schal, der zu meinem Mantel paßt.**

– **Dies hier ist echte Naturfaser, weich und dicht. Das da ist Kunstfaser, es fühlt sich weich an, aber die Farben sind grell.**

5d Evaluating things

abnormal **anormal**
I adore **ich liebe sehr**
all right **okay**
  it is all right **es geht**
appalling **entsetzlich**
bad **schlecht**
beautiful **schön**
better/best **besser, best-**
cheap **billig**
correct **richtig**
it costs **es kostet**
delicious **köstlich**
I detest **ich hasse**
difficulty **die Schwierigkeit(en)**

difficult/hard **schwierig**
disgusting **ekelhaft**
I dislike **ich mag nicht**
I enjoy **ich genieße, es macht mir**
  Spaß
easy **leicht**
essential (in-) **(un)wesentlich**
excellent **ausgezeichnet**
expensive **teuer**
I fail **es ist mir nicht gelungen**
failure **der Mißerfolg(e)**
  a total failure **eine totale Pleite**
false **falsch**
fine **schön**

– Would you like to try this wine? It's quite delicious.

– Möchten Sie diesen Wein probieren? Er schmeckt ausgezeichnet.

How do you like our neighbor's garden/yard? We do not like it at all.

Wie gefällt Ihnen der Nachbargarten? Wir mögen ihn gar nicht.

You cannot use the elevator today. It's momentarily out of order.

Sie können den Fahrstuhl heute nicht benutzen. Er ist zur Zeit außer Betrieb.

The chef in this restaurant prepares very delicious meals, and he uses only top quality ingredients.

Der Küchenchef dieses Restaurants bereitet sehr köstliche Mahlzeiten zu, und er verwendet nur Zutaten bester Qualität.

Did you hear? The new play at the City Theater was a total failure.

Hast du gehört? Das neue Schauspiel im Stadttheater war eine totale Pleite.

My brother says that the new manager in his department is not very nice, and that last week he was particularly unpleasant.

Mein Bruder sagt, daß der neue Manager in seiner Abteilung nicht sehr nett ist und daß er letzte Woche besonders unangenehm war.

good **gut**
good value **preiswert**
great/terrific **großartig**
I hate **ich hasse**
high **hoch**
important (un-) **(un)wichtig**
incorrect **falsch**
interesting (un-) **(un)interessant**
I like **ich mag, es gefällt mir**
mediocre **mittelmäßig**
necessary (un-) **(un)nötig**
normal **normal**
order **die Ordnung**
  in order **in Ordnung**
  out of order **außer Betrieb**
out of date **veraltet**
ordinary **normal**
pleasant **angenehm**
poor **arm**
practical (im-) **(un)praktisch**
I prefer **ich ziehe vor***

quality **die Qualität(en)**
  top quality **die beste Qualität**
  poor quality **die schlechte Qualität**
right **richtig**
strange **seltsam**
I succeed **es gelingt mir**
success **der Erfolg(e)**
successful **erfolgreich**
true **wahr, echt**
I try **ich versuche**
ugly **häßlich**
unpleasant **unangenehm**
unsuccessful **erfolglos**
I use **ich verwende, ich benutze**
use **der Gebrauch**
useful **praktisch**
well **gut**
worse/worst **schlimm/schlimmst-**
I would rather **ich möchte lieber**
wrong **falsch**

---

a bit **ein bißchen**
enough **genug**
extremely **äußerst**
fairly **ziemlich**
hardly ... at all **kaum**
litte **wenig** (invar)
  a little **ein wenig**
a lot **viel, eine Menge**
much (better) **viel (besser)**

not at all **gar nicht**
particularly **besonders**
quite **ganz**
rather **ziemlich**
really **wirklich**
so **so**
too (good) **zu (gut)**
very **sehr**

– Do you enjoy going to the movie theater? – Yes, I particularly enjoyed last week's movie.

Gehen Sie gern ins Kino? – Ja, der Film letzte Woche hat mir besonders gut gefallen.

If you're looking for an elegant sweater to go with those wool pants, I would recommend this creme colored cashmere one.

Wenn Sie einen eleganten Pullover suchen, der zu den Wollhosen paßt, würde ich diesen cremefarbenen aus Kaschmirwolle vorschlagen.

➤ EXPRESSING VIEWS 6d

43

5e Comparisons

Regular comparatives & superlatives

small	**klein**	smallest (*adj*)	**der kleinste**
small	**kleiner**	smallest (*adv*)	**am kleinsten**

Irregular comparatives & superlatives

big **groß, größer, größt-**
elderly **der/die/das ältere**
extremely **äußerst**
good **gut, besser, best-**
healthy **gesund, gesünder, gesündest-**
high **hoch, höher, höchst-**
highly **höchst**
little **wenig, weniger, wenigst-**
least of all **am wenigsten, am mindesten**
at least **wenigstens**
at the very least **mindestens**
much **viel, mehr, meist-**
mostly **meistens**

near **nah, näher, nächst-**
soon **bald, eher, am ehesten**
willingly **gern, lieber, am liebsten**
acrylic **das Acryl**
brick **der Backstein(e)**
camel hair **das Kamelhaar**
cashmere **die Kaschmirwolle**
cement **der Zement**
china **das Porzellan**
concrete **der Beton**
corduroy **der Cord**
cotton **die Baumwolle**
denim **der Jeansstoff**

NOTE: some common one-syllable adjectives take an Umlaut, e.g., **stark, stärker, stärkst-**

Have you seen our newest products already? They are of the highest quality.

Haben Sie unsere neuesten Produkte schon gesehen? Sie sind von höchster Qualität.

I know you're very busy, but at least give me a call if you're coming home later.

I weiß, daß du sehr beschäftigt bist, aber ruf wenigstens an, wenn du später nach Hause kommst.

Look at our children! Peter, our eldest, is now the tallest. He loves playing soccer, because that's what he enjoys most.

Sehen Sie sich unsere Kinder an! Peter, unser ältester, ist jetzt der größte. Er spielt am liebsten Fußball, weil ihm das am meisten Spaß macht.

If I were you, I would go to the gas station around the corner. You'll pay less for gas there.

An deiner Stelle würde ich zu der Tankstelle um die Ecke fahren. Da bezahlst du weniger für Benzin.

5f Materials

felt	**der Filz**	silk	**die Seide**
flannel	**der Flanell**	silk *(adj)*	**seiden**
gas	**das Gas**	silver	**das Silber**
glass	**das Glas**	steel	**der Stahl**
gold	**das Gold**	steel *(adj)*	**stählern**
iron	**das Eisen**	stone	**der Stein(e)**
iron *(adj)*	**eisern**	stone *(adj)*	**steinern**
lace	**die Spitze**	suede	**das Wildleder**
leather	**das Leder**	terylene	**das Trevira, Diolen**
leather *(adj)*	**ledern**	towelling	**das Frottee**
linen	**das Leinen**	velvet	**der Samt**
material	**der Stoff(e)**	viscose	**die Viskose**
metal	**das Metall(e)**	wood	**das Holz**
mineral	**das Mineral(e/ien)**	wooden	**hölzern**
nylon	**das Nylon**	wool	**die Wolle**
oil	**das Öl(e)**	woolen	**wollen**
paper	**das Papier(e)**	worsted	**das Kammgarn**
plastic	**der Kunststoff(e)**		
polyester	**der Polyester**		
pottery	**die Keramik**		
satin	**der Satin**		

NOTE: compound nouns are commonly used instead of adjectives, e.g., **das Backsteinhaus, der Wollpullover**.

– What do you think? Should I buy the green silk dress, or that one over there with the black lace?
– I like the lace dress the best.

– Was meinst du? Soll ich das grüne Seidenkleid oder das mit der schwarzen Spitze kaufen?
– Mir gefällt das Spitzenkleid am besten.

Next week all suede jackets and leather belts are on sale.

Nächste Woche sind alle Wildlederjacken und Ledergürtel im Angebot.

Nowadays many people prefer natural materials like cotton, linen and wool over synthetic ones.

Heutzutage ziehen viele Leute natürliche Stoffe, wie Baumwolle, Leinen und Wolle, den synthetischen vor.

– Did you succeed in finding something less expensive?
– Yes, this coat is particularly good value. And it's a very good quality.

– Ist es Ihnen gelungen, etwas weniger Teueres zu finden?
– Ja, dieser Mantel ist besonders preiswert. Und die Qualität ist auch sehr gut.

➤ CLOTHES 9c; MINERALS, CHEMICAL ELEMENTS App.23b

6 The human mind & character

6a Human characteristics*

active **aktiv**
I adapt **ich passe mich an***
I annoy **ich ärgere**
bad **schlecht**
bad-tempered **schlechtgelaunt**
I behave **ich benehme mich**
behavior **das Benehmen**
I boast **ich gebe an***
calm **ruhig**
care **die Vorsicht, die Sorge(n)**
careful **vorsichtig, sorgfältig**
careless **nachlässig**
character **der Charakter(e)**
characteristic **die Eigenschaft(en)**
characteristic **charakteristisch**
charming **charmant, anmutig**
cheerful **lustig, vergnügt**
clever **begabt, klug**
confident **voller Selbstvertrauen, selbstsicher**
discipline **die Disziplin**
dreadful **schrecklich**
evil **böse**
I forget **ich vergesse**

forgetful **vergeßlich**
friendly (un-) **(un)freundlich**
fussy **anspruchsvoll**
generous **großzügig**
I get along with **ich verstehe mich gut mit** +dat
gifted **begabt**
good **gut**
good-tempered **gutgelaunt, gutmütig**
guilty **schuldig**
habit **die Gewohnheit(en)**
hard-working **fleißig**
help **die Hilfe**
I help **ich helfe**
helpful **hilfreich, hilfsbereit**
honest (dis-) **(un)ehrlich**
humor **der Humor**
humorous **humorvoll**
immorality **die Unsittlichkeit, die Unmoral**
innocent **unschuldig**
intelligence **die Intelligenz**
intelligent **intelligent**

Gerhard's oldest daughter used to be so shy and quiet. But she has turned into a very self-confident woman.

Gerhards älteste Tochter war immer so schüchtern und ruhig. Aber sie hat sich zu einer sehr selbstbewußten Frau entwickelt.

Sonja is always so serious. I think she has no sense of humor at all.

Sonja ist immer so ernst. Ich glaube sie hat überhaupt keinen Humor.

Mr. Schumann's wife is very pleasant, and she is always so helpful.

Herrn Schumanns Frau ist sehr nett, und sie ist immer so hilfsbereit.

kind (un-) **nett, lieb, (un)freundlich**
kindness **die Liebenswürdigkeit, die Freundlichkeit**
lazy **faul**
laziness **die Faulheit**
lively **temperamentvoll, lebhaft**
manners **die Manieren**
mental(ly) **geistig**
moral (im-) **(un)moralisch**
morality **die Moralität**
morals **die Moral**
nervous **nervös, ängstlich**
nice **nett, freundlich**
I obey **ich gehorche** +dat
optimistic **optimistisch**
patient (im-) **(un)geduldig**
personality **das Temperament(e)**
pessimistic **pessimistisch**
pleasant **lieb, angenehm, nett**
polite (im-) **(un)höflich**
popular **beliebt**
quality **die Eigenschaft(en)**
reason **die Vernunft**
reasonable (un-) **(un)vernünftig**
respect **der Respekt**
respectful **respektvoll**
rude **unhöflich, grob, rüde**
self-confidence **das Selbstvertrauen**
self-esteem **die Selbstachtung**

sense **der Sinn(e)**
(common) sense **der gesunde Menschenverstand**
good sense **die Vernunft**
sense of humor **der Sinn für Humor**
sense of shame **das Schamgefühl**
sensible **vernünftig**
serious **ernst**
shy **schüchtern**
skillful **geschickt**
sociable (un-) **(un)freundlich, gesellig**
stupid **dumm**
stupidity **die Dummheit(en)**
suspicious **argwöhnisch, mißtrauisch**
sympathy **das Mitgefühl, das Mitleid**
tact/tactful **der Takt, taktvoll**
tactless **taktlos**
talented **begabt**
temperament **das Temperament(e)**
temperamental **launenhaft, temperamentvoll**
I trust **ich traue** +dat
trusting **vertrauensvoll**
well-known **bekannt**
wit **der Witz(e)**
witty **geistreich**

The pupils in this school are hard-working and well-behaved.
We encourage self-confidence and discipline.
Bad behavior is punished.

Die Schüler in dieser Schule sind fleißig und benehmen sich gut.
Wir fördern Selbstvertrauen und Disziplin.
Schlechtes Benehmen wird bestraft.

Henrik is well known as a talented, charming, but very temperamental artist.

Henrik ist als ein begabter, charmanter, aber sehr temperamentvoller Künstler bekannt.

➤ THOUGHT PROCESSES 6c; EXPRESSING VIEWS 6d

THE HUMAN MIND & CHARACTER

6b Feelings & emotions

I am afraid (of)   **ich habe Angst (vor +dat)**
I am amazed (at)   **ich staune (über +acc)**
amazement   **das Erstaunen**
I amuse   **ich amüsiere**
   I am amused by   **es amüsiert mich**
amusement   **das Vergnügen**
anger   **die Wut**
angry   **wütend**
I am annoyed (at/about)   **ich ärgere mich (über +acc)**
anxiety   **die Angst, Ängstlichkeit**
anxious   **ängstlich**
I approve (of)   **ich bewillige etw.**
I am ashamed (of)   **ich schäme mich (vor +dat)**
I am bored   **ich langweile mich**
boredom   **die Langeweile**
content (with)   **zufrieden (mit +dat)**
cross (with)   **böse (auf +acc)**
delighted (about)   **entzückt (über +acc)**
I dislike   **es gefällt mir nicht**
dissatisfaction   **die Unzufriedenheit(en)**

dissatisfied (with)   **unzufrieden (mit +dat)**
embarrassed (about)   **verlegen (wegen +gen)**
embarrassment   **die Verlegenheit(en)**
emotion   **das Gefühl(e)**
emotional(ly)   **emotional (emotionell)**
I enjoy ...   **... gefällt mir**
envy   **der Neid**
envious (of)   **neidisch (auf +acc)**
I feel   **ich fühle (mich)**
I forgive   **ich vergebe/verzeihe +dat**
forgiveness   **die Vergebung**
I am frightened (of)   **ich habe Angst (vor +dat)**
furious (about)   **wütend (über +acc)**
fussy   **pingelig**
grateful (to)   **dankbar (+dat)**
gratitude   **die Dankbarkeit**
happiness   **das Glück**
happy (about)   **glücklich (über +acc)**
hate   **der Haß**

My cousin is surprised how fast his son and his wife have adapted to country life. But their children are unhappy and are often bored.

Mein Cousin ist überrascht, wie schnell sich sein Sohn und dessen Frau dem Landleben angepaßt haben. Aber ihre Kinder sind unglücklich und haben oft Langeweile.

The boss is in a bad mood today, because he's annoyed at a customer. I hope he's in a better mood tomorrow.

Der Chef ist heute schlechtgelaunt, weil er sich über einen Kunden ärgert. Hoffentlich ist er morgen wieder besserer Laune.

I hate **ich hasse**
I have a grudge against him **ich bin ihm böse**
hope **die Hoffnung(en)**
I hope (for) **ich hoffe (auf** +acc)
I hope that **hoffentlich**
hopeful **hoffnungsvoll**
idealism **der Idealismus**
indifference **die Gleichgültigkeit**
indifferent (to) **gleichgültig (gegenüber** +dat)
I am indifferent **es macht mir nichts aus***
interest **das Interesse(n)**
I am interested (in) **ich interessiere mich (für** +acc)
jealous **eifersüchtig auf** +acc
jealousy **die Eifersucht**
joy **die Freude(n)**
joyful **freudig**
I like **ich mag**
love **die Liebe(n)**
I love **ich liebe**
miserable (about) **miserabel, unglücklich (über** +acc)
misery **das Elend**

mood **die Laune(n)**
in a good/bad mood **gut/schlecht gelaunt**
I prefer **ich ziehe vor***
I regret **ich bedauere**
satisfaction **die Zufriedenheit**
satisfied (with) **zufrieden (mit** +dat)
surprise **die Überraschung(en)**
I am surprised (at) **ich bin überrascht/erstaunt (über** +acc)
thankful **dankbar**
unhappy **unglücklich**
unhappiness **die Traurigkeit, die Trauer**
I am upset (about) **aufgeregt (wegen** +dat)
I wonder (at) **ich wundere mich (über** +acc)
I wonder if **ich bin gespannt, ob**
worried (about) **besorgt (wegen** +gen)
worry **die Sorge(n)**
I worry (about) **ich mache mir Sorgen (über** +acc)
it worries me **es beunruhigt mich**

– I am really ashamed of my behavior. I was so upset and worried. Please forgive me.

– It's okay. I'm just glad that you're feeling better now.

I wonder if Eckhart suspects that we're giving him a party or if it will really be a surprise.

I'm very interested in tennis, but I also like golf.

– Ich schäme mich wirklich wegen meines Benehmens. Ich war so aufgeregt und ängstlich. Bitte verzeihen Sie mir.

— Es ist schon gut. Ich bin nur froh, daß es Ihnen jetzt besser geht.

Ich bin gespannt, ob Eckhart ahnt, daß wir ihm eine Party geben, oder ob es wirklich eine Überraschung wird.

Ich interessiere mich sehr für Tennis, aber ich mag auch Golf.

49

6c Thought processes

advantage   der Vorteil(e)
   disadvantage   der Nachteil(e)
against   gegen +acc
   I am against it   ich bin dagegen
I analyze   ich analysiere
analysis   die Analyse(n)
I assume   ich nehme an*
assuming that ...   angenommen,
   daß ...
I base   ich gründe
basic   Grund-
basically   im Grunde genommen
basis   die Grundlage(n)
belief   der Glaube(n) (gen -ns)
I believe   ich glaube +dat
   I believe in   ich glaube an +acc
certainty   die Sicherheit(en)
certain/sure   sicher
I consider   ich überlege
   I consider ... (to be)   ich halte ...
   (für +acc)
consideration   der Faktor(en)
   I take into consideration   ich
   berücksichtige
   taking everything into

consideration   alles in allem
context   der Zusammenhang(¨e)
on the contrary   im Gegenteil
controversial   umstritten
I decide   ich beschließe, ich
   entschließe mich
decision   der Entschluß (¨sse)
I determine   ich stelle fest*
I disbelieve   ich glaube nicht
I distinguish   ich unterscheide
doubt   der Zweifel(-)
I doubt   ich bezweifle, ich zweifle
   an +dat
doubtful   zweifelhaft
doubtless/without a doubt   ohne
   Zweifel
exception   die Ausnahme(n)
evidence   der Beweis(e)
evidently   offensichtlich
fact   die Tatsache(n)
   in fact   in der Tat, tatsächlich
false   falsch
for   für +acc
   I am for it   ich bin dafür
I forbid   ich verbiete

– I suggest we try to analyze the problem carefully. But in my view, it will take some time. If you agree, I suggest we meet early on Thursday about it.

– Ich schlage vor, wir versuchen das Problem genau zu analysieren. Aber meiner Ansicht nach, wird es etwas dauern. Wenn Sie einverstanden sind, schlage ich vor, daß wir uns am Donnerstag früh treffen.

– From the beginning I would like to make our position clear. On the one hand we need to do more research. On the other hand we must cut the budget.

– Ich möchte unsere Lage von Anfang an klarmachen. Auf der einen Seite müssen wir mehr Forschung betreiben. Auf der anderen Seite müssen wir das Etat kürzen.

hypothesis **die Hypothese(n)**
implication **die Bedeutung(en)**
interesting **interessant**
issue **die Frage(n)**
I judge **ich beurteile**
judgement **das Urteil(e)**
justice **die Gerechtigkeit**
I justify **ich rechtfertige**
I know **ich weiß**
knowledge **das Wissen, die Kenntnis(se)**
logic **die Logik**
logical **logisch**
memory **das Gedächtnis(se)**
philosophy **die Philosophie(n)**
point of view **der Gesichtspunkt(e)**
I presume **ich nehme an***
principle **das Prinzip(ien), der Grundsatz(-e)**
in/on principle **im/aus Prinzip**
problem **das Problem(e)**
proof **der Beweis(e)**
I prove **ich beweise**
I reason **ich denke durch***
  I reason *(conclude)* **ich schließe**
reason *(faculty)* **der Verstand**

I recognize **ich erkenne**
I reflect **ich denke nach***
relevant **relevant**
I remember **ich erinnere mich** +acc
right **richtig**
  I am right **ich habe recht**
  it is right **es stimmt**
I see **ich sehe**
I solve **ich löse**
solution **die Lösung(en)**
I suppose **ich vermute**
theoretical **theoretisch**
theory **die Theorie(n)**
in theory **theoretisch**
I think **ich denke, ich meine**
thought **der Gedanke(n)** (gen -ns)
true **wahr**
truth **die Wahrheit(en)**
I understand **ich verstehe**
understanding **das Verständnis**
valid (in-) **gültig (un-)**
view **die Ansicht**
  in my view **in/nach meiner Ansicht**
wrong **falsch**
  I am wrong **ich habe unrecht**
  it is wrong **es stimmt nicht**

– What do you think of the speaker?
– In my opinion he did not consider the basic problem. I would have liked to ask more questions.

– In principle I agree with his views. Firstly, he proved the need for new housing. And secondly, he discussed the problems of finding a site.

– **Was halten Sie vom Referenten?**
– **Meiner Meinung nach hat er das Hauptproblem nicht in Betracht gezogen. Ich hätte gern noch einige Fragen gestellt.**
– **Im Prinzip bin ich mit seinen Ansichten einverstanden. Erstens hat er den Bedarf an neuen Häusern festgestellt. Und zweitens hat er die Probleme diskutiert, wie man ein Grundstück findet.**

6d Expressing views

I accept **ich nehme an***
I agree (with) **ich bin (mit** +dat)
  einverstanden
I agree **ich stimme zu***
we agree (about) **wir sind uns**
  einig über +acc
I answer **ich beantworte**
answer **die Antwort(en)**
I argue **ich diskutiere, ich streite**
argument **das Argument(e)**
I ask **ich frage**
I ask (a question) **ich stelle eine**
  Frage
I contradict **ich widerspreche** +dat
I criticize **ich kritisiere**
I define **ich definiere**
definition **die Definition(en)**
I deny **ich leugne, ich bestreite**

I describe **ich beschreibe**
description **die Beschreibung(en)**
I disagree (with) **ich bin (mit** +dat)
  nicht einverstanden
we disagree about **wir streiten**
  uns über +dat
I discuss **ich bespreche, ich**
  diskutiere
discussion **die Diskussion(en)**
I maintain **ich behaupte**
I mean **ich meine**
opinion **die Meinung(en)**
in my opinion **meiner Meinung**
  nach
question **die Frage(n)**
I question **ich bezweifle**
  a thorny question **eine heikle**
  Frage

If I may quote my colleague. As is well known, these statements are contradictory. For example, we can not have total freedom of the press, and censorship.

Wenn ich meinen Kollegen zitieren darf. Wie bekannt ist, widersprechen sich diese Behauptungen. Wir können zum Beispiel nicht die totale Pressefreiheit und die Pressezensur haben.

Norbert had stated from the beginning that it wouldn't be possible to build this machine like that.

Norbert hat von Anfang an behauptet, daß man diese Maschine nicht so bauen könne.

In my opinion he is asking too much.

Meiner Meinung nach verlangt er zu viel.

Would you please explain the pros and cons of the new program? I would also like to hear how it stands in comparison to our present program.

Würden Sie bitte die Vor- und Nachteile des neuen Programms erklären? Ich möchte auch gern hören, wie es im Vergleich zu unserem jetzigen Programm steht.

it is a question of **es handelt
sich um** +acc
I say **ich sage, ich meine**
I state **ich behaupte**
statement **die Behauptung(en)**
suggestion **der Vorschlag(̈-e)**
I suggest **ich schlage vor***
I summarize **ich fasse
zusammen***
summary **die
Zusammenfassung(en)**
I think (of/about) **ich denke
(an/über** +acc)
I think of **ich halte von** +dat
thought **der Gedanke**
I sum up **ich fasse zusammen***

Giving examples

as is known **wie bekannt**
etc./and so on **usw., und so
weiter**
example **das Beispiel(e)**
for example **zum Beispiel**
I give an example **ich gebe ein
Beispiel**
i.e. **das heißt, d.h.**
namely **und zwar**
I quote **ich zitiere**

such as **wie zum Beispiel**

Comparing & contrasting

advantage **der Vorteil(e)**
I compare **ich vergleiche**
comparison **der Vergleich(e)**
in comparison with **im
Vergleich mit** +dat
I contrast **ich stelle** +dat
gegenüber*
it contrasts with **es unterscheidet
sich von** +dat
contrast **der Gegensatz(̈-e)**
in contrast **im Gegensatz zu**
+dat
I differ **ich unterscheide mich**
difference **der Unterschied(e)**
different **unterschiedlich**
different (from) *(adv)* **anders
als**
disadvantage **der Nachteil(e)**
dissimilar **verschieden**
I distinguish **ich unterscheide**
pros and cons **die Vor- und
Nachteile**
relatively **verhältnismäßig**
same **gleich, der/die/dasselbe**
similar **ähnlich**

---

beginning **der Anfang(̈-e)**
from the beginning **von Anfang
an**
I am brief **ich fasse mich kurz**
in brief **kurz**
I conclude **ich schließe**
conclusion **der Schluß (̈-sse)**
in conclusion **zum Schluß**
final **Schluß-**
finally **schließlich**
first **der/die/das erste**
firstly **erstens**
furthermore **weiter**
on the one hand **auf der einen
Seite**

on the other hand **auf der
anderen Seite**
initially **zu Anfang**
last **der/die/das letzte**
lastly **schließlich**
at last **endlich**
next **der/die/das nächste**
place **die Stelle(n)**
in the first place **an erster
Stelle**
in the second place **an
zweiter Stelle**
secondly **zweitens**
in short **kurz**
and so on **und so weiter, usw.**

THE HUMAN MIND & CHARACTER

Arguing a point

admittedly	**zwar**
all the same	**trotzdem**
although	**obgleich**
anyway	**auf jeden Fall**
apart from	**abgesehen von** +dat
as for ...	**was ... betrifft**
as I see it	**nach meiner Ansicht**
as well	**auch**
despite this	**trotzdem**
in effect	**in Wirklichkeit**
however	**aber**
incidentally	**übrigens**
instead	**an seiner Stelle**
instead of	**statt** +gen
just as important	**genauso wichtig**
likewise	**gleichfalls**
no matter whether	**egal, ob**
that may be so	**ich glaube schon**
nevertheless	**trotzdem**
otherwise	**sonst**
in reality	**in Wirklichkeit**
in many respects	**in vielen Hinsichten**
in return	**dafür**
as a rule	**meistens**
so to speak	**gewissermaßen**
in spite of	**trotz** +gen
still, ...	**dennoch**

to tell the truth	**um ehrlich zu sein**
whereas	**indem, während**
on the whole	**im großen und ganzen, alles in allem**

Cause & effect

all the more (because)	**um so mehr, (da)**
as	**da**
because	**weil**
cause	**die Ursache(n)**
consequence	**die Folge(n)**
consequently	**infolgedessen**
effect	**die Wirkung(en), die Auswirkung(en)**
it follows that	**hieraus folgt, daß**
how?	**wie?**
if	**wenn**
reason	**der Grund(⁻e)**
for this reason	**deshalb**
result	**das Ergebnis(se)**
as a result	**infolgedessen**
provided that	**vorausgesetzt**
since	**da**
so long as (conj)	**solange**
that is why (adv)	**deshalb**
therefore/so	**so**
thus	**so**
when(ever)	**wenn**

In many respects things are not too bad.	**In vielen Hinsichten ist die Lage nicht zu schlimm.**
As a rule people try to obey the law.	**Meistens versuchen die Leute dem Gesetz zu gehorchen.**
However, crime is still common, in spite of the efforts of the police.	**Aber die Verbrechen sind immer noch weit verbreitet, trotz der Bemühungen der Polizei.**
– He is not very ill, is he?	**– Er ist nicht sehr krank, oder?**
– Yes he is. His brother is not well either. Therefore we have to postpone our meeting.	**– Doch. Sein Bruder ist auch nicht gesund. Deshalb müssen unsere Besprechung verschieben.**
– I hope they will be better soon.	**– Hoffentlich sind sie bald wieder gesund.**

when *(past event)* **als**
whether **ob**
why? **warum?, wozu?**

Emphasizing

above all **vor allem**
in addition **dazu**
all the more **um so mehr**
also **auch**
certainly **sicher**
clearly **offensichtlich**
under no circumstances **unter keinen Umständen**
completely **völlig, ganz**
especially **besonders**
even (more) **noch (mehr)**
without exception **ohne Ausnahme**
I emphasize **ich betone**
extremely **höchst, äußerst**
far and away **bei weitem**
fortunately **zum Glück**
honestly **ehrlich**
just when **gerade wo**
mainly **hauptsächlich**
moreover **übrigens**
naturally **natürlich, selbstverständlich**
not at all **keineswegs**
not in the least **keineswegs**

both ... and **sowohl ... wie/als**
obviously **offensichtlich, ja**
in particular **ins besondere**
particularly **besonders**
in every respect **in jeder Hinsicht**
I stress **ich betone**
thanks to **dank** +dat
undeniably **unleugbar**
very **sehr**
and what is more **und dazu**

Expressing reservations

even if **auch wenn**
even so **selbst dann**
to some extent **gewissermaßen**
at first sight **beim ersten Blick**
hardly **kaum**
in general **im allgemeinen**
in the main **zum größten Teil**
in part **zum Teil**
partly **teils, teilweise**
perhaps **vielleicht**
presumably **wohl, vermutlich**
probably **wahrscheinlich**
relatively **verhältnismäßig**
unfortunately **leider**
unusual(ly) **ungewöhnlich**
virtually **fast**
in a way **gewissermaßen**

Rolf is said to have gone abroad, in fact to the States.
Rolf is abroad, in fact he's in the States now. He'll probably be there for at least a week. So, unfortunately he won't attend our dinner.

Rolf soll ins Ausland gefahren sein, und zwar in die USA.
Rolf ist im Ausland, und zwar ist er gerade in den USA. Er wird wahrscheinlich mindestens eine Woche dort sein. Deshalb wird er leider nicht an unserem Essen teilnehmen.

Under no circumstances can we let the client wait for this shipment. All the more, because the last one was delayed as well.

Unter keinen Umständen können wir den Kunden auf diese Lieferung warten lassen. Um so mehr, da sich die letzte auch verzögert hatte.

7 | Human life & relationships

7a Family & friends

Friendship

acquaintance **der/die Bekannte**
   (adj/n)
boyfriend **der Freund(e)**
chum **der Kumpel(-)**
classmate **der Klassenkamerad**
   (wk)
companion **der Gefährte** *(wk)*, **die Gefährtin(nen)**
friend **der Freund(e) [-in]**
   close friend **der enge Freund(e) [-in]**
friendship **die Freundschaft(en)**
gang **die Gang(s)**
I get along/on with **ich komme mit jdm. gut zurecht*/aus***
we get together **wir treffen uns**
girl friend **die Freundin(nen)**
I get to know **ich lerne kennen***
human relationships **die menschlichen Beziehungen** *(pl)*
I introduce **ich stelle . . . vor***
mate/buddy **der Kamerad** *(wk)*

penfriend/pal **der Brieffreund(e) [-in]**
relationship **die Verwandtschaft(en)**
schoolfriend/pal **der Schulfreund(e) [-in]**

The family & close relatives

adopted **adoptiert, Adoptiv-**
ancestor **der Vorfahr** *(wk)* **[-in]**
ancestry **die Abstammung(en)**
aunt **die Tante(n)**
   maiden aunt **die unverheiratete Tante(n)**
baby **das Baby(s)**
brother **der Bruder(⁻)**
brothers and sisters **die Geschwister** *(pl)*
brother-in-law **der Schwager(⁻)**
child **das Kind(er)**
close relative **der/die enge Verwandte** *(adj/n)*
closely related **nah verwandt mit** +dat

We're old school friends. We get along very well and do a lot together.

Wir sind alte Schulfreunde. Wir kommen sehr gut miteinander aus und unternehmen viel gemeinsam.

Helmut and Siegfried met each other during their vacation and quickly became close friends.

Helmut und Siegfried haben sich im Urlaub kennengelernt und sind ganz schnell enge Freunde geworden.

I live with my grandparents.

Ich wohne bei meinen Großeltern.

common-law **eheähnlich**
common-law partner **der Partner(-) [-in]**
cousin **der Cousin(s), die Cousine(n)**
dad/daddy **der Vati(s)**
daughter **die Tochter(-)**
daughter-in-law **die Schwiegertochter(-)**
elder **älter**
eldest **der/die/das älteste**
family **die Familie(n)**
family-tree **der Familienstammbaum(-e)**
father **der Vater(-)**
father-in-law **der Schwiegervater(-)**
fiance(e) **der/die Verlobte** (adj/n)
foster **Pflege-**
genealogy **die Genealogie(n)**
godmother **die Patin(nen)**
grandad **der Opa(s)**
grandchild **das Enkelkind(er)**
granddaughter **die Enkeltochter(-)**
grandfather **der Großvater(-)**
grandma **die Großmama(s)**
grandmother **die Großmutter(-)**
grandpa **der Großpapa(s)**
grandparents **die Großeltern** (pl)
grandson **der Enkelsohn(-e)**
granny **die Oma(s)**
guardian **der Vormund(-er)**
half-brother **der Halbbruder(-)**

half-sister **die Halbschwester(n)**
husband **der Ehemann(-er)**
member of the family **der/die Familienangehörige** (adj/n)
mom **die Mutti(s)**
mother **die Mutter(-)**
mother-in-law **die Schwiegermutter(-)**
nephew **der Neffe(n)** (wk)
niece **die Nichte(n)**
only child **das Einzelkind(er)**
parents **die Eltern** (pl)
partner **der Partner(-) [-in]**
related **verwandt**
relation **der/die Verwandte** (adj/n)
sister **die Schwester(n)**
son **der Sohn(-e)**
son-in-law **der Schwiegersohn(-e)**
spouse **der Gatte** (wk), **die Gattin(nen)**
step- **Stief-**
stepfather **der Stiefvater(-)**
twin **der Zwilling(e)**
twin brother **der Zwillingsbruder(-)**
twin sister **die Zwillingsschwester(n)**
uncle **der Onkel(-)**
wife **die Ehefrau(en)**
younger **jünger**
youngest (adj) **der/die/das jüngste**

– Do you have a big family?
– Yes. I have three brothers, four sisters, a sister-in-law and two brothers-in-law. My oldest sister has three children.

I have no close family. I am an only child.

Can you imagine, Lisa's grandpa is getting married again!

– **Hast du eine große Familie?**
– **Ja. Ich habe drei Brüder, vier Schwestern, eine Schwägerin und zwei Schwager. Meine älteste Schwester hat drei Kinder.**

Ich habe keine engen Verwandten. Ich bin (ein) Einzelkind.

Kannst du dir das vorstellen, Lisas Opa heiratet wieder!

7b Love, marriage, & children

Love & marriage

adultery **der Ehebruch(̈e)**
affair **das Verhältnis(se)**
I have an affair with **ich habe ein Verhältnis mit** +dat
alimony **die Unterhaltszahlung(en)**
bachelor **der Junggeselle(n)** *(wk)*
betrothal **die Verlobung(en)**
betrothed **der/die Verlobte** *(adj/n)*
breakdown **der Zusammenbruch(̈e)**
bride **die Braut(̈e)**
bridegroom **der Bräutigam(e)**
bridesmaid **die Brautjungfer(n)**
I cheat on **ich betrüge**
couple **das Paar(e)**
  married couple **das Ehepaar(e)**
I court **ich mache jdm. den Hof**
divorce **die Scheidung(en)**
divorced **geschieden**
I get divorced **ich lasse mich scheiden**
divorcee **der/die Geschiedene** *(adj/n)*
engaged **verlobt**
engagement **die Verlobung(en)**
I fall for **ich bin in jdn. vernarrt**
I fall in love (with) **ich verliebe mich (in** +acc**)**
I get divorced (from) **ich lasse**

mich **(von jdm.) scheiden**
I get engaged to **ich verlobe mich mit** +dat
I get married (to) **ich verheirate mich (mit** +dat**)**
I go out with **ich gehe mit** +dat
we are incompatible **wir passen nicht zueinander**
love **die Liebe(n)**
I love **ich liebe**
lover **der/die Geliebte** *(adj/n)*
marriage **die Ehe(n), die Heirat(en)**
marriage guidance **die Eheberatung**
married **verheiratet**
I marry **ich heirate**
matrimony **der Ehestand** *(no pl)*
mistress **die Geliebte** *(adj/n)*
newly-weds **die Neuvermählten** *(pl)*
orgasm **der Orgasmus (-en)**
promiscuity **die Promiskuität**
he is promiscuous **er wechselt häufig seine Partnerin**
relationship **das Verhältnis(se)**
we separate **wir trennen uns**
separation **die Trennung(en)**
sexual intercourse **der Geschlechtsverkehr** *(no pl)*
we have sex **wir haben Sex**

– Are you married?
– No, but we are engaged.

– Seid ihr verheiratet?
– Nein, aber wir sind verlobt.

Tell me, what do you buy an old bachelor for his birthday?

Sag mal, was kauft man einem alten Junggesellen zum Geburtstag?

I was surprised to hear that your boss and his wife are separating after so many years.

Ich war überrascht zu hören, daß dein Chef und seine Frau sich nach so vielen Jahren trennen.

single **ledig**
single mother **die alleinstehende Mutter(⁻)**
unmarried **unverheiratet**
wedding **die Hochzeit(en)**
widow **die Witwe(n)**
widower **der Witwer(-)**

Birth & children

abortion **die Abtreibung(en)**
I have an abortion **ich lasse das Kind abtreiben**
I adopt **ich adoptiere**
adoption **die Adoption(en)**
baby **das Baby(s)**
babysitter **der Babysitter(-)**
baptism **die Taufe(n)**
I am baptized **ich werde/bin getauft**
birth **die Geburt(en)**
birth control **die Geburtenkontrolle**
birth rate **die Geburtsrate(n)**
birthday **der Geburtstag(e)**
I was born **ich wurde geboren**
boy **der Junge(n)** *(wk)*
I bring up **ich erziehe**
I breast feed **ich stille**
caesarian section **der Kaiserschnitt(e)**
child **das Kind(er)**
child maintenance **das Kindergeld**
child minder **der Kinderbetreuer(er) [-in]**
childhood **die Kindheit(en)**
christening **die Taufe(n)**
I conceive **ich empfange**
condom **das/der Kondom(e), das Präservativ(e)**
contraception **die Empfängnisverhütung**
contractions **die Wehen** *(pl)*
I deliver a baby **ich bringe ein Baby zur Welt**
I am expecting a baby **ich erwarte ein Baby**

family planning **die Familienplanung**
fertile (in-) **(un)fruchtbar**
fertility **die Fruchtbarkeit**
fertility drug **die Fruchtbarkeitspille(n)**
fetus **der Fötus (Foten/Fötusse)**
I give birth **Ich gebäre/bringe zur Welt**
girl **das Mädchen(-)**
infancy **die Kindheit(en)**
infant **das Kleinkind(er)**
infantile **kindlich**
insemination **die Befruchtung(en)**
artificial insemination **die künstliche Befruchtung**
lad **der Bursche(n), der Junge(n)** *(wk)*
lass **das Mädchen(-)**
he looks like his mother **er sieht wie seine Mutter aus***
I have a miscarriage **ich habe eine Fehlgeburt**
midwife **die Hebamme(n)**
nappy/diaper **die Windel(n)**
nanny **das Kindermädchen(-)**
new-born child **das neugeborene Kind(er)**
orphan **die Waise(n), das Waisenkind(er)**
ovary **der Eierstock(⁻e)**
pregnancy **die Schwangerschaft(en)**
I get pregnant **Ich werde schwanger**
period *(monthly)* **die Periode(n)**
I remind of **ich erinnere an** +acc
I spoil my child **ich verwöhne mein Kind**
stillbirth **die Totgeburt(en)**
teenage **Jugend-**
teenager **der Teenager(-)**
toddler **das Kleinkind(er)**
triplets **der Drilling(e)**

➤ FAMILY 7a

7c Life & death

Growing up

adolescent   der/die Jugendliche
   (adj/n)
adolescence   die Jugend
adult   der/die Erwachsene (adj/n)
age   das Alter(-)
aged   bejahrt
centenarian   der/die
   Hundertjährige (adj/n)
child   das Kind(er)
I come from   ich stamme aus +dat
early retirement   der Vorruhestand
elder(ly)   älter
elderly (adj)   der/die/das ältere
eldest (adj)   der/die/das älteste
female   die Frau(en)
   female (adj)   weiblich
foreigner   der Ausländer(-) [-in]
generation   die Generation(en)
generation gap   das
   Generationsproblem(e)
I grow old/older   ich werde größer
grown-up   der/die Erwachsene
   (adj/n)
I grow up   ich wachse auf*
life   das Leben(-)
life insurance   die
   Lebensversicherung(en)
male/man   der Mann(¨er)
   male (adj)   männlich
maturity   die Reife (no pl)
menopause   die Wechseljahre (pl)

middle age   das mittlere
   Lebensalter
new   neu
nickname   der Spitzname(n) (wk)
old   alt
old age   das hohe Alter
old man/woman   der/die Alte
   (adj/n)
old people's home   das
   Altenwohnheim(e)
pension   die Rente(n)
pensioner   der Rentner(-) [-in]
people   die Leute (pl)
person   die Person(en), der
   Mensch(en) (wk)
in the prime of his/her life   in der
   Blüte seiner/ihrer Jahre
puberty   die Pubertät (no pl)
responsible for   verantwortlich für
   +acc
I retire   ich gehe in den
   Ruhestand
retired   pensioniert
retirement   der Ruhestand
senility   die Senilität (no pl)
single   ledig
spinster   die ledige Frau(en)
stranger   der/die Fremde (adj/n)
surname   der Familienname(n)
   (wk)
I take after   ich bin jdm. ähnlich
well brought up   wohlerzogen

– When I grow up, I want to be an astronaut.
– And how old are you now?
– I'm ten.

– **Wenn ich groß bin, möchte ich Astronaut werden.**
– **Und wie alt bist du jetzt?**
– **Ich bin zehn Jahre alt.**

Werner respects his elders.

Werner respektiert ältere Menschen.

Young people often get into conflicts with their parents.

Junge Leute geraten oft in Konflikt mit ihren Eltern.

woman **die Frau(en)**
young **jung**
young person **der junge**
Mensch(en) *(wk)*
younger **jünger**
youngest *(adj)* **der/die/das jüngste**
youth **die Jugend**
youth *(persons)* **der/die**
Jugendliche *(adj/n)*

Death

afterlife **das Leben nach dem Tod**
angel **der Engel(-)**
ashes **die Asche** *(no pl)*
autopsy **die Autopsie(n)**
I bequeath **ich vererbe**
body/corpse **die Leiche(n)**
burial **das Begräbnis(se)**
I bury **ich begrabe**
he is cremated **er wird**
eingeäschert
cremation **die Einäscherung(en)**
crematorium/crematory **die**
Krematorium (-ien)
dead **tot**
death **der Tod(e), das**
Todesfall(-̈e)
death certificate **die**
Sterbeurkunde(n)
death rate **die Sterberate(n)**
I die **ich sterbe**
epitaph **die Grabinschrift(en)**
eulogy **die Lobesrede(n)**
fatal **tödlich**

funeral **die Beerdigung(en)**
grave **das Grab(-̈er)**
gravestone/tombstone **der**
Grabstein(e)
graveyard/cemetery **der**
Friedhof(-̈e)
heaven **der Himmel(-)**
he goes to heaven **er kommt in**
den Himmel
hell **die Hölle**
I inherit **ich erbe**
inheritance **die Erbschaft(en)**
I kill **ich töte**
I am killed **ich komme um***
late *(dead)* **selig**
last rites **die Letzte Ölung**
I lose my life **ich komme ums**
Leben
mortuary **die Leichenhalle(n)**
I mourn (for) **ich trauere um** +acc,
ich beklage
mourning **die Trauer** *(no pl)*
obituary **der Nachruf(e)**
he passes away **er scheidet hin***
remains **die Überreste** *(pl)*
tomb **das Grab(-̈er), das**
Grabmal(-̈e)
undertaker/mortician **der**
Leichenbestatter(-) [-in]
will **der Wille** *(no pl) (gen des*
***Willens) (wk)*
the last will and testament of …
der Letzte Wille des/der …

Mrs. Hansen went into retirement
last August.

Frau Hansen hat sich letzten
August in den Ruhestand
begeben.

It's a matter of life and death.

Es geht um Leben und Tod.

Aunt Gertrud bequeathed her
entire estate to her nephew and
his wife.

Tante Gertrud hat ihr ganzes
Vermögen ihrem Neffen und
seiner Frau vererbt.

➤ SICKNESS 11; WAR 27a

Daily life

8a The house

amenities **die Einrichtung(en)**
apartment **die Wohnung(en)**
block of flats/apartment house **der Wohnblock(-̈e)**
I build **ich baue**
building **das Gebäude(-)**
building plot **das Grundstück(e)**
building site **die Baustelle(n), das Baugelände(-)**
building society/savings & loan association **die Bausparkasse(n)**
bungalow **der Bungalow(s)**
caretaker **der Hausmeister(-)**
chalet **das Chalet(s)**
condominium **die Eigentumswohnung(en)**
council flat **die Sozialwohnung(en)**
council/public housing **der soziale Wohnungsbau** *(no pl)*
detached house **das Einzelhaus(-̈er)**

I build an extension **ich baue ein Zimmer an***
apartment **die Wohnung(en)**
furnished (un-) **(un)möbliert**
home **die Wohnung(en), das Haus(-̈er)**
at home **zu Hause**
house **das Haus(-̈er)**
housing **die Wohnverhältnisse** *(pl)*
landlord **der Grundbesitzer(-), der (Haus)wirt(e)**
lease **der Mietvertrag(-̈e)**
leasehold property **der Pachtbesitz**
I let/rent out **ich vermiete**
I modernize **ich modernisiere**
mortgage **die Hypothek(en)**
mortgage rate **der Zinssatz(-̈e)**
I move (house) **ich ziehe um***
I occupy **ich bewohne**
I own **ich besitze**

Renate and Karl are buying a new detached house.
Renate und Karl kaufen ein neues Einfamilienhaus.

We are having a house built.
Wir lassen ein Haus bauen.

I live in a rented, furnished apartment.
Ich wohne in einer möblierten Mietwohnung.

My tenancy has two weeks to run.
Mein Mietvertrag hat noch zwei Wochen zu laufen.

We moved two years ago. Our house has a pleasant view
Wir sind vor zwei Jahren um gezogen. Unser Haus hat einen schönen Ausblick.

owner-occupied house **das Eigentumshaus(¨er)**
penthouse **die Dachterrassenwohnung(en)**
prefabricated house **das Fertighaus(¨er)**
I rent **ich miete**
rent **die Miete(n)**
semidetached house **das Zweifamilienhaus(¨er)**
street lighting **die Straßenbeleuchtung** *(no pl)*
I take out a mortgage **ich nehme eine Hypothek auf***
tenancy **das Miet/Pachtverhältnis(se)**
tenant **der Mieter(-), der Pächter(-)**

Rooms

attic **die Dachstube(n), die Mansarde(n)**
balcony **der Balkon(s)**
basement **das Kellergeschoß (-sse)**
bathroom **das Badezimmer(-)**
bedroom **das Schlafzimmer(-)**
breakfast room **der Frühstücksraum(¨e)**
cellar **der Keller(-)**
corridor **der Gang(¨e)**

dining room **das Eßzimmer(-)**
en suite **mit Bad**
garage **die Garage(n)**
ground floor **das Erdgeschoß (-sse)**
hall(way) **der Hausflur(e)**
kitchen **die Küche(n)**
landing **der Treppenabsatz(¨e), der Flur(e)**
lavatory/bathroom **die Toilette(n)**
living room **das Wohnzimmer(-)**
loft **der Dachboden(¨)**
lounge **das Wohnzimmer(-)**
mezzanine floor **das Zwischengeschoß (-sse)**
passage **der Korridor(e)**
room **das Zimmer(-)**
shower room **der Duschraum(¨e)**
staircase **das Treppenhaus(¨er)**
stairs **die Treppe(n)**
study **das Arbeitszimmer(-)**
sunroom **die Veranda (-en)**
terrace **die Terrasse(n)**
toilet **die Toilette(n)**
toilet/W.C. **das WC(s)**
upper floor **das obere Stockwerk(e)**
utility room **die Waschküche(n)**
verandah **die Veranda(s)**

Anke's penthouse is for rent.

Ankes Dachterrassenwohnung ist zu vermieten.

Let's go home.

Laß uns nach Hause gehen.

We are renting an apartment at the moment. The rent is very high and I do not like the estate/housing development.

Wir mieten zur Zeit eine Wohnung. Die Miete ist sehr hoch, und ich mag die Wohnsiedlung nicht.

It's a large three-room apartment on the third floor.

Es ist eine geräumige Drei-Zimmer-Wohnung im dritten Stock.

8b The home

aerial **die Antenne(n)**
back door **die Hintertür(en)**
big **groß**
blind **das Rollo(s)**
button **der Knopf(:-e)**
carpet **der Teppich(e)**
ceiling **die Decke(n)**
central **Zentral-**
central heating **die Zentralheizung(en)**
chimney/smokestack **der Schornstein(e)**
clean **sauber**
clothes hanger **der Kleiderbügel(-)**
comfortable (un-) **bequem**
cosy **gemütlich**
curtain **der Vorhang(:-e), die Gardine(n)**
desk **der Schreibtisch(e)**
dirty **schmutzig**
door **die Tür(en)**
door handle **der Türgriff(e)**
door knob **der Türknauf(:-e)**
door mat **die Fußmatte(n)**
downstairs **(nach) unten**
dusty **staubig**
dustbin/trash can **die Mülltonne(n)**
electric **elektrisch**
electric plug **der (elektrische) Stecker(-)**
electric socket **die Steckdose(n)**
electricity **der Strom, die Elektrizität**
filthy **dreckig**
fire alarm **der Feueralarm(e)**
fire extinguisher **der Feuerlöscher(-)**
fireplace **der offene Kamin(e)**
extension cord **das Verlängerungskabel(-)**
floor **der (Fuß)boden(:-)**
floor *(storey/story)* **der Stock, das Stockwerk(e)**
on the first (second Am.) floor **im ersten Stock**

front door **die Haustür(en)**
furnished **möbliert**
furniture **die Möbel** *(pl)*
item of furniture **das Möbelstück(e)**
gas **das Gas**
glass *(material)* **das Glas(:-er)**
handle **der Griff(e)**
handle *(of broom, pan)* **der Stiel(e)**
handle *(on jug)* **der Henkel(-)**
hearth **der Kamin(e)**
hearth and home **Haus und Herd**
household **der Haushalt(e)**
included **inbegriffen**
key **der Schlüssel(-)**
keyhole **das Schlüsselloch(:-er)**
lamp **die Lampe(n)**
lampshade **der Lampenschirm(e)**
letterbox **der Briefkasten(:)**
lever **der Hebel(-)**
lift **der Lift(s), der Fahrstuhl(:-e)**
light bulb **die Birne(n)**
light **das Licht(er)**
light switch **der Lichtschalter(-)**
lock **das Schloß (:-sser)**
mantelpiece **der Kaminsims(e)**
mat **die Matte(n)**
modern **modern**
new **neu**
nice **schön, nett**
off *(switch)* **aus**
off *(tap/faucet)* **zu**
old **alt**
on *(switch, tap/faucet)* **an**
own **eigen**
pipe **das Rohr(e)**
plaster **der Verputz** *(no pl)*
plumbing **die Leitungen** *(pl)*
price **der Preis(e)**
radiator **der Heizkörper(-), die Heizung** *(no pl)*
roof **das Dach(:-er)**
rubbish/garbage **der Abfall(:-e)**
shelf **das Regal(e)**

shutters **der Fensterladen(ꞏ)**
situation **die Lage(n)**
skylight **das (Dach)Fenster(-)**
small **klein**
step **die Stufe(n)**
switch **der Schalter(-)**
tile *(roof)* **der Dachziegel(-)**
  tile *(ceramic)* **die Fliese(n)**
upstairs **(nach) oben**
vase **die Vase(n)**
view **die Aussicht(en)**
wall **die Mauer(n)**
  (inside) **die Wand(ꞏe)**
  (partition) **die Trennwand(ꞏe)**
wastepaper basket **der Papierkorb(ꞏe)**
water **das Wasser**
window **das Fenster(-)**
window sill **die Fensterbank(ꞏe)**
wire/flex **das Kabel(-)**
wiring **die elektrischen Leitungen** *(pl)*
wood **das Holz**

Electrical items

blender **der Mixer(-)**
cassette deck **das Kassettendeck(s)**
cassette recorder **der Kassettenrecorder(-)**
coffee machine **die Kaffeemaschine(n)**
compact-disc player **der CD-Spieler(-**
chest freezer **die Tiefkühltruhe(n)**

dishwasher **der Geschirrspüler(-)**
electric appliance **das Elektrogerät(e)**
electric razor/shaver **der Rasierapparat(e)**
electric stove **der Elektroherd(e)**
food mixer/processor **die Küchenmaschine(n)**
fridge/refrigerator **der Kühlschrank(ꞏe)**
freezer **der Tiefkühlschrank(ꞏe)**
hairdryer **der Fön(e)®**
iron **das Bügeleisen(-)**
microwave oven **der Mikrowellenherd(e)**
radio **das Radio(s)**
record player **der Schallplattenspieler(-)**
refrigerator **der Kühlschrank(ꞏe)**
stereo system **die Stereoanlage(n)**
tape player **der Kassettenspieler(-)**
tape recorder **der Kassettenrecorder(-)**
television (TV) **das Fernsehen** *(no pl)*
tumble drier **der Trockenautomat(en)**
TV set **der Fernseher(-)**
vacuum cleaner **der Staubsauger(-)**
video recorder **der Videorecorder(-)**
Walkman® **der Walkman(s)®**
washing machine **die Waschmaschine(n)**

Where did Alex put the toolbox? **Wo hat Alex den Werkzeugkasten hingestellt?**

Careful, there's a step. **Vorsicht, hier ist eine Stufe.**

If you're too cold, you can turn the heat up. **Wenn es dir zu kalt ist, kannst du die Heizung höher stellen.**

We have rented a furnished apartment. **Wir haben eine möblierte Wohnung gemietet.**

The electricity has been cut off. **Der Strom ist gesperrt.**

8c Furnishings

Lounge

armchair **der Lehnstuhl(¨e)**
ashtray **der Aschenbecher(-)**
bookshelf **das Bücherregal(e)**
bookcase **das Bücherregal(e), der Bücherschrank(¨e)**
bureau **der Sekretär(e)**
coffee table **der Kaffeetisch(e)**
cupboard/closet **der Schrank(¨e)**
cushion **das Kissen(-)**
easy chair **der Sessel(-)**
ornament **der Schmuck, der Ziergegenstand(¨e)**
picture **das Bildnis(se), das Gemälde(-)**
    picture *(portrait)* **das Porträt(s)**
photo **das Foto(s)**
poster **das Poster(-)**
pouffe **der Puff(e)**
rocking chair **der Schaukelstuhl(¨e)**
rug **der Läufer(-)**
settee **die Couch(en), das Sofa(s)**
sofa **das Sofa(s)**

Kitchen

bottle opener **der Flaschenöffner(-)**
bowl **die Schüssel(n)**
broom **der Besen(-)**
cloth **der Stoff(e), das Tuch(¨er)**
clothes line **die Wäscheleine(n)**
clothes peg **die Wäscheklammer(n)**
coffee pot **die Kaffeekanne(n)**
crockery/dishes **das Geschirr** *(no pl)*
cup **die Tasse(n)**
cupboard **der Schrank(¨e)**
    wall cupboard **der Wandschrank(¨e)**
cutlery **das Besteck(e)**
dish **die Schüssel(n)**
dishrag **der Spüllappen(-)**
dish washer **die Spülmaschine**

dish washing liquid **das Spülmittel(-)**
drain board **das Ablaufbrett(er)**
duster **das Staubtuch(¨er)**
fork **die Gabel(n)**
garbage can **der Mülleimer(-)**
gas oven **der Gasofen(¨)**
gas stove **der Gasherd(e)**
glass **das Glas(¨er)**
    wine glass **das Weinglas(¨er)**
jug **der Krug(¨e), die Kanne(n)**
knife **das Messer(-)**
    carving knife **das Tranchiermesser(-)**
leftovers **die Überreste** *(pl)*
mug **der Becher(-)**
oven **der Ofen**
peppermill **die Pfeffermühle(n)**
plate **der Teller(-)**
rag **der Lappen**
salt shaker **der Salzstreuer(-)**
saucer **die Untertasse(n)**
scouring pad **der Topfkratzer(-)**
sink **das Spülbecken(-)**
sink unit **die Spüle(n)**
spoon **der Löffel(-)**
stove **der Herd(e),**
tap/faucet **der Wasserhahn(¨e)**
teapot **die Teekanne(n)**
tea towel **das Geschirrtuch(¨er)**
tray **das Tablett(s)**
washing powder **das Waschmittel(-)**

Dining room

chair **der Stuhl(¨e)**
candle **die Wachskerze(n)**
candlestick **der Kerzenhalter(-)**
china cabinet **die Anrichte(n), der Geschirrschrank(¨e)**
hot warmer **die Warmhalteplatte(n)**
place setting **das Gedeck(e)**
serviette **die Serviette(n)**
sideboard **das Büffett(s)**

table **der Tisch(e)**
table cloth **die Tischdecke(n)**
table napkin/serviette **die Serviette(n)**

Bedroom

alarm clock **der Wecker(-)**
bed **das Bett(en)**
   bunk bed **das Etagenbett(en)**
   double bed **das Doppelbett(en)**
bedclothes **das Bettzeug** *(no pl)*
bedside table **der Nachttisch(e)**
bedspread **der Bettüberwurf(-̈e)**
blanket **die Decke(n)**
chest of drawers **die Kommode(n)**
dressing table **die Frisierkommode(n)**
duvet **das Federbett(en)**
pillow **das Kopfkissen(-)**
quilt **die Steppdecke(n)**
sheet **das Bettuch(-̈er)**
wardrobe **der Kleiderschrank(-̈e)**

Bathroom

basin **das (Wasch)becken(-)**
bath **das Bad(-̈er)**
bathplug **der Stöpsel(-)**
bath mat **die Badematte(n)**
clothes brush **die Kleiderbürste(n)**
flannel **der Waschlappen(-)**
laundry basket **der Waschkorb(-̈e)**
mirror **der Spiegel(-)**
nail brush **die Nagelbürste(n)**
plug **der Stecker(-)**
shampoo **das Shampoo(s)**
shower **die Dusche(n)**
sink **das Waschbecken(-)**
soap **die Seife(n)**
tap **der Wasserhahn(-̈e)**
toilet **das Klo(s), die Toilette(n)**
toilet paper **das Toilettenpapier**
toothbrush **die Zahnbürste(n)**
toothpaste **die Zahnpasta(s)**
towel **das Handtuch(-̈er)**
towel rail **der Handtuchhalter(-)**
washbasin **das Waschbecken(-)**

The washing machine doesn't work! Can you repair it?

Die Waschmaschine funktioniert nicht. Können Sie sie reparieren?

Please come into the living room.

Bitte kommen Sie ins Wohnzimmer.

Would you please take the teapot out of the china cabinet?

Würdest du mal bitte die Teekanne aus der Anrichte nehmen?

Could we have some clean towels?

Könnten wir einige saubere Handtücher bekommen?

During the winter, our grandma likes to sit in her rocking chair by the fireplace.

Im Winter sitzt unsere Oma gerne in ihrem Schaukelstuhl am Kamin.

Tell your brother to clear the table and put the dishes in the sink.

Sag deinem Bruder, er soll den Tisch abräumen und das Geschirr ins Spülbecken stellen.

▶ GARDENING 24c; TOOLS App.8b; TOILETRIES 9b

8d Daily routine

bath	**das Bad(-̈er)**
bed	**das Bett(en)**
breakfast	**das Frühstück(e)**
clean	**sauber**
cleaner	**die Putzperson(en)**
daily routine	**der Alltag** *(no pl)*
dinner *(evening)*	**das Abendessen(-)**
dirty dishes	**der Abwasch**
evening meal	**das Abendbrot(e)**
home	**das Heim(e), das Haus(-̈er)**
home *(at home)*	**zu Hause**
home *(to one's home)*	**nach Hause**
housekeeper/maid	**die Haushälterin(nen)**
housework	**die Hausarbeit(en)**
laundry	**die Wäsche**
lunch	**das Mittagessen(-)**
school	**die Schule(n)**
shop	**der Laden(-̈)**
sleep	**der Schlaf** *(no pl)*
spare *(left over)*	**der Rest(e)**
spare *(available)*	**übrig, frei**
spare time	**die Freizeit**
spring cleaning	**der Frühjahrsputz**
supper	**das Abendessen(-)**
time	**die Zeit(en)**
work	**die Arbeit(en)**

Actions

I break	**ich breche**
I bring	**ich bringe**
I buy	**ich kaufe**
I carry	**ich trage**
I change *(clothes)*	**ich ziehe mich um***
I chat	**ich plaudere**
I clean	**ich putze, ich mache sauber***
I clear away	**ich räume weg***
I clear the table	**ich räume/decke den Tisch ab***
I cook	**ich koche**
I close *(door)*	**ich mache zu***

I darn	**ich stopfe**
I dirty	**ich mache schmutzig**
I do	**ich tue, ich mache**
I drink	**ich trinke**
I drop	**ich lasse fallen***
I dry up	**ich trockne ab***
I dust	**ich wische Staub**
I eat	**ich esse**
I empty	**ich leere**
I enter	**ich betrete**
I extend	**ich baue aus*/an***
I fall	**ich falle**
I fasten	**ich verschließe**
I fasten *(attach)*	**ich mache fest***
I fill	**ich fülle**
I get dressed	**ich ziehe mich an***
I get undressed	**ich ziehe mich aus***
I get up	**ich stehe auf***
I go to bed	**ich gehe ins Bett**
I go to sleep	**ich gehe schlafen***
I go to the toilet	**ich gehe zur Toilette**
I have breakfast	**ich frühstücke**
I have lunch	**ich esse zu Mittag**
I have tea/coffee	**ich trinke Tee/den Nachmittagskaffee**
I heat	**ich heize**
I iron	**ich bügele**
I knit	**ich stricke**
I knock	**ich klopfe, schlage**
I lay the table	**ich decke den Tisch**
I leave	**ich verlasse** +acc
I let *(allow)*	**ich erlaube**
I let/rent	**ich vermiete**
I live	**ich wohne**
I lock	**ich schließe ab***
I make	**ich mache**
I make wet/dampen	**ich befeuchte**
I mend	**ich repariere, flicke**
I move (house)	**ich ziehe um***
I move in	**ich ziehe ein***
I move out	**ich ziehe aus***
I move	**ich bewege mich**

it is on **es ist an**
it is off **es ist aus**
I paint **ich streiche an*, ich male an***
I pick up **ich hebe auf***
I polish **ich poliere**
I prepare **ich bereite vor***
I press *(button)* **ich drücke (den Knopf)**
  I press *(iron)* **ich bügele**
I put on *(clothes)* **ich ziehe an***
  I put on *(radio, TV)* **ich mache an***
I put away **ich räume weg***
I put right **ich stelle zurecht***
I repair/fix **ich repariere**
I rest **ich ruhe mich aus***
I ring *(telephone)* **ich telefoniere**
  I ring *(doorbell)* **ich klingele**
I rinse **ich spüle**
I sew **ich nähe**
I share **ich teile**
I shine **ich poliere**
I shop **ich kaufe ein***
I shower **ich dusche**
I shut/close **ich schließe**
I sit down **ich setze mich (hin*)**

I sit **ich sitze**
I sleep **ich schlafe**
I speak **ich spreche**
I stand **ich stehe**
I stand up **ich stehe auf***
I start **ich beginne**
I stop **ich beende**
I sweep **ich kehre, ich fege**
I switch/turn off **ich schalte aus***
I switch/turn on **ich schalte ein***
I take off **ich ziehe aus***
I tear **ich zerreiße**
I throw away **ich werfe weg***
I tidy/straighten up **ich räume auf***
I tie **ich binde**
I unblock **ich schließe auf***
I undo **ich mache auf***
I use **ich benutze**
I wake up **ich wache auf***
I wake up someone **ich wecke jdn.**
I wallpaper **ich tapeziere**
I wash **ich wasche**
I wash up/wash dishes **ich wasche ab***
I watch TV **ich sehe fern***
I wear **ich trage**

I get up at seven o'clock, get dressed and go to work.

Ich stehe um sieben Uhr auf, ziehe mich an und gehe zur Arbeit.

Dinner will be at 9 p.m.

Das Abendessen ist um 9 Uhr.

Mrs. Fischer does the cleaning and dusting for us on Fridays.

Freitags macht Frau Fischer bei uns sauber und wischt Staub.

Shopping

9a General terms

article **der Artikel(-)**
assistant/sales clerk **der Verkäufer(-) [-in]**
automatic door **die automatische Tür(en)**
banknote **der Geldschein(e)**
bargain **das Sonderangebot(e)**
basement **das Untergeschoß (-sse)**
business **das Geschäft(e)**
cash desk/register **die Kasse(n)**
change *(coinage)* **das Wechselgeld(er)**
cheap **billig, preiswert**
checkout **die Kasse(n)**
choice **die Auswahl** *(no pl)*
closed **geschlossen, zu**
coin **die Münze(n)**
color **die Farbe(n)**
costly **kostspielig**
credit **der Kredit(e)**
credit card **die Kreditkarte(n)**
customer information **die Kundeninformation(en)**
customer service **der Kundendienst(e)**
day off/closed **am ... geschlossen**

dear **teuer**
department **die Abteilung(en)**
deposit **die Anzahlung(en)**
discount **der Rabatt(e)**
elevator **der Fahrstuhl(-e)**
entrance **der Eingang(-e)**
escalator **die Rolltreppe(n)**
exit **der Ausgang(-e)**
expensive **teuer**
fashion **die Mode(n)**
fire door **die Feuertür(en)**
fire exit **der Notausgang(-e)**
fitting room **der Anproberaum(-e)**
free **frei, kostenlos**
free gift **(die Ware) umsonst**
it is good value **es ist preisgünstig**
handbag **die Handtasche(n)**
instructions for use **die Gebrauchsanweisung(en)**
item **die Ware(n), der Gegenstand(-e)**
manager **der Manager(-), der Geschäftsführer(-) [-in]**
open **geöffnet, auf**
opening hours **die Öffnungszeiten** *(pl)*

Eight questions

Anything else?/Is that all?	**Sonst noch etwas?/Ist das alles?**
Are you being served?	**Werden Sie bedient?**
Can I help you?	**Kann ich Ihnen helfen?**
Do you want anything in particular?	**Möchten Sie etwas Bestimmtes?**
Sliced or whole?	**Geschnitten oder im Stück?**
What would you like?	**Was möchten Sie?**
Whose turn is it?	**Wer ist dran?**

packet **das Päckchen(-)**
I pay **ich bezahle**
pocket **die Tasche(n)**
I pull **ich ziehe**
purse **der Geldbeutel(-)**
I push **ich drücke**
quality **die Qualität(en)**
real/genuine **echt**
receipt **die Quittung(en)**
reduced **ermäßigt**
reduction **die Ermäßigung(en)**
refund **das Geld zurück**
sale **der Ausverkauf(-̈e)**
security guard/store detective **der/ die Sicherheitsbeamte** *(adj/n)* **[-in]**
self-service **die Selbstbedienung(en)**
shop/store **der Laden(-̈)**
shop assistant/sales person **der Verkäufer(-) [-in]**
shop keeper **der Geschäftsinhaber(-) [-in]**
shoplifter **der Ladendieb(e)**
shopping list **der Einkaufszettel(-)**
shopping basket **der Einkaufskorb(-̈)**
shopping trolley/cart **der Einkaufswagen(-)**
shut **zu**
it shuts **es schließt**
special offer **das Sonderangebot(e)**
I spend **ich gebe aus***
summer sale **der Sommerschlußverkauf** *(no pl)*

till **die Kasse(n)**
till receipt **der Kassenbon(s)**
trader **der Händler(-)**
traveler's check **der Reisescheck(s)**
wallet **die Brieftasche(n)**
way in **der Eingang(-̈e)**
way out **der Ausgang(-̈e)**

Actions

I change **ich wechsle**
I choose **ich wähle**
I decide **ich entscheide**
I dress **ich ziehe mich an***
I exchange **ich tausche**
I have on/wear **ich trage**
I push in **ich drücke ein***
I put on **ich ziehe an***
line up **ich stehe an***
I select **ich sortiere aus***
I sell **ich verkaufe**
I serve **ich bediene**
I shop **ich kaufe ein***
I shoplift **ich stehle, ich klaue**
I show **ich zeige**
I spend (money) **ich gebe aus***
I steal **ich stehle**
I take off **ich ziehe aus***
I try on **ich probiere (an*)**
I wait **ich warte**
I wear **ich trage**
I weigh **ich wiege**
I wrap up **ich packe/wickle ein***

How much is it? Have you anything cheaper?
Can I pay by check?
Do you take credit cards?
I've no change.
Can you change this note?

– Is there a deposit on the bottle?
– No, the bottle is nonreturnable.

Wieviel kostet das? Haben Sie (irgend)was Billigeres?
Kann ich mit Scheck bezahlen?
Nehmen Sie Kreditkarten?
Ich habe kein Kleingeld.
Können Sie mir diesen (Geld)schein wechseln?

– Ist auf der Flasche Pfand?
– Nein, es ist eine Einwegflasche.

➤ HOUSEHOLD GOODS & TOILETRIES 9b; CLOTHING 9c

9b Household goods & toiletries

Toiletries

acne cream   **die Aknesalbe(n)**
aftershave (lotion)   **das After-shave/Rasierwasser**
antiperspirant   **das Anti-transpirant**
bubble bath   **das Schaumbad**
brush   **die Bürste(n)**
cologne   **das Kölnischwasser**
comb   **der Kamm(¨e)**
condom   **das Kondom(e)**
cotton wool   **die Watte**
cosmetics   **das Kosmetikum (-a)**
deodorant   **der (Deo-)spray(s)**
eye liner   **der Eyeliner**
face cream   **die (Haut)creme(s)**
foot powder   **der/das Fußpuder(-)**
glasses   **die Brille(n)**
hairbrush   **die Haarbürste(n)**
dental floss   **die Zahnseide(n)**
lipsalve   **die Lippenpomade(n)**
lipstick   **der Lippenstift(e)**
makeup   **das Make-up**
makeup remover pad   **die Abschminkwatte**
mascara   **die Wimperntusche(-)**
mouthwash   **das Mundwasser**
nail file   **die Nagelfeile(n)**
paper handkercief   **das Papiertaschentuch(¨er)**
perfume   **das Parfüm(e/s)**
razor   **der Rasierapparat(e)**

razor blades   **die Rasierklinge(n)**
sanitary towels   **die Binde(n)**
shampoo   **das Shampoo(s), das Haarwaschmittel(-)**
soap   **die Seife(n)**
spray   **der/das Spray(s)**
sunglasses   **die Sonnenbrille(n)**
suntan lotion   **das Sonnenöl(e)**
talcum powder   **der/das Talkumpuder**
tampon   **der Tampon(s)**
tissues   **das Papiertaschentuch(¨er)**
toilet water   **das Toilettenwasser**
toilet paper   **das Toilettenpapier**
toiletries   **die Toilettenartikel** *(pl)*
toothpaste   **die Zahnpasta(s)**
toothbrush   **die Zahnbürste(n)**

Household items

airfreshener   **der Luftreiniger(-)**
bleach   **das Reinigungsmittel(-), Bleichmittel(-)**
cellophane wrapping   **die Frischhaltefolie**
clothes pegs   **die Wäscheklammer(n)**
dishwashing liquid   **das Spülmittel(-)**
fire lighter   **der Feueranzünder(-)**
foil/aluminum foil   **die (Aluminium)folie(n)**

Expressions of quantity

a bar of ...	**ein Stück/ein Riegel/eine Tafel...**
a bottle of ...	**eine Flasche ...**
a hundred gram(me)s of ...	**hundert Gramm ...**
a kilo of ...	**ein Kilo ...**
a liter of ...	**ein Liter ...**
a packet of ...	**ein Päckchen ...**
a slice of ...	**eine Scheibe ...**
a tin/can of ...	**eine Büchse/Dose ...**
half a pound of ...	**ein halbes Pfund ...**

insect spray **das Insektenbekämpfungsmittel(-)**
kitchen roll **das Papierhandtuch(¨er)**
match **das Streichholz(¨er)**
mouse trap **die Mausefalle(n)**
paper napkin/serviette **die Papierserviette(n)**
paper towel **das Papiertuch(¨er)**
scouring pad **der Topfkratzer(-)**
string **die Schnur(¨e)**
washing/wash powder **das Waschpulver(-)**

Basic foodstuffs

bacon **der Schinkenspeck**
beef **das Rindfleisch**
beer **das Bier(e)**
biscuit/cookie **der Keks(e)**
bread **das Brot(e)**
   black bread **der Pumpernickel, das Schwarzbrot(e)**
   bread and butter **das Butterbrot(e)**
   rye bread **das Roggenbrot(e)**
   slice **die Scheibe(n)**
   sliced bread **das Brot in Scheiben**
   toast **der Toast(e)**
   white bread **das Weizenbrot(e)**
   wholemeal bread **das Vollkornbrot(e)**
butter **die Butter**
cakes **der Kuchen(-)**
cereal **das Getreide, die Getreideflocken**
cheese **der Käse**
chips/french fries **die Pommes Frites**
chocolate spread **der Schokoladenaufstrich(e)**
cola **die Cola(s)**
coffee **der Kaffee(s)**
   instant coffee **der Pulverkaffee(s)**
crisps/chips *(US)* **die Chips**
custard **die Vanillesoße(n)**

egg **das Ei(er)**
fish **der Fisch(e)**
fruit **die Frucht(¨e), das Obst**
ham **der Schinken**
jam **die Marmelade(n)**
juice **der Saft(¨e)**
lemonade **die Limonade(n)**
loaf **das Brot(e), der Laib(e)**
macaroni **die Makkaroni(s)**
margarine **die Margarine**
marmalade **die Orangenmarmelade(n)**
mayonnaise **die Mayonnaise**
meat **das Fleisch**
milk **die Milch**
mustard **der Senf**
oil **das Öl(e)**
olive-oil **das Olivenöl(e)**
pasta **die Nudel(n)**
paté **die Pastete(n)**
peanut-butter **die Erdnußbutter**
pepper **der Pfeffer**
pizza **die Pizza(s)**
pork **das Schweinefleisch**
pudding **der Pudding(s)**
roll *(bread)* **die Semmel(n), das Brötchen**
salt **das Salz(e)**
sandwich **das Sandwich(es)**
   open sandwich **das belegte Brot(e)**
sardine **die Sardine(n)**
sauce **die Soße(n)**
sausage **die Wurst(¨e)**
soup **die Suppe(n)**
spaghetti **die Spaghetti** *(pl)*
spice **das Gewürz(e)**
sugar **der Zucker**
   cube/lump sugar **der Würfelzucker**
sunflower oil **das Sonnenblumenöl(e)**
tea **der Tee(s)**
teabag **der Teebeutel(-)**
vegetables **das Gemüse(-)**
vinegar **der Essig**
wine **der Wein(e)**

➤ FOOD & DRINK 10; MEAT 10b; VEGETABLES 10c

9c Clothing

anorak/parka der Anorak(s)
beautiful schön
big groß
bikini der Bikini(s)
blouse die Bluse(n)
boot der Stiefel(-)
bra der BH, der Büstenhalter(-)
brand new funkelnagelneu
briefs der Slip(s)
cagoule das Windhemd(en)
cap die Mütze(n)
cardigan die Strickjacke(n)
check kariert
clothes die Kleider (pl)
clothing die Kleidung
coat der Mantel(-)
colorfast waschecht
colorful bunt
cravate die Krawatte(n)
dress das Kleid(er)
elegant elegant
embroidered bestickt
fashion die Mode(n)
fashionable modisch
glove der Handschuh(e)
handkerchief das
  Taschentuch(-er)
hat der Hut(-e)
headscarf das Kopftuch(-er)
heel der Absatz(-e)
jacket die Jacke(n)
jeans die Jeans (pl)
jersey der Pullover(-)
jumper der Pulli(s)
knitted gestrickt
knitwear die Strickware(n)
ladies' wear die
  Damenbekleidung
the latest fashion die neueste
  Mode
linen die Wäsche
lingerie die Damenunterwäsche
long lang
long-sleeved langärm(e)lig
loose locker, lose

loud/brash laut
low-heeled mit flachem Absatz
manmade fiber die Kunstfaser(n)
matching passend zu +dat
men's wear die Herrenbekleidung
non-iron bügelfrei
pair das Paar(e)
panties der (Damen)slip(s)
pants die Hose(n)
plain einfach, schlicht
printed gedruckt, bedruckt
pyjamas der Schlafanzug(-e)
raincoat der Regenmantel(-)
sandal die Sandale(n)
scarf der Schal(s)
shirt das (Ober)hemd(e)
shoe der Schuh(en)
shoelace der Schnürsenkel(-)
short sleeves kurzärm(e)lig
silky seidig
size die Größe(n)
skirt der Rock(-e)
slip der Unterrock(-e)
small klein
smart elegant, schick
sneakers der Freizeitschuh(e)
sock die Socke(n)
soft weich
stocking der Strumpf(-e)
striped gestreift
suit der Anzug(-e)
sweater der Pullover(-)
sweatshirt das Sweatshirt(s)
swimming trunks die Badehose(n)
swimsuit der Badeanzug(-e)
T-shirt das T-Shirt(s)
tie der Schlips(e)
tight eng
tights die Strumpfhose(n)
trainers der Sportschuh(e)
ugly häßlich
umbrella der Regenschirm(e)
underpants die Unterhose(n)
underwear die Unterwäsche
unfashionable unmodern

vest **die Weste(n), das Unterhemd(en)**

Alterations & repairs

alteration **die Änderung(en)**
I alter **ich ändere**
belt **der Gürtel(-)**
buckle **die Schnalle(n)**
button **der Knopf(-e)**
collar **der Kragen(-)**
dressmaker **der Damenschneider(-) [-in]**
dressmaking **das Schneidern**
dry cleaning **die chemische Reinigung**
hat pin **die Hutnadel(n)**
hem **der Saum(-e)**
I hem **ich säume**
I iron/press **ich bügele**
jewellery/jewelry **der Schmuck**
knitting machine **die Strickmaschine(n)**

knitting needle **die Stricknadel(n)**
material **der Stoff(e)**
needle **die Nadel(n)**
patch **der Flicken(-)**
pin **die Stecknadel(n)**
pocket **die Tasche(n)**
press stud/snap fastener **der Druckknopf(-e)**
I repair **ich bessere aus***
safety pin **die Sicherheitsnadel(n)**
I sew **ich nähe**
sewing machine **die Nähmaschine(n)**
sleeve **der Ärmel(-)**
I stitch **ich nähe**
I take in/let out **ich mache enger/weiter**
tailor **der Schneider(-) [-in]**
tailored **geschneidert**
thread **der Faden(-)**
turn-up/cuff **der Aufschlag(-e)**
zip(per) **der Reißverschluß (-sse)**

Expressions in clothes shops/stores

I'm next. **Ich bin der /die Nächste.**
I would like a … **Ich möchte …**
What color? **Welche Farbe?**
Do you have the same in red? **Haben Sie das gleiche in Rot?**
I would like it in brown. **Ich hätte es gern in braun.**
I prefer … **Ich bevorzuge …**
I would rather have … **Ich würde lieber das … nehmen/haben.**
I take/wear size … **Ich trage Größe …**
I'd like it two sizes bigger. **Ich hätte es gern zwei Größen größer.**

Can I try it on? **Kann ich es anprobieren?**
That's not quite right. **Das ist nicht ganz richtig/das Richtige.**
They don't go together. **Das paßt nicht zusammen.**
It suits me. **Es paßt/steht mir.**
I like it. **Mir gefällt es.**
I'll take it. **Ich nehme es.**
I'll take the big one. **Ich nehme das große.**
I bought it at the sale. **Ich habe es im Schlußverkauf gekauft.**
I would like to change it. **Ich möchte es gern (um)tauschen.**

Food & drink

10a Drinks & meals

Drinks

alcoholic **der Alkoholiker(-) [-in]**
alcoholic **alkoholisch**
aperitif **der Aperitif(s)**
beer **das Bier(e)**
black coffee **der schwarze Kaffee(s)**
brandy **der Weinbrand(-e), der Kognak(s)**
champagne **der Champagner(-), der Sekt(e)**
chocolate (drinking) **die (heiße) Schokolade(n)**
cider **der Apfelwein(e)**
cocktail **der Cocktail(s)**
coffee **der Kaffee(s)**
cola **die Cola(s)**
draught beer **das Bier(e) vom Faß**
drink **das Getränk(e)**
dry **herb**
fruit juice **der Fruchtsaft(-e)**
heavy **schwer**
juice **der Saft(-e)**
lemonade **die Limonade(n)**
light **leicht**
low alcohol **alkoholarm**
orange juice/squash **der Orangensaft(-e)**
milk **die Milch**
milkshake **das Milchmixgetränk(e)**
mineral **das Mineral(-e)**
mineral water **das Mineralwasser(-)**
    fizzy **mit Kohlensäure**
    still **ohne Kohlensäure**
nonalcoholic **alkoholfrei**
punch **die Bowle(n)**
red wine **der Rotwein(e)**

sherry **der Sherry(s)**
sour **sauer**
sparkling wine **der Schaumwein(e)**
spirits **die Spirituosen** *(pl)*
sweet **süß**
tea **der Tee(s)**
water **das Wasser(-)**
whisky **der Whisky(s)**
white coffee **der Kaffee (mit Sahne)**
white wine **der Weißwein(e)**
wine **der Wein(e)**

Drinking out

bar **die Bar(s)**
barman/barmaid **der Kellner(-) [-in]**
beer hall **die Bierhalle(n)**
bottle **die Flasche(n)**
cafe **das Café(s)**
coffee bar **die Kaffeebar(s)**
cellar **der Keller(-)**
coffee shop **der Kaffeeladen(-)**
counter/bar **der Ladentisch(e), die Theke(n)**
I drink **ich trinke**
I get drunk **ich betrinke mich**
pub **die Kneipe(n)**
public house **das Lokal(e)**
refreshments **die Erfrischungen** *(pl)*
saucer **die Untertasse(n)**
sip **das Schlückchen(s)**
straw **der Trinkhalm(e)**
teaspoon **der Teelöffel(-)**
wine cellar **der Weinkeller(-)**
wine glass **das Weinglas(-er)**
wine tasting **die Weinprobe(n)**

Meals

appetizer/starter **die Vorspeise(n)**
breakfast **das Frühstück(e)**
course **der Gang(⁻e)**
dessert **der Nachtisch** *(no pl)*
I dine **ich speise**
dinner **das Mittag-/Abendessen**
dish **das Gericht(e)**
I eat **ich esse**
I have/take **ich nehme**
I have a snack **ich esse eine Kleinigkeit**
I have breakfast **ich frühstücke**
I have dinner **ich esse zu Abend**
I have lunch **ich esse zu Mittag**
lunch **das Mittagessen(-)**
main **Haupt-**
meal **das Essen(-), die Mahlzeit(en)**
snack **der Imbiß(e)**
supper **das Abendessen(-)**

Eating out

I add up the bill **ich mache die Rechnung**
bill/check **die Rechnung(en)**
bowl **die Schüssel(n)**
charge **der Preis(e)**
I charge **ich verlange**
cheap **billig, preiswert**
I choose **ich wähle**
it costs **es kostet**
cup **die Tasse(n)**
I decide **ich entscheide mich**
dessert **der Nachtisch(e)**

expensive **teuer**
first course **der erste Gang(⁻e)**
fixed price **der Festpreis(e)**
fork **die Gabel(n)**
glass **das Glas(⁻er)**
inclusive **inklusiv, einschließlich**
knife **das Messer(-)**
main course **das Hauptgericht(e)**
menu **die Speisekarte(n)**
menu of day **das Tagesangebot(e), das Tagesmenü(s)**
napkin **die Serviette(n)**
I order **ich bestelle**
order **die Bestellung(en)**
place setting **das Gedeck(e)**
plate **der Teller(-)**
portion **die Portion(en)**
reservation **die Reservierung(en)**
I serve **ich bediene**
service **die Bedienung**
set menu **die Tageskarte(n)**
side-dish **die Beilage(n)**
spoon **der Löffel(-)**
table **der Tisch(e)**
tablecloth **die Tischdecke(n)**
I take away/out **ich nehme mit***
tip/gratuity **das Trinkgeld(er)**
I tip **ich gebe ein Trinkgeld**
toothpick **der Zahnstocher(-)**
tourist menu **die Touristenspeisekarte(n)**
tray **das Tablett(s)**
waiter/waitress **der Kellner(-) [-in]**
wine list **die Weinkarte(n)**

---

cafeteria **das Selbstbedienungsrestaurant(s)**
canteen **die Kantine(n)**
hot-dog stall **die Wurstbude(n)**
ice-cream parlor **die Eisdiele(n)**
pizza parlor **die Pizzeria(s)**

pub/inn **das Wirtshaus(⁻er)**
restaurant **das Restaurant(s)**
self-service **die Selbstbedienung(en)**
snack bar **die Imbißstube(n)**
take-away/out **zum Mitnehmen**

➤ COOKING, EATING 10d; BASIC FOODSTUFFS 9b

10b Fish & meat

Fish & seafood

anchovy	**die Sardelle(n)**
carp	**der Karpfen(-)**
clam	**die Venusmuschel(n)**
cockle	**die Herzmuschel(n)**
cod	**der Kabeljau(e)**
crab	**der Krebs(e)**
crayfish/crawfish	**die Languste(n)**
eel	**der Aal(e)**
fish	**der Fisch(e)**
hake	**der Seehecht(e)**
herring	**der Hering(e)**
langouste	**die Languste(n)**
lobster	**der Hummer(-)**
mussels	**die Miesmuschel(n)**
octopus	**der Tintenfisch(e)**
oyster	**die Auster(n)**
perch	**der Flußbarsch(e)**
pike	**der Hecht(e)**
plaice	**die Scholle(n)**
prawn	**die Krabbe(n)**
salmon	**der Lachs(e)**
sardine	**die Sardine(n)**
scampi	**die Scampi** (pl)
seafood	**die Meeresfrüchte** (pl)
shell	**die Muschel(n)**
shellfish	**die Meeresfrüchte** (pl)
shrimp	**die Krabbe(n), die Garnele(n)**
snails	**die Schnecke(n)**
sole	**die Seezunge(n)**
squid	**der Tintenfisch(e)**
sturgeon	**der Stör(e)**
trout	**die Forelle(n)**
tuna/tunny	**der Thunfisch(e)**
turbot	**der Steinbutt(e)**
whitebait	**der Breitling(e)**

Where can we get a drink around here?	**Wo können wir hier in der Nähe etwas zu trinken bekommen?**
I would like a white wine with soda.	**Ich möchte einen Weißwein gespritzt.**
Two white coffees, please.	**Zweimal Kaffee mit Sahne bitte.**
I'd like a pot of coffee, please.	**Ich hätte gerne ein Kännchen Kaffee.**
Can I have a mineral water, please?	**Könnte ich bitte ein Mineralwasser bekommen?**
I'd rather have tuna than crab.	**Ich nehme lieber den Thunfisch als den Krebs.**
Would you prefer cod or sole?	**Möchtest Du lieber Kabeljau oder Seezunge?**
One trout with boiled potatoes.	**Einmal Forelle mit Salzkartoffeln.**
Shall we try the chicken?	**Wollen wir das Hühnchen probieren?**
I'll have a rare steak with french fries and salad, please.	**Ich möchte bitte ein leicht durchgebratenes Steak mit Pommes frites und Salat.**

Meat & meat products

bacon **der Schweinespeck**
beef **das Rindfleisch**
beefburger **der Beefburger(-)**
bolognese **die Bolognese**
chop **das Kotelett(s)**
cold meats **der Aufschnitt** *(no pl)*
cold table **das kalte Büffet(s)**
cutlet **der/das Schnitzel(-)**
escalope **das Schnitzel(-)**
ham **der Schinken**
hamburger **der Hamburger(-)**
hare **der Hase(n)**
hotdog **der Hot-Dog(s)** *(wk)*, **das heiße Würstchen(-)**
kidney **die Niere(n)**
lamb **das Lammfleisch**
liver **die Leber**
liver sausage **die Leberwurst(-e)**
meat **das Fleisch**
meatball **der Fleischklops(-e)**
mixed grill **gemischte Grillplatte(n)**
mutton **das Hammelfleisch**
pate **die Pastete(n)**
pork **das Schweinefleisch**
rissole **die Frikadelle(n)**

salami **die Salami(s)**
sausage **die Wurst(-e)**
sirloin **das Rindfleischfilet(s)**
steak **das Steak(s)**
stew **der Eintopf(-e)**
veal **das Kalbfleisch**
venison **das Reh(e), das Wild** *(no pl)*

Poultry

chicken **das Hühnchen(-)**
duck **die Ente(n)**
goose **die Gans(-e)**
partridge **das Rebhuhn(-er)**
pheasant **der Fasan(e)**
pigeon **die Taube(n)**
poultry **das Geflügel**
quail **die Wachtel(n)**
turkey **die Pute(n)**

Egg dishes

egg **das Ei(er)**
boiled egg **das gekochte Ei(er)**
fried egg **das Spiegelei(er)**
omelette **das Omelett(s)**
poached egg **das pochierte Ei(er)**
scrambled egg **das Rührei(er)**

Traditional German dishes

die Gulaschsuppe beef soup
die Leberknödelsuppe liver dumpling soup
eingelegte Heringe pickled herrings
Forelle in Mandelbutter trout in almond butter
der Heringsalat herring salad
Lachs vom Grill grilled salmon
der Matjes young herring
der Rollmops(-e) pickled herring
der Salzhering(e) salted herring

der Aufschnitt cold, sliced meat
die Blutwurst blood sausage
die Bockwurst boiled sausage

das Eisbein mit Sauerkraut pork knuckle with sauerkraut
das Geschnetzelte meat cut in strips and stewed
der/das Gulasch beef stew
der Hasenpfeffer jugged hare
der Sauerbraten braised beef (marinaded in vinegar)
das Schweinekotelett(s) pork chop
die Thüringer Rostbratwurst fried sausage
das Wiener Schnitzel veal schnitzel
das Zigeunerschnitzel(-) veal in spicy sauce

10c Vegetables, fruit, & dessert

Vegetables

artichoke **die Artischocke(n)**
asparagus **der Spargel**
avocado **die Avocado(s)**
baked beans **gebackene Bohnen**
beans **die Bohne(n)**
beetroot **die rote Bete(n)**
broccoli **der Brokkoli** *(pl)*
Brussels sprout **der Rosenkohl**
 (no pl)
cabbage **der Kohl** *(no pl)*, **der**
 Kohlkopf(-e)
carrot **die Mohrrübe(n)**
cauliflower **der Blumenkohl**
celeriac **der Knollensellerie**
celery **der Sellerie**
chickpea **die Kichererbse(n)**
chicory/endive **der Endivensalat**
corn **der Mais**
corn on the cob **der Maiskolben(-)**
cucumber **die Gurke(n)**
eggplant **die Aubergine(n)**
French bean **die Brechbohne(n)**
gherkin **die saure Gurke(n)**
haricot bean **die Gartenbohne(n)**
herb **das Kraut(-er)**
leek **der Lauch(e), der Porree(s)**
lentil **die Linse(n)**
lettuce **der Kopfsalat(e)**
marrow **der Kürbis(e)**
mushroom **der Pilz(e), der**
 Champignon(s)
onion **die Zwiebel(n)**
parsnip **die Pastinake(n)**
pea **die Erbse(n)**
pepper **die Paprikaschote(n)**

potato **die Kartoffel(n)**
 boiled **die Salzkartoffel(n)**
 jacket **die Pellkartoffel(n)**
 mashed **der Kartoffelbrei**
 roast **die Röstkartoffel(n)**
pumpkin **der Kürbis(e)**
radish **das Radieschen(-)**
rice **der Reis**
salad **der Salat(e)**
spinach **der Spinat**
sweetcorn **der Mais**
tomato **die Tomate(n)**
turnip **die Steckrübe(n)**
vegetable **das Gemüse(-)**
watercress **die Kresse(n)**
zucchini **die Zucchini** *(pl)*

Fruit

apple **der Apfel(-)**
apricot **die Aprikose(n)**
banana **die Banane(n)**
berry **die Beere(n)**
bilberry **die Heidelbeere(n)**
blackberry **die Brombeere(n)**
blackcurrant **die schwarze**
 Johannesbeere(n)
cherry **die Kirsche(n)**
chestnut **die Kastanie(n)**
coconut **die Kokosnuß (-sse)**
currant **die Korinthe(n)**
date **die Dattel(n)**
fig **die Feige(n)**
fruit **die Frucht(-e), das Obst** *(no*
 pl)
fruit pie **die Obsttorte(n)**
gooseberry **die Stachelbeere(n)**

I want a tomato salad. **Ich möchte einen Tomatensalat.**
Does it have garlic in it? **Ist da Knoblauch drin?**

grape   **die Weinbeere(n)**
bunch of grapes   **die Weintraube(n)**
grapefuit   **die Pampelmuse**
hazelnut   **die Hazelnuß (ˉsse)**
kiwifruit   **die Kiwi(s)**
lemon   **die Zitrone(n)**
lime   **die Limone(n)**
melon   **die Melone(n)**
nut   **die Nuß (ˉsse)**
olive   **die Olive(n)**
orange   **die Orange(n)**
passion fruit   **die Passionsfrucht(ˉe)**
peach   **der Pfirsich(e)**
peanut   **die Erdnuß (ˉsse)**
pear   **die Birne(n)**
peel   **die Schale(n)**
I peel   **ich schäle**
piece of fruit   **das Obststück(e)**
pineapple   **die Ananas(se)**
pip   **der Kern(e)**
plum   **die Pflaume(n)**
pomegranate   **der Granatapfel(ˉ)**
prune   **die Backpflaume(n)**
raisin   **die Rosine(n)**
raspberry   **die Himbeere(n)**
redcurrant   **die rote Johannisbeere(n)**
rhubarb   **der Rhabarber** *(no pl)*
stone   **der Kern(e)**
strawberry   **die Erdbeere(n)**
sultana   **die Sultanine(n)**

tangerine   **die Mandarine(n)**
walnut   **die Walnuß(ˉe)**

Dessert

biscuit/cookie   **der Keks(e)**
blancmange   **der Pudding(s)**
caramel   **die Karamelle(n)**
chocolate   **die Schokolade(n)**
chocolates   **die Praline(n)**
cake   **der Kuchen(-)**
cream   **die Sahne, die Creme**
creme caramel   **die Karamelcreme**
custard   **die Vanillesoße(n)**
dessert   **der Nachtisch**
flour   **das Mehl**
fresh fruit   **das Frischobst** *(no pl)*
fruit of the day/season   **die Früchte der Saison**
fruit salad   **der Fruchtsalat(e)**
gateau   **die Torte(n)**
ice cream   **das Eis**
mousse   **das Mousse**
pancake   **der Pfannkuchen(-)**
pastry   **der Blätterteig(e)**
pie   **die Pastete(n)**
pudding   **der Pudding(s)**
stewed apple   **das/der Apfelmus**
stewed fruit   **das Kompott(e)**
sweet   **der Nachtisch**
tart   **das Obsttörtchen(-)**
vanilla   **die Vanille**
whipped cream   **die Schlagsahne**
yoghurt   **der Joghurt(s)**

Traditional dishes

Bratkartoffeln   fried potatoes
Butterreis   fried rice
Himmel und Erde   potato and apples with black pudding
Kartoffelklöße/knödel   potato dumplings
Kartoffelpuffer(-)   potato pancake
Sauerkraut   pickled cabbage

Spätzle   Swabian noodles
der Kaiserschmarren   pancake with raisins
die rote Grütze   red fruit pudding
Salzburger Nockerln   sweet soufle
Schwarzwälder Kirschtorte   Black Forest Gateau
Zwetschenknödel   plum dumplings

FOOD & DRINK

10d Cooking & eating

Food preparation

I bake **ich backe**
I beat **ich schlage**
I boil **ich koche**
bone **der Knochen(-)**
  bone *(of fish)* **die Gräte(n)**
I bone **ich entferne die**
  Knochen/Gräten
I braise **ich schmore**
in breadcrumbs **paniert**
breast **die Brust(-̈e)**
I carve **ich tranchiere**
I chop **ich hacke**
I clear the table **ich räume den**
  Tisch ab*
I cook **ich koche**
cooking/cuisine **die Küche, die**
  Kochkunst
creamed **-püree**
I cut **ich schneide**
I dice **ich schneide in Würfel**
diced **gehackt**
I dry up **ich trockne ab***
flavoring **der Geschmack** *(no pl)*
I fry **ich brate**

I garnish with **ich garniere mit**
  +dat
I grate **ich reibe**
gravy **die Bratensoße(n)**
I grill **ich grille**
grilled **vom Grill**
with ice **mit Eis**
ingredients **die Zutaten** *(pl)*
large **groß**
leg **die Keule(n)**
I lay/set the table **ich decke den**
  Tisch
I marinate **ich mariniere**
I mix **ich mixe**
I mix in **ich mische ein***
I peel **ich schäle**
I pour **ich gieße**
preparation **die Vorbereitung(en)**
I prepare **ich bereite vor***
rare **leicht durchgebraten**
recipe **das Rezept(e)**
roast **der Braten**
I roast **ich brate**
roasted **gebraten**
in sauce **in Soße(n)**

Potato cakes
Peel and grate 1 kg raw potatoes.

Add a grated onion, 50g flour and salt to the potatoes. Mix into a dough.

Heat plenty of cooking oil in a frying pan.
Put spoonfuls of the mixture into the hot pan and make about 4 cakes.
Fry golden brown on both sides and serve with stewed apples.

Kartoffelpuffer
1 kg rohe Kartoffeln schälen und grob reiben.

Eine geriebene Zwiebel, 50g Mehl, Salz unter den rohen Kartoffelbrei mischen. Zu einem Teig verrühren.

In einer Pfanne reichlich Backöl erhitzen.
Mit einem Löffel den Teig in die heiße Pfanne geben und etwa 4 Plätzchen machen.
Die Reibekuchen an beiden Seiten goldgelb backen und mit Apfelmus servieren.

I sift/sieve **ich siebe durch***
sliced **in Scheiben**
I spread **ich streiche**
stewed **gedämpft**
I stir **ich verrühre**
stuffed **gefüllt**
I toast **ich toaste**
toasted **getoastet, überbacken**
I wash up **ich wasche ab***
I weigh **ich wiege**
well done **gut durchkocht**
I whip/whisk **ich schlage**

Eating

additive **der Zusatz(ˉe)**
appetite **der Appetit**
appetizing **appetitanregend**
bad **schlecht**
I bite **ich beiße**
bitter **bitter**
calorie **die Kalorie(n)**
  low-calorie **kalorienarm**
I chew **ich kaue**
cold **kalt**
delicious **lecker**
diet **die Diät**
  I'm on a diet **ich mache eine Schlankheitskur**
fatty/oily **fett**
food **die Lebensmittel** *(pl)*
fresh(ly) **frisch**
healthy **gesund**
I help myself **ich bediene mich**
hot **heiß**
hunger **der Hunger**

hungry **hungrig**
  I am hungry **ich bin hungrig, ich habe Hunger**
I like **ich mag**
mild **mild**
I offer **ich biete**
I pass (the salt) **ich reiche jdm. (das Salz)**
piece **das Stück(e)**
I provide **ich versorge (jdn.) mit** +dat, **ich besorge (etw.)**
salty **salzig**
I serve **ich serviere, ich trage auf***
serving **die Portion(en)**
sharp **scharf**
I smell **ich rieche**
soft **weich**
sour **sauer**
spicy **pikant, würzig**
stale *(bread)* **altbacken**
strong **stark, fest**
I swallow **ich (ver)schlucke**
sweet **süß**
taste **der Geschmack**
  it tastes of **es schmeckt nach** +dat
tasty **schmackhaft**
thirst **der Durst**
thirsty **durstig**
  I am thirsty **ich habe Durst**
I try **ich probiere, ich versuche**
vegan **der radikale Vegetarier(-) [-in]**
vegetarian **der Vegetarier(-) [-in]**
  vegetarian *(adj)* **vegetarisch**

Enjoy your meal!	**Guten Appetit!**
Did you enjoy it?	**Hat's geschmeckt?**
Dinner is served.	**Darf ich zu Tisch bitten?**
It tastes of lemon.	**Es schmeckt nach Zitrone.**
Pour the wine.	**Schenk' den Wein ein!**
Pass the salt, please.	**Reich` (mir) bitte das Salz rüber.**

➤ HOUSEHOLD ITEMS, BASIC FOODSTUFFS 9b

Sickness & health

11a Accidents & emergencies

accident **der Unfall(-̈e)**
alive **am Leben**
ambulance **der Krankenwagen(-)**
black eye **das blaue Auge**
bomb **die Bombe(n)**
break **der Bruch(-̈e)**
I break **ich breche**
I break my arm **ich breche mir den Arm**
I have broken my leg **ich habe mir ein Bein gebrochen**
break **die Bruchstelle(n)**
breakage **der Bruch(-̈e)**
broken **gebrochen**
bruise **der blaue Fleck(e/en)**
I bruise **ich bekomme einen blauen Fleck**
burn **die Verbrennung(en)**
I burn **ich verbrenne (mich)**

casualty **der/die Verunglückte** *(adj/n)*
casualty department **die Unfallabteilung(en)**
it catches fire **es fängt Feuer**
I collide **ich stoße zusammen***
collision **der Zusammenstoß(-̈e)**
I have cut my finger **ich habe mich in den Finger geschnitten**
I crash (into) **ich knalle (gegen +acc)**
I crush **ich quetsche**
dead **tot**
death **der Tod, der Todesfall(-̈e)**
I die **ich sterbe**
emergency **der Notfall(-̈e)**
emergency department **die Notaufnahme(en)**
emergency exit **der Notausgang(-̈e)**

– What's happened?

– Was ist los?

– There has been an accident!
We need an ambulance quickly!

**– Es ist ein Unfall passiert!
Wir brauchen schnellstens einen Krankenwagen!**

Call the fire department!

Rufen Sie die Feuerwehr!

It was his fault, not mine!

Es war seine Schuld, nicht meine!

My friend is injured!
Are you a doctor?
Where's the nearest hospital?

**Mein Freund ist verletzt!
Sind Sie Arzt?
Wo befindet sich das nächste Krankenhaus?**

Calm down!

Beruhigen Sie sich!

emergency services **der Notdienst(e)**
it explodes **es explodiert**
explosion **die Explosion(en)**
I extinguish **ich lösche**
I fasten my seatbelt **ich schnalle mich an***
fatal **tödlich**
fire **der Brand(ẽe)**
fire brigade **die Feuerwehr**
fire engine **das Feuerwehrauto(s)**
fire extinguisher **der Feuerlöscher(-)**
fireman **der Feuerwehrmann(ẽer)**
first aid **die erste Hilfe**
graze **die Schramme(n)**
I graze **ich schramme mich**
I have an accident **ich habe einen Unfall**
hospital **das Krankenhaus(ẽer)**
impact **der Zusammenprall(ẽe)**
incident **der Vor-/Zwischenfall(ẽe)**
I injure **ich verletze**
injury **die Verletzung(en)**
injured **verletzt**
insurance **die Versicherung(en)**

I insure **ich versichere**
I kill **ich töte**
killed **getötet**
life belt **der Rettungsgurt(e)**
life jacket **die Schwimmweste(n)**
oxygen **der Sauerstoff**
paramedic **der Sanitäter(-) [-in]**
I recover consciousness **ich komme wieder zu mir**
I rescue **ich rette**
rescue **die Rettung(en)**
rescue services **der Rettungsdienst(e)**
I run over **ich überfahre**
I rush **ich renne, ich eile**
safe **sicher**
safe and sound **gesund und wohlbehalten**
safety belt **der Sicherheitsgurt(e)**
I save **ich rette**
seat belt **der Sitzgurt(e)**
terrorist attack **das Terroristenattentat(e)**
third party **die dritte Person(en)**
witness **der Zeuge(n)** *(wk)* **[-in]**

Fasten safety belts.

Bitten anschnallen!

I think I have broken my arm. It hurts a lot.

Ich glaube, ich habe mir den Arm gebrochen. Es tut sehr weh.

Sylvia has cut her hand badly.

Sylvia hat sich tief in die Hand geschnitten.

Statistics show that the most likely place for accidents is in the home.

Laut Statistik sollen die meisten Unfälle zu Hause passieren.

SICKNESS & HEALTH

11b Illness & disability

arthritis **die Arthritis**
I am asleep **ich schlafe**
asthma **das Asthma**
awake **wach**
bacillus **der Bazillus (-en)**
bacteria **die Bakterie(n)**
I bleed **ich blute**
blind **blind**
blood **das Blut**
breath **der Atem, der Atemzug(-e)**
I breathe **ich atme**
breathless **atemlos**
catarrh **der Katarrh(e)**
I catch a cold **ich erkälte mich**
circulatory problem **die Kreislaufstörung(en)**
constipated **verstopft**
constipation **die Verstopfung(en)**
convalescence **die Genesung**
I am convalescing **ich genese**
cough **der Husten**
I cough **ich huste**
I cry **ich weine**
I cut **ich schneide**
dead **tot**
deaf **taub**

deafness **die Taubheit**
death **der Tod(-e)**
depressed **deprimiert**
depression **die Depression(en)**
diarrhea **der Durchfall**
I die **ich sterbe**
diet **die Diät**
disabled **behindert**
disease **die Krankheit(en)**
dizziness **das Schwindelgefühl(e)**
dizzy **schwindelig**
Down's syndrome **das Down-Syndrom**
drug **die Droge(n), die Arznei(en)**
drugged **betäubt**
drunk **betrunken**
dumb **stumm**
earache **die Ohrenschmerzen** (pl)
I fall **ich falle**
I feel **ich fühle mich, mir ist ...**
fever **das Fieber**
I'm feverish **ich habe Fieber**
flu **die Grippe(n)**
I get drunk **ich betrinke mich**
I got better **mir geht es besser**
I have an operation **ich habe eine Operation**

I don't feel well. I think I've got the flu.

Ich fühle mich nicht wohl. Ich glaube, ich habe eine Grippe.

I've had a sore throat since yesterday, and now I have a headache.

Seit gestern tut mir der Hals weh, und jetzt habe ich Kopfschmerzen.

Your boss must be sick too. He's been sneezing all morning.

Ihr Chef muß auch krank sein. Er niest schon den ganzen Morgen.

If you have a fever, you should stay in bed.

Wenn Sie Fieber haben, sollten Sie im Bett bleiben.

I have a cold   **ich habe eine Erkältung**
I have a temperature   **ich habe Fieber**
headache   **die Kopfschmerzen** *(pl)*
health   **die Gesundheit**
healthy   **gesund**
heart attack   **der Herzanfall(ˑe), der Herzinfarkt(e)**
high blood pressure   **der Bluthochdruck**
hurt   **der Schmerz(en)**
    hurt *(adj)*   **verletzt**
I hurt   **es tut mir weh**
it hurts   **es schmerzt**
I am ill/sick   **ich bin krank**
illness   **die Krankheit(en)**
I live   **ich lebe**
I look ill   **Ich sehe krank aus***
mental illness   **die Geisteskrankheit(en)**
mentally sick   **geisteskrank**
microbe   **die Mikrobe(n)**
migraine   **die Migräne(n)**
nervous breakdown   **der Nervenzusammenbruch(ˑe)**
overdose   **die Überdosis (-en)**

pain   **der Schmerz(en)**
painful   **schmerzhaft**
pale   **blaß, bleich**
pregnancy   **die Schwangerschaft(en)**
I recover/get well   **ich erhole mich**
recovery   **die Erholung(en)**
rheumatism   **der Rheumatismus**
I sneeze   **ich niese**
sore throat   **die Halsschmerzen** *(pl)*
sting   **der Stich(e)**
it stings   **es sticht**
stomach   **der Magen(-/-)**
stomach ache   **die Magen-/Bauchschmerzen** *(pl)*
stomach upset   **die Magenverstimmung(en)**
I take drugs   **ich nehme Medikamente**
temperature   **die Temperatur(en)**
I vomit   **ich übergebe mich**
Where does it hurt?   **Wo tut es weh?**
I wound   **ich verletze**
wounded   **verletzt**

My children have diarrhea.

Meine Kinder haben Durchfall.

I don't know what was wrong with Max last week. He looked very ill, but he seems to have recovered.

Ich weiß nicht, was letzte Woche mit Max los war. Er sah sehr krank aus, aber er scheint sich wieder erholt zu haben.

I can't breathe very well

Ich kann nur schwer atmen.

My husband suffers from high blood-pressure.

Mein Mann leidet an Bluthochdruck.

➤ PARTS OF THE BODY App.5a

SICKNESS & HEALTH

11c Medical treatment

antibiotic **das Antibiotikum (-a)**
appointment **der Termin(e)**
bandage **der Verband(ꞏe)**
blood **das Blut**
blood test **die Blutprobe(n)**
blood pressure **der Blutdruck**
capsule **die Kapsel(n)**
chemotherapy **die Chemotherapie(n)**
cure **die Heilung(en)**
danger to life **die Lebensgefahr(en)**
dangerous **gefährlich**
death **der Tod(e)**
I diet **ich halte eine Diät.**
doctor (Dr.) **der Arzt(ꞏe), die Ärztin(nen)**
dressing **der Verband(ꞏe)**
drop **der Tropfen(-)**
drug **die Arznei(en)**
I examine **ich untersuche**
examination **die Untersuchung(en)**
I fill **ich fülle**
I have **ich habe**
heating **die Heizung(en)**
hospital **das Krankenhaus(ꞏer)**
I improve **ich erhole mich**
I inject **ich spritze**
injection **die Spritze(n)**

insurance certificate **der Krankenschein(e)**
intensive care **die Intensivpflege(n)**
I look after **ich pflege**
medical **medizinisch**
medicine **die Medizin, das Medikament(e), das Mittel(-)**
alternative medicine **die alternative Medizin**
midwife **die Hebamme(n)**
nurse **die Krankenschwester(n), der Krankenpfleger(-)**
I nurse **ich pflege**
I operate **ich operiere**
operation **die Operation(en)**
I have an operation **ich lasse mich operieren**
operating theater/room **der Operationsaal (-säle)**
pastille **die Pastille(n)**
patient **der Patient(en)** *(wk)* **[-in]**
pharmacist **der Apotheker(-) [-in]**
physiotherapy **die Physiotherapie(n)**
physiotherapist **der Physiotherapeut(en)** *(wk)* **[-in]**
pill **die Tablette(n), die Pille(n)**
plaster (of Paris) **der Gipsverband(ꞏe)**

Call a doctor! This man needs help immediately!
Rufen Sie einen Arzt! Dieser Mann braucht sofort Hilfe!

Lisas mother is having an operation next week, and afterwards she has to go to physiotherapy.
Lisas Mutter läßt sich nächste Woche operieren, und danach muß sie zur Physiotherapie gehen.

I'll prescribe an antibiotic for you that you have to take twice a day for five days.
Ich verschreibe Ihnen ein Antibiotikum, das Sie fünf Tage zweimal täglich nehmen müssen.

Ernst has never had an X-ray.
Ernst wurde noch nie geröntgt.

I prescribe **ich verschreibe**
prescription **das Rezept(e)**
radio therapy **die Röntgentherapie(n)**
service **der Dienst(e)**
I set *(in plaster)* **ich richte ein*, ich gipse**
smear test **der Abstrich(e)**
spa resort **der Kur- und Erholungsort(e)**
specialist **der Facharzt(¨e)**
stitch **der Faden(¨)**
sticking plaster/Bandaid® **das Heftpflaster(-)**
surgery **die Chirurgie**
syringe **die Spritze(n)**
tablet **die Tablette(n)**
therapeutic **therapeutisch**
therapy **die Therapie(n)**
therapist **der Therapeut(en)** *(wk)* **[-in]**
thermometer **das Thermometer(-)**
transfusion **die Transfusion(en)**
I treat **ich behandle**
treatment **die Behandlung(en)**
ward **die (Kranken)station(en)**
wound **die Wunde(n)**
X-ray **die Röntgenaufnahme(n)**
I X-ray **ich röntge**

Dentist & optician

abscess **der Abszeß (-sse)**
bifocals **die Bifokalbrille(n)**

contact lens **die Kontaktlinse(n)**
hard/soft lenses **harte/weiche Linsen**
contact lens fluid **die Flüssigkeit für Kontaktlinsen**
crown **die Krone(n)**
dental treatment **die zahnärtliche Behandlung(en)**
dentist **der Zahnarzt(¨e) [-in]**
dentures **das Gebiß (-sse)**
I drill **ich bohre**
I extract **ich ziehe heraus***
eye **das Auge(n)**
eyesight **die Sehkraft**
eye test **der Augentest(e)**
false teeth **das künstliche Gebiß**
far-sighted **weitsichtig**
I fill **ich plombiere**
filling **die Plombe(n)**
frame **das Gestell(e)**
glasses **die Brille(n)**
gum **das Zahnfleisch** *(no pl)*
lens **die Linse(n)**
near-sighted **kurzsichtig**
optician **der Optiker(-)**
pupil **die Pupille(n)**
spectacle case **das Brillenetui(s)**
stye **das Gerstenkorn(¨er)**
sunglasses **die Sonnenbrille(n)**
tinted **dunkel**
tooth **der Zahn(¨e)**
toothache **die Zahnschmerzen** *(pl)*

In order to determine what's wrong with you, we have to take a blood test.

Wir müssen Ihnen Blut abnehmen, um festzustellen was mit Ihnen nicht in Ordnung ist.

I have a terrible toothache, and I urgently need an appointment with Dr. Brenner.

Ich habe fürchterliche Zahnschmerzen, und ich brauche dringend einen Termin mit Herrn Dr. Brenner.

Detlef has been working in the city hospital as a nurse since last year.

Detlef arbeitet seit letztem Jahr im städtischen Krankenhaus als Krankenpfleger.

11d Health & hygiene

Physical state

ache **der Schmerz(en)**
aching **schmerzen**
  aching *(adj)* **schmerzend**
all right/OK **in Ordnung**
I am asleep **ich schlafe**
awake **wach**
blister **die Blase(n)**
boil **das Furunkel(-)**
bruise **der blaue Fleck(en)**
I am cold **mir ist kalt**
comfort **der Trost**
I comfort **ich tröste**
comfortable (un-) **(un)bequem**
corn **das Hühnerauge(n)**
discomfort **die Beschwerden** *(pl)*
drowsiness **die Schläfrigkeit**
drowsy **schläfrig**
faint **ohnmächtig**
I faint **ich falle in Ohnmacht**
I feel **ich fühle mich, mir ist …**
I am hot **mir ist warm**
I get fat **ich werde dick, ich nehme zu***
I get fit **ich trimme mich**
I get thin **ich werde mager/dünn**
hunger **der Hunger**
hungry **hungrig**
  I am hungry **ich habe Hunger**
it hurts **es tut weh**
ill/sick **krank**
I lie down **ich lege mich hin***
I look **ich sehe, ich gucke**
I lose weight **ich nehme ab***
I put on weight **ich nehme zu***
queasy **übel, schlecht**
I relax **ich ruhe mich aus***
I rest/have a rest **ich mache eine Pause**
I sleep **ich schlafe**
sleepy **schläfrig**
I slim **ich mache eine Schlanksheitskur**
strange **komisch, sonderbar**
thirst **der Durst**

thirsty **durstig**
I am thirsty **ich bin durstig, ich habe Durst**
tired **müde**
I am tired **ich bin müde**
tiredness **die Müdigkeit**
under the weather **angeschlagen**
unwell **nicht wohl**
I wake up **ich wache auf***
well **wohl**
well-being **das Wohlbefinden**

Beauty & hygiene

acne **die Akne**
bath **das Bad(¨er)**
beauty **die Schönheit**
beauty contest **der Schönheitswettbewerb**
beauty queen **die Schönheitskönigin(nen)**
beauty salon/parlor **der Schönheitssalon(s)**
beauty specialist **der Kosmetiker(-) [-in]**
beauty treatment **die kosmetische Behandlung**
body odor **der (üble) Körpergeruch**
I burp/belch **ich rülpse**
I brush **ich bürste**
brush **die Bürste(n)**
I clean **ich putze**
clean **sauber**
I clean my teeth **ich putze mir die Zähne**
comb **der Kamm(¨e)**
I comb my hair **ich kämme meine Haare**
complexion **der Teint**
condom **das Kondom(e)**
contraceptive **das Verhütungsmittel(-)**
contraception **die Empfängnisverhütung(en)**
cosmetics **die Kosmetika** *(pl)*

cosmetic/plastic surgery **die Schönheitsoperation(en)**
I cut **ich schneide**
dandruff **die Schuppen** *(pl)*
dirty **schmutzig**
electric razor **der elektrische Rasierapparat(e)**
I exercise **ich bewege mich**
exercise bike **der Heimtrainer(-)**
face-lift **das Facelift(s)**
face-pack **die Gesichtspackung(en)**
fit (un-) **(nicht) gesund**
fitness **die Fitness**
flea **der Floh(¨e)**
hair **das Haar(e)**
  unwanted hair **das unerwünschte Haar**
hairbrush **die Haarbürste(n)**
haircut **der Haarschnitt(e)**
I have my hair cut **ich lasse mir die Haare schneiden**
hairdo **die Frisur(en)**
hairdryer **der Fön(e)**
head lice **die Kopfläuse** *(pl)*
healthy *(person)* **gesund**
hygiene **die Hygiene**
hygienic **hygienisch**
laundry *(establishment)* **die Wäscherei(en)**
  laundry *(linen)* **die Wäsche**
I'm losing my hair **die Haare fallen mir aus***
I make up **ich schminke mich**
I menstruate **ich menstruiere**
menstruation **die Menstruation(en)**

mole **der Leberfleck(e)**
nailbrush **die Nagelbürste(n)**
nit **die Nisse(n)**
period **die Periode(n)**
period pains **die Periodenschmerzen** *(pl)*
permanent wave **die Dauerwelle(n)**
pill **die Pille(n)**
razor **der Rasierer(-)**
I remove unwanted hair **ich enthaare**
sanitary **hygienisch**
sanitary towel **die Monatsbinde(n)**
scissors **die Schere(n)**
shampoo **das Shampoo(s)**
I shave **ich rasiere mich**
shower **die Dusche(n)**
soap **die Seife(n)**
spot **der Fleck(en)**
spotty **fleckig**
smell *(odor)* **der Geruch(¨e)**
I smell (bad) **ich rieche (übel)**
sweat **der Schweiß**
I sweat **ich schwitze**
I take a bath **ich nehme ein Bad**
I take a shower **ich dusche (mich)**
tampon **der Tampon(s)**
toothbrush **die Zahnbürste(n)**
toothpaste **die Zahnpasta(s)**
toupee **das Toupet(s)**
towel **das Handtuch(¨er)**
wart **die Warze(n)**
I wash **ich wasche mich**
washcloth **der Waschlappen(-)**
wig **die Perücke(n)**

I need a haircut. But please don't cut it too short, just a little shorter in the back and on the sides.

Ich brauche einen Haarschnitt. Aber bitte schneiden Sie es nicht zu kurz, nur hinten und an den Seiten etwas kürzer.

Rainer bought an exercise bike, because he really wants to lose weight now.

Rainer hat sich einen Heimtrainer gekauft, weil er jetzt unbedingt abnehmen will.

➤ TOILETRIES 9b

Social issues

12a Society

abnormal **anormal, abnormal**
alternative **alternativ**
amenity **die Unterhaltungsmöglichkeit(en)**
anonymous **anonym**
attitude **die Einstellung(en)**
available **verfügbar**
it is available **es steht zur Verfügung**
basic **grundlegend**
basis **die Grundlage(n)**
burden **die Last(en)**
campaign **die Initiative(n)**
care **die Sorge, die Fürsorge**
cause **die Ursache(n)**
change **der Wandel(-)**
circumstance **der Umstand(ˉe)**
community **die Gemeinde(n), die Gemeinschaft(en)**
compulsory **Pflicht-**
contribution **der Beitrag(ˉe)**
cost **die Kosten** (pl), **die Unkosten** (pl)
I counsel **ich berate**
counselling **die (soziale) Beratung**
criterion **das Kriterium (-ien)**
dependence **die Abhängigkeit**
dependent **abhängig**
depressed **deprimiert**
depression **die Depression(en)**
deprived **benachteiligt, depriviert**
difficulty **die Schwierigkeit(en)**
effect **die Auswirkung(en)**
effective **wirksam**
fact **die Tatsache(n)**
finance **die Finanzen** (pl)
financial **finanziell**
frustrated **frustriert**
frustration **die Frustration(en)**
guidance **die Orientierung(en)**

increase **die Zunahme**
inner city **die Innenstadt(ˉe)**
institution **die Anstalt(en)**
loneliness **die Einsamkeit**
lonely **einsam**
long-term **langfristig**
measure **die Maßnahme(n)**
negative **negativ**
normal **normal**
policy **die Politik**
policies **die Politik**
positive **positiv**
power **die Macht(ˉe)**
prestige **das Prestige** (no pl)
problem **das Problem(e)**
protest movement **die Protestbewegung(en)**
I provide (with) **ich versorge jdn. (mit** +dat)
provision **die Versorgung**
psychological **psychologisch**
quality of life **die Lebensqualität**
question/issue **die Frage(n)**
rate **die Rate(n), die Quote(n)**
responsibility **die Verantwortung(en)**
responsible (ir-) **(un)verantwortlich**
result **die Folge(n)**
right **das Recht(e)**
role **die Rolle(n)**
rural **ländlich**
scarcity **der Mangel(ˉ)**
scheme **die Maßnahme(n)**
I belong on the scrap heap **ich gehöre zum alten Eisen**
secure (in-) **(un)sicher**
security (in-) **die (Un)sicherheit(en)**
self-esteem **die Selbstachtung**

short-term **kurzfristig**
situation **die Lage(n)**
social **sozial**
society **die Gesellschaft(en)**
stable (un-) **(un)stabil**
stability (in-) **die (Un)stabilität**
statistics **die Statistik(en)**
status **der Status**
stigma **das Brandmal(e)**
stress **der Streß (no pl.)**
stressful **stressig**
structure **die Struktur(en), der Aufbau**
superfluous **überflüssig**
support **die Unterstützung(en)**
urban **Stadt-**
urge to conform **der Anpassungsdruck**
value **der Wert(e)**

Some useful verbs

I adapt/conform **ich passe mich +dat an***
it affects **es beeinflußt**
I afford **ich leiste mir (etw.)**
I alienate **ich entfremde**
I am ashamed **ich schäme mich**
I break down **ich breche zusammen***
I campaign **ich kämpfe**
I care for **ich sorge für +acc**
I cause **ich verursache**
it changes **es wandelt sich**

I contribute **ich trage zu +dat bei***
I cope **ich komme gut zurecht***
I depend on **ich hänge von +dat ab***
I deprive **ich benachteilige**
I discourage **ich entmutige**
I dominate **ich beherrsche, ich dominiere**
I encourage **ich ermutige**
I help **ich helfe +dat**
I increase **ich vergrößere**
I lack **es mangelt mir an +dat**
I look after **ich kümmere mich um +acc**
I need **ich brauche**
I neglect **ich vernachlässige**
I owe **ich bin jdm. etw. schuldig**
I protest **ich protestiere**
I provide for **ich versorge jdn. mit +dat**
I put up with **ich gebe mich mit +dat**
I rely on **ich bin auf jdn. angewiesen.**
I respect **ich achte, respektiere**
I share **ich teile**
I solve **ich löse**
I suffer from **ich leide an +dat**
I support **ich unterstütze**
I tackle **ich befasse mich mit +dat**
I value **ich schätze**

There are immense social problems in the inner city.

Es gibt ungeheuere Sozialprobleme der Innerstadt.

Since our cousin lost his job, he's financially dependent on his father.

Seitdem unser Cousin seine Stelle verloren hat, ist er finanziell von seinem Vater abhängig.

What measure did the police take against the demonstrations in the city?

Welche Maßnahmen hat die Polizei gegen die Demonstrationen in der Stadt ergriffen?

➤ ADDICTION & VIOLENCE 12d; PREJUDICE 12e

12b Social services & poverty

Social services

aid **die Sozialhilfe**
agency **die Agentur(en)**
authority **die Gemeinde(n)**
benefit **die Unterstützung(en)**
I benefit **ich profitiere**
charity **die Wohlfahrtsorganisation(en)**
I give to charity **ich spende**
claim **der Anspruch(¨e), der Antrag(¨e)**
I claim **ich beantrage**
claimant **der Antragsteller(-)**
disability **die Arbeitsunfähigkeit**
disabled **arbeitsunfähig**
eligible (for) **berechtigt zu** +dat
I am eligible for **ich habe Anspruch auf** +acc
frail **schwach**
frailty **die Schwäche(n)**
grant **der Zuschuß (¨sse)**
handicap **die Behinderung(en)**
handicapped **behindert**
ill health **die schlechte Gesundheit**
income support **die Beihilfe(n)**
loan **die Anleihe(n)**
maintenance **die finanzielle Unterstützung(en)**
official **amtlich, offiziell**
reception center **das Aufnahmelager(-)**

Red Cross **das Rote Kreuz**
refuge **der Zufluchtsort(e)**
refugee **der Flüchtling(e)**
I register **ich melde mich an***
registration **die Anmeldung(en)**
Salvation Army **die Heilsarmee**
service **der Dienst(e)**
social security **die soziale Sicherheit**
social service **der Sozialdienst(e)**
social worker **der Sozialarbeiter(-) [-in]**
support **die Hilfe**
I support **ich unterstütze**
welfare **die Wohlfahrt**

Wealth & poverty

I beg **ich bettele**
beggar **der Bettler(-) [-in]**
I am broke **ich bin abgebrannt**
debt **die Schuld(en)**
I am in debt **ich habe Schulden**
deprivation **die Benachteiligung**
deprived **benachteiligt**
destitute **mittellos**
living standards **der Lebensstandard(s)**
millionaire **der Millionär(e)**
need **die Not(¨e)**
those in need **die Notleidenden** *(adj/n) (pl)*

The physically handicapped can apply for help.

Die körperlich Behinderten können einen Antrag auf Hilfe stellen.

Not everyone gets unemployment benefits.

Nicht jeder bekommt Arbeitslosenunterstützung.

Mr. Karsten is eligible for his pension beginning January 1.

Herr Karsten kann ab 1. Januar Anspruch auf seine Rente stellen.

nutrition **die Ernährung**
poor **arm**
poverty **die Armut**
rich **reich**
subsistence **der Lebensunterhalt**
tramp/vagrant **der Landstreicher(-) [-in]**
wealth **der Reichtum(ˉer), der Wohlstand**
well off **wohlhabend**

Unemployment

I cut back *(on jobs)* **ich baue ab***
I dismiss **ich entlasse**
dole/unemployment benefits **das Arbeitslosengeld**
I employ **ich beschäftige**
employee **der Arbeitnehmer(-) [-in]**
employer **der Arbeitgeber(-) [-in]**
employment **die Arbeit**
employment office **das Arbeitsamt(ˉer)**
full-time **Vollzeit-**
I give notice **ich kündige jdm.**
income support **die Sozialhilfe**
job **der Job(s), die Arbeit, der Arbeitsplatz(ˉe)**
job/workplace **die Arbeitsstelle(n)**
job-sharing **das Jobsharing**
job creation scheme **die Arbeits- beschaffungsmaßnahme(n)**

long-term unemployed **der/die Langzeitarbeitslose** *(adj/n)*
occupation **der Beruf(e)**
occupational **beruflich**
part-time **Teilzeit-**
qualification **die Qualifikation(en)**
qualified **qualifiziert**
redundancy/layoff **die Entlassung(en)**
redundant/laid off **arbeitslos**
I am made redundant/I was layed off **mir wird gekündigt**
retraining **die Umschulung(en)**
I am retrained **ich lasse mich umschulen**
short-time work **die Kurzarbeit**
skill **die Fertigkeit(en)**
staffing **die Arbeitskräfte** *(pl)*
I take on **ich stelle an***
training scheme/program **die Ausbildungsmaßnahme(n)**
unemployed **arbeitslos**
unemployment figure **die Arbeitslosenzahl(en)**
unemployment rate **die Arbeitslosenrate(n)**
unskilled worker **der Hilfsarbeiter(-)**
vacancy **die leere Stelle(n)**
wage costs **die Lohnkosten** *(pl)*

– How high is the level of unemployment? – In the South it is about 15%.
– Can people retrain or work part-time?

– Some yes, but many retire early.

My brother was laid off some months ago. Now he has to report every two weeks to the job centre/employment office.

– **Wie hoch ist die Arbeitslosenrate? – Im Süden ist sie ungefähr 15%.**
– **Können die Leute umgeschult werden oder Teilzeitarbeit machen?**
Manche ja, aber viele treten vorzeitig in den Ruhestand.
Mein Bruder hat vor einigen Monaten seine Arbeitsstelle verloren. Jetzt muß er sich alle zwei Wochen beim Arbeitsamt melden.

➤ JOB APPLICATION 14c

12c Housing & homelessness

accommodation **die Unterkunft**
apartment **die Wohnung(en)**
I build **ich baue**
building **das Gebäude(-)**
comfortable/homey **gemütlich**
commune **die Wohngemeinschaft(en)**
I commute **ich pendle**
commuter **der Pendler(-)**
delapidated **baufällig**
I demolish **ich reiße ab***
demolition **der Abbruch**
it deteriorates **es verfällt**
digs/unfurnished rooms **die Bude(n)**
drab **trist, traurig**
estate/real estate agent **der Immobilienmakler(-)**
it falls down **es stürzt ab***
house **das Haus(ᵉer)**

council house **die Sozialwohnung(en)**
housing **die Wohnungen** *(pl)*
housing association **die Wohnungsbaugesellschaft(en)**
housing policy **die Wohnungspolitik**
inner city **die Innenstadt(ᵉe)**
landlord **der Vermieter(-)**
I let/rent out **ich vermiete**
I maintain **ich halte instand**
I modernize **ich modernisiere**
I move (house) **ich ziehe um***
own **eigen**
public housing **die Sozialwohnung(en)**
redevelopment **die Sanierung**
I renovate **ich saniere**
I rent **ich miete**
rent **die Miete(n)**

– Will the downtown area really be redeveloped?

– Yes, some of the old houses will be torn down. But most of them will be restored or renovated.

– Are you going to buy your own home soon?
– Yes, we are trying to get a mortgage. We have found an older property that we want to modernize.

At the moment we are renting an apartment.

It is impossible to find a furnished apartment to rent.

– **Wird die Stadtmitte wirklich saniert?**

– **Ja, einige der alten Häuser werden abgerissen. Aber die meisten werden restauriert oder renoviert.**

– **Wollen Sie bald ein Eigenheim kaufen?**
– **Ja, wir versuchen eine Hypothek aufzunehmen. Wir haben ein älteres Haus gefunden, das wir modernisieren wollen.**

Zur Zeit wir mieten eine Wohnung.

Es ist unmöglich, eine möblierte Mietwohnung zu finden.

I repair **ich repariere**
repair **die Reparatur(en)**
shelter **die Unterkunft(-̈e)**
speculator **der Spekulant(en)** *(wk)*
squalid **elend**
squatter **der Hausbesetzer(-) [-in]**
suburb **der Vorort(e)**
tenant **der Mieter(-) [-in]**
town planning **die Stadtplanung**
urban **städtisch**
urban renewal **die Stadterneuerung**

Housing shortage

camp **das Lager(-)**
commune **die Wohngemeinschaft(en)**
container town **die Containerstadt(-̈e)**
delapidated **verfallen**
I evict **ich weise aus***

homeless **obdachlos**
homelessness **die Obdachlosigkeit**
hostel **das Wohnheim(e)**
housing shortage **die Wohnungsnot**
living conditions **die Wohnverhältnisse** *(pl)*
overcrowded **überfüllt**
overcrowding **die Überfüllung**
I pull down **ich reiße ab***
shanty town **das Armenviertel(-)**
I sleep rough **ich übernachte im Freien**
slum **die Baracke(n)**
slum clearance **die Slumsanierung(en)**
squalid **dreckig**
I squat **ich besetze ein Haus**
it stands empty **es steht leer**
wasteland **das Ödland**

There's such a housing shortage that they've built a container town on the outskirts.

– Is the municipality still building public housing?

Wir haben so eine Wohnungsnot, daß man eine Containerstadt am Stadtrand gebaut hat.

– Baut die Stadtbehörde immer noch Sozialwohnungen?

12d Addiction & violence

abuse der Mißbrauch(-e)
I abuse ich mißbrauche
act of violence die Gewalttat(en)
addict der/die Abhängige *(adj/n)*
addiction die (Drogen)Abhängigkeit
addictive zur Abhängigkeit führend
aggression die Agression(en), die Agressivität(en)
aggressive aggressiv
alcohol der Alkohol
alcoholic der Alkoholiker(-) [-in]
alcoholism der Alkoholismus
anger die Wut
angry wütend
I attack ich greife an*
attack der Angriff(e), das Attentat(e)
I beat up ich verprügele, ich haue zusammen*
I bully ich tyrannisiere
bully der Schlägertyp(en)
consumption der Konsum
I cure, I dry out ich entwöhne mich
dangerous gefährlich
I drink ich trinke
I get drunk ich betrinke mich

drunk betrunken
drunken driving die Trunkenheit am Steuer
effect die Wirkung(en)
fatal tödlich
fear die Angst(-e)
I fear ich habe Angst (vor +dat)
force die Gewalt
gang die Bande(n)
I harass ich schikaniere, ich haue an*
hooligan der Rowdy (-ies)
hostile feindlich
hostility die Feindseligkeit(en)
insult die Beleidigung(en)
I insult ich beleidige
intoxication der Rausch
legal (il-) (il)legal
I legalize ich gebe frei*
I mug ich überfalle
mugger der Straßenräuber(-)
nervous ängstlich
nervousness die Ängstlichkeit
pimp der Zuhälter(-)
porno der Porno(s)
pornography die Porno(graphie)
prostitution die Prostitution
punk der Punk(s)

Many alcoholics meet in the inner city and are often aggressive.

Viele Alkoholiker treffen sich in der Innenstadt, und verhalten sich oft sehr aggressiv.

Older people and women are sometimes afraid to go out alone.

Ältere Leute und Frauen haben manchmal Angst, allein auszugehen.

Some young people have a drug problem. They start by sniffing solvents, or by taking soft drugs.

Einige Jugendliche haben ein Drogenproblem. Es fängt damit an, daß sie schnüffeln oder weiche Drogen nehmen.

rehabilitation **die Rehabilitation**
I revert **ich falle zurück***
rocker **der Rocker(-)**
I seduce **ich verführe**
sexual harassment **die sexuelle Belästigung(en)**
skinhead **der Skinhead(s)**
I smoke **ich rauche**
stimulant **das Anregungsmittel(-)**
stimulation **der Rausch**
I terrorize **ich terrorisiere**
I threaten **ich bedrohe**
thug **der Schlägertyp(en)**
vandal **der Vandale(n)** *(wk)*
vandalism **der Vandalismus**
victim **das Opfer(-)**
violent **gewalttätig**
   act of violence **die Gewalttat(en)**

Drugs

addicted to drugs **süchtig**
cannabis **das Marihuana**
cocaine **das Kokain**
crack **das Crack**
I deal **ich handle**
dealer **der Dealer(-)**
drug **das Rauschmittel(-), die Droge(n)**
drug scene **die Drogenszene**
drug traffic **der Drogenhandel**
I get infected **ich infiziere mich**
glue **der Klebstoff(e)**
hard drug **die harte Droge(n)**
hashish **der Haschisch, das Heu**
I have a fix **ich setze mir einen Druck**
heroin **das Heroin**
I inject **ich spritze**
junkie **der Fixer(-)**
I kick *(the habit)* **ich gewöhne mich ab***
LSD **das LSD**
narcotic **das Rauschgift(e)**
pusher **der Dealer(-)**
I sniff **ich schnüffele**
soft drugs **weiche Drogen**
solvent **das Lösungsmittel(-)**
stimulant **das Anregungsmittel(-)**
syringe **die Spritze(n)**
I take drugs/a fix **ich nehme ein***
tranquilizer **das Betäubungsmittel(-) /Beruhigungsmittel(-)**
withdrawal **die Entwöhnung**

Cannabis is the most common. It gives a feeling of intoxication. People become psychologically dependent. Then they go onto hard drugs.

All drugs are dangerous, but injecting them brings risks of AIDS.

Junkies inject or smoke drugs.

Marihuana wird am häufigsten gebraucht. Es gibt einen Rausch. Die Leute werden psychologisch abhängig. Dann greifen sie zu den harten Drogen.

Alle Drogen sind gefährlich, aber das Spritzen hat das Risiko, daß man sich mit AIDS infiziert.

Die Fixer spritzen oder rauchen die Drogen.

12e Prejudice

asylum seeker **der Asylant(en)**
  (wk)
I call names **ich beschimpfe**
citizenship **die
  Staatsangehörigkeit(en)**
country of origin **das
  Geburtsland(⁻er)**
cultural **kulturell**
culture **die Kultur(en)**
I discriminate **ich diskriminiere**
discrimination **die Diskriminierung**
dual nationality **die doppelte
  Staatsangehörigkeit**
emigrant **der Auswanderer(-)**
emigration **die Auswanderung**
equal (un-) **gleich (un-)**
equal opportunities **die
  Chancengleichheit**
equal pay **der gleiche Lohn(⁻e)**
equal rights **die
  Gleichberechtigung**
equality (in-) **die (Un)gleichheit**
ethnic **ethnisch**
far-right (adj.) **rechtsradikal**
fascism **der Faschismus**
fascist **der Faschist(en)** *(wk)* **[-in]**,
  der/die Rechtsradikale *(adj/n)*
foreign **fremd, ausländisch**

foreign worker **der Gastarbeiter(-)**
freedom **die Freiheit**
  freedom of movement **die
  Bewegungsfreiheit**
  freedom of speech **die
  Redefreiheit**
ghetto **das Ghetto(s)**
I immigrate **ich wandere ein***
immigrant (from Eastern block) **der
  Aussiedler(-) [-in]**
immigration **die Einwanderung**
I integrate **ich integriere mich**
integration **die Integration**
intolerance **die Intoleranz**
intolerant **intolerant**
majority **die Mehrheit(en)**
minority **die Minderheit(en)**
mother tongue **die
  Muttersprache(n)**
I persecute **ich verfolge**
persecution **die Verfolgung**
prejudice **das Vorurteil(e)**
prejudiced **voreingenommen
  gegenüber** +dat
rabid **rabiat**
race riot **der Rassenkrawall(e)**
racism **der Rassismus**
racist **der Rassist(en) [-in]**
  racist *(adj)* **rassistisch**

Unfortunately, many people are
prejudiced against foreigners.

**Leider sind viele Leute gegen
Ausländer voreingenommen.**

In recent years many immigrants
from the Eastern block countries
have come to Germany.

**In den letzten Jahren sind viele
Aussiedler aus den
Ostblockländern nach
Deutschland gekommen.**

Immigration is now restricted.
Many immigrants are often refused
a residence permit or work permit.

**Die Immigration ist jetzt
eingeschränkt. Einwanderer
erhalten oft keine Aufenthalts-
oder Arbeitserlaubnis.**

refugee **der Flüchtling(e)**
I repatriate **ich sende in das Heimatland zurück***
residence permit **die Aufenthaltserlaubnis(se)**
right **das Recht(e)**
    right to asylum **das Asylrecht**
    right to residence **das Wohnrecht**
second language **die zweite Sprache(n)**
stereotypical **stereotypisch**
tolerance **die Toleranz**
tolerant **tolerant**
I tolerate **ich toleriere**
work permit **die Arbeitserlaubnis(se)**

Race

anti-Semitic **antisemitisch**
anti-Semitism **der Antisemitismus**
Asian **asiatisch**
black **schwarz**
    black **der/die Schwarze** (adj/n)
Caribbean **der Karibe(n), die Karibin(nen)**
Caribbean **karibisch**
colored **farbig**
dark-skinned **dunkelhäutig**
Jew **der Jude(n)** (wk)
Jewess **die Jüdin(nen)**
Jewish **jüdisch**
National Front **die Nationale Front**

Neo-Nazism **der Neonazismus**
white **weiß**
    white **der/die Weiße** (adj/n)

Sexuality

female **weiblich**
feminine **weiblich**
feminism **der Feminismus**
feminist **feministisch**
gay **schwul**
heterosexual **der Hetero(s)**
    heterosexual (adj) **heterosexuell**
homophobic **homophobisch**
homosexual **der/die Homosexuelle** (adj/n)
    homosexual (adj) **homosexuell**
homosexuality **die Homosexualität**
lesbian **die Lesbierin(nen), die Lesbe(n)**
lesbian **lesbisch**
male **männlich**
sexual **sexuell**
sexuality **die Sexualität**
women's lib **die Frauenbewegung(en)**
women's libber **die Frauenrechtlerin(nen)**
women's rights **die Frauenrechte**

– What about the ethnic minority population resident here?

– Wie ist es mit den ethnischen Minderheiten, die hier seßhaft sind?

– Many have no right to citizenship.

– Viele haben kein Recht auf Staatsangehörigkeit.

The feminist movement is still demanding equal rights for women

Die Frauenbewegung verlangt immer noch die Gleichberechtigung der Frauen.

---

13 Religion

13a Ideas & doctrines

agnostic **der Agnostiker(-) [-in]**
anglican **der Anglikaner(-) [-in]**
anti-Semitism **der Antisemitismus**
apostle **der Apostel(-)**
atheism **der Atheismus**
atheist **der Atheist(en)** *(wk)* **[-in]**
atheistic **atheistisch**
authority **die Autorität(en)**
belief **der Glaube (***gen* **-ns)** *(wk)*
I believe (in) **ich glaube (an +acc)**
believer **der/die Gläubige** *(adj/n)*
Bible **die Bibel(n)**
biblical **biblisch**
blessed **gesegnet**
Buddha **der Buddha(s)**
Buddhism **der Buddhismus**
Buddhist **der Buddhist(en)** *(wk)*
[-in]
Calvinist **der Calvinist(en)** *(wk)*
[-in]
cantor **der Kantor(en)** *(wk)* **[-in]**
Catholic **der Katholik(en)** *(wk)* **[-in]**
catholic *(adj)* **katholisch**
charismatic **charismatisch**
charity **die Nächstenliebe**
charity *(adj)* **karitativ**
charity organization **die**
Wohlfahrtsorganisation(en)
Christ **Christus**
Christian *(adj)* **christlich**
all Christians **alle Christen**
Christianity **die Christenheit**
church **die Kirche(n)**
commentary **der Kommentar(e)**
consciousness **das Bewußtsein**
covenant **der Bund(-̈e)**
disciple **der Jünger(-)**
divine **göttlich**
doctrine **die Lehre(n)**

duty **die Aufgabe(n), die**
Pflicht(en)
ecumenicism **der Ökumenismus**
ethical **ethisch**
evil **das Böse** *(adj/n)*
evil *(adj)* **böse, übel**
I forgive **ich vergebe** +dat
forgiveness **die Vergebung(en)**
free will **der freie Wille (***gen* **-ns)**
(wk)
fundamentalism **der**
Fundamentalismus
fundamentalist **der**
Fundamentalist(en) *(wk)* **[-in]**
god **der Gott(-̈er)**
goddess **die Göttin(nen)**
Gospel **das Evangelium (-ien)**
grace **die Gnade**
heaven **der Himmel(-)**
Hebrew **der Hebräer(-)**
hell **die Hölle(n)**
heretical **ketzerisch**
Hindu **der Hindu(s)**
Hinduism **der Hinduismus**
holiness **die Heiligkeit**
holy **heilig**
Holy Spirit **der Heilige Geist**
hope **die Hoffnung(en)**
human **menschlich**
human being **der Mensch(en)**
(wk)
humanism **der Humanismus**
humanity **die Menschheit, die**
Menschlichkeit
infallibility **die Unfehlbarkeit**
infallible **unfehlbar**
Islam **der Islam**
Islamic **islamisch**
Jesus **Jesus**

Jew   **der Jude(n)** *(wk)*, **die Jüdin(nen)**
Jewish   **jüdisch**
Judaic   **judäisch**
Judaism   **der Judaismus**
Lord   **der Herr(en)** *(wk)*
merciful   **gnadenvoll**
mercy   **die Gnade(n)**
Messiah   **der Messias**
Mohammed   **Mohammed**
moral   **moralisch**
morality   **die Moral, die Moralität**
Muslim   **der Moslem(s)**
   Muslim *(adj)*   **moslemisch**
myth   **der Mythos (-en)**
New Testament   **das neue Testament**
nirvana   **das Nirwana**
Old Testament   **das alte Testament**
orthodox   **orthodox**
pagan   **der Heide(n)** *(wk)* **[-in]**
parish   **der Pfarrer, die Gemeinde(n)**
Pentateuch   **der Pentateuch**
prophet   **der Prophet(en)** *(wk)* **[-in]**
Q'uran/Koran   **der Koran**
redemption   **die Erlösung**
religion   **die Religion(en)**

Roman Catholic   **römisch-katholisch**
sacred   **heilig**
saint   **der/die Heilige** *(adj/n)*
Saint Peter   **Sankt Peter, der Heilige Petrus**
Salvation Army   **die Heilsarmee**
he sanctifies   **er heiligt**
Satan   **der Satan**
he saves   **er rettet**
scripture   **die Heilige Schrift(en)**
service   **der Gottesdienst(e)**
Sikh   **der Sikh(s)**
Sikhism   **der Sikhismus**
sin   **die Sünde(n)**
sinful   **sündig**
soul   **die Seele(n)**
spirit   **der Geist(er)**
spiritual   **geistlich**
spirituality   **die Geistlichkeit**
Talmud   **der Talmud**
Taoism   **der Taoismus**
theological   **theologisch**
theology   **die Theologie(n)**
traditional   **traditionell**
Trinity   **die Trinität, die Dreiheiligkeit**
true   **wahr**
truth   **die Wahrheit(en)**

Religious fundamentalism can lead to fanaticism and intolerance in any religion.

Religiöser Fundamentalismus kann in jeder Religion zu Fanatismus und Intoleranz führen.

Freedom of faith, of conscience and freedom of religious and ideological belief are inviolable. (Article 4 of the German constitution)

Die Freiheit des Glaubens, des Gewissens und die Freiheit des religiösen und weltanschaulichen Bekenntnisses sind unverletzlich. (Artikel 4 des Grundgesetzes)

There is considerable disagreement about the ordination of women to the priesthood.

Es bestehen beträchtliche Differenzen über die Ordination von Frauen ins Priesteramt.

archbishop **der Erzbischof(-̈e)**
baptism **die Taufe(n)**
I baptise **ich taufe**
bar mitzvah **das Bar-Mizvah**
I bear witness to **ich bekenne**
bishop **der Bischof(-̈e)**
bishopric/see **das Bistum(-̈er)**
he canonises **er spricht heilig**
cathedral **die Kathedrale(n)**
I celebrate **ich feiere**
chapel **die Kapelle(n)**
christening **die Taufe(n)**
clergy **der Klerus**
clergyman **der Geistliche(n)**
  (adj/n), **der Pfarrer(-)**
communion *(catholic)* **die**
  Kommunion
  holy communion **die heilige**
  Kommunion
  communion *(protestant)* **das**
  Abendmahl
community **die Gemeinde(n)**
I confess *(faith)* **ich bekenne mich**
  zu +dat

I confess *(sins)* **ich beichte**
confession **die Beichte(n)**
confirmation **die Konfirmation**
congregation **die Gemeinde(n)**
  (of cardinals) **die**
  Kongregation
conversion **die Bekehrung(en)**
convent **das Kloster(-̈)**
I convert *(others)* **ich bekehre**
I convert *(self)* **ich konvertiere**
Eucharist **die Eucharistie**
evangelical **evangelisch**
evangelist **der Evangelist(en)** *(wk)*
faith **der Glaube** *(gen* **-ns)** *(wk)*
faithful **treu, gläubig**
the faithful **die Gläubigen** *(pl)*
I give alms **ich gebe Almosen, ich**
  spende
I give thanks **ich sage Dank**
Imam **der Imam**
intercession **die Fürsprache(n)**
laity **der Laienstand** *(no pl)*
lay **Laien-**
layperson **der Laie(n)** *(wk)*

Those who are called to ministry must demonstrate their vocation before being accepted in theological colleges.

Wer Pfarrer werden will, muß seine Berufung demonstrieren, bevor er in eine theologische Fakultät aufgenommen wird.

The sacrament of Holy Communion will be celebrated on Sunday at nine o'clock.

Das Sakrament der heiligen Kommunion wird am Sonntag um neun Uhr gefeiert.

We work for charity.

Wir arbeiten für eine Wohlfahrtsorganization.

Aunt Anna always contributes to the Red Cross.

Tante Anna spendet für das Rote Kreuz.

The Baptist tradition is very strong in the American South.

Die baptistische Tradition ist sehr stark im Süden der USA.

the Lord's Supper **das Abendmahl**
Mass **die Messe**
I meditate **ich meditiere**
meditation **die Meditation**
minister **der Pfarrer(-)**
I minister to the parish **ich diene der Gemeinde**
ministry **das geistliche Amt(-̈er)**
mission **die Mission(en)**
missionary **der Missionar(e) [-in]**
monastery **das Kloster(-̈)**
monk **der Mönch(e)**
mosque **die Moschee(n)**
mullah **der Mullah(s)**
nun **die Nonne(n)**
parish **die Gemeinde(n)**
parishioner **das Gemeindemitglied(er)**
pastor **der Pastor(en)** *(wk)*
pastoral **seelsorgerisch**
Pope **der Papst(-̈e)**
I praise **ich lobe**
I pray (for) **ich bete (für** +acc**)**

prayer **das Gebet(e)**
morning prayer **die Morgenandacht**
prayerful **fromm**
priest **der Priester(-)**
rabbi **der Rabbi(s)**
I repent **ich empfinde Reue**
repentance **die Reue**
repentant **reuevoll**
I revere **ich verehre**
reverence **die Verehrung(en)**
reverent **ehrfürchtig**
rite **der Ritus (Riten)**
ritual **das Ritual(e)**
sacrament **das Sakrament(e)**
sermon **die Predigt(en)**
synagogue **die Synagoge(n)**
synod **die Synode(n)**
temple **der Tempel(-)**
vision **die Vision(en)**
vocation **die Berufung(en)**
witness **der Zeuge(n)** *(wk)* **[-in]**
I witness **ich bezeuge**
I worship **ich bete an*, ich verehre**

About 85% of the population belongs to one of the Christian faiths.
The Protestants predominate in the north, the Catholics in the south of Germany.

Etwa 85% der Bevölkerung bekennen sich zu einer der christlichen Konfessionen.
Die Evangelischen überwiegen im Norden, die Katholiken im Süden Deutschlands.

In England there is an Established Church. In Germany state and church are separate.

In England gibt es eine Staatskirche. In Deutschland sind Staat und Kirche getrennt.

Bishops in the Church of England are not afraid to speak about social problems.

Die Bischöfe der anglikanischen Kirche scheuen sich nicht, über soziale Probleme zu sprechen.

Business & economics

14a Economic life

I administer **ich verwalte**
we agree (to) **wir beschließen (zu +inf)**
agreement **die Übereinkunft(-̈e)**
bureaucracy **die Bürokratie(n)**
business **das Geschäft(e), die Unternehmung(en)**
a business **ein Geschäft(e)**
capacity *(industrial)* **die Kapazität(en)**
commerce **der Kommerz, der Handel**
commercial **kommerziell**
company **die (Handels)gesellschaft(en)**
competition **die Konkurrenz**
competitive **konkurrenzfähig**
deal **das Geschäft(e)**
I deliver **ich liefere**
demand **die Nachfrage(n)**
in demand **gefragt**
development **die Entwicklung(en)**
I dismiss **ich kündige**
I earn (a living) **ich verdiene**
economy **die Wirtschaft(en), die Konjunktur** *(no pl)*
I employ **ich beschäftige**
employee **der Arbeitnehmer(-)**
employer **der Arbeitgeber(-)**
employment **die Arbeit**
executive **der Geschäftsführer(-) [-in]**
I export **ich exportiere**
export(s) **der Export(e)**
it falls **es sinkt, es fällt**
firm **die Firma (Firmen), der Betrieb(e)**
goods **die Ware(n)**
it grows **es wächst**
I import **ich importiere**

I increase **ich erhöhe, ich erweitere**
increase **der Anstieg, die Zunahme**
industrial **industriell**
industrial output **die Produktion(en)**
industry **die Industrie(n), der Industriebetrieb(e)**
I invest **ich investiere**
investment **die Investition(en)**
job **der Arbeitsplatz(-̈e)**
job creation scheme **die Arbeitsbeschaffungsmaßnahme(n)**
lay off **die Entlassung(en)**
living standards **der Lebensstandard(s)**
I manage **ich leite**
management **das Management(s), die Leitung(en)**
multinational **multinational**
I negotiate **ich verhandle**
priority **die Priorität(en)**
I produce **ich produziere, ich stelle her***
producer **der Hersteller(-)**
product **der Produkt(e)**
production line **das Fließband(-̈er)**
productivity **die Produktivität(en)**
public company **die Aktiengesellschaft(en)**
quality **die Qualität(en)**
I raise (prices) **ich erhöhe (die Preise)**
reliability **die Zuverlässigkeit**
rise **der Anstieg(e)**
wage rise/raise **die Gehaltserhöhung(en)**
semiskilled **angelernt**
service **der Service**

service industry **der Dienstleistungsbetrieb(e)**

I set (priorities) **ich setze (Prioritäten)**

I am on sick leave **ich bin krankgeschrieben**

sick pay **das Krankengeld(er)**

I sign (contracts) **ich unterzeichne (Verträge)**

skilled labor **der Facharbeiter(-) [-in]**

I strengthen **ich stärke**

supply **das Angebot(e)**

trade-unionism **das Gewerkschaftswesen**

turnover **der Umsatz(ー̈e)**

unemployment **die Arbeitslosigkeit(en)**

unemployment benefit **das Arbeitslosengeld(er)**

unskilled labor **der ungelernte Arbeiter(-)**

work **die Arbeit(en)**

worker **der Arbeiter(-) [-in]**

work ethic **die Arbeitsmoral** *(no pl)*

workforce **die Arbeitskräfte** *(pl)*

working week **die Arbeitswoche(n)**

workplace **der Arbeitsplatz(ー̈e)**

working conditions **die Arbeitsbedingungen** *(pl)*

Industrial/Labor dispute

ballot **die Abstimmung(en)**

I boycott **ich boykottiere**

demonstration **die Demonstration(en)**

dispute **der Streit(e), die Auseinandersetzung(en)**

I go slow/slow down **ich mache einen Bummelstreik**

industrial/labor dispute **der Arbeitskonflikt(e)**

industrial relations **die Beziehungen zwischen Arbeitgeber und Gewerkschaften**

I lock out **ich sperre aus***

lockout **die Aussperrung(en)**

minimum wage **der Mindestlohn**

I picket **ich stelle Streikposten auf***

picket **der Streikposten(-)**

productivity bonus **die Prämie(n)**

I resume work **ich nehme die Arbeit wieder auf***

social unrest **die soziale Not/Unruhe(n)**

stoppage **der Stopp(s)**

strike **der Streik(s)**

unofficial strike **der wilde Streik(s)**

I am on strike **ich streike**

I go on strike **ich trete in den Streik**

striker **der Streiker(-)**

strikebreaker **der Streikbrecher(-)**

trade union **die Gewerkschaft(en)**

unfair dismissal **die ungerechtfertigte Entlassung(en)**

unrest **die Unruhe(n)**

wage costs **die Lohnkosten** *(pl)*

wage demand **die Lohnforderung(en)**

wage settlement **das Lohnabkommen(-)**

| The unions called for a reduction in working hours. | **Die Gewerkschaften forderten eine Verkürzung der Arbeitszeit.** |
| Unemployment is rising to 12%. | **Die Arbeitslosenquote steigt auf 12 Prozent an.** |

➤ AT WORK 14b; UNEMPLOYMENT 12c; JOBS & PROFESSIONS.14b

14b At Work

agenda **die Tagesordnung(en)**
  on the agenda **auf dem Programm**
on business **geschäftlich**
boring **langweilig**
business lunch **das Geschäftsessen(-)**
business meeting **das Treffen(-), die Konferenz(en), die Besprechung(en)**
business trip **die Geschäftsreise(n)**
I buy **ich kaufe**
canteen **die Kantine(n)**
career **der Beruf(e)**
I chair a meeting **ich führe den Vorsitz**
I delegate **ich delegiere**
disciplinary proceeding **das Disziplinarverfahren(-)**
I do **ich mache**
I follow a training course **ich lasse mich ausbilden**
free **kostenlos**
grant **das Stipendium (-ien)**
holiday/vacation **die Ferien** *(pl)*, **der Urlaub(e)**
job **der Job(s)**

I have job satisfaction **ich bin mit meiner Arbeit zufrieden**
I market **ich bringe ... auf den Markt, ich vermarkte**
meal **die Mahlzeit(en)**
meeting **die Sitzung(en)**
misconduct **das Vergehen(-)**
occupation **die Beschäftigung(en), der Beruf(e)**
I'm absent **ich fehle**
I pay taxes **ich zahle Steuern**
post **die Stelle(n), die Stellung(en)**
profession **der Beruf(e)**
professional **der Fachmann(-̈er)**
  professional *(adj)* **beruflich, professionell**
publicity **die Öffentlichkeit**
I qualify **ich qualifiziere**
I report to **ich unterstehe jdm.**
research **ich forsche**
I am responsible for **ich bin für +acc verantwortlich**
I sell **ich verkaufe**
I teach **ich lehre**
I toil **ich schufte**
training **die Ausbildung(en)**

Please tell Mrs. Weber in reception that I'm expecting Mr. Hartmann at 10 o'clock.

Bitte sagen Sie Frau Weber am Empfang, daß ich Herrn Hartmann um 10 Uhr erwarte.

– What kind of work does your daughter do?

– Was macht Ihre Tochter beruflich?

– She took a training course as a computer programmer and is now looking for a job.

– Sie hat sich als Computerprogrammiererin ausbilden lassen und sucht jetzt eine Stelle.

Our meeting will be in the conference room next to my office.

Unsere Besprechung findet im Konferenzzimmer neben meinem Büro statt.

training course **das Ausbildungsprogramm(e)**
I transfer **ich werde versetzt**
unskilled **ungelernt**
vocation **die Berufung(en)**
warning *(verbal)* **die Verwarnung(en)**
written warning **die schriftliche Warnung(en)/Abmahnung(en)**
I work as ... **ich arbeite als ...**

In the office

computer **der Computer(-)**
conference room **der Konferenzsaal (-säle)**
desk **der Schreibtisch(e)**
I dictate **ich diktiere**
dictating machine **das Diktiergerät(e)**
electronic mail **die elektronische Post**
extension **der Apparat(e)**
fax **das Fax**
fax machine **das Faxgerät(e)**
I fax **ich faxe**
file **die Akte(n)**
I file **ich ordne/lege Akten an***
filing cabinet **der Aktenschrank(-̈e)**
intercom **die Sprechanlage(n)**
memorandum **die Mitteilung(en)**
open plan **offen angelegt**
photocopier **der Fotokopierer(-)**
photocopy **die Kopie(n)**
I photocopy **ich kopiere**
pigeonhole **das Lesefach(-̈er)**
reception **die Rezeption(en)**
receptionist **der Herr/die Dame am Empfang**
shorthand **die Stenographie**
swivel chair **der Drehstuhl(-̈e)**
telephone **das Telefon(e)**
typing pool **die Schreibzentrale(n)**
wastebasket **der Papierkorb(-̈e)**
word processor **der Textverarbeiter(-)**
work station **die Arbeitssplatz(-̈e)**

At the factory & on site

automation **die Automatisierung**
blue-collar worker **der manuelle Arbeiter(-) [-in]**
bulldozer **die Planierraupe(n)**
car/automobile industry **die Autoindustrie(n)**
component **der Bestandteil(e)**
concrete **der Beton**
construction industry **die Bauindustrie(n)**
crane **der Kran(-̈e)**
forklift truck **der Gabelstapler(-)**
I forge **ich schmiede**
industry **die Industrie(n)**
heavy industry **die Schwerindustrie(n)**
light industry **die Leichtindustrie(n)**
I manufacture **ich stelle her***
manufacture **das Herstellen**
mass production **die Massenproduktion**
mining **der Bergbau**
power industry **die Energieindustrie(n)**
precision tool **das Präzisionswerkzeug(e)**
prefabricated **vorgefertigt**
process **der Prozeß (-sse)**
I process **ich verarbeite**
product **das Produkt(e)**
on the production line **am Fließband**
raw materials **der rohe Werkstoff(e)**
road building **der Straßenbau**
robot **der Roboter(-)**
scaffolding **das Gerüst(e)**
shipbuilding **der Schiffbau**
I smelt **ich schmelze**
steamroller **die Dampfwalze(n)**
steel smelting **das Stahlschmelzen**
textile industry **die Textilindustrie(n)**

WORKING CONDITIONS 14c; COMPUTERS 15f; STATIONERY 22b **109**

BUSINESS & ECONOMICS

14c Working conditions

I am employed   **ich bin angestellt**
apprenticeship   **die Lehre(n), die Lehrzeit(en)**
benefit   **der Nutzen(-)**
bonus   **die Prämie(n), der Zuschlag(ːe)**
I clock (in/out)   **ich stemple (den Arbeitsbeginn/beim Herausgehen)**
commission   **die Kommission(en)**
on commission   **auf Provision**
company car   **der Firmenwagen(-)**
conditions of employment   **die Arbeitsbedingungen** *(pl)*
contract   **der Vertrag(ːe)**
expenses   **die Spesen** *(pl)*
expense account   **das Spesenkonto (-en)**
flextime   **die flexible Arbeitszeit(en)**
freelance   **freiberuflich**
I work freelance   **ich arbeite freiberuflich**
full-time   **ganztägig, ganztags**
full-time job   **die Ganztagsstelle(n)**

income   **das Einkommen**
overtime   **die Überstunde(n)**
overworked   **überfordert**
part-time   **Teilzeit-**
pay   **der Lohn(ːe)**
payday   **der Zahltag(e)**
pay raise   **die Gehaltserhöhung(en)**
payslip   **die Lohnabrechnung(en)**
pension   **die Rente(n), die Pension(en)**
perk   **die Vergünstigung(en)**
permanent   **permanent**
professional association   **die Berufsgenossenschaft(en)**
remuneration   **die Vergütung(en)**
I retire   **ich trete in den Ruhestand**
retirement   **der Ruhestand**
salary   **das Gehalt(ːer)**
self-employed   **selbständig**
shift   **die Schicht(en)**
   day shift   **die Tagesschicht(en)**
   night shift   **die Nachtschicht(en)**
shiftworking   **die Schichtarbeit**

The conditions in this office are intolerable. The place is cold, badly lit, and poorly ventilated.

Die Zustände in diesem Büro sind unerträglich. Der Raum ist kalt, schlecht beleuchtet und nicht ausreichend gelüftet.

Many people who are in part-time work choose not to work full-time because of family commitments.

Viele Leute, die in Teilzeitjobs beschäftigt sind, wählen diese, um Familienverpflichtungen nachzukommen.

Our policy is to create more part-time jobs, and to protect the rights of the part-time workers.

Unsere Geschäftspolitik ist mehr Teilzeitstellen zu schaffen und die Rechte der Teilzeitkräfte zu stärken.

temporary **für kurze Zeit, befristet**
trial period **die Probezeit(en)**
working-hours **die Arbeitsstunden**
wage **der Lohn(¨e)**

Job application

I advertise the position **ich inseriere die Stelle**
advertisement **die Anzeige(n)**
I apply for a job **Ich bewerbe mich für eine Stelle.**
classified ad **die Kleinanzeige(n)**
curriculum vitae/resumé **der Lebenslauf(¨e)**
discrimination **die Diskriminierung(en)**
  racial discrimination **die Rassendiskriminierung(en)**
  sexual discrimination **die sexuelle Diskriminierung(en)**
employment agency **die Arbeitsvermittlungsagentur(en)**
job centre/employment office **das Arbeitsamt(¨er)**
I find a job **ich finde einen Job**
interesting **interessant**

interview **das Vorstellungsgespräch(e)**
I interview **ich interviewe**
job application **die Bewerbung(en)**
job offer **das Stellenangebot(e)**
I look for **ich suche**
opening **die freie Stelle(n)**
vacant positions **die Stellenangebote** *(pl)*
I promote (someone) **ich befördere (jdn.)**
I am promoted **ich werde befördert**
promotion **die Beförderung(en)**
qualification **die Qualifikation(en)**
qualified **qualifiziert, ausgebildet**
I start work (for) **Ich fange (bei** +dat**) zu arbeiten an***
I take on *(employee)* **ich stelle ein***
vacancy **die offene Stelle(n)**
wage **der Lohn(¨e), die Bezahlung(en)**
work experience **das Praktikum (-a)**

- Hello. Could I speak to the personnel manager, please.
- Speaking. What can I do for you?
- I saw your advertisement in the local paper for a sales executive. Could you send me the application forms?

How many references do you require?
- Two, including your present or last employer.

- **Hallo, könnte ich bitte den Personalchef sprechen.**
- **Am Apparat. Was kann ich für Sie tun?**
- **Ich habe Ihre Anzeige für einen Verkaufsleiter in der Lokalzeitung gesehen. Können Sie mir die Bewerbungsunterlagen zusenden?**

Wie viele Referenzen benötigen Sie?
- **Zwei, einschließlich die Ihres jetzigen oder letzten Arbeitgebers.**

➤ UNEMPLOYMENT 12c

BUSINESS & ECONOMICS

14d Finance & industry

account **die Rechnung(en), das Konto (-en)**
advance **der Vorschuß ("-sse)**
I audit **ich prüfe**
bill **die Rechnung(en)**
bond **die Staatsanleihe(n)**
branch *(of company)* **die Zweigstelle(n)**
budget **das Budget(s), der Haushalt(e), der Etat(s)**
capital **das Kapital**
capital expenditure **die Kapitalaufwendungen** *(pl)*
chamber of commerce **die Handelskammer(n)**
collateral **die Sicherheit(en)**
company **die Gesellschaft(en)**
competition **die Konkurrenz**
I consume *(resources)* **ich verbrauche**
consumer goods **die Konsumgüter** *(pl)*
consumer protection **der Verbraucherschutz**
consumer spending **die Verbraucherausgaben** *(pl)*
cost of living **die Lebenshaltungskosten** *(pl)*
costing **die Kostenberechnung(en)**
costs **die Kosten** *(pl)*
credit **der Kredit(e)**
debit **die Abhebung(en)**
deflation **die Deflation**
economic **wirtschaftlich**
economy **die Wirtschaft(en)**
government spending **die öffentlichen Ausgaben** *(pl)*
income **das Einkommen**
income tax **die Einkommenssteuer(n)**
installment **die Rate(n)**
interest rate **die Zinsrate(n)**
I invest in **ich investiere in** +acc

investment **die Investierung(en)**
invoice **die Rechnung(en)**
labour/labor costs **die Arbeitskosten** *(pl)*
liability **die Verpflichtung(en)**
limited liability company **die Gesellschaft mit beschränkter Haftung (GmbH)**
loan **der Kredit(e)**
manufacturing industry **die herstellende Industrie(n)**
market **der Markt("-e)**
market economy **die Marktwirtschaft**
marketing **das Marketing**
merchandise **die Güter** *(pl)*
national debt **die Staatsschulden** *(pl)*
I nationalize **ich verstaatliche**
output **die Leistung(en), die Produktion(en)**
pay **der Lohne("-e)**
price **der Preis(e)**
private sector **der Privatsektor(en)**
I privatize **ich privatisiere**
product **das Produkt(e)**
production **die Produktion(en)**
public sector **der öffentliche Sektor(en)**
quota **die Quote(n)**
rate (going) **der Kurs(e)**
real estate/realty **die Immobilien** *(pl)*
retail sales **der Einzelhandelsverkauf** *(no pl)*
retail trade **der Einzelhandel** *(no pl)*
salaries **das/der Gehalt("-er)**
sales tax **die Verkaufssteuer(n)**
service sector **der Dienstleistungssektor(en)**
share **die Aktie(n)**
shares are going up/down **die Aktien fallen/steigen**
share index **der Aktienindex(e)**

statistics **die Statistik(en)**
stock exchange **die Börse(n)**
I subsidize **ich subventioniere**
subsidy **der Zuschuß (¨-sse)**
supply and demand **Angebot und Nachfrage**
supply costs **die Lieferkosten** *(pl)*
I tax **ich versteuere**
tax **die Steuer(n)**
    after tax **nach Abzug und Steuer**
tax cut **die Steuersenkung(en)**
tax relief **die Steuerbegünstigung(en)**
tax increase **die Steuererhöhung(en)**
taxation **die Steuern** *(pl)*
taxation level **das Steuerniveau(s)**
turnover **der Umsatz(¨-e)**
VAT/sales tax **die Mehrwertsteuer, MwSt**
viable **rentabel**
wage(s) **der Lohn(¨-e)**

Financial personnel

accountant **der Wirtschaftsprüfer(-) [-in]**
actuary **der Versicherungsmathematiker(-) [-in]**
auditor **der Prüfer(-) [-in]**
banker **der Bankier(s)**
    investment banker **der Investitionsbankier(s)**
    merchant banker **der Handelsbankier(s)**
bank manager **der Bankmanager(-) [-in]**
broker **der Makler(-) [-in]**
    insurance broker **der Versicherungsmakler(-) [-in**
consumer **der Verbraucher(-) [-in]**
investor **der Investor(en)**
speculator **der Spekulant(en)** *(wk)*
stockbroker **der Börsenmakler(-) [-in]**
trader *(Wall St.)* **der Händler(-) [-in], der Makler(-) [-in]**

Industry is recovering.	**Die Industrie nimmt Aufschwung.**
In spite of the increase in the value of the Deutschmark, there is an export surplus.	**Trotz der DM-Aufwertungen gibt es einen Ausfuhrüberschuß.**
Inflation is slowing down.	**Die Inflation nimmt ab.**
A stable economy, free trade and an organized monetary system are important for the EU/European Union.	**Eine stabile Wirtschaft, freier Handel und ein geordnetes Währungssystem sind wichtig für die EU.**
We have to pay for the import of raw materials.	**Wir müssen die Einfuhr von Rohstoffen bezahlen.**
The fall in value of the dollar is the cause of the recession.	**Der Rückgang des Dollarkurses ist Ursache der Rezession.**
I have overdrawn my account.	**Ich habe mein Konto überzogen.**

➤ ADVERTISING 18d

14e Banking & the economy

Banking & personal finance

account **das Konto (-en)**
automatic teller/cash point **der Geldautomat(en)** *(wk)*
bank **die Bank(en)**
I bank *(money)* **ich zahle Geld ein***
banking **das Bankwesen**
bank loan **das Bankdarlehen(-)**
bank charge **die Bankgebühr(en)**
bank statement **der Kontoauszug(-̈e)**
building society/savings and loan association **die Bausparkasse(n)**
cash **das Bargeld(er)**
I cash a cheque/check **ich löse einen Scheck ein***
cashcard **die Scheckkarte(n)**
cashdesk **die Kasse(n)**
I change **ich wechsle**
cheque/check **der Scheck(s)**
credit card **die Kreditkarte(n)**
I'm in credit **Ich habe Geld auf dem Konto**
currency **die Währung(en)**
deficit **das Defizit(e)**
deposit *(in a bank)* **die Einzahlung(en)**
deposit *(returnable)* **die Kaution(en)**

I deposit **ich zahle … ein***
direct debit **die Einzugsermächtigung(en)**
down payment/deposit **die Anzahlung(en)**
Eurocheque **der Euroscheck(s)**
exchange rate **der Wechselkurs(e)**
hire purchase/installment plan **der Teilzahlungskauf(-̈e)**
I invest **ich lege an***
I lend **ich leihe**
loan **das Darlehen(-)**
mortgage **die Hypothek(en)**
I mortgage **ich nehme eine Hypothek auf***
I open an account **ich eröffne ein Konto**
overdraft **der Überziehungskredit(e)**
I overdraw **ich überziehe**
I pay cash **ich bezahle bar**
in the red **in den roten Zahlen**
repayment **die Zurückzahlung(en)**
I save **ich spare**
savings **die Ersparnisse** *(pl)*
savings bank **die Sparkasse(n)**
standing order **der Dauerauftrag(-̈e)**
I transfer (to) **ich überweise auf** +acc

I have opened an account at the (savings) bank. You only need an identity card and an initial deposit. Now I have my salary automatically transferred into my account.

Ich habe bei der Sparkasse ein Konto eröffnet. Man braucht nur einen Personalausweis und eine erste Einzahlung. Jetzt lasse ich mein Gehalt automatisch auf das Konto überweisen.

I pay my rent by standing order.

Ich begleiche meine Miete per Dauerauftrag.

Gas and electricity are withdrawn from my account by direct debit.

Gas und Strom werden durch Einzugsermächtigungen von meinem Konto abgebucht.

travellers' cheque/traveler's check
der Reisecheck(s)
I withdraw **ich hebe ab***

Growth

appreciation **die
Wertsteigerung(en)**
asset **der Aktivposten(-)**
assurance **die Versicherung(en)**
auction **die Auktion(en)**
boom **die Hochkunjunktur, der
Boom(s), der Aufschwung(Ꞌe)**
I diversify **ich diversifiziere**
economic miracle **das
Wirtschaftswunder(-)**
efficiency **die Wirtschaftlichkeit**
I grow/expand **ich wachse**
growth **das Wachstum**
it increases **es steigt**
joint venture **die
Gemeinschaftunternehmen(-)**
they merge **sie fusionieren**
we merge **wir schließen uns
zusammen***
merger **die Fusion(en)**
plan **der Plan(Ꞌe)**
profit **der Gewinn(e)**
profitable **rentabel**
progress **der Fortschritt(e)**
prosperity **der Wohlstand** *(no pl)*
prosperous **wohlhabend**

recovery **der neue Aufschwung**
takeover **die Übernahme(n)**
takeover bid **das
Übernahmeangebot(e)**

Decline

bankrupt **bankrott, pleite**
I go bankrupt **ich mache bankrott**
credit squeeze **die
Kreditbeschränkung(en)**
debt **die Schuld(en)**
it is declining **es fällt, es geht
zurück**
deficit **das Defizit(e)**
depreciation **der
Kaufkraftverlust(e)**
I dump **ich verkaufe zu
Dumpingpreisen**
inflation **die Inflation(en)**
inflation rate **die Inflationsrate(n)**
loss **der Verlust(e)**
no-growth economy **die
stagnierende Wirtschaft**
recession **die Rezession(en)**
it slows down **es geht zurück**
slump **der Rückgang(Ꞌe)**
it slumps **es stürzt**
spending cuts **die Kürzungen im
Etat**
stagnant **stagnierend**
stagnation **die Stagnation(en)**

Nobody accepts a check today
without a check card. The bank
guarantees that every check is
honored.

**Niemand nimmt heute einen
Scheck ohne eine Scheckkarte.
Die Bank garantiert, daß jeder
Scheck eingelöst wird.**

We have a record surplus of 8
million marks.

**Wir haben einen Rekordüberschuß
von 8 Millionen Mark.**

The cost of oil imports is rising
steeply.

**Die Kosten der Öleinfuhren
steigen enorm.**

115

15 Communicating with others

15a Meetings & greetings

Meetings

I accept *(invitation)* **ich nehme an***
appointment **die Verabredung(en), der Termin(e)**
at home **zu Hause**
ball **der Ball(¨e)**
banquet **das Bankett(e)**
I bump into **ich begegne jdm.**
I'm busy **ich habe keine Zeit**
I celebrate **ich begehe, ich feiere**
celebration **die Feier(n) , die Gedenkfeier(n)**
club **der Klub(s), der Club(s)**
dance **der Tanz(¨e)**
date *(appointment)* **die Verabredung(en), das Rendezvous(-)**
diary/datebook **der (Termin)kalender(-)**
I drop in **ich komme vorbei**
I'm expecting ... for dinner **ich erwarte +acc zum Abendessen**
I greet **ich begrüße**
guest **der Gast(¨e)**

I have guests **ich habe Besuch**
handshake **der Händedruck(¨e)**
I invite **ich lade ein***
invitation **die Einladung(en)**
I join **ich trete +dat bei***
we meet **wir treffen uns**
meeting **die Begegnung(en), das Treffen(-)**
party **die Party(s), die Feier(n), das Fest(e)**
I throw a party **ich gebe eine Party**
reception **der Empfang(¨e)**
I shake hands with (someone) **ich gebe (jdm.) die Hand**
social life **das gesellschaftliche Leben**
I socialize **ich komme viel unter die Leute**
I spend *(an evening)* **ich verbringe**
I take part **ich mache mit***
I talk to someone **ich unterhalte mich mit jdm.**

– Please come in and take a seat.

– **Kommen Sie bitte herein und nehmen Sie Platz.**

– I'm delighted you were able to come. How are you?

– **Ich freue mich, daß Sie kommen konnten. Wie geht es Ihnen?**

– Very well thank you, and you?

– **Sehr gut, danke, und Ihnen?**

– Excellent.

– **Ausgezeichnet.**

– Hello, Otto! May I introduce my cousin Martina?

– **Servus, Otto! Darf ich dir meine Cousine Martina vorstellen?**

– I'm delighted to meet you.

– **Es freut mich dich kennenzulernen.**

I visit *(someone)* **ich besuche**
visit **der Besuch(e)**

Greetings

Good day **Guten Tag!**
Good morning! **Guten Morgen!**
Good evening! **Guten Abend!**
Hello! **Guten Tag! Grüß Gott!**
Hello! *(fam)* **Hallo! Servus!**
Hey you! **Heh! Du!**
Doctor Braun, ... **Herr Doktor Braun, ...**
greetings to you all **ich begrüße Sie alle**
I say, did you know? **Du, weißt du schon?**
welcome to our home! **herzlich willkommen bei uns!**
what is it? **was ist's?**
what's up? **was gibt's?**
yes? **ja, bitte?**

Introductions

I am called ... **ich heiße ...**
can I introduce you? **darf ich (Sie) bekanntmachen?**
delighted to meet you **es freut mich, Sie kennenzulernen**
do you know Doctor Schmidt?
kennen Sie schon Herrn Doktor Schmidt?
I am a friend of Peter's **ich bin ein Freund von Peter**
how do you do! **angenehm! freut mich!**
may I introduce my friend Peter?
darf ich meinen Freund Peter vorstellen?
my name is ... **mein Name ist ...**

what are you called? **wie heißt du?**
what's your surname? **wie heißt du mit Nachnamen?**

Congratulations

all the best! **alles Gute!**
cheers! **zum Wohl! prost!**
congratulations! **herzlichen Glückwunsch!**
merry Christmas! **frohe Weihnachten**
happy Easter! **frohe Ostern!**
happy New Year! **ein gutes neues Jahr!, einen guten Rutsch ins neue Jahr!**
I congratulate you on **ich gratuliere (Ihnen) zu** +dat
I wish you ... **ich wünsche Ihnen ...**
my deepest sympathy! **mein herzliches Beileid!**
thank you so much! **ich bedanke mich (sehr)!**
to your good health! **auf Ihr Wohl!**

Pleasantries

I address (someone) **ich rede (jdn.) an*, ich spreche zu** +dat
I address as "du" **ich duze**
I address as "Sie" **ich sieze**
may I come in? **darf ich reinkommen?**
come in! **herein!**
am I disturbing you? **störe ich?**
Am I in your way? **Störe ich?**
not at all! **nein, keineswegs!**

We were so lucky with the weather.

Wir haben wirklich Glück mit dem Wetter gehabt.

Mrs. Eilers, best wishes on your birthday!

Frau Eilers, recht herzlichen Glückwunsch zum Geburtstag!

➤ FAREWELLS 15d; POST/MAIL, TELEPHONE 15e; COMPUTERS 15f

COMMUNICATING WITH OTHERS

15b Approving, thanking, & disapproving

Approval

all right **in Ordnung**
that's all right **es ist ganz in Ordnung**
all right by me! **meinetwegen!**
that's all right by me! **von mir aus!**
fabulous **fabelhaft**
fantastic **phantastisch**
I'm in favor of **ich bin (wäre) dafür**
delighted **erfreut**
I'm delighted **das freut mich**
I enjoy **ich genieße**
exactly **genau**
I feel **ich fühle mich**
I feel like (doing) **ich habe Lust, zu** +inf
fun **der Spaß(-e)**
that's fun **das macht Spaß**
fine! **schön!, prima!, gut!**
I am fond of him **ich habe ihn sehr gern**
glad **froh**
I'm glad **ich bin froh, ich freue mich**
great! **toll!, prima!, phantastisch!, Klasse!**
that would be great **das wäre gut/prima!**
interesting **interessant**
it interests me **das interessiert mich**

I am interested in **ich interessiere mich für** +acc
just so! **so ist das einfach/eben**
I like it a lot **ich mag es sehr**
I like reading **ich lese gern**
I like it **es gefällt mir**
I really like you **ich mag dich wirklich gern**
I like her **ich kann sie gut leiden**
I would like **ich würde gern, ich möchte**
I look forward to **ich freue mich auf** +acc
I love **ich liebe**
lovely **schön**
marvellous **herrlich**
I don't mind **das ist (mir) egal/gleich**
nice **nett, schön, sympathisch**
how nice! **wie schön!**
pleased **zufrieden**
with pleasure **mit Vergnügen**
rather **lieber**
I would rather **ich möchte lieber**
right **korrekt**
that's right **das stimmt**
I want **ich will/möchte**
wonderful **großartig, wunderbar**
it works out **es klappt**

I am really looking forward to my vacation. It is exactly what I need.

Ich freue mich sehr auf meine Ferien. Es ist genau das, was ich brauche.

I really like it in Bavaria. I feel great there.

Es gefällt mir sehr gut in Bayern. Ich fühle mich dort sehr wohl.

Last year I spent two marvelous weeks at the Chiemsee. This summer I would like to go to Reit-im-Winkl.

Letztes Jahr habe ich zwei herrliche Wochen am Chiemsee verbracht. Diesen Sommer möchte ich nach Reit-im-Winkl.

Thanking

please! **bitte!**
I thank **ich danke** +dat
thank you! **danke!**
many thanks! **vielen Dank!, danke sehr!**
thank you very much! **danke schön!**
thank you very much indeed! **herzlichen Dank!**
thanks a lot! **schönen Dank auch!**
don't mention it! **nichts zu danken!**
glad to help! **gern geschehen!**
no need to thank me! **keine Ursache!**
not at all! **bitte!, bitteschön!**
it was the least I could do! **das ist doch selbstverständlich!**

Disapproval

I annoy **ich störe**
you're annoying me! **du störst mich!**
bad **schlecht**
that's too bad! **das geht zu weit**
bad luck **das Pech**
we had bad luck **wir hatten Pech**
what bad luck! **so ein Mist!**
damn! **verdammt!**
dreadful **schrecklich, furchtbar**
fed up **sauer**

furious **wütend**
how dreadful! **wie schrecklich!**
I hate doing **ich hasse es, zu** +inf
it hurts! **das tut weh!**
impossible **unmöglich**
that's impossible **das geht (doch) nicht, unmöglich!**
leave me in peace! **laß mich in Ruhe!**
are you mad? **bist du verrückt?**
I mind a lot **es macht mir viel aus***
miserable **miserabel**
nonsense! **Quatsch!, (das ist) Unsinn!**
it's nothing to do with me **das geht mich nichts an***
ouch! **au!**
there's no point! **das hat keinen Zweck/Sinn**
rubbish **Quatsch!**
shit! **Scheiße!**
I can't stand him **ich kann ihn nicht leiden**
stop that! **laß das!, hör doch auf!**
stupid **dumm**
that's stupid! **das ist zu dumm!**
that won't do **das geht nicht**
that's enough **das genügt**

The weather was dreadful. Such bad luck! | **Das Wetter war schrecklich. So ein Pech!**

– Thanks a lot for your help, Willi. | **– Vielen Dank für deine Hilfe, Willi.**

– Don't mention it. Glad to help. | **– Nichts zu danken. Gern geschehen.**

There's no point planning a picnic for Sunday. It's supposed to rain. | **Es hat keinen Zweck ein Picknick für Sonntag zu planen. Es soll regnen.**

I have to concentrate on my work. Please leave me in peace! | **Ich muß mich auf meine Arbeit konzentrieren. Bitte laß mich in Ruhe!**

➤ INTERJECTIONS, APOLOGIZING, & FAREWELLS 15d

15c Permission, obligation, & clarification

Permission

can I? **kann ich?**
could I? **könnte ich?**
OK? **geht das?**
may I? **darf ich?**
might I? **dürfte ich?**
will you allow me to **erlauben Sie mir zu** +inf?
would it be possible? **wäre es möglich?**
Why of course! **ja natürlich!**
sure! **ja klar!**
OK! **okay!, in Ordnung!**
yes, that's OK! **ja, das geht!**
allowed **erlaubt/gestattet**
I allow you to.... **ich erlaube Ihnen zu** +inf
it doesn't bother me, if you ... **es stört mich nicht, wenn Sie ...**
carry on! **machen Sie ruhig weiter!**
of course you can ... **Sie dürfen selbstverständlich ...**
you can if you want **du kannst, wenn du willst**
as far as I'm concerned, you can ... **meinetwegen können Sie ...**
do you mind if ...? **stört es Sie wenn ...?**
yes, if you must **ja, wenn es sein muß**
do you object? **haben Sie was dagegen?**
permission **die Erlaubnis(se)**
as you wish **wie Sie wollen**
you are not allowed to **du darfst nicht**
no, you can't ... **nein, du kannst/darfst nicht ...**
certainly not! **durchaus nicht!**
certainly not **auf keinen Fall, keinesfalls**
it is just not done! **das tut man nicht!**
forbidden **untersagt, verboten**

smoking forbidden **kein Rauchen, Rauchverbot**
impossible! **ausgeschlossen!**
no, certainly not **nein, keineswegs**
not at all **gar/überhaupt nicht**
it's not possible **es geht leider nicht**
of course not! **überhaupt nicht!**
out of the question! **es kommt nicht in Frage!**
please don't! **bitte nicht!**
I'd rather you didn't! **lieber nicht!**
I have no right to ... **ich habe kein Recht zu** +inf
I'm sorry! **tut mir leid!**
under no circumtances **auf keinen Fall**

Obligation

it's compulsory **es ist Vorschrift/obligatorisch**
I have got to **ich muß unbedingt/auf jeden Fall**
you've got to! **das muß sein!**
I have to **ich muß**
do I have to? **muß ich?**
you don't have to **du mußt nicht**
I have a lot to do **ich habe viel zu tun**
I intend to ... **ich habe vor zu** +inf
I intend to **ich habe die Absicht**
I must **ich muß**
you must pay a fee **es ist gebührenpflichtig**
it is not necessary **es ist nicht nötig**
not necessarily **nicht unbedingt**
you do not need to **du brauchst nicht zu** +inf
you needn't do it **du kannst es ruhig lassen**
I am obliged to **ich bin verpflichtet zu** +inf

I am not supposed to   **ich soll nicht**
I want to   **ich will**
what is to be done?   **was ist zu tun?**

Clarifying

and so on, etc.   **und so weiter, usw.**
I ask   **ich frage**
may I ask a question?   **dürfte ich eine Frage stellen?**
example   **das Beispiel(e)**
for example   **zum Beispiel, beispielsweise**
I explain   **ich erkläre**
I hear   **ich höre**
can you still hear me?   **hören Sie mich noch?**
are you still there?   **sind Sie noch da?**
I didn't hear   **ich habe nicht gehört**
I forget   **ich vergesse**
in other words   **mit anderen Worten, anders gesagt**
I know   **ich weiß**
I don't know how you say …   **ich weiß nicht, wie man sagt …**
loud   **laut**
louder   **lauter**
not so loud!   **nicht so laut!**
I mean   **ich meine**
it means   **es bedeutet**
what does it mean?   **was heißt das?**
what do you mean   **was meinen Sie?**
what do you mean by that?   **was meinen Sie damit?**

I pronounce   **ich spreche aus***
how do you pronounce it?   **wie spricht man das aus?**
I have a question   **ich habe eine Frage**
quick(ly)   **schnell**
not so quick   **nicht so schnell**
quiet please!   **Ruhe bitte!**
quietly!   **leise!**
I repeat   **ich wiederhole**
could you repeat that?   **können Sie das wiederholen?**
I say   **ich sage**
how do you say that in German?   **wie sagt man das auf deutsch?**
what would you say?   **was würden Sie sagen?**
what did you say?   **was haben Sie gesagt?**
slow   **langsam**
slower   **langsamer**
sorry   **Entschuldigung!**
I translate into German   **ich übersetze ins Deutsche**
I understand   **ich verstehe**
can you understand me?   **können Sie mich verstehen?**
what is it in English?   **wie/was heißt das auf Englisch?**
what do you call it in German?   **wie nennt man das auf deutsch?**
what was that?   **wie war das? was war das gleich?**

Excuse me, could you say that a little louder? I didn't hear you.

Entschuldigung, könnten Sie das ein bißchen lauter sagen? Ich habe Sie nicht gehört.

– May I interrupt you for a moment?
– Certainly.
– Would you please repeat that last point? I didn't understand it.

– Darf ich Sie mal unterbrechen?
– Selbstverständlich.
– Würden Sie bitte den letzten Punkt wiederholen? Ich habe ihn nicht verstanden.

15d Interjections, apologizing, & farewells

Surprise

at last!	**endlich!**
amazed	**erstaunt**
Fancy that!	**Na, so was!**
funny	**komisch!**
funny he never told me!	**komisch, daß er mir nicht Bescheid sagte!**
God!	**O Gott!**
God be praised!	**Gott sei Dank!**
Good God!	**meine Güte!**
goodness	**um Himmels willen**
I surprise	**ich überrasche**
impossible	**unmöglich**
that's incredible!	**das ist ja unglaublich!**
possible	**möglich**
that can't be possible!	**das ist doch nicht möglich!**
really?	**(also) wirklich?**
so what?	**na, und?**
surely	**doch**
surely you know	**du weißt doch ...**
surprised	**überrascht**
surprising	**überraschend**
what a surprise!	**das ist aber eine Überraschung!**
I think	**ich denke**
I would never have thought that	**das hätte ich nicht gedacht**
true	**wahr**
that can't be true!	**das darf doch nicht wahr sein!**
is that true?	**ist das wahr? stimmt das?**
Well I never!	**Na, so was!**
what!	**was!**
luck	**das Glück**
what luck (that)!	**ein Glück (daß)!**
wow!	**Mensch!**

Hesitating

aha	**aha, ach so**
as it were	**sozusagen**
but ...	**aber ...**
by the way	**nebenbei**
definitely?	**bestimmt? sicher?**
is that so?	**ist das so?**
I don't know	**ich weiß nicht**
you know	**wissen Sie**
maybe	**es kann sein**
moreover	**übrigens**
oh!	**ach!**
one minute please	**eine Minute, einen Moment bitte**
one moment!	**(einen) Moment mal**
or?	**oder? gell?**
or not?	**oder nicht?**
pardon	**bitte? Verzeihung?**
I beg your pardon	**bitte?**
perhaps	**vielleicht**

– I just don't know what to do.

It can't be true! I have to go to a meeting shortly and my husband took the car!

– You've got time on Friday, don't you?

– I don't know. Just a moment, let me check my calendar.

– **Ich weiß einfach nicht, was ich machen soll.**

Das darf doch nicht wahr sein! Ich muß gleich zu einer Besprechung, und mein Mann hat das Auto genommen!

– **Du hast doch am Freitag Zeit, oder nicht?**

– **Ich weiß nicht. Einen Moment mal, laß mich mal in meinem Kalender nachsehen.**

please go on   **mach weiter**
really?   **wirklich? tatsächlich?**
something like that   **so etwas**
I suppose   **ich vermute**
supposedly   **vermutlich, wohl**
that is, i.e.   **das heißt, d.h.**
that is to say   **das heißt**
what next?   **was nun?**
what shall I do now?   **was mache ich jetzt?**
well …   **na, nun …**
well OK!   **na gut!**
well then …   **also**
what now?   **was jetzt/nun?**
why?   **warum**
why not?   **warum nicht?**
yes, but …   **(ja) schon aber, schon gut aber …**

Agreeing

I agree   **das finde ich auch**
agreed!   **einverstanden!, abgemacht!**
both … and   **sowohl … als auch**
certain   **sicher**
certainly!   **bestimmt!, allerdings!, eben!**
definitely   **bestimmt, gewiß**
exactly!   **genau!**
firstly   **erstens**
in short   **kurz (gesagt)**
I know   **ich weiß**
no!   **nein!**
not only … but also   **nicht nur … sondern auch**
obviously!   **selbstverständlich!**
that's obvious   **das ist klar**
of course!   **freilich!**
it occurs to me   **es fällt mir ein***
right!   **richtig!**
is that right?   **ist das richtig?**
isn't that so/right?   **nicht wahr?**
secondly   **zweitens**
something else   **was anderes**
I tell   **ich erzähle**
tell us   **erzählen Sie mal**
I think so too!   **das glaub ich auch!**

do you think so?   **finden/glauben/ meinen Sie?**
true   **wahr**
that's true!   **das stimmt!**
is that true?   **ist das wahr?**
I want   **ich will**
as you want   **wie Sie wollen/meinen**
if you want   **wenn Sie Lust haben**
well, that's that   **so, das wär's**
yes!   **ja!**

Apologizing

I apologize (for)   **ich entschuldige mich (für** +acc)
apology   **die Entschuldigung(en)**
excuse me   **entschuldigen Sie**
sorry!   **Entschuldigung!, Verzeihung!**
I'm sorry   **das tut mir leid!**
I am so sorry!   **Entschuldigen Sie bitte!**
it doesn't matter!   **das macht nichts!**
that's OK!   **schon gut!**

Farewells

Goodbye!   **Auf Wiedersehen!**
Goodbye! *(telephone)*   **Auf Wiederhören!**
Bye!   **Tschüß!**
See you soon!   **Bis bald!**
See you tomorrow!   **Bis morgen!**
greetings to the family!   **viele Grüße an die Familie!**
greet Manfred from me!   **grüß Manfred von mir!**
all the best!   **alles Gute!, mach's gut!**
best wishes to your wife!   **einen schönen Gruß an Ihre Frau!**
have fun!   **viel Spaß!**
have a good time!   **viel Vergnügen!**
have a good journey!   **gute Reise!**
have a safe journey!   **komm gut nach Hause!**
have a good holiday/vacation!   **schöne Ferien!**
same to you!   **danke gleichfalls!**

COMMUNICATING WITH OTHERS

15e Post/Mail & telephone

Post/Mail

abroad **im/ins Ausland**
addressee **der Adressat(en)** *(wk)* **[-in]**
answer **die Antwort(en)**
any news? **irgendwelche Nachricht(en)?**
by air **per Luftpost**
airmail **die Luftpost**
collection/pickup **die Leerung(en)**
I correspond **ich korrespondiere**
correspondent **der Korrespondent(en)** *(wk)* **[-in]**
counter **der Schalter(-)**
customs declaration **die Zollerklärung(en)**
express delivery **das Eilgut**
first-class **erster Klasse**
franking-machine/postage meter **die Frankiermaschine(n)**
freepost **Gebühr bezahlt Empfänger**
I get/receive **ich bekomme**
I hand in **ich reiche ein***
letter **der Brief(e)**
letter rate **die Briefgebühr(en)**
mailbox **der Briefkasten(-̈e)**
I finish *(letter)* **ich beende**
news **die Neuigkeit(en), die Nachricht(en)**
I note down **ich schreibe auf, ich notiere**

package **das Päckchen(-)**
parcel **das Paket(e)**
parcel rate **die Paketgebühr(en)**
pen pal **der Brieffreund(e) [-in]**
post/mail **die Post**
post office **das Postamt(-̈er)**
poste restante **postlagernd**
postage **die Postgebühr(en)**
postal order **der Geldgutschein(e)**
postman/mail carrier **der Briefträger(-) [-in]**
I receive **ich erhalte**
recorded delivery **per Einschreiben**
registered mail **die eingeschriebene Post**
reply **die Antwort(en)**
sealed **versiegelt**
I send **ich schicke**
I send (greetings) **ich bestelle (Grüße)**
sender **der Absender(-)**
stamp **die Briefmarke(n)**
I write **ich schreibe**
zip code **die Postleitzahl(en)**

Telephoning

I call **ich rufe an**
I connect **ich verbinde**
I dial **ich wähle**
I fax **ich faxe**
I hang up **ich lege auf***
I hold **ich warte**

Jan corresponds a lot with clients abroad.

Jan korrespondiert viel mit Kunden im Ausland.

When does the mail arrive?

Wann trifft die Post ein?

I am writing on behalf of my father, concerning …

Ich schreibe im Namen meines Vaters, bezüglich …

I look forward to hearing from you.

Ich hoffe bald von Ihnen zu hören.

➤ LETTER WRITING FORMULAE App.15e; STATIONERY App.22b

I pick up **ich hebe ab***
I press **ich drücke**
I put ... through (to) **ich stelle zu +dat ... durch***
I speak to ... **ich spreche mit** +dat
I telephone/phone **ich telefoniere**

Telephone & telecommunications

answering machine **der Anrufbeantworter**
booth **die Telefonzelle(n)**
button **der Knopf(-̈e)**
  push the button **auf den Knopf drücken!**
call-box **die Telefonzelle(n)**
communication **die Kommunikation(en)**
conversation **das Gespräch(e)**
I dial **ich wähle**
E-mail **Daten-Fernübertragung (DFÜ), das Teletex**
electronic mail **die elektronische Post**
engaged/busy *(phone)* **besetzt**
I am ex-directory/not listed **ich stehe nicht im Telefonbuch**
extension **der Anschluß (-̈sse)**
fax **das Fax-Gerät(e), das Fax**
fax modem **das Fax-Modem**
information highway **das Integrierte Breitband-Fernmeldenetz**
line **die Telefonverbindung(en)**
link **der Anschluß (-̈sse)**

local call **das Ortsgespräch(e)**
long-distance call **das Ferngespräch(e)**
nought/zero/0 **Null**
number **die Nummer(n)**
operator **die Zentrale(n)**
optical fibre/fiber **das Glasfaserkabel(-)**
order **in Betrieb**
out of order **außer Betrieb**
receiver **der Hörer(-)**
reverse charge call/collect call **das R-Gespräch(e)**
satellite **der Satellit(en)** *(wk)*
slot **der Schlitz(e)**
subscriber **der Telefonteilnehmer(-)**
telecommunications **die Telekommunikation(en)**
telegram(me) **das Telegramm(e)**
telegraph **der Telegraf(en)**
telephone **das Telefon(e)**
  car phone **das Autotelefon(e)**
  cellular/mobile phone **das Funktelefon(e), das Handy(s)**
telephone directory **das Telefonbuch(-̈er)**
telephone kiosk **die Telefonzelle**
teletext **der Videotext**
telex **das Telex**
I transmit **ich übertrage**
wrong number **falsch verbunden**

Can I dial direct? | **Kann ich direkt durchwählen?**
– Who's speaking? | **– Wer ist am Apparat?**
– This is John Smith (speaking). | **– Hier spricht John Smith.**
Could you put me through to Mr. Müller? | **Können sie mich mit Herrn Müller verbinden?**
– Please hold! Are you still there? | **–Bitte bleiben Sie am Apparat.**
I'm afraid Mr. Müller's not in. | **Sind sie noch dran? Herr Müller ist leider nicht da.**

– I will call back later. | **–Ich werde später zurückrufen.**
Good-bye! | **Auf Wiederhören.**

➤ COMPUTERS 15f

125

15f Computers

Computer applications

adventure game **das Abenteuerspiel(e)**
application **die Anwendung(en)**
artificial intelligence **die künstliche Intelligenz**
barcode **der Bar-Code(s)**
barcode reader **der Bar-Code-Leser(-)**
barcoded **mit Bar-Code**
calculator **der Rechner(-)**
computer control **die Computerkontrolle(n)**
computer-controlled lathe **die computergesteuerte Drehmaschine(n)**
computer science/studies **die Informatik**
computerized **computerisiert**
desktop publishing/DTP **das DTP-Programm(e)**
game **das Spiel(e)**
grammar checker **der Grammatiküberprüfer**
information **die Information(en)**
information technology **die Informatik**

office automation **die Büroautomation**
simulation **die Simulatation(en)**
simulator **der Simulator(en)** *(wk)*
spell-check **die Rechtschreibkontrolle(n)**
synthesizer **der Synthesizer(-)**
thesaurus **das Synonymwörterbuch(⁻er)**
word processor **der Textverarbeiter(-)**
word processing **die Textverarbeitung**

Word processing & operating

I abort **ich breche ab***
I access **ich rufe auf***
I append **ich hänge an***
I back-up **ich sichere**
I block *(text)* **ich markiere**
I boot up **ich boote**
I browse **ich schmöckere**
I cancel *(command)* **ich deaktiviere**
I click on **ich klicke an***
I communicate **ich kommuniziere**
I copy **ich kopiere**
I count **ich zähle**

It's all done by computer.

Das geht alles per Computer.

In a spreadsheet you can fill the cells with text, figures or formulas.

In einer Tabellenkalkulation kann man die Zellen mit Text, Zahlen oder Formeln füllen.

You must analyze the problem and decide what formulas to use.

Sie müssen die Aufgabe analysieren und entscheiden, welche Formeln Sie einsetzen müssen.

– This disk is corrupted. It has wiped out my file!
– Have you checked for a virus?

– Diese Diskette ist defekt. Sie hat meine Datei gelöscht!
– Haben Sie ein Virusprogramm ablaufen lassen?

I create **ich erstelle**
I cut and paste **ich schneide aus***
I debug **ich beseitige den Fehler**
I delete **ich lösche**
I download **ich lade**
I drag **ich ziehe**
I embolden **ich formatiere in Fettschrift**
I emulate **ich emuliere**
I enter (text) **ich gebe (Text) ein***
I erase **ich lösche**
I exit (the program) **ich beende (das Programm)**
I export **ich exportiere**
I file **ich lege an***
I format **ich formatiere**
I handle *(text)* **ich verarbeite**
I import **ich importiere**
I insert **ich füge ein***
I install **ich installiere**
keyboard operator **der Tastaturbearbeiter(-) [-in]**
keyboarding skills **die Eingabefähigkeit**
I key in **ich gebe ein***
I list **ich liste auf***
I log off **ich beende das Progamm**
I log on/off **ich logge ein/aus***
I merge **ich schließe zusammen***
I move *(a file)* **ich versetze**

I move **ich versetze, ich verschiebe**
I network **ich vernetze**
I open (a file) **ich öffne (eine Datei)**
I paste **ich füge ein***
I print **ich drucke**
I print out **ich drucke aus***
I (word) process **ich verarbeite**
I program **ich programmiere**
I read **ich lese**
I receive **ich empfange**
I record **ich nehme auf***
I remove **ich streiche**
I replace **ich ersetze**
I retrieve **ich rufe ab*/auf***
I run **ich lade, ich lasse laufen***
I save **ich speichere**
I search **ich suche**
I send **ich (ver)sende**
I shift **ich speichere**
I simulate **ich simuliere**
I sort **ich sortiere**
I store **ich speichere, ich lege an***
I switch on/off **ich schalte ein/aus***
I tabulate **ich tabuliere**
I underline **ich unterstreiche**
I update **ich aktualisiere**

The data is in memory. **Die Daten befinden sich im Arbeitsspeicher.**

Copy the files onto a floppy disk. **Kopieren Sie die Dateien auf eine Diskette.**

Make a backup copy. **Machen Sie eine Sicherheitskopie.**

Which operating system do you use? **Welches Betriebssystem verwenden Sie?**

How easy is this spreadsheet to use? **Wie einfach ist es, diese Bildschirmtabelle zu bedienen?**

I don't like the software package with this PC. **Ich mag die Software an diesem PC nicht.**

16 Leisure & sport

16a Leisure

activity   die Aktivität(en)
I am free   ich bin frei
archery   das Bogenschießen
bar   die Bar(s)
I begin   ich beginne
book   das Buch(¨er)
boring   langweilig
camera   der Fotoapparat(e), die Kamera(s)
card   die (Spiel)karte(n)
card game   das Kartenspiel(e)
card table   der Spieltisch(e)
carpentry   das Tischlern
casino   das Kasino(s)
chess   das Schach, das Schachspiel(e)
cinema   das Kino(s)
closed   geschlossen
club   der Klub(s)
I collect   ich sammle
coin   die Münze(n)
crosswords   das Kreuzworträtsel(-)
collection   die Sammlung(en)
collectors fair   die Sammlerausstellung(en)
discotheque   die Diskothek(en)

I draw (etch)   ich zeichne
holiday/vacation   die Ferien (pl)
interest   das Interesse(n)
energy   die Energie(n)
enthusiasm   die Begeisterung
enthusiastic   begeistert
entrance   der Eingang(¨e)
entry fee   die Eintrittsgebühr(en)
excitement   die Aufregung(en), die Erregung(en)
exciting   aufregend, erregend
excursion   der Ausflug(¨e)
excursionist   der Ausflügler(-) [-in]
exit   der Ausgang(¨e)
fair   die Ausstellung(en), die Messe(n)
fascinating   faszinierend
finished   beendet, zu Ende
I fish   ich angle
free time   die freie Zeit, die Freizeit
fun   der Spaß(¨e)
I gamble   ich spiele um Geld
I go out   ich gehe aus*
guide   der Reiseführer(-) [-in]
guided tour   die Reisetour(en)

Do you do a lot of sport?
I like going for long walks.

Treibst du viel Sport?
Ich wandere gern.

Sometimes I go fishing, which can be highly recommended for stressed executives!

Manchmal gehe ich fischen, was sehr empfehlenswert für gestreßte Manager ist.

I can meet you at the swimming pool or, if you prefer, at the gym.

Wir können uns an der Schwimmhalle oder, wenn du willst, an der Turnhalle treffen.

hobby **das Hobby(s)**
energetic **energisch**
interesting **interessant**
it is over **es ist vorbei**
I join **ich trete in** +acc **ein*, ich schließe mich (jdm.) an***
leisure **die Freizeit**
line **die Schlange(n)**
I get in line **ich ordne mich ein***
I listen to **ich höre** +dat **zu***
I look **ich sehe, ich blicke**
market **der Markt(¨e)**
   antiques market **der Antiquitätenmarkt(¨e)**
   flea market **der Flohmarkt(¨e)**
I meet **ich treffe**
meeting place **der Treffpunkt(e)**
member **das Mitglied(er)**
membership **die Mitgliedschaft(en)**
nightclub **der Nachtklub(s)**
open **offen, auf**
organization **die Organisation(en)**
I organize **ich organisiere**
photograph **die Fotografie(n), die Aufnahmen(n)**
picnic **das Picknick(s)**
place **der Ort(e)**
I play **ich spiele**
pleasure **das Vergnügen(-), die Freude(n)**
politics **die Politik**
I prefer **ich bevorzuge, ich ziehe**

vor*
private **privat**
public **öffentlich**
line **die Schlange(n)**
I queue **ich stehe an***
I read **ich lese**
season **die Jahreszeit(en)**
secluded **abgelegen, ruhig**
I sew **ich nähe**
slide/chute **die Rutsche(n)**
I slide **ich rutsche**
sold out **ausverkauft**
spectator **der Zuschauer(-) [-in]**
I start (doing) **ich beginne, zu** +inf
I stop (doing) **ich höre auf*, zu** +inf
I stroll **ich schlendere, ich spaziere**
subscription **das Abonnement(s)**
I take photos **ich fotografiere**
television **der Fernseher(-)**
ticket **die Karte(n)**
time **die Zeit(en)**
theatre **das Theater(-)**
tour **die Tour(en)**
vacation **die Ferien, der Urlaub**
I visit **ich besuche**
visit **der Besuch(e)**
I walk **ich gehe spazieren***
I watch **ich schaue** +dat **zu*, ich sehe** +dat **zu***
youth club **der Jugendklub(s)**
zoo **der Zoo(s)**

– What do you like doing on a rainy day?
– Perhaps playing cards, but not with my brother: he cheats!

– Are there any special rates for students?
– Yes, but only on Friday nights.

– **Was machst du gern, wenn es regnet?**
– **Vielleicht Karten spielen, aber nicht mit meinem Bruder: er mogelt!**

– **Gibt es besondere Studentenermäßigungen?**
– **Ja, aber nur Freitag abends.**

➤ LEISURE WEAR, LEISURE EQUIPMENT 16c; PHOTOGRAPHY App.16a

16b Sporting activity

aerobics **das Aerobic**
against **gegen** +acc
athlete **der Athlet(en)** *(wk)* **[-in],**
  der Sportler(-) [-in]
athletic **sportlich**
I attack **ich greife an***
bathtowel **das Badetuch(¨er)**
I defend **ich verteidige**
I bet **ich wette**
boat **das Boot(e)**
I box **ich boxe**
boxer **der Boxer(-)**
I bowl **ich bowle, ich gehe**
  bowlen
captain **der Kapitän(e)**
I catch **ich fange**
champion **der Meister(-) [-in]**
championship **die**
  Meisterschaft(en)
changing/locker room **der**
  Umkleideraum(¨e)
I climb **ich klettere**
climber **der Bergsteiger(-) [-in]**
club **der Klub(s)**
coach **der Trainer(-) [-in]**
crew **die Mannschaft(en)**
cup *(tournament)* **der Pokal(e)**
cycle **das Fahrrad(¨er)**
I cycle **ich fahre Rad**
defeat **die Niederlage(n)**
I dive **ich tauche**
I do (sport) **ich treibe (Sport)**
I draw **ich spiele unentschieden**
it was a draw **es war**
  unentschieden
effort **die Anstrengung(en)**
  I make an effort **ich strenge**
  mich an*
endurance **die Ausdauer**
equipment **die Ausstattung(en)**
I exercize **ich bewege mich**
exercize **die Bewegung(en)**
I fall **ich falle, ich stürze**
fall **der Sturz(¨e)**
field **das Feld(er)**

finals **das Finale(s), das**
  Endspiel(e)
fit **fit**
fitness **die Fitness** *(no pl)*
game **das Spiel(e)**
I get fit **ich trimme mich**
goal **das Tor(e)**
ground **der Boden**
gym(nasium) **die Turnhalle(n)**
I hit **ich schlage, ich treffe**
hit **der Schlag(¨e), der Treffer(-)**
horse race **das Pferderennen(-)**
I ice-skate **ich laufe Schlittschuh**
ice rink **die Eisbahn(en)**
injury **die Verletzung(en)**
instructor **der Lehrer(-) [-in]**
I jog **ich jogge**
jogger **der Jogger(-) [-in]**
I jump **ich springe**
jump **der Sprung(¨e)**
lawn **der Rasen(-)**
league **die Liga(s)**
league leader **der Ligaführer(-)**
locker room **der**
  Umkleideraum(¨e)
I lose **ich verliere**
marathon **der Marathon(s)**
match **das Spiel(e)**
medal **die Medaille(n)**
  bronze/gold/silver **Bronze-/**
  Gold-/Silber-
muscle **der Muskel(n)**
Olympic Games (Winter) **die**
  Olympischen (Winter)spiele
I pass (ball) **ich spiele jdm. (den**
  Ball) zu*
pedal **das Pedal(e)**
I pedal **ich strample, ich trete**
physical **körperlich**
I pitch **ich werfe**
pitcher **der Werfer(-)**
pitch/field **das Spielfeld(er)**
I play **ich spiele**
player **der Spieler**

point **der Moment(e), der Zeitpunkt(e)**
professional **professionell**
I race **ich renne (um die Wette)**
race **das Wettrennen(-)**
referee **der Schiedsrichter(-) [-in]**
rest **die Pause(n)**
result **das Ergebnis(se)**
I ride **ich reite, ich fahre**
riding **das Reiten**
riding school **die Reitschule(n)**
I row **ich rudere**
I run **ich renne, ich laufe**
run **der Lauf(ːe)**
runner **der Läufer(-) [-in]**
sailing school **die Segelschule(n)**
I sail **ich segle**
I save (goal) **ich halte, ich verhindere**
I score (a goal) **ich schieße (ein Tor)**
score **das Spielergebnis(se), die Punktzahl(en), der Spielstand(ːe)**
I ski **ich laufe Ski**
I shoot (ball, puck) **ich schieße**
show **die Show(s)**
skier **der Skiläufer(-) [-in]**
ski lift **der Skilift(e)**
sponsor **der Sponsor(en)**
sponsorship **die Förderung**
sport **der Sport (Sportarten)**

sports field/pitch **der Sportplatz(ːe)**
sprint **der Sprint(s)**
stadium **das Stadion (-ien)**
stamina **das Durchhaltevermögen**
strength **die Kraft(ːe)**
supporter **der Anhänger(-) [-in]**
I swim **ich schwimme**
team **die Mannschaft(en)**
team sport **das Mannschaftsspiel(e)**
I throw **ich werfe**
timing **das Timing**
tournament **das Turnier(e)**
track **die Rennbahn(en), die Piste(n)**
I train **ich trainiere**
trainer **der Trainer(-) [-in]**
training **das Training**
triumph **der Sieg(e)**
trophy **die Trophäe(n)**
I am unfit **ich bin nicht fit**
victory **der Sieg(e)**
I win **ich gewinne**
weight training **das Krafttraining**
workout **das Training**
world championship **die Weltmeisterschaft(en)**
world cup (soccer) **die Fußballweltmeisterschaft(en)**

The victory was a remarkable achievement for the national team, which played extremely well.

Der Sieg war eine bemerkenswerte Leistung der Nationalmannschaft, die besonders gut gespielt hat.

The team has been training in very trying weather conditions. Each athlete was ready to give his best.

Die Mannschaft hat unter äußerst schwierigen Wetterverhältnissen trainiert. Jeder Spieler war bereit, das Beste zu geben.

Unfortunately, a member of the team was seriously injured during the last race.

Unglücklicherweise hat sich ein Mitglied der Mannschaft während des letzten Rennens ernsthaft verletzt.

16c Sports & equipment

Sports

athletics **die Leichtathletik**
badminton **das Badminton, der Federball**
baseball **der Baseball**
basketball **der Basketball**
billiards **das Billiard**
bowling **das Bowling**
boxing **das Boxen**
car racing **das Autorennen, der Rennsport**
climbing **das Bergsteigen, das Klettern**
   free climbing **freies Klettern**
   rock climbing **das Felsenklettern**
cricket **das Cricket**
cycling **das Radfahren**
decathlon **der Zehnkampf(-̈e)**
diving **das Tauchen**
deep-sea diving **das Tiefseetauchen**
football **der amerikanische Fußball**
handball **der Handball**
hockey **das Hockey**
horse racing **das Pferderennen**
horse riding **das Pferdereiten**

ice hockey **das Eishockeyspiel(e)**
ice skating **das Schlittschuhlaufen**
jogging **das Joggen**
paragliding **das Fallschirmgleiten**
pentathlon **der Fünfkampf(-̈e)**
polo **das Polo**
pool **das Poolbilliard**
racing **das Rennen, der Wettlauf(-̈e)**
roller skating **das Rollschuhlaufen**
rugby **das Rugbyspiel(e)**
sailing **das Segeln**
skiing **das Skilaufen**
   alpine skiing **das Abfahrtslaufen**
   cross-country skiing **das Langlaufen**
   downhill skiing **das Schußfahren**
snooker **das Snooker**
soccer **der Fußball**
swimming **das Schwimmen**
table tennis **das Tischtennis**
tennis **das Tennis**
volleyball **der Volleyball**
water polo **der Wasserball**
weightlifting **das Gewichtheben**

– Did you watch the match?
– No, I had to leave before the end. Who won?
– We lost three to one. I still cannot understand how our team could lose so disastrously after a brilliant season.

– **Hast du das Spiel gesehen?**
– **Nein, ich mußte vor dem Ende gehen. Wer hat gewonnen?**
– **Wir haben drei zu eins verloren. Ich kann immer noch nicht verstehen, wie unsere Mannschaft nach einer sehr guten Saison so verheerend verlieren konnte.**

Leisure wear & sports clothes

anorak   **der Anorak(s)**
bathing suit   **der Badeanzug(⁼e)**
boots   **die Stiefel(-)**
cycling shorts   **die Radlerhose(n)**
dancing shoes   **der Tanzschuh(e)**
gardening gloves   **der Gartenhandschuh(e)**
leotard   **der Gymnastikanzug(⁼e)**
parka   **der Parka(s)**
swimsuit   **der Badeanzug(⁼e)**
swimming trunks   **die Badehose(n)**
rugby shirt   **das Rugbyshirt(s)**
track suit   **der Trainingsanzug(⁼e)**
trainers athletic shoes   **der Turnschuh(e)**
walking boot   **der Wanderschuh(e)**
waterproof jacket   **die Wetterjacke(n)**
Wellington boot   **der Gummistiefel(-)**
wet suit   **der Wetteranzug(⁼e)**

Leisure & sports equipment

arrow   **der Pfeil(e)**
ball   **der Ball(⁼e)**
bat   **der Schläger(-)**
binoculars   **das Fernglas(⁼er)**
boxing gloves   **der Boxhandschuh(e)**
bow   **der Bogen(-)**
camera   **die Kamera(s)**
crash helmet   **der Schutzhelm(e)**

exercise bike   **der Heimtrainer(-)**
equipment   **die Ausrüstung(en)**
fishing rod   **die Angelrute(n)**
headphone   **der Kopfhörer(-)**
hi-fi   **das Hi-Fi**
knapsack   **der Rucksack(⁼e)**
knitting needles   **die Stricknadel(n)**
javelin   **der Speer(e)**
mountain bike   **das Mountainbike(s)**
net   **das Netz(e)**
oar   **das Ruder(-)**
puck   **die Scheibe(n), der Puck(s)**
racket   **der Schläger(-)**
rifle   **das Gewehr(e)**
roller skate   **der Rollschuh(e)**
rowing machine   **das Motorboot(e)**
rowing boat   **das Ruderboot(e)**
rucksack   **der Rucksack(⁼e)**
sailing-boat   **das Segelboot(e)**
sewing kit   **das Nähzeug**
skate   **der Schlittschuh(e)**
skis   **der Ski(er)**
ski boot   **der Skistiefel(-)**
ski pole   **der Skistock(⁼e)**
stick *(hockey)*   **der Hockeyschläger(-)**
spinning wheel   **das Spinnrad(⁼er)**
sports bag   **die Sporttasche(n)**
surf board   **das Surfbrett(er)**
weight   **das Gewicht(e)**
yacht   **die Yacht(en)**

All the sports commentators agreed that it was particularly unfortunate when the referee insisted on the penalty kick.

– Do you develop your own photos?
– I would like to, but I do not have a dark room.

Alle Sportreporter waren sich einig, daß es besonderes Pech war, als der Schiedsrichter auf dem Strafstoß bestand.

– Entwickelst du deine Fotos selbst?
– Ich würde es gern, aber ich habe keine Dunkelkammer.

➤ PHOTOGRAPHY App.16a; GARDENING 8c   **133**

17 The arts

17a Appreciation & criticism

abstract **abstrakt**
abstruse **schwerverständlich**
action **die Handlung(en)**
aesthete **der Ästhet(en)** *(wk)*
aesthetics **die Ästhetik**
I analyze **ich analysiere**
I appreciate **ich schätze**
appreciation **das Verständnis(se)**
art **die Kunst(¨e)**
artist **der Künstler(-) [-in]**
artistic **künstlerisch**
atmosphere **die Atmosphäre(n)**
atmospheric **atmosphärisch**
author **der Verfasser(-) [-in]**
award **der Preis(e)**
avant-garde **die Avantgarde**
believable **glaubhaft**
character **der Charakter(e)**
characterization **die Charakterisierung(en)**
characteristic **charakteristisch**
climax **der Höhepunkt(e)**
I close **ich schließe**
comic **der Komiker(-) [-in]**
comic *(adj)* **lustig, komisch**
commentary **der Kommentar(e)**
conflict **der Konflikt(e)**
contemporary **zeitgenössisch, modern**
contrast **der Kontrast(e)**
it creates **es schafft**
creative **kreativ**
creativity **die Kreativität** *(no pl)*
credible **glaubwürdig**
critic **der Kritiker(-) [-in]**
criticism **die Kritik(en)**
cultivated **gebildet**
culture **die Kultur(en)**
it deals with **es handelt von** +dat
it describes **es beschreibt**

it develops **es entwickelt (sich)**
development **die Entwicklung(en)**
device **der Kunstgriff(e)**
dialog **der Dialog(e)**
disturbing **störend**
empathy **das Einfühlungsvermögen**
ending **der Schluß (¨sse)**
endless **endlos**
it ends **es endet**
entertaining **amüsant**
entertainment **die Unterhaltung**
epic **die Epik**
epic *(adj)* **episch**
event **das Ereignis(se)**
eventful **ereignisreich**
example **das Beispiel(e)**
excited **aufgeregt**
exciting **aufregend, spannend**
I explain **ich erläutere**
explanation **die Erläuterung(en)**
it explores **es untersucht**
it expresses **es drückt aus***
extravagant **überschwenglich**
fake **die Fälschung(en)**
fake *(adj)* **gefälscht**
fantastic **phantastisch**
fantasy **die Phantasie(n)**
farcical **possenhaft**
figure **die Figur(en)**
funny **komisch**
genre **das Genre(s)**
image **das Bild(er)**
imaginary **frei erfunden**
imagination **die Phantasie(n)**
inspiration **die Inspiration(en)**
inspired by **inspiriert durch** +acc
intense **intensiv**
intensity **die Intensität**
interpretation **die Deutung(en)**

interpreter **der Interpret(en)** *(wk)* **[-in]**
interpretation **die Interpretation(en)**
invention **die Erfindung(en)**
inventive **erfinderisch**
inventiveness **die schöpferische Kraft(⁻e)**
ironic **ironisch**
irony **die Ironie(n)**
issue **die Frage(n)**
long-winded **umständlich**
lyrical **lyrisch**
modern **modern**
mood **die Stimmung(en)**
moral **die Moral, die Ethik**
moral *(adj)* **moralisch**
morality **die Sittlichkeit(en)**
moving **ergreifend**
mystery **das Geheimnis(se)**
mysterious **geheimnisvoll**
mystical **mystisch**
mysticism **die Mystik(en)**
nature **die Natur**
obscure **unklar, undeutlich**
obscene **obszön**
obscenity **die Obszönität(en)**
opinion **die Meinung(en)**
optimism **der Optimismus**
optimistic **optimistisch**
parody **die Parodie(n)**
passion **die Leidenschaft(en)**
passionate **leidenschaftlich**
pessimism **der Pessimismus**
pessimistic **pessimistisch**
poetic **poetisch**
it portrays **es zeigt, es schildert**
portrayal **die Schilderung(en)**

precious **gekünstelt, affektiert**
protagonist **der Protagonist(en), der Held(en)** *(wk)*
I read **ich lese**
reader **der Leser(-) [-in]**
readership **die Leserschaft**
realistic **realistisch**
reference **die Erwähnung(en), die Anspielung(en)**
I reflect **ich denke nach***
it reflects **es widerspiegelt**
reflection **die Reflektion(en)**
relationship **die Beziehung(en)**
it represents **es stellt dar***
representation **die Darstellung(en)**
review **die Kritik(en)**
romantic **romantisch**
sad **traurig**
satire **die Satire(n)**
it satirizes **es verspottet**
satirical **satirisch**
style **der Stil(e)**
in the style of **im Stil des/der**
stylish **stilvoll**
subject **das Thema (-en)**
Surrealism **der Surrealismus**
technique **die Technik(en)**
tension **die Spannung(en)**
theme **das Thema (-en)**
tone **der Ton(⁻e)**
tragedy **die Tragödie(n)**
tragic **tragisch**
true **wahr**
vivid **lebhaft**
vividly **anschaulich**
viewpoint **der Gesichtspunkt(e)**
witty **witzig, geistreich**
work of art **das Kunstwerk(e)**

The predominant theme of painting of the period was the landscape.
The painters tried to represent moral values symbolically.

Das entscheidende Motiv der Malerei dieser Zeit war die Landschaft.
Die Maler versuchten Moralwerte symbolisch zu veranschaulichen.

➤ MUSIC, DANCE 17d; THEATER & CINEMA/THEATER & MOVIES 17e

17b Art & architecture

antique   die Antiquität(en)
   antique *(adj)*   antik
antiquity   das Altertum, die Antike
architect   der Architekt(en) *(wk)*
   [-in]
art   die Kunst(-̈e)
artifact   das Artefakt(e)
artist   der Künstler(-)
art student   der Kunststudent(en)
   (wk) [-in]
I auction   ich versteigere
auction sale   die Auktion(en)
auctioneer   der Auktionator(en)
balance   das Gleichgewicht(e)
beam   der Balken(-)
bronze   die Bronze(n)
brush   der Pinsel(-)
I build   ich baue
building   das Gebäude(-)
bust   die Büste(n)
caricature   die Karikatur(en)
I carve   ich schnitze, ich haue
I cast   ich gieße
ceramics   die Keramik(en)
charcoal   die Holzkohle(n)
chisel   der Meißel(-)
clay   der Ton
collage   die Collage(n)
decorated   dekoriert
decoration   die Verzierung(en)
I design   ich entwerfe
design   der Entwurf(-̈e), das
   Design(s)
dimension   die Dimension(en)
I draw   ich zeichne
drawing   die Zeichnung(en)
drawing board   das Reißbrett(er)
easel   die Staffelei(en)
elevation   der Aufriß (-sse)
enamel   die Emaille(n)
I engrave   ich graviere ein*
engraving   der (Kupfer-/
   Stahl)stich(e)
I etch   ich ätze

etching   der Kupferstich(e)
exhibition   die Ausstellung(en)
figure   die Form(en), Figur(en)
figurine   die Figurine(n)
fine arts   die schönen Künste *(pl)*
form   die Gestalt(en)
freehand   Freihand-
fresco   die Freskomalerei(en)
frieze   das Fries(-)
gouache   die Gouache
graphic arts   die Grafik(en)
holography   die Holographie(n)
interior   das Innere, die
   Innengestaltung
intricate   kompliziert, fein
iron   das Eisen
landscape *(painting)*   das
   Landschaftsbild(er)
landscape architect   der
   Landschaftsarchitekt(en) *(wk)*
landscape painter   der
   Landschaftsmaler(-)
large-scale   in großem Maßstab
late works   die späten Arbeiten
light   das Licht
   light *(adj)*   leuchtend, hell
lithograph(y)   die Lithographie(n)
luminosity   die Helligkeit
luminous   leuchtend
masterpiece   das Meisterwerk(e)
metal   das Metall(e)
miniature   die Miniatur(en)
model   das Modell(e)
monostyle   der Monostil(e)
mosaic   das Mosaik(en)
museum   das Museum (-en)
oil painting   das Ölgemälde(-)
ornate   geschmückt
I paint   ich male
paint   die Farbe(n)
painting   das Gemälde(-)
pastel   das Pastell(e)
pattern   das Muster(-)
portrait   das Porträt(s)

potter   **der Töpfer(-) [-in]**
pottery   **die Töpferware(n)**
reproduction   **die Reproduktion(en)**
restoration   **die Restaurierung(en)**
I restore   **ich restauriere**
restored   **restauriert**
restorer   **der Restaurierer(-) [-in]**
roughcast   **der Rauhputz**
school   **die Schule(n)**
I sculpt   **ich bildhauere**
sculptor   **der Bildhauer(-) [-in]**
sculpture   **die Skulptur(en)**
seascape   **die Seegemälde(-)**
shadow   **der Schatten(-)**
shape   **die Form(en)**
I shape   **ich forme, ich gestalte**
sketch   **die Skizze(n)**
I sketch   **ich skizziere**
stained glass   **das farbige Glas(-̈er)**

statuary   **die Plastik(en)**
statue   **die Statue(n)**
still life   **das Stilleben(-)**
studio   **das Studio(s)**
symbolic   **symbolisch**
tapestry   **der Wandbehang(-̈e)**
town planning   **die Stadtplanung(en)**
translucent   **lichtdurchlässig**
transparent   **durchsichtig**
visual arts   **die bildenden Künste** *(pl)*
watercolor   **das Aquarell(e)**
weathering   **die Verwitterung(en)**
wood   **das Holz**
wood-carving   **die Holzschnitzerei(en)**
woodcut   **der Holzschnitt(e)**

Historical periods

Alemannic   **alemannisch**
Charlemagne   **Karl der Große**
Enlightenment   **die Aufklärung**
First World War   **der Erste Weltkrieg**
Frankish   **fränkisch**
Hitler period   **die Hitlerzeit, das Dritte Reich**
Holy Roman Empire   **das Heilige Römische Reich**
Hundred Years War   **der Hundertjährige Krieg**
Middle Ages   **das Mittelalter**
migration of peoples   **die Völkerwanderung**
Reformation   **die Reformation**
Roman age   **die Römerzeit**
Roman Empire   **das Römische Reich**

Second World War   **der Zweite Weltkrieg**
Thirty Years War   **der Dreißigjährige Krieg**
Weimar Republic   **die Weimarer Republik**

Bronze Age   **die Bronzezeit**
Iron Age   **die Eisenzeit**
Neolithic Age   **die Jungsteinzeit**
Palaeolithic Age   **die Altsteinzeit**
prehistoric   **vorgeschichtlich**
prehistory   **die Vorgeschichte**
Stone Age   **die Steinzeit**

the 20th Century   **das zwanzigste (20.) Jahrhundert**
in the 13th Century   **im dreizehnten Jahrhundert**

17c Literature

autograph **die Originalhandschrift(en)**
book **das Buch(¨er)**
bookshop/store **der Buchladen(¨e)**
bookseller **der Buchverkäufer(-) [-in]**
character **die Figur(en), die Gestalt(en)**
comic **lustig**
it concerns **es handelt (sich) um** +acc
dialog **der Dialog(e)**
fictional **frei erfunden**
hardback **eine gebundene Ausgabe(n)**
I imagine **ich stelle mir vor***
imagination **die Einbildungskraft(¨e)**
inspiration **die Inspiration(en)**
inspired by **inspiriert durch**
it introduces **es führt ein***
introduction **die Einleitung(en)**
I leaf through **ich blättere durch***
librarian **der Bibliothekar(e) [-in]**
library **die Bibliothek(en)**
   public library **die öffentliche Bibliothek(en)**
   reference library **die Präsenzbibliothek(en)**

library ticket **der Leserausweis(e)**
literal(ly) **wörtlich**
main character **die Hauptfigur(en)**
myth **der Mythos (-en)**
mythology **die Mythologie(n)**
it narrates **es erzählt**
narrative **die Erzählung(en)**
narrator **der Erzähler(-) [-in]**
note **die Anmerkung(en)**
page **die Seite(n)**
paperback **das Taschenbuch(¨er)**
poem **das Gedicht(e)**
poetic **poetisch**
poetry **die Poesie, die Dichtkunst**
quotation **das Zitat(e)**
I quote **ich zitiere**
I read **ich lese**
I recount **ich erzähle**
review **die Rezension(en), die Kritik(en)**
rhyme **der Reim(e)**
secondary character **die Nebenfigur(en)**
it is set in **es spielt in** +dat
subtitle **der Untertitel(-)**
table **der Tabelle(n)**
text **der Text(e)**
title **der Titel(-)**
verse **der Strophe(n)**

Buddenbrooks is the great epic novel of the early 20th Century.

***Buddenbrooks* ist der große Bildungsroman des frühen zwanzigsten Jahrhunderts.**

After the war, the "Gruppe 47" played an important role. Poetry blossomed again, above all in East Germany.

Nach dem Krieg spielte die "Gruppe 47" eine wichtige Rolle. Die Lyrik blühte wieder auf, vor allem in der DDR.

Günter Grass shows intense political involvement and an inexhaustible imagination.

Günter Grass zeigt großes politisches Engagement und eine unerschöpfliche Phantasie.

Types of books

adventure story **die Abenteuergeschichte(n)**
atlas **der Atlas(se/Atlanten)**
(auto)biography **die (Auto)biographie(n)**
children's literature **die Kinderliteratur**
comic novel **die humoristische Erzählung(en)**
cookbook **das Kochbuch(-̈er)**
crime novel **der Kriminalroman(e), der Krimi(s)**
dictionary **das Wörterbuch(-̈er)**
bilingual **zweisprachiges**
monolingual **einsprachiges**
diary **das Tagebuch(-̈er)**
encyclopedia **die Enzyklopädie(n)**
epic poem **das Epos (-en), das epische Gedicht(e)**
epic poetry **die Epik**
essay **der Aufsatz(-̈e)**
fable **die Fabel(n)**
fairy tale **das Märchen(-)**
feminist literature **die Frauenliteratur**
fiction **die Belletristik**
Greek tragedy **die griechische Tragödie(n)**

horror story **die Horrorgeschichte(n)**
letters **die Literatur(en)**
light reading **die Unterhaltungslektüre(n)**
manual **das Handbuch(-̈er)**
memoirs **die Memoiren** *(pl)*
mystery play **das Mysterienspiel(e)**
novel **der Roman(e)**
novella **die Novelle(n)**
non-fiction **das Sachbuch(-̈er)**
parody **die Parodie(n)**
picaresque novel **der Schelmenroman(e)**
poetry **die Dichtkunst**
reference book **das Nachschlagewerk(e)**
satire **die Satire(n)**
science fiction story **die Science-Fiction-Erzählung(en)**
short story **die Kurzgeschichte(n)**
spy story **die Spionagegeschichte(n)**
teenage fiction **die Jugendliteratur**
travel book **der Reisebericht(e)**
war novel **der Kriegsroman(e)**

Heinrich Böll received the Nobel prize for literature. A central theme of his novels is Roman Catholicism. He describes the troubles and worrries of the "little people."

Heinrich Böll erhielt den Nobelpreis für Literatur. Ein zentrales Thema seiner Romane ist das katholische Christentum. Er schildert die Nöte und Sorgen der "kleinen Leute".

Baroque richness, precision of description and autobiographical details are typical of the period.

Barocke Fülle, Genauigkeit der Darstellung, und autobiographische Details kennzeichnen diese Periode.

THE ARTS

17d Music & dance

accompaniment **die Begleitung**
accompanist **der Begleiter(-) [-in]**
I accompany **ich begleite**
acoustics **die Akustik**
agent **der Agent(en)** *(wk)*
album **das Album (-en)**
alto **der Alt(e), die Altstimme(n)**
amplifier **der Verstärker(-)**
audience **das Publikum**
audition **das Vorspielen(-)**
I audition **ich spiele/singe vor***
auditorium **das Auditorium (-ien)**
ballet **das Ballett**
baton **der Taktstock(¨e)**
brass band **die Blaskapelle(n)**
canned music **die Musikberieselung**
cassette tape **die Kassette(n)**
cassette deck **das Kassettendeck(s)**
chamber music **die Kammermusik**
chart **die Hitliste(n)**
choir **der Chor(¨e)**
choral society **der Gesangverein(e)**
choreography **die Choreographie(n)**
chorus **der Refrain(s)**
classical music **die klassische Musik**
compact disc/disk **die Compact Disc(s)**

competition **der Wettbewerb(e)**
I compose **ich komponiere**
composer **der Komponist(en)**
composition **die Komposition(en)**
concert **das Konzert(e)**
concert hall **die Konzertsaal (-säle)**
dance **der Tanz(¨e)**
I dance **ich tanze**
dancer **der Tänzer(-) [-in]**
dance music **die Tanzmusik**
discotheque **die Diskothek(en)**
disc jockey **der Discjockey(s)**
ensemble **das Ensemble(s)**
folk music **die Volksmusik**
folksong **das Volkslied(er), der Folksong(s)**
gig **das Konzert(e)**
group **die Gruppe(n)**
harmony **die Harmonie(n)**
harmonic **harmonisch**
hit *(song)* **der Hit(s)**
hit parade **die Hitparade(n)**
I hum **ich summe**
instrument **das Instrument(e)**
instrument maker **der Instrumentenbauer**
I interpret **ich interpretiere**
interpretation **die Interpretation(en)**
jazz **der Jazz**
juke box **die Musikbox(en)**

Phillip always sings out of tune.
His sister Natalie, on the other
Hand, has perfect pitch.
You must tune your violin. It is flat.

Phillip singt immer falsch.
Seine Schwester Natalie
hingegen, hat absolutes Gehör.
Du mußt die Violine stimmen.
Sie ist zu tief.

The poem was set to music by
Wolf.
My parents love going to concerts.
Last week they went to a recital at
the city theater.

Das Gedicht wurde von Wolf
vertont.
Meine Eltern gehen sehr gern
ins Konzert. Letzte Woche sind
sie zu einem Liederabend im
Stadttheater gegangen.

lesson **der Musikunterricht** *(no pl)*
librettist **der Librettist(en)** *(wk)*
I listen to **ich höre** +dat **zu***
microphone **das Mikrofon(e)**
music **die Musik**
musically **musikalisch**
musician **der Musiker(-) [-in]**
musicologist **der Musikwissenschaftler(-) [-in]**
note **die Note(n)**
orchestra **das Orchester(-)**
orchestration **die Orchesterbearbeitung(en)**
part **die Stimme(n)**
I perform **ich führe vor/auf**
performance **die Aufführung(en)**
performer **der Künstler(-) [-in]**
piano tuner **der Klavierstimmer(-) [-in]**
piece **das Stück(e)**
I play **ich spiele**
player **der Spieler(-) [-in]**
popular music/pop **die Popmusik**
I practice **ich übe**
promotional video **das Werbevideo(s)**
I put on a record **ich lege eine Schallplatte auf***
recital **das Konzert(e), der Liederabend(e)**
record **die Schallplatte(n)**
I record **ich nehme auf***
recording **die Aufnahme(n)**

recording studio **das Aufnahmestudio(s)**
I rehearse **ich probe**
rehearsal **die Probe**
rhythm **der Rhythmus (-en)**
rhythmic **rhythmisch**
rock music **der Rock**
I rock **ich rocke**
show **die Show**
I sing **ich singe**
singer **der Sänger(-) [-in]**
solo **das Solo(s)**
soloist **der Solist(en)** *(wk)* **[-in]**
song **das Lied(er)**
song writer **der Liederschreiber(-) [-in]**
string **die Saite(n)**
string orchestra **das Streichorchester(-)**
tape **das Tonband(¨er)**
tour **die Tournee(n)**
on tour **auf Tournee**
tune **der Klang**
I sing in tune **ich singe richtig**
out of tune **falsch, verstimmt**
I tune **ich stimme**
tuning fork **die Stimmgabel(n)**
voice **die Stimme(n)**
I whistle **ich pfeife**
wind band **die Blaskapelle(n)**
wind instrument **das Blasinstrument(e)**

– We play a lot of music at home.
– Do you play an instrument?

– **Wir musizieren viel zu Hause.**
– **Spielst du ein Instrument?**

– Yes, I've been playing the piano since I was little.

– **Ja, ich spiele schon seitdem ich klein war Klavier.**

During the summer, you can often hear street musicians in many European cities.

Während des Sommers kann man in vielen europäischen Städten oft Straßenmusikanten hören.

17e Theater & film/Theater & the movies

act   der Akt(e)
I act   ich spiele
acting school   die
   Schauspielschule(n)
actor   der Schauspieler(-) [-in]
I applaud   ich klatsche Beifall
applause   der Beifall
audience   die Zuschauer(-)
auditorium   der Zuschauerraum(-e)
I book   ich buche
box   die Loge(n)
box office   die (Theater)kasse(n)
cabaret   das Kabarett(s)
camera   die Kamera(s)
camera crew   das Kamerateam(s)
cameraman   der Kameramann(-er)
cartoon   der Trickfilm(e)
choreographer   der
   Choreograph(en) (wk) [-in]
cinema/movies   das Kino(s)
cinema/movie buff   der Kinofan(s)
circle/gallery   der Rang(-e)
circus   der Zirkus(se)
I clap   ich klatsche Beifall
cloakroom   die Garderobe(n)
comedian   der Komiker(-) [-in]
contract   der Vertrag(-e)
critic   der Kritiker(-) [-in]
curtain   der Vorhang(-e)
I design   ich entwerfe
I direct   ich führe Regie
director   der Regisseur(e)

distribution system   das
   Vertriebssystem(e)
drama   das Drama (-en)
dress rehearsal   die
   Generalprobe(n)
dubbed   synchronisiert
dubbing   die Synchronisation
I enter   ich trete auf*
exciting   spannend
I exit   ich gehe ab*
expectation   die Erwartung(en)
farce   der Schwank(-e), die
   Farce(n)
film/movie   der Film(e)
I film   ich filme, ich verfilme
film/movie maker   der
   Filmemacher(-)
filmstar/movie star   der Filmstar(s)
film/movie producer   der
   Filmproduzent(en) (wk)
first night   die Uraufführung(en)
floor show   die Vorstellung(en)
flop   der Reinfall(-e)
intermission/interval   die Pause(n)
lights   die Beleuchtung(en)
limelights   das Rampenlicht(er)
lobby   das Foyer(s)
location work   die
   Außenaufnahmen (pl)
I make a film/movie   ich drehe
   einen Film
masterpiece   das Meisterwerk(e)

The play begins at eight p.m.

**Das Theater beginnt um acht
Uhr abends.**

Have you seen the latest
production of Faust? The principal
actors are excellent. Its been
playing to full houses for weeks
already.

**Hast du die neueste
FaustInszenierung gesehen?
Die Hauptdarsteller sind
vortrefflich. Das Stück läuft
schon seit Wochen vor
ausverkauften Häusern.**

matinée   **die Matinee(s)**
melodrama   **das Melodrama (-en)**
mime   **die Pantomime(n)**
movie   **der Film(e)**
music hall   **das Varieté(s)**
off-stage   **hinter den Kulissen**
one-act play   **der Ein-Akter(-)**
opening night   **die Eröffnungsvorstellung(en)**
ovation   **der Beifallssturm(ˉe)**
performance   **die Aufführung(en)**
photography   **die Aufnahmen** *(pl)*
play   **das (Theater)stück(e)**
I play   **ich spiele**
playwright   **der Dramatiker(-) [-in]**
premiere   **die Premiere(n)**
I produce   **ich produziere, ich inszeniere**
producer   **der Regisseur(e)**
production   **die Inszenierung(en)**
projector   **der Projektor(en)**
public   **die Öffenlichkeit, die Zuschauer** *(pl)*
retrospective   **der Rückblick**
  retrospective *(adj)* **rückblickend**
review   **die Rezension(en)**
role   **die Rolle(n)**
row   **die Reihe(n)**
scene   **die Szene(n)**
scenery   **das Bühnenbild(er)**
screen   **die Leinwand(ˉe)**
screen test   **die Probeaufnahmen** *(pl)*

screening   **die Vorführung(en)**
I shoot *(a film/movie)* **ich drehe, ich filme**
script   **das Drehbuch(ˉer)**
scriptwriter   **der Drehbuchautor(en)**
script girl   **das Scriptgirl(s)**
seat   **der Sitzplatz(ˉe)**
sequel   **die Folge(n)**
sequence   **die Reihenfolge(n)**
I show *(film/movie)* **ich führe auf*, ich bringe**
it is shown at   **es wird im ... gezeigt/gegeben**
sold out   **ausverkauft**
sound track   **der Ton, die Filmmusik**
special effects   **die Spezialeffekte** *(pl)*
stage   **die Bühne(n)**
stage directions   **die Bühnenanweisungen** *(pl)*
stage designer   **der Bühnenbildner(-) [-in]**
stage effects   **die Bühneneffekte** *(pl)*
stage-fright   **das Lampenfieber**
stalls   **die Parterre**
stunt person   **der Stuntman**
it takes place in   **es spielt in**
trailer/preview   **die Vorschau**
understudy   **die zweite Besetzung**
usherette   **die Platzanweiserin(nen)**
walk-on part   **die Statistenrolle(n)**
I zoom   **ich zoome**

An exciting film was shown on TV last evening. It was set in Vienna. The time and place of the action are Berlin in the 20s.

The latest book by John Grisham is being adapted to the screen. Despite their experience, many actors still suffer from stage fright every time they get on stage.

Ein spannender Film wurde gestern abend im Fernsehen gezeigt. Er spielte in Wien. Ort und Zeit der Handlung sind Berlin in den 20er Jahren.

Das neueste Buch von John Grisham wird verfilmt. Trotz ihrer Erfahrung leiden viele Schauspieler immer noch unter Lampenfieber, wenn sie auf die Bühne treten.

The media

18a General terms

admission **der Eintritt(e), der Einlaß**
I analyze **ich analysiere**
analysis **die Analyse(n)**
I appeal to **ich appelliere an** +acc
I argue **ich argumentiere**
argument **das Argument(e)**
attitude **die Einstellung(en), die Weltanschauung(en)**
biased **voreingenommen**
campaign **die Aktion(en)**
censorship **die Zensur**
  press censorship **die Pressezensur**
cogent **überzeugend**
comment **der Kommentar(e)**
conspiracy **die Verschwörung(en)**
criticism **die Kritik(en)**
cultural **kulturell**
culture **die Kultur(en)**
cultured **kultiviert**
current events **die aktuellen Ereignisse** *(pl)*
declaration **die Erklärung(en)**

I declare **ich erkläre**
detailed **detailliert**
it discriminates **es diskriminiert**
disaster **die Katastrophe(n)**
disinformation **die Fehlinformation(en)**
educational **Bildungs-**
I entertain **ich unterhalte**
ethical **ethisch**
event **das Ereignis(se)**
example **das Beispiel(e)**
expectation **die Erwartung(en)**
I exploit **ich beute aus***
fallacious **trügerisch**
fallacy **der Irrtum(¨er)**
freedom **die Freiheit(en)**
  freedom of the press **die Pressefreiheit**
full/detailed **voll**
gullible **leichtgläubig**
hidden **versteckt**
homophobic **homophobisch**
ignorance **die Unwissenheit**

During the recent elections it was difficult to find an example of unbiased reporting.

Während der letzten Wahlen war es schwierig, ein Beispiel unbeeinflußter Berichterstattung zu finden.

In recent years many war correspondents have lost their lives while reporting from the front or have been taken hostage.

In den letzten Jahren wurden viele Kriegskorrespondenten bei der Berichterstattung getötet oder als Geiseln genommen.

I am a freelance journalist.

Ich bin ein freischaffender Journalist.

I ignore **ich sehe über** +acc
hinweg*
influential **einflußreich**
information **die Information(en)**
informative **informativ**
interview **das Interview(s)**
I intrude **ich störe**
intrusion **die Zudringlichkeit(en)**
intrusive **zudringlich**
issue *(problem)* **das Problem(e)**
journalese **der Pressejargon**
I keep up with (news) **ich bleibe
auf dem laufenden**
libel **die Verleumdung(en)**
libellous **verleumderisch**
local **Orts-, Regional-**
material **der Stoff(e)**
I meddle **ich mische mich ein***
medium **das Medium (-ien)**
media **die Medien** *(pl)*
news **die Nachrichten** *(pl)*
news agency **die
Nachrichtenagentur(en)**
news item **die Neuigkeit(en)**
partisan **parteiisch**
persuasion **die Überzeugung(en)**
persuasive **überzeugend**
prejudice **das Vorurteil(e)**
political **politisch**
politician **der Politiker(-) [-in]**
politics **die Politik** *(no pl)*

policy **die Politik** *(no pl)*
press **die Presse**
privacy **das Privatleben**
problem **das Problem(e)**
I report **ich berichte**
reportage **der Bericht(e)**
reporter **der Reporter(-) [-in]**
review **die Kritik(en)**
I review **ich bespreche**
it comes under review **es wird
geprüft**
scoop **der Knüller(-)**
sensational **sensationell**
sensationalism **die
Sensationsgier**
sexism **der Sexismus**
sexist **der Sexist(en)** *(wk)*
shrewd **klug, scharf**
summary **der Überblick(e)**
summary *(adj)* **kurzgefaßt**
it takes place **es findet statt***
trust **das Vertrauen**
I trust **ich glaube** +dat
trustworthy **glaubwürdig**
truth **die Wahrheit(en)**
truthful **ehrlich**
unbiased **unparteiisch**
untrustworthy **unzuverlässig**
up to date **aktuell**
weekly **wöchentlich**

Although British newspapers have correspondents in all the European capitals, they do not always report/cover current events.

Obwohl die britische Presse in allen europäischen Hauptstädten Berichterstatter hat, berichten diese nicht immer über aktuelle Ereignisse.

Media barons dominate the press in many western countries.

Die Medienbarone beherrschen die Presse in vielen westlichen Ländern.

145

THE MEDIA

article   der Artikel(-)
back page   die Rückseite(n)
barons   der Pressezar(en) *(wk)*
broadsheet flyer   das Flugblatt(-er)
cartoon   der/das Cartoon(s), der Zeichentrick(s)
chief editor   der Chefredakteur(e)
circulation   die Auflagenziffer(n)
color supplement   das Magazin(e), die Beilage(n)
column (of print)   die Spalte(n)
column *(article)*   die Kolumne(n)
comic   das Comic-Heft(e)
correspondent   der Korrespondent(en) *(wk)* [-in]
foreign correspondent   der Auslandskorrespondent
sports correspondent   der Sportkorrespondent
war correspondent   der Kriegskorrespondent
daily newspaper   die Tageszeitung(en)
I edit   ich gebe heraus*
edition   die Ausgabe(n)
editor   der Redakteur(-) [-in]

glossy magazine   das Hochglanzmagazin(e)
gutter press   die Boulevardpresse
headline   die Schlagzeile(n)
heading   die Überschrift(en)
illustration   die Illustration(en)
I publish   ich veröffentliche
it is published   es ist erschienen
journalist   der Journalist(en) *(wk)* [-in]
layout   das Layout(s)
local paper   die Lokalzeitung(en)
magazine   die Illustrierte(n)
monthly   die Monatsschrift(en)
national newspaper   die nationale Zeitung(en)
newsagent   der Zeitungs-händler(-)
newspaper   die Zeitung(en)
news stand   der Zeitungskiosk(e)
page   die Seite(n)
pamphlet   die Broschüre
periodical   die Zeitschrift(en)
power   die Macht(-e)
powerful   einflußreich

The constitution guarantees the right of freedom of expression and the freedom of the press.

Das Grundgesetz garantiert das Recht der freien Meinungsäußerung und die Pressefreiheit.

Die Frankfurter Allgemeine, die Süddeutsche Zeitung and *Die Welt* are the best known newspapers in the country. They are national newspapers.

***Die Frankfurter Allgemeine, Die Süddeutsche Zeitung* und *Die Welt* sind die bekanntesten Zeitungen im Land. Sie sind überregionale Zeitungen.**

Die *Bild Zeitung* is the most widely read newspaper in Germany.

Die *Bild Zeitung* ist die meist-gelesene Zeitung in Deutschland.

press agency **die Presseagentur(en)**
press conference **die Pressekonferenz(en)**
I print **ich drucke**
I publish **ich veröffentliche**
publisher **der Verleger(-) [-in]**
publishing company **der Verlag(e)**
quality press **die Qualitätspresse**

reader **der Leser(-) [-in]**
special issue **die Sonderausgabe(n)**
I subscribe to **ich abonniere**
subscription **das Abonnement(s)**
tabloid **die Boulevardzeitung(en)**
type(face) **die Schriftart(en)**
weekly **die Wochenzeitung(en)**

Newspaper sections & features

announcements **Anzeigen**
arts **bildenden Künste**
crossword puzzles **Kreuzwort-rätsel**
economy **Wirtschaft**
editorial **Kommentar**
entertainment **Kulturangebot**
finance **Finanzen, Börse**
food and drink **Speise und Getränk**
front page **die erste Seite**
editorials **Leitartikel**
gossip column **Klatschspalte**
home news **Landesspiegel, Meldungen aus dem Inland**

horoscope **Horoskop**
international news **internationale Nachrichten**
leaders **Leitartikel**
obituaries **Todesanzeigen**
politcs **Politik**
problem page **Problemseite**
property **Immobilien**
small ads **Kleinanzeigen, Inserate**
sports page **Sport**
travel **Reisen**
women's page **Frauen**

Der Spiegel is an influential news magazine.

***Der Spiegel* ist ein einfluß-reiches Nachrichtenmagazin.**

Many local newspapers are disappearing as a result of mergers.

Viele Lokalzeitungen sind infolge Fusionen verschwunden.

Many people think that diversity and independence will be lost.

Viele Leute meinen, daß Vielfalt und Unabhängigeit verloren gehen.

The gutter press has a surprisingly high readership.

Die Klatschpresse hat eine überraschend hohe Leserzahl.

Uncle Richard always reads the obituaries and the sports page.

Onkel Richard liest immer die Todesanzeigen und die Sportseite.

➤ PUBLISHING 17c; ADVERTISING 18d

THE MEDIA

18c Television & radio

aerial/antenna **die Antenne(n)**
anchor **der
    Nachrichtensprecher(-) [in]**
announcer **der Ansager(-) [in]**
audience **die Zuhörer/-schauer**
    (pl)
I broadcast **ich sende**
broadcasting station **die
    Sendestation(en)**
cable TV **das Kabelfernsehen**
    by cable **über Kabel**
cameraman **der Kameramann(-̈er)
    [-frau]**
I change channel **ich schalte um***
channel **der Kanal(-̈e), das
    Programm(e)**
commercial **die Fernsehwerbung**
couch potato **der Dauerglotzer(-)
    [-in]**
dubbed **synchronisiert**
earphone **der Kopfhörer(-)**
episode **die Fortsetzung(en)**
goggle box **die Glotzkiste(n)**
high frequency **die
    Hochfrequenz(en)**
interactive **interaktiv**
light entertainment **die
    Unterhaltungssendung(en)**

listener **der Zuhörer(-) [-in]**
live broadcast **die
    Liveübertragung(en)**
live coverage/commentary **die
    Liveberichterstattung(en)**
loudspeaker **der Lautsprecher(-)**
low frequency **die niedrige
    Frequenz(en)**
microphone **das Mikrofon(e)**
news flash **die Kurzmeldung(en)**
newsreader/caster **der
    Nachrichtensprecher(-) [-in]**
production studio **das
    Aufnahmestudio(s)**
program(me) **die Sendung(en)**
radio **das Radio(s), der Hörfunk**
    on radio **im Radio**
I receive **ich empfange**
I record **ich nehme auf***
recording **die Aufnahme(n)**
remote control **die
    Fernbedienung(en)**
I repeat **ich wiederhole**
repeat **die Wiederholung(en)**
satellite **der Satellit(en)** *(wk)*
satellite dish **die
    Satellitenschüssel(n)**

– What! You're still glued to the
TV? You've been sitting there all
evening. I'm afraid you're
becoming a real couch potato.

– I'm just going to record this film
then I'll join you. Do we have a
blank videocassette somewhere?

Was the Pavarotti concert
broadcast live?

– Was! Du klebst immer noch
vor dem Fernseher? Du sitzt
schon den ganzen Abend da.
Ich fürchte du wirst ein echter
Stubenhocker.

– Ich möchte nur diesen Film
aufnehmen, danach mache ich
bei euch mit. Haben wir
irgendwo eine leere
Videokassette?

Wurde das Pavarotti-Konzert
live übertragen?

satellite TV **das Satellitenfernsehen**
screen **der Bildschirm(e)**
I show **ich zeige**
signal **das Signal(e)**
station **der Sender(-)**
subtitles **der Untertitel(-)**
I switch off **ich schalte ab***
I switch on **ich schalte an***
teletext **der Bildschirmtext(e)**
television/TV **das Fernsehen**
on TV **im Fernsehen**
television set **das Fernsehgerät(e), der Fernseher(-)**
television studio **das Fernsehstudio(s)**
I transmit **ich übertrage, ich sende**
video clip **der Videoclip(s)**
videogame **das Videospiel(e)**
video library **die Videothek(en)**
video nasty **die verbotene Aufnahme(n)**
video recorder **der Videorecorder(-)**
video recording **die Videoaufnahme(n)**
viewer **der Zuschauer(-) [-in]**
I watch **ich schaue zu*, ich sehe mir an***

TV and radio programs
cartoon **der Zeichentrickfilm(e), der/das Cartoon(s)**

children program(me) **das Kinderprogramm(e)**
comedy **die Komödie(n)**
current affairs program(me) **die Tagesschau**
drama **das Drama (-en)**
documentary **der Dokumentarfilm(e)**
education program(me) **das Bildungs-/Lehrprogramm(e)**
feature film/movie **der Spielfilm(e)**
light entertainment **die leichte Unterhaltung** *(no pl)*
newscast **die Nachrichtensendung(en)**
quiz program(me) **das Quizprogramm(e), die Quizsendungen** *(pl)*
radio play **das Hörspiel(e)**
regional news **die Regionalnachrichten** *(pl)*
soap **die Fernsehserie(n)**
science program(me) **die Wissenschaftssendung(en)**
school broadcasting **die Schulsendung(en), der Schulfunk**
sports program(me) **die Sportsendung(en)**
TV film/movie **der Fernsehfilm(e)**
weather report **der Wetterbericht(e)**

Public broadcasting companies

ARD Arbeitsgemeinschaft der öffentlich-rechtlichen Rundfunkanstalten Deutschlands
ORF der Österreichische Rundfunk

SRG die Schweizerische Radio- und Fernsehgesellschaft
ZDF Zweites Deutsches Fernsehen
Deutsche Welle
Deutschlandfunk *(radio)*

18d Advertising

I advertise **ich werbe für** +acc
advertisement **die Anzeige(n), die Reklame(n)**
advertising **die Werbung(en)**
advertising column **die Litfaßsäule(n)**
advertising industry **die Werbeindustrie**
appeal **der Reiz(e)**
it appeals to **es spricht jdn. an***
billboard **das Werbeplakat(e)**
brand **die Marke(n)**
brand awareness **das Markenbewußtsein**
brochure **die Broschüre(n)**
campaign **die Kampagne(n)**
it catches the eye **es ist auffallend**
commercial **der Werbespot(s)**
commercial *(adj)* **kommerziell**
commercial break **die Werbepause(n)**
competition *(rival)* **die Konkurrenz *(no pl)***
competition *(game)* **das Preisausschreiben(-)**
consumer **der Verbraucher(-)**

consumer society **die Verbrauchergesellschaft(en)**
copywriter **der Werbetexter(-)**
I covet **ich begehre**
it creates a need **es schafft den Bedarf**
demand **die Nachfrage**
direct/junk mail **die Postwurfsendung(en)**
disposable income **das verfügbare Einkommen**
distributor **der Händler(-) [-in]**
ethical **ethisch**
good(s) **die Ware(n)**
hidden persuasion **die versteckte Beeinflussung**
image **das Image(s)**
launch **die Einführung**
lifestyle **der Lebensstil(e)**
I manipulate **ich manipuliere**
market **der Markt(ˉe)**
model **das Modell(e)**
I motivate **ich motiviere**
need **das Bedürfnis(se), der Mangel(ˉ)**
persuasion **die Überredung**

It's important that our advertising campaign is targeted to young women with a high income.

Es ist wichtig, daß sich unsere Werbekampagne auf junge Frauen mit hohem Einkommen richtet.

It pays to advertise!

Werbung zahlt sich aus!

The buildings are covered by ugly advertising billboards.

Die Gebäude sind mit häßlichen Werbeplakaten bedeckt.

Until recently most TV spots portrayed women in exclusively traditional roles.

Bis vor kurzem schilderten die meisten Fernsehspots Frauen in ausschließlich traditionellen Rollen.

poster **das Poster(-)**
product **das Produkt(e)**
I promote **ich fördere, ich werbe
für** +acc
promotion (of) **das Werbung (für)**
publicity **die Werbung(en)**
I publicize **ich mache Werbung
für** +acc
purchasing power **die Kaufkraft**
radio advertisement **die
Radiowerbung(en)**
slogan **der Slogan(s), der
Werbespruch(̈e)**
status symbol **das
Statussymbol(e)**
stunt **der Gag(s)**
I target **ich ziele auf** +acc **ab***
target group **die Zielgruppe(n)**
I tempt **ich locke an***
trademark **der Handelsname(n)**
trend **der Trend(s)**
truthful **wahrhaft**
TV advertisement **die
Fernsehwerbung(en)**
unethical **unethisch**

Small ads

---

accommodation **Häusermarkt**
appointments
Stellenangebote
births **Geburten**
courses and conferences
Kurse und Konferenzen
deaths **Todesanzeigen**
engagement(s)
Verlobungsannonce(n)
exchange **Wechselkurs**
exhibitions **Ausstellungen**
for sale **zum Verkauf**
health **Gesundheit**
holidays **Ferien**
lonely hearts
Kontaktanzeigen
marriages **Heiratsanzeigen**
personal services
Persönliches
property **Immobilien** *(pl)*
travel **Reisen**
wanted **Kaufgesuche,
gesucht**

A Mercedes is still considered a
status symbol.

**Ein Mercedes wird immer noch
als Statussymbol angesehen.**

Coca Cola is a world renowned
trademark.

**Coca Cola ist ein weltbekannter
Markenname.**

We absolutely have to hire a new
ad-writer.

**Wir müssen unbedingt einen
neuen Werbetexter einstellen.**

Do you think that TV advertisements are more effective than
advertisements in newspapers?

**Denkst du, daß Fernsehwerbung
effektiver ist als
Zeitungsanzeigen?**

➤ THE PRESS 18b; TELEVISION & RADIO 18c

19 TRAVEL

19a General terms

accident **der Unfall(-̈e)**
adult **der/die Erwachsene** *(adj/n)*
announcement **die Ansage(n)**
  special announcement **die Sondermeldung(en)**
arrival **die Ankunft(-̈e)**
I arrive at **ich komme in ... an**
assistance **die Hilfe** *(no pl)*
automatic **automatisch**
available **zu haben**
bag **die Tasche(n), der Beutel(-)**
baggage **das Gepäck** *(no pl)*
bar **die Bar(s)**
I book **ich buche**
booking office **der Fahrkartenschalter(-)**
business trip **die Geschäftsreise(n)**
I buy a ticket **ich kaufe/löse eine Fahrkarte**
he calls/stops at **er hält in** +dat
I cancel *(trip)* **ich sage ab***
  I cancel *(ticket)* **ich entwerte**
I carry **ich trage**
I catch **ich erwische, ich erreiche**
I check *(tickets)* **ich überprüfe, ich kontrolliere**
child **das Kind(er)**
class **die Klasse(n)**
coin **die Münze(n)**
I confirm **ich bestätige**
connection **die Verbindung(en)**
I cross **ich überquere**
delay **die Verspätung(en)**
delayed **verspätet, verzögert**
he is delayed **er hat Verspätung**
I depart **ich fahre ab***
departure **die Abfahrt(en)**
destination **das Reiseziel(e)**
direct **direkt**

direction **die Richtung(en)**
disabled **behindert**
distance **die Entfernung(en)**
document **das Dokument(e)**
early **früh**
emergency **der Notfall(-̈e)**
emergency call **der Notruf(e)**
I enquire about **ich erkundige mich nach** +dat
enquiry **die Erkundigung(en)**
en route **auf dem Weg**
entrance **der Eingang(-̈e)**
exit **der Ausgang(-̈e)**
extra charge **der Zuschlag(-̈e)**
fare **der Fahrpreis(e)**
fast **schnell**
I fill in a form **ich fülle ein Formular aus***
free *(not occupied)* **frei**
I go away **ich verreise**
information **die Information(en), die Auskunft**
information office **das Informationsbüro(s)**
insurance **die Versicherung(en)**
help **die Hilfe**
helpful **hilfsbereit**
holdall/travel bag **die Reisetasche(n)**
late **(zu) spät**
I leave **ich fahre ab***
I leave *(person/object)* **ich verlasse**
luggage/baggage office **die Gepäckaufbewahrung(en)**
lost **verloren**
lost & found office **das Fundbüro(s)**
loudspeaker **der Lautsprecher(-)**
luggage/baggage **das Gepäck** (no pl)
message **die Nachricht(en)**
I miss *(train)* **ich verpasse**

money **das Geld(er)**
nonsmoker **der Nichtraucher(-) [-in]**
notice **die Anzeige(n), die Mitteilung(en)**
nuisance **das Ärgernis(se)**
occupied **besetzt**
on board **an Bord**
on time **pünktlich**
I pack **ich packe**
passenger **der Passagier(e)**
porter *(hotel)* **der Portier(s)**
reduced fare **zu ermäßigtem Preis**
reduction **die Ermäßigung(en)**
reservation **die Reservierung(en)**
I reserve **ich reserviere**
I return **ich komme zurück***
return **die Rückkehr**
round-trip ticket **die Rückfahrkarte(n)**
round-trip **die Rundreise(n)**
safe **sicher**
safety **die Sicherheit(en)**
seat **der (Sitz)platz(⁻e)**
seatbelt **der Sicherheitsgurt(e)**
I set/take off **ich setze mich in Gang, ich mache mich auf den Weg**
slow **langsam**
I slow down **ich fahre langsamer**
small change **das Wechselgeld**
smoking **das Rauchen**
speed **die Geschwindigkeit(en)**

I speed up **ich fahre schneller**
staff **das Personal**
I start from **ich fahre von ... ab***
stop **der Halt, die Haltestelle(n)**
I stop **ich halte**
suitcase **der Koffer(-)**
I take *(bus, train)* **ich nehme**
ticket **die Fahrkarte(n)**
ticket desk **der Fahrkartenschalter(-)**
timetable **der Fahrplan(⁻e)**
to **nach, Richtung**
toilet/restroom **die Toilette(n)**
I travel **ich reise**
travel **die Reise(n)**
   document **das Reisedokument(e)**
   office **das Reisebüro(s)**
   pass **der Reisepaß (⁻sse)**
   sickness **die Reisenkrankheit**
traveller **der/die Reisende(n)** *(adj/n)*
tunnel **der Tunnel(s/-)**
unexpected **unerwartet**
I unpack **ich packe aus***
valid **gültig**
visitor **der Besucher(-) [-in]**
warning **die Warnung(en)**
way in/entrance **der Eingang(⁻e)**
way out/exit **der Ausgang(⁻e)**
on weekdays **an Wochentagen**
weekend **das Wochenende(n)**
welcome **der Empfang(⁻e)**
welcoming **freundlich**

---

by air **mit dem Flugzeug**
by car **mit dem Auto**
by ferry **mit der Fähre**
on foot **zu Fuß**

on horseback **mit dem Pferd**
by sea **auf dem Seeweg**
by train **mit dem Zug, mit der Bahn**

I usually fly, but today I am taking the train.

Meistens fliege ich, aber heute nehme ich den Zug.

Are you walking or driving to the movies?

Fährst du oder gehst du zu Fuß zum Kino?

➤ HOLIDAYS/VACATION 20a; DIRECTIONS 2b; MOVEMENT 2c

19b Going abroad & travel by boat

Going abroad

Channel Tunnel **der Kanaltunnel(s/-)**

I cross the English Channel **ich überquere den Ärmelkanal**

currency **die Währung(en)**

currency exchange office **die Wechselstube(n)**

customs **der Zoll(¨e)**

customs control **die Zollkontrolle(n)**

customs officer **der Zollbeamte(n)** *(wk)*

customs regulation **die Zollbestimmung(en)**

declaration **die Zollerklärung(en)**

I declare **ich verzolle**

duty **der Einfuhrzoll(¨e)**

duty-free goods **die zollfreie Ware(n)**

duty-free shop **das zollfreie Geschäft(e)**

exchange rate **der Wechselkurs(e)**

foreign currency **die Devisen** *(pl)*

frontier/border **die Grenze(n)**

I go through customs **ich gehe durch den Zoll**

I go through passport control **ich gehe durch die Paßkontrolle**

immigration office **die Einwanderungsbehörde(n)**

immigration rules **die Einwanderungsgesetze** *(pl)*

passport **der Paß(¨sse)**

I pay duty on **ich zahle Zoll auf** +acc

smuggler **der Schmuggler(-)**

smuggling **das Schmuggeln**

visa **das Visum (-en/-a)**

Travel by boat

bridge **die Brücke(n)**

cabin **die Kabine(n)**

calm **still**

captain **der Kapitän(e)**

car ferry **die Autofähre(n)**

Channel **der (Ärmel)kanal**

choppy **bewegt**

coast **die Küste(n)**

crew **die Besatzung(en)**

crossing **die Überfahrt(en)**

cruise **die Kreuzfahrt(en)**

deck **das Deck(s)**

below deck **unter Deck**

lower deck **das Unterdeck**

on deck **auf Deck**

upper deck **das Oberdeck**

deck chair **der Liegestuhl(¨e)**

I disembark **ich gehe von Bord**

disembarkation **die Landung(en)**

dock **die Landungsbrücke(n)**

I embark (for) **ich schiffe mich (nach** +dat**) ein***

The passport and customs formalities have been taken care of.

Die Paß- und Zollformalitäten sind erledigt.

What is the fastest way to Zürich?

Wie kommt man am schnellsten nach Zürich?

My final destination is Milan.

Mein Reiseziel ist Mailand.

embarkation card **die Bordkarte(n)**
I go on board **ich gehe an Bord**
harbor **der Hafen(⁻)**
heavy *(sea)* **schwer**
lifejacket **die Schwimmweste(n)**
lifeboat **das Rettungsboot(e)**
lounge **der Salon(s)**
luggage **das Gepäck**
ocean **der Ozean(e), das Meer(e)**
officer **der Offizier(e)**
offshore **vor der Küste**
on board **an Bord**
overboard **über Bord**
port **der Hafen(⁻)**
purser **der Zahlmeister(-)**
quay **der Kai(s)**
reclining seat **der Liegesitz(e)**
sea **die See**
seasickness **die Seekrankheit(en)**
seaman **der Seemann (-leute)**
shipping forecast **der Seewetterbericht(e)**
shipyard **die Werft(en)**
smooth **ruhig**
storm **der Sturm(⁻e)**
stormy **stürmisch**
tide **die Gezeiten** *(pl)*
  high tide **die Flut**
  low tide **die Ebbe**

waves **die Wellen**
wind **der Wind(e)**
windy **windig**

Ships & boats

aircraft carrier **der Flugzeugträger(-)**
canoe **das Kanu(s)**
cargo boat **das Transportschiff(e)**
dinghy *(rubber)* **das Schlauchboot(e)**
ferry **die Fähre(n)**
hovercraft **das Hovercraft(s)**
hydrofoil **das Tragflächenboot(e)**
life boat **das Rettungsboot(e)**
merchant ship **das Handelsschiff(e)**
motorboat **das Motorboot(e)**
ocean liner **der Überseedampfer(-)**
oil tanker **der Öltanker(-)**
rowing boat **das Ruderboot(e)**
sailing boat **das Segelboot(e)**
ship **das Schiff(e)**
speed boat **das Rennboot(e)**
submarine **das U-Boot(e)**
towboat **der Schlepper(-)**
warship **das Kriegsschiff(e)**
yacht **die Yacht(en)**

Can we meet on deck?

Können wir uns auf Deck treffen?

In stormy weather the ship pitches a lot.

Bei stürmischem Wetter schaukelt das Schiff sehr.

I felt very sick on the crossing.

Bei der Überfahrt war mir sehr übel.

The boat docked at 10:00 p.m.

Das Boot legte um 22.00 Uhr an.

➤ COUNTRIES App.20a; CURRENCIES 9a

19c Travel by road

I accelerate **ich gebe Gas**
access **der Zugang(ˉe)**
alley **die Gasse(n), der Durchgang(ˉe)**
I allow **ich erlaube**
avenue **die Allee(n)**
I back up/reverse **ich setze zurück***
bend/curve **die Kurve(n)**
bike/bicycle **das Fahrrad(ˉer)**
black ice **das Glatteis**
bottleneck **der Engpaß(ˉsse)**
breathalyzer test **die Alkoholkontrolle(n)**
I break down **ich habe eine Panne**
breakdown **die Panne(n)**
breakdown service **der Pannendienst(e)**
bridge **die Brücke(n)**
broken **kaputt**
built-up/residential area **das Wohngebiet(e)**
bump **die Beule(n), der Stoß(ˉe)**
bus **der Bus(se)**
bus fare **der Busfahrpreis(e)**
bus stop **die Bushaltestelle(n)**
bypass **die Umgehungsstraße(n)**
car **das Auto(s)**
car rental **der Autoverleih**
car part **das Ersatzteil(e)**
carwash **die Autowaschanlage(n)**
caravan/camping trailer **der Wohnwagen(-)**
careful **vorsichtig**
caution **die Vorsicht** *(no pl)*
  caution *(legal)* **die Warnung(en)**
central reservation/median **der Mittelstreifen(-)**
I change gear **ich schalte um***
chauffeur **der Chauffeur(e)**
I check **ich (über)prüfe**
closed *(road)* **gesperrt**
I collide with **ich stoße mit** +dat **zusammen***

collision **der Zusammenstoß(ˉe)**
company car **der Firmenwagen(-)**
conductor *(bus)* **der Schaffner(-) [-in]**
corner **die Ecke(n), die Kurve(n)**
I cross **ich überquere**
crossing **der Übergang(ˉe)**
crossroad **die Kreuzung(en)**
cul-de-sac **die Sackgasse(n)**
dangerous **gefährlich**
detour **der Umweg(e)**
diesel **der Diesel, das Dieselöl**
I do 30 km **ich fahre 30**
I drive **ich fahre**
drive **die Fahrt(en)**
driver **der Fahrer(-) [-in]**
driving **Fahr-**
  instructor **der Fahrlehrer(-)**
  lesson **die Fahrstunde(n)**
  licence/driver's license **der Führerschein(e)**
  school **die Fahrschule(n)**
  test **die Fahrprüfung(en)**
drunken driving **betrunken am Steuer**
emergency stop **die Vollbremsung(en)**
engine trouble **der Motorschaden (ˉen)**
entrance/exit **die Ein-/Ausfahrt(en)**
eyewitness **der Augenzeuge(n)** *(wk)*
I fasten my seatbelt **ich schnalle mich an***
fatality **das Todesopfer(-)**
I fill up **ich tanke**
I find my way **ich finde mich zurecht***
I fix **ich repariere**
forbidden **verboten**
for hire/rent **zu vermieten**
garage **die Garage(n), Werkstatt (ˉtten)**
gas station **die Tankstelle(n)**
gasoline **das Benzin**
  premium **das Superbenzin**

regular **das Normalbenzin**
gear **der Gang(ˉe)**
   in gear **der Gang ist eingelegt**
   in first gear **im ersten Gang**
   in neutral **im Leerlauf**
   in reverse **im Rückwärtsgang**
I get in the car **ich steige ein***
I get in lane **ich ordne mich ein***
I get out **ich steige aus***
I give way/yield **ich lasse (jdm.)
die Vorfahrt**
green card *(insurance)* **die grüne
Versicherungskarte**
I have it repaired **ich lasse es
reparieren**
highway **die Landstraße(n)/die
Autobahn**
highway code **die
Straßenverkehrsordnung**
highway police **die
Autobahnpolizei**
I hire/rent **ich miete**
hired/rented car **der Mietwagen(-)**
I hitchhike **ich trampe, ich fahre
per Anhalter**
hitchhiker **der Tramper(-) [-]**
I honk **ich hupe**
inside lane **die Innenspur(en)**
insurance **die Versicherung(en)**
insurance policy **die
Versicherungspolice(n)**
I am insured **ich bin versichert**
intersection **die Kreuzung(en)**
international driving licence **der
Internationale Führerschein(e)**
jack **der Wagenheber(-)**
it is jammed **es klemmt**
jughandle **die Verkehrsschleife(n)**
junction **der Kreuzweg(e)**
key **der Schlüssel(-)**
keyring **der Schlüsselring(e)**
kilometer **der Kilometer(-)**
lane **die Fahrspur(en)**
lay-by/rest stop **der Rastplatz(ˉe)**
lead-free **bleifrei**
leaded **verbleit**
learner driver **der Fahrschüler(-)**

level/railroad crossing **der
Bahnübergang(ˉe)**
limit **die (Geschwindigkeits)-
begrenzung(en)**
line of cars **die Autoschlange(n)**
liter **der Liter(-)**
logbook/vehicle registration **der
Kraftfahrzeugschein(e)**
main **Haupt-**
main street **die Hauptstraße(n)**
I make a statement **ich mache
eine Aussage**
make of car **die Automarke(n)**
MOT/vehicle validation/inspection
der TÜV
maximum speed **die
Höchstgeschwindigkeit(en)**
mechanic **der Mechaniker(-) [-in]**
mechanic *(adj)* **mechanisch**
motel **das Motel(s)**
motor caravan/trailer **der
motorisierte Wohnwagen**
motor/car show **die
Automobilausstellung(en)**
motorway/expressway **die
Autobahn(en)**
   entry **die Auffahrt(en)**
   exit **die Ausfahrt(en)**
   hard shoulder **die
   Standspur(en)**
   junction **die Kreuzung(en)**
   police **die (Autobahn)polizei**
   services **die Raststätte(en)**
   toll **die Autobahngebühr(en)**
one-way **Einbahn-**
one-way street **die
Einbahnstraße(n)**
outside lane **die Überholspur(en)**
I overtake/pass **ich überhole**
overtaking/passing **das Überholen**
I park **ich parke**
parking **das Parken**
parking ban **das Parkverbot(e)**
parking deck **die Hochgarage(n)**
   underground parking **die
   Tiefgaragen(n)**
parking lot **der Parkplatz(ˉe)**

parking meter **die Parkuhr(en)**
parking ticket **der Strafzettel(-)**
I pass **ich fahre vorbei***
passenger **der Passagier(e)**
pedestrian **der Fußgänger(-) [-in]**
pedestrian crossing **der Fußgängerübergang(-e)**
pedestrian zone **die Fußgängerzone(n)**
picnic area **der Picknickplatz(-e)**
police **die Polizei**
policeman **der Polizist(en)** *(wk)* **[-in]**
police station **das Polizeirevier(e)**
private car **der eigene Wagen(-)**
private property **das Privateigentum**
public transport **das öffentliche Verkehrsmittel(-)**
puncture/flat **der platte Reifen(-)**
I put on my seat belt **ich schnalle mich an***
ramp **die Rampe(n)**
registration papers **die Autopapiere** *(pl)*

rental charge **der Mietpreis(e)**
repair **die Reparatur(en)**
I repair **ich repariere**
I reverse **ich fahre zurück***
(in) reverse **im Rückwärtsgang**
right of way **die Vorfahrt**
ring road/bypass **die Umgehungsstraße(n)**
road **die Straße(n)**
 accident **der Unfall(-e)**
 block **die (Straßen)sperrung(en)**
 hog **der Verkehrsrowdy(s)**
 map **die Straßenkarte(n)**
 sign **das Straßenschild(er)**
 signals/traffic light **die Ampel(n)**
 side **der Straßenrand(-er)**
 works **der Straßenbau**
roundabout/circle **der Kreisverkehr**
route **die Route(n)**
I run over **ich überfahre**
rush hour **der Berufsverkehr**
secondhand car **der Gebrauchtwagen(-)**

If you don't put money into the parking meter immediately, you'll get a parking ticket.

Wenn du nicht sofort Geld in die Parkuhr steckst, kriegst du einen Strafzettel.

Fill her up!

Bitte volltanken!

When the engine starts, step on the clutch, put the car into first gear and step on the gas pedal.

Wenn der Motor anspringt, treten Sie die Kupplung, dann legen Sie den ersten Gang ein, und geben Gas.

In heavy traffic you have to go slowly.

Im dichten Straßenverkehr muß man langsam fahren.

Keep to the right!

Rechts halten!

This morning I almost hit a man at a pedestrian crossing.

Heute morgen habe ich fast einen Mann an einem Fußgängerüberweg überfahren.

service **die Inspektion(en)**
I set off **ich mache mich auf den Weg**
side street **die Nebenstraße(n)**
signpost **der Wegweiser(-), das Schild(er)**
I skid **ich rutsche aus***
slippery **glatt**
slow **langsam**
I slow down **ich fahre langsamer**
speed **die Geschwindigkeit(en)**
I speed up **ich fahre schneller**
speed limit **die Geschwindigkeits-begrenzung(en)**
spot traffic fine **die Geldstrafe(n)**
I start *(engine)* **ich lasse an***
street **die Straße(n)**
I switch off **ich schalte ab***
taxi/cab **das Taxi(s)**
taxi driver **der Taxifahrer(-)**
taxi rank/stand **der Taxistand(¨e)**
I test **ich prüfe**
tool **das Werkzeug(e)**
I tow away **ich schleppe ab***
town plan/map **der Stadtplan(¨e)**
town traffic **der Stadtverkehr**
traffic **der Verkehr**

traffic jam **der Stau(s)**
traffic light **die Ampel(n)**
traffic offence **das Verkehrsdelikt(e)**
traffic news **die Verkehrsmeldung(en)**
traffic police **die Verkehrspolizei**
traffic-free zone **die verkehrsfreie Zone(n)**
truck **der Lastwagen(-)**
truck driver **der LKW-Fahrer(-) [-in]**
I turn **ich biege**
I turn left **ich biege nach links**
I turn right **ich biege nach rechts**
I turn off at **ich biege ab***
I turn off *(engine)* **ich schalte ... ab***
underground garage **die Tiefgarage(n)**
underground passage **die Unterführung(en)**
unleaded/*(gasoline)* **bleifrei**
U-turn **das Wenden** *(no pl)*
vehicle **das Fahrzeug(e)**
I wait **ich warte**
warning **die Warnung(en)**
warning triangle **das Warndreieck(e)**

We must take a detour because of the road construction.

Wir müssen wegen der Baustelle einen Umweg fahren.

Can you please tell me where the next police station is?

Können Sie mir bitte sagen, wo das nächste Polizeirevier ist?

Be careful around the next turn. It's always very slippery when it rains.

Sei bei der nächsten Kurve vorsichtig. Die ist bei Regen immer sehr glatt.

When you come to visit us, take the Autobahn in the direction of Hannover and get off at the exit Gütersloh-Verl.

Wenn du uns besuchen kommst, nimm die Autobahn in Richtung Hannover und fahr an der Ausfahrt Gütersloh-Verl ab.

The rental price for the car is 350 DM per week.

Der Mietpreis für den Wagen beträgt 350 DM pro Woche.

➤ PARTS OF THE CAR, ROAD SIGNS App.19c; DIRECTIONS 2b

19d Travel by air

aeroplane/airplane **das Flugzeug(e)**
airline **die Fluglinie(n)**
airline desk **der Flugschalter(-)**
air travel **der Flugverkehr**
airport **der Flughafen(-)**
I am airsick **mir wird schlecht beim Fliegen**
baggage **das Gepäck**
baggage reclaim **die Gepäckausgabe**
body search **die Leibeskontrolle(n)**
I board a plane **ich gehe an Bord eines Flugzeugs**
boarding card **die Bordkarte(n)**
business class **die Businessklasse(n)**
by air **per Flugzeug**
cabin **die Kabine(n)**
cancelled **gestrichen**
carousel **das Gepäckband(-er)**
charter flight **der Charterflug(-e)**
I check in **ich checke ein***
check-in operations **das Einchecken**

control tower **der Kontrollturm(-e)**
co-pilot **der Co-Pilot(en)** *(wk)* **[-in]**
crew **die Besatzung(en)**
direct flight **der Direktflug(-e)**
domestic flights **der Inlandflug(-e)**
during landing **während der Landung**
during take-off **während des Starts**
during the flight **während des Fluges**
duty-free goods **die zollfreie Ware(n)**
economy class **die Touristenklasse(n)**
emergency exit **der Notausgang(-e)**
emergency landing **die Notlandung(en)**
excess baggage **das Übergewicht**
flight **der Flug(-e)**
flight attendant **der Flugbegleiter(-) [-in]**
I fly **ich fliege**
I fly at a height of **ich fliege in einer Höhe von**

We are about to land in Zürich.	**Wir befinden uns im Anflug auf Zürich.**
Please fasten your safety belt and stop smoking.	**Wir bitten Sie, sich jetzt anzuschnallen und das Rauchen einzustellen.**
Rosie and Tony are flying on the early flight to Mallorca.	**Rosie und Tony fliegen mit der Frühmaschine nach Mallorca.**
Your ticket is waiting at the Lufthansa desk, Mr. Richter.	**Ihr Ticket liegt am Lufthansa-Schalter bereit, Herr Richter.**
When you go downtown, you can park in the underground garage at Hertie's.	**Wenn du in die Stadt fährst, kannst du bei Hertie in der Tiefgarage parken.**
Can I change my reservation?	**Kann ich umbuchen?**

flying **das Fliegen**
fuselage **der Flugzeugrumpf(⁼e)**
gate **der Ausgang(⁼e)**
instructions **die Gebrauchsanweisung(en)**
hand luggage **das Handgepäck**
headphone **der Kopfhörer**
highjacker **der Luftpirat(en)** *(wk)*
immigrant **der Immigrant(en)** *(wk)* **[-in]**
immigration **die Einwanderung**
immigration rules **die Einwanderungsgesetze**
information desk **die Information**
I land **ich lande**
landing **die Landung(en)**
landing lights **die Landebeleuchtung**
no-smoking sign **das Rauchen-verboten-Schild**
nonstop **Non-stop-**
on board **an Bord**
parachute **der Fallschirm(e)**
passenger **der Passagier(e)**
passengers lounge **die Wartehalle(n)**

passport control **die Paßkontrolle(n)**
pilot **der Pilot(en)** *(wk)*
plane **die Maschine(n)**
refreshments **die Erfrischungen** *(pl)*
runway **die Start- und Landebahn(en)**
safety jacket **die Sicherheitsjacke(n), die Rettungsweste(n)**
security measures **die Sicherheitsmaßnahmen** *(pl)*
security staff **das Sicherheitspersonal**
I take off **ich starte, ich fliege ab***
takeoff **der Abflug(⁼e)**
terminal **das Terminal(s)**
tray **das Tablett(s/e)**
turbulence **die Turbulenzen** *(pl)*
view **die Aussicht(en)**
window **das Fenster(-)**
window seat **der Fensterplatz(⁼e)**

There was a problem in the baggage hall. The flight to London has been delayed by half an hour.

Es gab ein Problem bei der Gepäckaufgabe. Der Flug nach London hat eine halbe Stunde Verspätung.

There are still some seats available on the plane.

In der Maschine sind noch Plätze frei.

Passengers continuing to Rome please go to gate 18.

Passagiere im Weiterflug nach Rom bitte nach Ausgang 18 gehen.

I need a wheelchair for a disabled passenger.

Ich brauche einen Rollstuhl für einen behinderten Passagier.

Frankfurt Airport is called the gateway to the world.

Man nennt den Frankfurter Flughafen das Tor zur Welt.

19e Travel by rail

buffet **das Büffet(s)**
buffet car/dining car **der Speisewagen(-)**
coach **der Waggon(s)**
compartment **das Abteil(e)**
connection **der Anschluß (-̈sse)**
direct train **der durchgehende Zug(-̈e)**
express train **der Schnellzug(-̈e)**
fare **der Fahrpreis(e)**
first class **erster Klasse**
inspector **der Kontrolleur(e)**
Intercity train **der Intercity, der IC-Zug**
level crossing **der Gleisübergang(-̈e)**
luggage/baggage rack **die Gepäckablage(n)**
nonrefundable **keine Rückzahlung**
occupied **besetzt**
on time **pünktlich**

platform **der Bahnsteig(e), das Gleis(e)**
porter **der Gepäckträger(-)**
I punch *(ticket)* **ich entwerte**
railway/railroad **die Eisenbahn(en)**
station **der Bahnhof(-̈e)**
track **das Gleis(e)**
reduction **die Ermäßigung(en)**
reservation **die Reservierung(en)**
reserved **reserviert**
return/round trip ticket **die Rückfahrkarte(n)**
second class **zweiter Klasse**
single/one-way ticket **die einfache Karte(n)**
sleeper **der Schlafwagen(-)**
(non) smoking compartment **das (Nicht)raucherabteil(e)**
station master **der Bahnhofsvorsteher(-)**
stop **die Station(en)**

Have you checked the timetable?

Hast du im Fahrplan nachgesehen?

– When is the first train to Cologne? – At four p.m. from platform 3.

– Wann fährt der erste Zug nach Köln? – Um sechzehn Uhr von Gleis 3.

The train from Vienna arrived punctually.

Der Zug aus Wien ist pünktlich eingelaufen.

Have you got your ticket?

Haben Sie Ihren Fahrschein?

Paul travelled without a ticket.

Paul ist schwarzgefahren.

Don't forget to pay the supplement for the Inter-City train.

Vergessen Sie nicht, den Zuschlag für den Intercityzug zu bezahlen.

Where do I change?

Wo muß ich umsteigen?

I stop **ich halte**
suitcase **der Koffer(-)**
supplement **der Zuschlag(-e)**
taxi rank/stand **der Taxistand(-e)**
ticket **die Fahrkarte(n)**
  collector **der Schaffner(-)**
  office **der Fahrkartenschalter(-)**
timetable **der Fahrplan(-e)**
  change **die Fahrplanänderung(en)**
  summer timetable **der Sommerfahrplan(-e)**
  winter timetable **der Winterfahrplan(-e)**
toilets **die Toilette(n)**
track **das Gleis(e)**
traveller **der/die Reisende** (wk)

train **der Zug(-e)**
  express train **der Schnellzug(-e)**
  fast stopping train **der Eilzug(-e)**
  Intercity train **der Intercity-Zug(-e)**
  local train **die Ortsbahn, die Stadtbahn(en)**
  night train **der Nachtzug(-e)**
  through train **der D-Zug(-e)**
trolley **der Kofferkuli(s)**
waiting-room **der Wartesaal (-säle)**
wagon-lits **der Waggon(s)**
warning **die Warnung(en)**
window **das Fenster(-)**
window seat **der Fensterplatz(-e)**

– Is there a connection to Basle? – Yes, but only runs on Sundays and holidays.

– Gibt es eine Verbindung nach Basel? – Ja, aber nur an Sonn- und Feiertagen.

This is a no-smoking compartment.

Dies ist ein Nichtraucher-Abteil.

The German Federal Railway is the largest transport business in Germany.

Die Deutsche Bundesbahn (DB) ist das größte Transportunternehmen in Deutschland.

There is a lot of commuter traffic, above all in large built up areas.

Es gibt einen starken Pendelverkehr, vor allem in den großen Ballungsgebieten.

On Sundays and holidays ...

An Sonn- und Feiertagen ...

On weekdays ...

An Werktagen ...

Holidays/Vacation

20a General terms

abroad **im/ins Ausland**
accommodation **die Unterkunft(⁼e)**
alone **allein**
amenities **die Möglichkeiten** *(pl)*
area **das Gebiet(e)**
arrival **die Ankunft(⁼e)**
it is available **er steht zur Verfügung**
beach **der Strand(⁼e)**
camera **die Kamera(s), der Fotoapparat(e)**
clean **sauber**
climate **das Klima(s)**
closed **geschlossen**
clothes **die Kleidung**
cold **kalt**
comfortable **bequem**
congested **überfüllt**
cost **die Kosten** *(pl)*
country **das Land(⁼er)**
   in the country **auf dem Land(e)**
countryside **die Landschaft(en)**
departure **die Abfahrt(en)**
dirty **schmutzig**
disorganized *(untidy)* **unordentlich**
I am disorganized **ich bin schlecht organisiert**
exchange *(money)* **die Wechselstube(n)**
folding chair **der Klappstuhl(⁼e)**
folding table **der Klapptisch(e)**
food **das Essen**
free **frei, kostenlos**
full **voll**
I get tan **ich werde braun**
I go away **ich verreise**
group **die Gruppe(n)**
group travel **die Gruppenreise(n)**
guide **der Reiseführer(-) [-in]**
guided tour **die Reisetour(s)**

guided walk **die Führung(en)**
holidays/vacation **die Ferien** *(pl)*, **der Urlaub** *(no pl)*
I go on holiday/vacation **ich fahre in Urlaub**
holiday/vacation dates **die Ferientermine** *(pl)*
land **das Land(⁼er)**
landscape **die Landschaft(en)**
journey **die Reise(n)**
map **die Landkarte(n)**
mild *(climate)* **mild**
money **das Geld(er)**
in the mountains **im Gebirge**
no vacancy *(hotel)* **ausgebucht**
open **offen, geöffnet**
it is open **es ist offen**
organization **die Organisation(en)**
I organize **ich organisiere**
organized **organisiert**
I pack **ich packe ein***
I plan **ich plane**
portable **tragbar**
postcard **die Ansichtskarte(n)**
rucksack/knapsack **der Rucksack(⁼e)**
sea **das Meer(e), die See(n)**
seaside resort **der Badeort(e)**
shade **der Schatten(-)**
I shop **ich kaufe ein***
show **die Vorstellung(en)**
sight **die Sehenswürdigkeit(en)**
I spend (time) **ich verbringe (Zeit)**
stay **der Aufenthalt(e)**
I stay **ich wohne**
sun **die Sonne(n)**
I sunbathe **ich liege in der Sonne**
tour **die Tour(en), die Fahrt(en)**
tourism **der Tourismus**
tourist **der Tourist(en)** *(wk)*

tourist menu **die Touristenspeisekarte(n)**
tourist office **das Verkehrsamt(¨er)**
town **die Stadt(¨e)**
town plan **der Stadtplan(¨e)**
travel **das Reisen**
I travel **ich reise**
travel adaptor **der Adapter(-)**
trip **der Ausflug(¨e)**
uncomfortable **unbequem**
I understand **ich verstehe**
I unpack **ich packe aus***
visit **der Besuch(e)**
I visit **ich besuche**
visiting hours **die Besuchszeit(en)**
visitor **der Besucher(-)**
welcome **der Empfang(¨e)**
I welcome **ich begrüße**
worth seeing **sehenswert**

Holidays/Vacation activities

beach holiday/vacation **der Urlaub am Meer**
boating **das Bootsfahren(-)**
camping **das Zelten**
canoeing **das Kanufahren**
coach holiday/vacation bus tour **die Busreise(n)**

cruise **die Kreuzfahrt(en)**
cycling **das Radfahren**
exchange (school) **der Austausch(e)**
fishing **das Angeln, das Fischen**
fruit picking **das Obstpflücken**
hunting **die Jagd** *(no pl)*
I go hunting **ich gehe auf die Jagd**
mountain climbing **das Bergsteigen**
package holiday/tour **die Pauschalreise(n)**
rock climbing **das Klettern**
safari **die Safari(s)**
sailing **das Segeln**
shopping **das Einkaufen**
sightseeing **die Besichtigungstour(en)**
skiing **das Skilaufen**
study holiday **die Informationstour(en)**
sunbathing **das Sonnenbaden**
trekking **das Trekking**
volunteer work **für die Wohlfahrt arbeiten**
walking/hiking tour **das Wandern**
wine tasting **die Weinprobe(n)**

– When are you on vacation? Do you have your holiday/vacation dates already?

– We are going on vacation in July.

– I hope you had a restful vacation.

– Yes, we spent it on a farm. We did a lot of walking and cycling.

– **Wann hast du Urlaub? Hast du schon deine Ferientermine?**

– **Wir fahren im Juli in Urlaub.**

– **Hoffentlich haben Sie einen erholsamen Urlaub gehabt.**

– **Ja, wir haben ihn auf einem Bauernhof verbracht. Wir sind viel gewandert und Rad gefahren.**

➤ COUNTRIES App.20a; HOBBIES 16a; ON THE BEACH App.20a **165**

20b Accommodation & hotel

Accommodation

accommodation **die Unterkunft(ːe)**
apartment **die Wohnung(en)**
bed and breakfast **die Übernachtung mit Frühstück**
"Bed & Breakfast"
"Fremdenzimmer"
campsite **der Campingplatz(ːe)**
caravan/trailer **der Wohnwagen(-)**
guest **der Gast(ːe)**
farm **der Bauernhof(ːe)**
full board **die Vollpension**
half board **die Halbpension**
holiday flat/vacation apartment **die Ferienwohnung(en)**
home exchange **der Haustausch(e)**
hotel **das Hotel(s)**
mobile home **das Wohnmobil(e)**
inn **das Wirtshaus(ːer)**
self-catering/service **mit Selbstverpflegung**
villa **die Villa(s)**
youth hostel **die Jugendherberge(n)**

Booking & payment

I afford **ich leiste mir**
all included **(alles mit) inbegriffen, inklusiv**
bill **die Rechnung(en)**
I book **ich buche**
cash (money) **das (Bar)geld**
I cash **ich löse ein***
cheap **billig, preiswert**
check **der Scheck(s)**
cost **der Preis(e)**
credit **der Kredit(e)**
credit card **die Kreditkarte(n)**
Eurocheque **der Euroscheck(s)**
exclusive **exklusiv**
expensive **teuer**
extra charge **zusätzliche Kosten (pl)**
I fill in **ich fülle aus***
form **das Formular(e)**

free **kostenlos, frei**
I pay **ich bezahle**
payment **die Bezahlung(en)**
by cheque/check **mit Scheck**
with cash **in bar**
price **der Preis(e)**
price list **die Preisliste(n)**
receipt **die Quittung(en)**
reduction **der Ermäßigung(en)**
refund **die Rückvergütung(en)**
reservation **die Reservierung(en)**
I reserve **ich reserviere**
I sign **ich unterschreibe**
signature **die Unterschrift(en)**
traveller's check **der Reisescheck(s)**
VAT/sales tax **die Mehrwertsteuer, MWS**

In the hotel

amenities **die Einrichtungen** (pl)
balcony **der Balkon(s)**
ball **der Ball(ːe)**
bank card **die Bankkarte(n)**
basement **das Kellergeschoß(ːe)**
bath **das Bad(ːer)**
bed **das Bett(en)**
double bed **das Doppelbett(en)**
single bed **das Einzelbett(en)**
twin beds **mit zwei Betten**
bedding **das Bettzeug** (no pl)
bedspread **die Überwurf(ːe)**
billiard room **der Billardraum(ːe)**
breakfast **das Frühstück(e)**
English breakfast **das englische Frühstück**
broken **kaputt**
it is broken **es ist zerbrochen**
business conference **die Geschäftskonferenz(en)**
button **der Knopf(ːe)**
call **der Anruf(e)**
I call **ich rufe an***
I check in **ich melde mich an***
I check out **ich fahre/reise ab***

coathanger **der Kleiderbügel(-)**
comfortable **bequem**
I complain (about) **ich beschwere mich (über** +acc)
complaint **die Beschwerde(n)**
conference **die Konferenz(en)**
conference facilities **die Konferenzeinrichtungen** (pl)
damage **der Schaden(-)**
dining room **der Speiseraum(-e)**
dry cleaning **die Reinigung**
early morning call **der Weckruf(e)**
en-suite bathroom **mit Bad**
evening meal **das Abendessen(-)**
extravagant **luxuriös**
facilities **die Einrichtungen** (pl)
fax **das (Tele)fax(e)**
it is on fire **es brennt!**
fire alarm **der Feueralarm**
fire exit **der Notausgang(-e)**
fire extinguisher **der Feuerlöscher(-)**
first floor **die erste Etage**
ground floor **das Erdgeschoß (-sse)**
guest **der Gast(-e)**
hairdresser **der Friseur(e)**
hairdryer **der Fön(s)**
heating **die Heizung(en)**
key **der Schlüssel(-)**
laundry **die Wäsche** (no pl)
laundry bag **der Wäschebeutel(-)**

laundry service **der Wäscheservice**
elevator **der Fahrstuhl(-e), der Aufzug(-e)**
night porter **der Nachtportier(s)**
noisy **laut**
nuisance **das Ärgernis(se)**
overnight bag **die Übernachtungstasche(n)**
parking space **der Parkplatz(-e)**
pleasant **angenehm, freundlich**
plug **der Stecker(-)**
porter **der Portier(s)**
private **privat**
privacy **die Ruhe**
proof of identity **der Ausweis(e)**
quality **die Qualität(en)**
quiet **still, ruhig**
reception **die Rezeption(en)**
receptionist **der Empfangschef/dame**
room **das Zimmer(-)**
double room **das Doppelzimmer**
family room **der Familienraum(-e)**
room service **der Zimmerservice**
service **die Bedienung**
stay **der Aufenthalt(e)**
I stay **ich wohne**
suitcase **der Koffer(-)**
terrace **die Terrasse(n)**
view **die Aussicht(en)**

Our hotel room was large and sunny. And from our balcony, we had a great view of the mountains.

Unser Hotelzimmer war groß und sonnig. Und von unserem Balkon aus hatten wir einen wunderbaren Ausblick auf die Berge.

The children spent a lot of time in the swimming pool.

Die Kinder verbrachten viel Zeit im Swimmingpool.

You can pay the bill by credit card if you'd like.

Sie können die Rechnung gern mit Kreditkarte bezahlen.

We have a large parking lot for our guests behind the hotel.

Wir haben einen großen Parkplatz für unsere Gäste hinter dem Hotel.

➤ ROOMS 8a; FURNISHINGS 8c; EATING OUT 10a

20c Camping & self-service

At the campsite

air bed **die Luftmatratze(n)**
antihistamine cream **die Antihistamincreme(n)**
ant **die Ameise(n)**
barbeque **der Grill(s), das Grillfest(e)**
battery **die Batterie(n)**
I camp **ich zelte**
camp bed **das Campingbett(en)**
camper **der Camper(-)**
camping **das Zelten**
camping equipment/gear **die Campingausrüstung(en)**
camping gas **das Campinggas**
campsite **der Zeltplatz(ˉe)**
caravan/trailer **der Wohnwagen(-)**
connected **mit elektrischem Anschluß**
cooking facilities **die Kochmöglichkeiten** *(pl)*
dark **dunkel**
disconnected **ohne elektrischen Anschluß**
drinking water **das Trinkwasser**
dry **trocken**
dustbin/trash can **der Mülleimer(-)**

extension lead/cord **das Verlängerungskabel(-)**
forbidden **verboten**
fun **der Spaß** *(no pl)*
gas cooker **der Gaskocher(-)**
gas cylinder **die Gasflasche(n)**
ground sheet **der Zeltboden(ˉ)**
we make friends **wir freunden uns an***
medicine box **der Arzneikasten(ˉ)**
mosquito **der Moskito(s)**
mosquito bite **der Moskitostich(e)**
mosquito net **das Moskitonetz(e)**
pan **der Kochtopf(ˉe)**
peg **der Pflock(ˉe)**
pillow **das Kissen(-)**
I pitch/put up *(tent)* **ich stelle auf***
potty **das Töpfchen(-)**
private **privat**
proprietor **der Eigentümer(-) [-in]**
registration **die Anmeldung(en)**
reservation **die Reservierung(en)**
services **der Strom- und Wasseranschluß (ˉsse)**
shadow **der Schatten(-)**
sheet **das Bettlaken(-)**
site **der Platz(ˉe)**

Last week we went camping. We pitched our tent in the shade near the lake. Unfortunately, there were many bugs, because it was damp. I didn't sleep well, because the ground was hard and I only had a sleeping bag. Next time I'm taking an air bed along.

Letzte Woche haben wir gezeltet. Wir haben das Zelt im Schatten dicht am See aufgeschlagen. Leider gab es dort viel Ungeziefer, weil es feucht war. Ich habe nicht gut geschlafen, weil der Boden hart war und ich nur einen Schlafsack hatte. Das nächste Mal nehme ich eine Luftmatratze mit.

sleeping bag **der Schlafsack(-̈e)**
space **der Platz(-̈e)**
I take down (tent) **ich baue (das Zelt) ab***
tent **das Zelt(e)**
tin/can opener **der Dosenöffner(-)**
toilet **die Toilette(n)**
flashlight **die Taschenlampe(n)**
uncomfortable **unbequem, ungemütlich**
vehicle **das Fahrzeug(e)**
washing facilities **die Waschgelegenheiten** (pl)
water filter **der Wasserfilter(-)**

Self-catering/service

agency **die Agentur(en)**
agreement **der Vertrag(-̈e)**
amenity **die Annehmlichkeit(en)**
apartment **die Wohnung(en)**
clean **sauber**
I clean **ich mache sauber***
I cook **ich koche**
damaged **defekt**
damages **der Schadensersatz** (no pl)
electricity **die Elektrizität**

equipment **die Austattung(en)**
facilities **die Einrichtungen** (pl)
farm **der Bauernhof(-̈e)**
furniture **die Möbel** (pl)
ironing board **das Bügelbrett(er)**
landlord **der Wirt(e) [-in]**
maid **das Dienstmädchen(-)**
meter **der Zähler(-)**
owner **der Besitzer(-) [-in]**
rent **die Miete(n)**
I rent **ich miete**
I rent out **ich vermiete**
repair **die Reparatur(en)**
I repair **ich repariere**
I return (give back) **ich gebe wieder***
ruined **zerstört**
self-service **die Selbstbedienung**
set of keys **der Schlüsselbund(-̈e)**
I share **ich teile**
shutters **die Fensterläden** (pl), **die Rolladen** (pl)
smelly **übelriechend**
spare key **der Ersatzschlüssel(-)**
well **der Brunnen(-)**
well kept **gut gepflegt**

Klaus and Ursula rented a vacation cottage this summer.

Klaus und Ursula haben diesen Sommer ein Ferienhaus gemietet.

It was really worthwhile.

Es hat sich wirklich gelohnt.

The cottage had two double bedrooms, one with bunk beds, a modern kitchen and a bathroom with shower.

Das Haus hatte zwei Doppelzimmer, eins Zimmer mit Etagenbetten, eine modern eingerichtete Küche und Bad mit Dusche.

It was in a quiet location. The advertisement said there was a view, and that was really true.

Die Lage war ruhig. In der Anzeige hieß es, daß man eine gute Aussicht hatte, und das stimmte wirklich.

➤ FURNISHINGS 8c; COOKING UTENSILS App. 10d

Language

21a General terms

accuracy **die Genauigkeit**
accurate **genau sein**
I adapt **ich passe mich an***
I adopt **ich übernehme**
advanced **fortgeschritten**
aptitude **die Begabung**
artificial language **die künstliche Sprache(n)**
it is based on **es basiert auf** +dat
bilingual **zweisprachig**
bilingualism **die Zweisprachigkeit**
branch **der Zweig(e)**
classical language **die klassische Sprache(n)**
it derives from **es stammt aus** +dat
development **die Entwicklung(en)**
difficult **schwer**
easy **leicht**
error **der Fehler(-)**
foreign language **die Fremdsprache(n)**
I forget **ich vergesse**
grammar **die Grammatik(en)**
grammatical **grammatisch**

I improve **ich verbessere (mich)**
influence **der Einfluß (⁻sse)**
isolation **die Isoliertheit**
known **bekannt**
language **die Sprache(n)**
language course **der Sprachkurs(e)**
language family **die Sprachfamilie(n)**
language school **die Sprachschule(n)**
language skill **die (Sprach)fertigkeit(en)**
I learn **ich lerne**
learning **das Lernen**
level **das Sprachniveau(s)**
linguistics **die Sprachwissenschaft(en)**
link **die Verbindung(en)**
living **lebendig**
loan-word **das Lehnwort(⁻er)**
major language **die Weltsprache(n)**
it means **das bedeutet**
I mime **ich mime**

– You speak such good German, Mr. Brown. Did you learn it in school?

– No, but my mother is German, and she always spoke German to me at home.

I am not very good at languages, but my sister is a good linguist.

– **Sie sprechen sehr gut Deutsch, Herr Brown. Haben Sie es in der Schule gelernt?**

– **Nein, aber meine Mutter ist Deutsche, und sie hat zu Hause immer mit mir Deutsch gesprochen.**

Ich bin nicht sehr gut in Sprachen, aber meine Schwester ist sehr sprachbegabt.

minor language **die weniger bedeutende Sprache(n)**
mistake **der Fehler(-)**
monolingual **einsprachig**
mother tongue **die Muttersprache(n)**
mutation/change **der Wandel** *(no pl)*
name **der Name(n)** (gen **des Namens)** *(wk)*
nation **das Volk(ˉer)**
national **national**
native **Mutter-, Heimat-**
natural **natürlich**
official **offiziell**
offshoot **der Zweig(e)**
origin **die Herkunft(ˉe)**
phenomenon **die Erscheinung(en)**
I practise/practice **ich übe**
preserved **erhalten**
question **die Frage(n)**
register **das Verzeichnis (-sse), das Register(-)**
separate **einzeln**
sign language **die Zeichensprache(n)**
survival **das Überleben**
it survives **es überlebt**
I translate **ich übersetze, ich übertrage**

translation **die Übersetzung(en)**
I understand **ich verstehe**
unknown **unbekannt**
widely used **weit verbreitet**
witticism **die witzige Bemerkung(en)**

Words & vocabulary

antonym **das Antonym(e)**
colloquial **umgangssprachlich**
consonant **der Konsonant(en)**
dictionary **das Wörterbuch(ˉer)**
expression **der Ausdruck(ˉe)**
idiom **die Redewendung(en)**
idiomatic **idiomatisch**
jargon **der Jargon(s)**
lexicographer **der Lexikograph(en)** *(wk)* **[-in]**
lexicon **das Lexikon(s/-a)**
phrase **die Phrase(n)**
phrase book **der Sprachführer(-)**
sentence **der Satz(ˉe)**
slang **der Slang** *(no pl)*
syllable **die Silbe(n)**
synonym **das Synonym(e)**
vocabulary **der Wortschatz(ˉe)**
vowel **der Vokal(e)**
word *(individual)* **das Wort(ˉer)**
word *(in text)* **das Wort(e)**
word game **das Wortspiel(e)**

Claudia and her boyfriend always talk French.

Claudia und ihr Freund unterhalten sich immer auf französisch.

I practice my Spanish with a native speaker.

Ich übe mein Spanisch mit einem Muttersprachler.

Writing Urdu is a problem for me as the alphabet is quite different. They use the Arabic script.

Es ist für mich ein Problem, Urdu zu schreiben, da das Alphabet ganz anders ist. Man verwendet die arabische Schrift.

LANGUAGE

21b Using language

Speaking & listening

accent **der Akzent(e)**
  regional accent **die regionale**
  Aussprache(n)
I am articulate **ich spreche (mich)**
  klar aus*
I articulate **ich artikuliere**
clear **klar, deutlich**
colloquial language **die**
  Umgangssprache
I communicate **ich kommuniziere,**
  ich teile jdm. mit* +dat
conversation **das Gespräch(e)**
I converse (with) **ich unterhalte**
  mich (mit +dat)
dialect **der Dialekt(e)**
diction **die Ausdrucksweise(n)**
I express (myself) **ich drücke**
  (mich) aus*
fluent(ly) **fließend**
I interpret **ich dolmetsche**
interpreter **der Dolmetscher(-)**
  [-in]
intonation **die Betonung(en)**
lisp **das Lispeln**
I lisp **ich lisp(e)le**
I listen to **ich höre jdm. zu*** +dat
listening **das Hören**
listening skills **das**
  Hörverständnis(se)

I mispronounce **ich spreche**
  falsch aus*
mispronunciation **die falsche**
  Aussprache
oral **mündlich**
I pronounce **ich spreche aus***
pronunciation **die Aussprache(n)**
rhythm **der Rhythmus (-en)**
I say **ich sage**
sound **der Laut(e)**
I sound **ich klinge**
I speak **ich spreche, ich rede**
speaking **das Sprechen**
speaking skills **die**
  Sprechfähigkeit(en)
speech **die Sprache(n), die**
  Rede(n)
I give a speech **ich halte eine**
  Rede
speed **die Schnelligkeit(en)**
spoken **gesprochen**
spoken language **die**
  gesprochene Sprache
stress **die Betonung(en)**
stressed (un-) **(un)betont**
I stutter/stammer **ich stottere**
I talk **ich spreche, ich rede**
I tell **ich sage, ich erzähle**
unpronouncable **unaussprechbar**
verbal(ly) **verbal**

When you travel in a foreign
country, it's very useful to take
along a phrase book.

Wenn man ins Ausland reist, ist
es sehr nützlich einen
Sprachführer mitzunehmen.

How do you pronounce that?

Wie spricht man das aus?

How do you spell that?

Wie schreibt man das?

Could you please translate that
into English?

Könnten Sie das bitte ins
Englische übersetzen?

Writing & reading

accent mark **das Akzentzeichen(-)**
alphabet **das Alphabet(e)**
alphabetically **alphabetisch**
in bold **fett**
Braille **die Blindenschrift**
character **der Charakter(e)**
code **der Kode**
I correct **ich korrigiere**
I correspond with **ich korrespondiere mit** +dat
correspondence **die Korrespondenz**
I decypher **ich entziffere**
I draft **ich entwerfe**
graphic **graphisch**
handwriting **die Handschrift**
illiterate **der Analphabet(en)** *(wk)* **[-in]**
italic **der Kursivdruck**
in italics **kursivgedruckt**
letter *(alphabet)* **der Buchstabe(n)** *(wk)*
he is literate **er kann lesen und schreiben**
literature **die Literatur(en)**
note **die Anmerkung(en)**
paragraph **der Absatz(̈e)**
philology **die Sprachwissenschaft(en)**
philologist **der Sprachwissenschaftler(-) [-in]**

pictogram(me) **das Piktogramm(e), die Bilddarstellung(en)**
I print **ich drucke**
I read **ich lese**
reading **das Lesen, die Lektüre**
reading matter **die Lektüre(n), der Lesestoff**
reading skills **das Leseverständnis(se)**
I re-write **ich schreibe neu, ich schreibe um***
scribble **das Gekritzel**
I scribble **ich kritz(e)le**
sign **das Zeichen(-)**
I sign **ich unterschreibe**
signature **die Unterschrift(en)**
I spell **ich buchstabiere**
spelling **die Rechtschreibung**
text **der Text(e)**
I transcribe **ich schreibe ab*/nieder***
transcription **die Abschrift(en), die Umschrift(en)**
umlaut **der Umlaut(e)**
I underline **ich unterstreiche**
I write **ich schreibe**
writing **das Schreiben**
writing skills **die Schreibfähigkeit(en)**
written language **die Schriftsprache(n)**

What is the right spelling? | **Was ist die richtige Schreibweise?**

Don't worry about spelling mistakes. | **Mach dir keine Sorgen um Schreibfehler.**

The stem is modified by an umlaut. | **Der Stamm wird umgelautet.**

The verb goes to the end. | **Das Verb steht am Ende.**

That is colloquial German. | **Das ist Umgangssprache.**

Education

22a General terms

absent **abwesend**
achievement **die Leistung(en)**
admission **die Einschulung**
   I am admitted to school **ich werde eingeschult**
after school activity **die Arbeitsgemeinschaft(en)**
age group **die Altersstufe(n)**
aptitude **die Fertigkeit(en), das Talent(e)**
I analyze **ich analysiere**
answer **die Antwort(en)**
I answer **ich antworte**
   I answer (someone) **ich beantworte (jdn.)**
   I answer (a question) **ich antworte auf (eine Frage)**
I ask (a question) **ich stelle (eine Frage)**
   I ask (someone) **ich frage (jdn.)**
I attend (a school) **ich besuche (eine Schule)**
career **die Berufslaufbahn(en)**
career advice **die Berufsberatung(en)**
career education **die Berufsorientierung(en)**
career advisor **der Berufsberater(-)**
caretaker **der Hausmeister(-)**
I catch up **ich hole nach***
chapter **das Kapitel(-)**
I cheat **ich mogele, ich betrüge**
class **die Klasse(n)**
class council **der Klassenrat(ⁿe)**
class representative **der Klassensprecher(-)**
class teacher **der Klassenlehrer(-)**
class trip **die Klassenfahrt(en)**
club **der Klub(s), der Verein(e)**
I complete **ich vollende**

comprehension **das Verständnis(se)**
compulsory schooling **die Schulpflicht**
computer **der Computer(-)**
concept **das Konzept(e)**
I copy (out) **ich kopiere ... aus***
copy **die Kopie(n)**
course **der Kurs(e), das Seminar(e)**
deputy head **der/die stellvertretende Schulleiter(-) [in]**
detention **das Nachsitzen**
   I am in detention **ich sitze nach***
difficult **schwierig**
discuss **besprechen**
easy **leicht**
education **die Bildung, die Erziehung**
educational system **das Bildungssystem(e)**
I encourage **ich fördere**
essay **der Aufsatz(ⁿe)**
example **das Beispiel(e)**
excellent **ausgezeichnet, vortrefflich**
favorite **der Liebling(e), Lieblings-**
favorite subject **das Lieblingsfach(ⁿer)**
I forget **ich vergesse**
governing body **der Schulausschuß(ⁿe)**
grade **die Klasse(n)**
holidays/vacation **die Ferien** *(pl)*
principal **der Schulleiter(-)[-in]**
homework **die Hausaufgabe(n)**
instruction **der Unterricht**
interesting **interessant**
I learn **ich lerne**

I leave **ich verlasse**
lesson **die Stunde(n)**
   lesson *(chapter)* **die Lektion(en)**
   lessons **der Unterricht**
I listen **ich höre** +dat **zu***
local education authority **die**
   Schulbehörde(n)
I look at **ich sehe ... an***
I misunderstand **ich mißverstehe**
modular **aus Elementen**
   zusammengesetzt
module **die Einheit(en), das**
   Element(e)
oral **mündlich**
outdoor **im Freien**
parents' evening **der**
   Elternabend(e)
I play truant **ich schwänze die**
   Schule
principal **der Direktor(en) [-in]**
project **das Projekt(e), die**
   Projektarbeit(en)
punctual **pünktlich**
I punctuate **ich setze die**
   Satzzeichen
punctuation mark **das**
   Satzzeichen(-)
I punish **ich bestrafe**
punishment **die Strafe(n)**
pupil **der Schüler(-)[-in]**
qualification **die Qualifikation(en)**
I qualify **ich qualifiziere**
question **die Frage(n)**
I question **ich befrage (jdn.)**
I read **ich lese**
reading **das Lesen**
I repeat a year **ich wiederhole das**
   Jahr
report **das Zeugnis(se)**
research **die Forschung(en)**
I research **ich forsche**
resources centre/center **die**
   Mediathek(en)
scheme of work **der Lehrplan(-̈e)**

school book **das Schulbuch(-̈er)**
school council **der Schulausschuß**
   (-̈sse)
school friend **der**
   Klassenkamerad(en)
set **die Leistungsgruppe(n)**
   setted *(by ability)* **differenziert**
   nach Leistung
skill **die Fertigkeit(en)**
special achievement course **die**
   Leistungsgruppe(n)
specialist teacher **der Fachlehrer(-)**
spelling **die Rechtschreibung, die**
   Orthographie
I stay down/fail **ich bleibe sitzen***
strict **streng**
I study **ich studiere, ich lerne**
sum **die Rechenaufgabe(n)**
I summarize **ich fasse zusammen***
I swot **ich büffele, ich pauke**
task **die Aufgabe(n)**
I teach **ich lehre, unterrichte**
teacher **der Lehrer(-) [-in]**
teaching **der Unterricht**
teaching staff/falculty **das**
   Lehrerkollegium (-ien)
term/semester **das Semester(-)**
I train **ich lasse mich ausbilden**
training **die Ausbildung(en)**
I translate **ich übersetze**
translation **die Übersetzung(en)**
tutor **der Privatlehrer(-) [-in]**
I understand **ich verstehe**
understanding **das**
   Verständnis(se), der Verstand
unit (of work) **die Einheit(en)**
I work **ich arbeite**
   I work at ... **ich arbeite an** +dat
work experience **das**
   Betriebspraktikum (-a)
I write **ich schreibe**
written work **die schriftliche**
   Arbeit(en)

EDUCATION

22b School

blackboard **die Tafel(n)**
blackout **das Blackout**
book **das Buch(-̈er)**
break **die Pause(n)**
briefcase **die Mappe(n)**
canteen **die Kantine(n)**
cassette *(audio/video)* **die Kassette(n)**
cassette recorder **der Kassettenrecorder(-)**
classroom **das Klassenzimmer(-)**
computer **der Computer(-)**
desk **das Pult(e)**
dormitory **das Schlafsaal (-säle)**
gym(nasium) **die Turnhalle(n)**
headphone **der Kopfhörer(-)**
interactive TV **das interaktive Fernsehen**
laboratory **das Laboratorium (-ien)**
language laboratory **das Sprachlabor(s)**
library **die Bibliothek(en)**
lunch hour **die Mittagspause(n)**
note **die Anmerkung(en)**
office **das Büro(s)**
playground **der Schulhof(-̈e)**
radio **das Radio(s)**
rubber/eraser **das Radiergummi(s)**
ruler **das Lineal(e)**
slide **das Dia(s)**

satellite TV **das Satellitenfernsehen**
school hall **der Saal(Säle), die Halle(n)**
schoolbag/satchel/bookbag **die Schulmappe(n)**
sports field **der Sportplatz(-̈e)**
sports hall **die Sporthalle(n)**
staffroom **das Lehrerzimmer(-)**
studio **das Studio(s)**
timetable **der Stundenplan(-̈e)**
video **das Video(s)**
   video player **das Videogerät(e)**
video camera **die Videokamera(s)**
video cassette **die Videokassette(n)**
video recorder **der Video-recorder(-)**
workshop **das Werkstatt(-̈en)**

Type of school

boarding school **das Internat(e)**
comprehensive school **die Gesamtschule(n)**
day school **das Externat(e)**
further education **die Weiterbildung**
infant school **die Vorschule(n)**
nursery school **der Kindergarten(-̈)**
playgroup **die Spielgruppe(n)**
primary school **die Grundschule(n)**
school **die Schule(n)**

– At what age do children start school in Germany?

– They have to go to school when they are six. Our son already goes to kindergarten and is looking forward to school.

I would like to go to college to study math.

– In welchem Alter kommen die Kinder in Deutschland in die Schule?
– Mit sechs werden sie schulpflichtig. Unser Sohn geht schon zum Kindergarten und freut sich auf die Schule.

Ich möchte gern auf die Hochschule gehen, um Mathematik zu studieren.

school type **die Schulform(en)**
of school age **schulpflichtig**
secondary **Sekundar-**
secondary school/junior high school
  die Sekundarschule(n)
secondary modern school/senior
  high school **die Hauptschule(n)**
sixth form/senior year **die
  Oberstufe(n)**
sixth-form college **das
  Oberstufenzentrum (-en)**
special school **die Sonderschule(n)**
technical school **die Realschule(n)**

Classroom commands

Answer the question! **Beantworte
  die Frage!**
Be careful! **Vorsicht!, Passen Sie
  auf!**
Be quiet! **Ruhe!**
Be quick! **Macht schnell!**
Bring me your work! **Bring' mir
  deine Aufgabe!**
Clean the blackboard! **Mach' die
  Tafel sauber!**
Close the door! **Machen Sie die Tür
  bitte zu!**
Come here! **Komm' mal her!**
Come in! **Kommen Sie bitte herein!**
Copy these sentences! **Kopieren
  Sie diese Sätze!**

Do your homework! **Macht eure
  Hausaufgaben!**
Don't talk/chatter! **Bitte nicht reden!**
Go out! **Geht hinaus!**
Learn by heart! **Lernt auswendig!**
Learn the vocabulary! **Lern' die
  Vokabeln!**
Listen carefully! **Hören Sie gut zu!**
Make less noise! **Machen Sie nicht
  so viel Krach!**
Make notes! **Macht Notizen!**
Open the window! **Mach' das
  Fenster auf!**
Pay attention! **Paßt gut auf!**
Put on the headphones! **Legt die
  Kopfhörer auf!**
Read the text! **Lies' den Text (vor)!**
Show me your book! **Zeig' mir dein
  Heft!**
Sit down! **Setzt euch!**
Stand up! **Aufstehen!**
Tick the boxes! **Abhaken!**
Work in pairs! **Jetzt Partnerarbeit!**
Work in groups! **Jetzt
  Gruppenarbeit!**
Write an essay! **Jetzt schreiben wir
  einen Aufsatz!**
Write it down! **Schreiben Sie es auf!**
Write out in rough! **Macht einen
  Entwurf!**
Write out in neat/neatly! **Bitte schön
  ausschreiben!**

Our daughter goes to elementary
school. She reads to her teacher
every day and can read well now.

**Unsere Tochter geht zur
Grundschule. Jeden Tag liest
sie ihrer Lehrerin vor und kann
jetzt gut lesen.**

– Have you moved up a class every
year?
– No, last year I had to stay back a
year.

**– Bist du jedes Jahr versetzt
worden?
– Nein, letztes Jahr bin ich
sitzengeblieben.**

EDUCATION

22c School subjects & examinations

School subjects

arithmetic **das Rechnen**
art **die Kunst, das Zeichnen**
biology **die Biologie**
business studies **die Wirtschaftkunde**
career education **die Berufslehre**
chemistry **die Chemie**
CDT/crafts, design and technology **das Werken**
commerce **die Betriebswirtschaft**
compulsory subject **das Pflichtfach(⁻er)**
computer studies **die Informatik**
design technology **die Technologie**
economics **die Wirtschaftskunde**
elective/option(al subject) **das**

Wahlfach(⁻er)
English **das Englisch**
foreign language **die Fremdsprache(n)**
French **das Französisch**
geography **die Erdkunde, die Geographie**
German **das Deutsch**
Greek **das Griechisch**
gymnastics **das Turnen**
history **die Geschichte**
home economics **die Hauswirtschaft**
Italian **das Italienisch**
information technology **die Informatik**
Latin **das Latein**

Examinations in Germany

das Abitur   A-level exam
der Abiturient(en) [-]   A-level candidate
das Staatsexamen(-)   final examination
die mittlere Reife   16+ examination
die Abschlußprüfung(en)   school-leaving exam/finals

der Hauptschulabschluß(üsse)   school-leaving certificate
der Realschulabschluß(üsse)   school-leaving certificate

Marks

1 sehr gut very good
2 gut good
3 befriedigend satisfactory
4 ausreichend pass
5 mangelhaft poor
6 ungenügend unsatisfactory

– Is your son now at the university?

– Yes, and he likes it a lot. His favorite subjects are law, history and economics.

– My daughter is also studying. She'll graduate next year.

– **Ist Ihr Sohn jetzt an der Universität?**

– **Ja, und es gefällt ihm sehr gut. Seine Lieblingsfächer sind Rechtskunde, Geschichte und Wirtschaftskunde.**

– **Meine Tochter studiert auch. Sie macht nächstes Jahr ihren Abschluß.**

law **die Rechtskunde**
main subject **der Leistungskurs(e)**
mathematics **die Mathematik**
metalwork **die Metallarbeit**
music **die Musik**
philosophy **die Philosophie**
physical education **der Sport**
physics **die Physik**
religious education **die Religion**
science **die Naturwissenschaft(en)**
sex education **die Sexualerziehung**
social studies **die Gemeinschaftskunde**
sociology **die Sozialkunde**
Spanish **das Spanisch**
sport **der Sport**
   type of sport **die Sportart(en)**
subject **das Fach(-̈er)**
subsidiary subject **das Nebenfach(-̈er)**
technical drawing **das technische Zeichnen**
technology **die Technologie**
textiles **die Textilarbeit(en)**
woodwork **die Holzarbeit(en)**

Examinations

I assess **ich bewerte, ich benote**
assessment **die Bewertung(en)**
certificate **das Zertifikat(e)**
degree **das Diplom(e)**
diploma **das Diplom(e)**
dissertation **die Dissertation(en)**

distinction **die Auszeichnung(en)**
doctorate **das Doktorat(e)**
examination **die Prüfung(en), das Examen(-)**
external **extern**
final **Schluß-**
grade **die Zensur(en), die Note(n)**
I grade **ich benote, ich zensiere**
graduate engineer **der Diplomingenieur(-)**
listening comprehension **das Hörverständnis(se)**
mark **die Note(n)**
mark system **das Notensystem(e)**
masters **die Magisterarbeit(en)**
merit **die Auszeichnung(en)**
oral **mündlich**
point **der Punkt(e)**
post-graduate course **der Anschlußkurs(e)**
reading comprehension **das Leseverständnis(se)**
I pass (an exam) **ich lege (ein Examen) ab***
I test **ich teste, ich prüfe**
test **der Test(s)**
thesis **die Doktorarbeit(en)**
trainee **der Azubi(s)/ Auszubildende(n)** *(adj/n)*
written test **die schriftliche Prüfung(en)**

My favorite subject is physical education.	**Mein Lieblingsfach ist Sport.**
Since Robert was an exchange student in the USA, he speaks fluent English.	**Seitdem Robert Austauschschüler in den USA war, spricht er fließend Englisch.**
After school I do sports, and I am on the soccer team in our town.	**Nach der Schule mache ich Sport, und ich bin Mitglied bei der Fußballmannschaft in unserer Stadt.**

▶ SCHOOL 22b; USING LANGUAGE 21b

EDUCATION

22d Further & higher education

adult **der/die Erwachsene(n)** *(adj/n)*
adult *(adj)* **erwachsen**
adult education **die Erwachsenenbildung**
alumnus **der ehemalige Schüler(-)**
apprentice **der Lehrling(e)**
apprenticeship **die Lehre(n)**
chair **der Lehrstuhl (¨e)**
college **die Hochschule(n)**
college of FE **die berufsbildende Schule(n)**
college of HE **die Fachhochschule(n)**
continuing education **der zweite Bildungsweg**
course of study **das Studium (-ien)**
diploma **das Diplom(e)**
dual system **das duale System**
faculty **das Seminar(e), die Fakultät(en)**
hall of residence/residence hall **das Wohnheim(e)**
in-service training **die Weiterbildung**
lecture **das Referat(e), die Vorlesung(en)**
lecture hall **der Hörsaal (-säle)**
lecturer **der Referent(en)** *(wk)* **[-in]**
masters degree **der Magisterabschluß(¨e)**
part-time FE **die Berufschule(n)**

part-time education **die Teilzeitschule(n)**
polytechnic **die technische Hochschule(n)**
practical **das Praktikum (-a)**
principal **der Direktor(en) [-in]**
professor/college professor **der Professor(en) [-in]**
quota (for university entry) **der Numerus clausus**
research **die Forschung(en)**
retraining **die Umschulung**
I retrain **ich lasse mich umschulen**
scholarship **das Stipendium (-ien)**
seminar **das Seminar(e)**
sorority/fraternity **die Studentenverbindung(en)**
student **der Student(en)[-in]**wk
student council **der Studentenrat(¨e)**
student grant **das Bafög (Bundesausbildungsausförde-rungsgesetz), die Studienbeihilfe**
student association **die Studentenvereinigung(en)**
teacher training college **die pädagogische Hochschule(n)**
technical college **die technische Hochschule(n)**

The technical colleges now belong to the university sector.

Die Fachhochschulen gehören jetzt zum Universitätsbereich.

Admission to the technical colleges is possible without the *Abitur.*
The length of course is four years (eight semesters).

Der Zugang zu den Fachhochschulen ist auch ohne Abitur möglich. Die Studiendauer beträgt vier Jahre (acht Semester).

Financial support is of the greatest importance.

Die finanzielle Förderung ist von größter Bedeutung.

university/college **die Universität(en)**
university entrance qualification **die Hochschulreife**

Subjects

accountancy/accounting **die Buchführung**
architecture **die Architektur**
business management **die Betriebswirtschaftslehre**
catering **das Gaststättengewerbe**
classics **die Altphilologie**
civil engineering **der Hoch- und Tiefbau**
commerce **das Betriebswesen**
construction **das Bauwesen**
education **die Pädagogik**
electronics **die Elektronik**
electrical engineering **die Elektroinstallation**
economics **die Ökonomie**
engineering **das Ingenieurwesen**

environmental sciences **die Umweltkunde**
foreign languages **die Fremdsprachen** *(pl)*
history of art **die Kunstgeschichte**
hotel management **das Hotelwesen**
law **die Rechtswissenschaft, Jura**
leisure and tourism **(die) Freizeit und (der)Tourismus**
literature **die Literatur**
mechanical engineering **der Maschinenbau**
medicine **die Medizin**
pharmacy **die Pharmarzie**
nuclear science **die Kernwissenschaft**
office skills **das Bürowesen**
philosophy **die Philosophie**
psychology **die Psychologie**
sociology **die Soziologie**
theology **die Theologie**

Many students get a state grant.

Viele Studenten erhalten staatliche Beihilfe.

Many students apply for places to study but they cannot all be admitted.

Viele Studenten bewerben sich um einen Studienplatz, aber sie können nicht alle zugelassen werden.

There is now an entrance restriction. Admission depends on marks in the *Abitur*.
Particularly high marks are required for medicine.

Es gibt jetzt den Numerus clausus. Die Zulassung hängt von den Noten im Abitur ab. Für Medizin braucht man besonders gute Zensuren.

Our results are always outstanding.

Unsere Prüfungsergebnisse sind immer hervorragend.

▶ LANGUAGES App.21a; SCIENTIFIC DISCIPLINES App.23a

23 Science: the changing world

23a Science & biology

Scientific method

academic paper **die theoretische/ akademische Arbeit(en)**
I analyze **ich analysiere**
authentic **authentisch**
I challenge **ich stelle in Frage**
I check **ich prüfe**
classification **die Klassifizierung(en), die Einteilung(en)**
I classify **ich klassifiziere, ich ordne**
I conduct *(an experiment)* **ich führe durch*, ich leite**
control **die Kontrolle(n)**
I control **ich kontrolliere**
dial **die Skala (-en)**
experiment **das Experiment(e), der Versuch(e)**
I experiment **ich experimentiere**
flask **der Kolben(-)**
gauge **das Meßgerät(e)**
hypothesis **die Hypothese(n)**
I identify **ich identifiziere**
invention **die Erfindung(en)**

I investigate **ich untersuche**
laboratory **das Laboratorium (-ien)**
material **das Material(ien)**
I measure **ich messe**
measurement **die Messung(en), das Maß(e)**
(electron) microscope **das (Elektronen)mikroskop(e)**
I observe **ich beobachte**
observation **die Beobachtung(en)**
origin **der Ursprung(¨e)**
pipette **die Pipette(n)**
research **die Forschung(en)**
I research **ich (er)forsche**
result **das Resultat(e)**
scientific **wissenschaftlich**
I solve (a problem) **ich löse (ein Problem)**
I sort **ich sortiere**
test **die Probe(n)**
I test **ich teste, ich prüfe**
test tube **das Reagenzglas(¨er)**
theory **die Theorie(n)**
I transfer **ich versetze/übertage**

Research on human embryo tissue is likely to remain highly controversial.

Die Forschung am menschlichen Embryogewebe wird wohl sehr umstritten bleiben.

The researcher took a sample, mounted it on a slide and put it under the microscope for examination. All the results from the experiments support her hypothesis.

Die Forscherin nahm eine Probe, gab sie auf einen Objektträger und legte sie zum Untersuchen unter das Mikroskop. Alle Untersuchungsergebnisse unterstützen ihre Hypothese.

Life sciences

bacteria **das Bakterium(en)**
botanical **botanisch**
I breathe **ich atme**
cell **die Zelle(n)**
chlorophyll **das Chlorophyl**
it circulates **es zirkuliert, es fließt**
decay **der Verfall**
it decays **es verfault**
decline **der Nieder-/Rückgang(Ꞌe)**
it declines **es geht zurück***
it excretes **es scheidet aus***
excretion **die Ausscheidung(en)**
it feeds (on) **es frißt, es ernährt
  sich (von** +dat)
food chain **die Nahrungskette(n)**
gene **das Gen(e)**
gene bank **die Gen-Bank(en)**
genetic **genetisch**
genetics **die Genetik**
genetic disorder **die genetische
  Krankheit(en)**
it grows **es wächst**
growth **das Wachstum**
habitat **der Lebensraum(Ꞌe)**
I inherit **ich erbe**
mammal **das Säugetier(e)**
membrane **die Membran(en)**
it mutates **es verändert sich, es
  mutiert**
nucleus **der Nukleus (Nuklei)**
organic **organisch**
organism **der Organismus (-en)**
photosynthesis **die
  Photosynthese(n)**
population **die Menge(n), die
  Bevölkerung**
process **der Prozeß (-sse)**
it reproduces **es reproduziert sich**
respiration **die Atmung(en)**
sample **die Probe(n)**
sensitivity **die Empfindlichkeit(en)**
slide **der Objektträger(-)**
survival **das Überleben**
it survives **es überlebt**
virus **der Virus (-en)**

Medical science & research

ante-natal tests (on foetus) **die
  Schwangerschaftsunter-
  suchung(en)**
cosmetic surgery **die
  Schönheitsoperation(en)**
DNA **die DNS**
donor **der Blutspender(-) [-in]**
embryo **der Embryo(s)**
embryo research **die
  embryonische
  Untersuchung(en)**
ethical consideration **ethische
  Ansichten** (pl)
ethics of human reproduction **die
  Ethik** (pl) **der menschlichen
  Fortpflanzung**
experiment on animals **der
  Tierversuch(e)**
hereditary illness **die
  Erbkrankheit(en)**
IVF (in vitro fertilization) **die in
  vitro Befruchtung**
I justify **ich rechtfertige**
microorganism **der
  Mikroorganismus (-en)**
organ transplant **die
  Organtransplantation(en)**
pacemaker **der
  (Herz)schrittmacher(-)**
I permit **ich erlaube jdm.**
plastic surgery **die plastische
  Chirurgie**
psychology **die Psychologie**
recipient **der Empfänger(-) [-in]**
I reject (an organ) **ich stoße (ein
  Organ) ab***
risk **das Risiko (-en)**
I risk **ich riskiere**
survival rate **die Überlebensrate**
test-tube baby **das Retortenbaby (
  -ies)**
transplant **das Transplantat(e)**
X-ray **die Röntgenstrahlung(en)**
I X-ray **ich röntge**

▶ MEDICAL TREATMENT 11c; THE ANIMAL WORLD 24b

23b Physical sciences

Chemistry

acid **die Säure(n)**
air **die Luft(⁼e)**
alkali **das Alkali**
alkaline **basisch**
alkaline solution **die Lauge(n)**
boiling point **der Siedepunkt(e)**
Bunsen burner **der Bunsenbrenner(-)**
I calculate **ich berechne, ich kalkuliere**
chemical **chemisch**
compound **die Verbindung(en)**
composition **die Zusammensetzung(en)**
it dissolves **es löst sich (auf)***
it dissolves in water **es ist wasserlöslich**
element **das Element(e)**
emulsion **die Emulsion(en)**
equation **die Gleichung(en)**
gas **das Gas(e)**
inorganic **anorganisch**
insoluble **unlöslich**
liquid **die Flüssigkeit(en)**
   liquid *(adj)* **flüssig**
Litmus paper **das Lackmuspapier**
matter **die Materie, der Stoff(e)**
metal **das Metall(e)**
natural gas **das Erdgas(e)**
opaque **undurchsichtig**
periodic table **das Periodensystem**
physical **physikalisch**
pure **rein**
it reacts **es reagiert**
reaction **die Reaktion(en)**
salt **das Salz(e)**
solid **der Festkörper(-)**
   solid *(adj)* **fest**
soluble **löslich**
solution **die Lösung(en)**
stable **fest, stabil**
substance **die Substanz(en)**
transparent **durchsichtig**

Physics & mechanics

it accelerates **es beschleunigt**
acceleration **die Beschleunigung(en)**
acoustic(s) **die Akustik**
analysis **die Analyse(n)**
artificial **künstlich**
automatic **automatisch**
ball bearing **das Kugellager(-)**
conservation **die Erhaltung**
density **die Dichte(n)**
distance **die Distanz(en)**
energy **die Energie**
engine **der Motor(en)**
it expands **es dehnt sich aus***
fiber **die Faser(n)**
force **die Kraft(⁼e), die Stärke(n)**
it freezes **es gefriert**
formula **die Formel(n)**
freezing point **der Gefrierpunkt(e)**
friction **die Reibung(en), die Friktion**
gear **das Getriebe**
gravity **die Schwerkraft(⁼e)**
   center of gravity **der Schwerpunkt(-)**
   law of gravity **das Gravitationsgesetz**
I heat **ich erhitze**
heat **die Hitze, die Wärme**
heat loss **der Wärmeverlust(e)**
laser **der Laser(-)**
laser beam **der Laserstrahl(en)**
light **das Licht(er)**
light beam **der Lichtstrahl(en)**
lubricant **das Schmiermittel(-)**
machinery **der Mechanismus (-en), die Maschinerie(n)**
magnetism **der Magnetismus**
magneto **der Magnetzünder(-)**
mass **die Masse(n)**
mechanics **der Maschinenbau**
mechanical **mechanisch**
mechanism **der Mechanismus (-en)**
mechanics **die Mechanik**

metallurgy **die Metallurgie**
microscope **das Mikroskop(e)**
microwave **die Mikrowelle(n)**
mineral **das Mineral(e)**
missile **das Geschoß (-sse), die Rakete(n)**
model **das Modell(e)**
motion **die Bewegung(en)**
I operate *(machinery)* **ich bediene**
optics **die Optik**
pressure **der Druck(ˉe)**
property **die Eigenschaft(en)**
proportional **proportional**
ray **der (Licht)strahl(en)**
reflection **die Reflexion(en)**
refraction **die Brechung(en)**
relativity **die Relativität**
  relativity theory **die Relativitätstheorie**
resistance **der Widerstand(ˉe)**
resistant **widerstandsfähig**
robot **der Roboter(-)**
sound **der Schall(ˉe)**
speed **die Geschwindigkeit(en)**
structure **die Struktur(en)**
synthetic **synthetisch, künstlich**
temperature **die Temperatur(en)**
theory **die Theorie(n)**
transmission **die Übertragung(en)**
I transmit **ich übertrage**
vapor **der Dampf(ˉe)**
it vibrates **es vibriert**
vibration **die Vibration(en)**
wave **die Welle(n)**
  long wave **die Langwelle(n)**
  medium/short wave **die Kurzwelle(n)**
wavelength **die Wellenlänge(n)**

Electricity

alternating current **der Wechselstrom**
battery **die Batterie(n)**
charge **die Ladung(en)**
I charge the battery **ich lade die Batterie auf***
circuit **der Stromkreis(e)**
current **der Strom(ˉe), die Strömung(en)**
direct current **der Gleichstrom**
electrical **elektrisch**
electricity **die Elektrizität**
electrode **die Elektrode(n)**
electron **das Elektron(en)**
electronic **elektronisch**
electronics **die Elektronik**
positive **positiv**
negative **negativ**
voltage **die Spannung(en)**

Nuclear physics

atom **das Atom(e)**
atomic **atomar, Atom-**
fission **die Spaltung(en)**
fusion **die Verschmelzung(en)**
molecular **molekular**
molecule **das Molekül(e)**
neutron **das Neutron(en)**
nuclear **Nuklear-, Kern-**
nuclear energy **die Nuklearenergie**
nuclear reactor **der Kernreaktor(en)**
nucleus **der Nukleus, der Kern(e)**
particle **das Partikel(-)**
proton **das Proton(en)**
quantum theory **die Quantentheorie(n)**
radiation **die (Aus)strahlung(en)**

Water has a boiling point of 100 degrees centigrade.

Der Siedepunkt des Wassers liegt bei 100 Grad Celsius.

What is the wattage of this appliance?

Wieviel Watt hat dieses Gerät?

➤ MEASURING 4b; DESCRIBING THINGS 5c; ENERGY 23c

23c The earth & space

Energy & fuels

coal **die Kohle(n)**
concentration **die Konzentration(en)**
coolant **das Kühlmittel(-)**
energy **die Energie(n)**
energy conservation **die Energiesparmaßnahmen** *(pl)*
energy consumption **der Energieverbrauch**
energy crisis **die Energiekrise(n)**
energy needs **der Energiebedarf**
energy source **die Energiequelle(n)**
energy waste **die Energieverschwendung**
fossil fuel **der fossile Brennstoff(e)**
fuel **der Treibstoff**
fuel consumption **der Kraftstoffverbrauch**
it generates **es erzeugt**
geothermal energy **die geothermische Energie**
global warming **die globale Erwärmung**
greenhouse effect **der Treibhauseffekt**
hole in the ozone layer **das Ozonloch(¨er)**
hydroelectric dam **der hydro-elektrische Damm(¨e)**
hydroelectric power **die Wasserkraft**
insulation **die Isolation**
natural gas **das Erdgas(e)**
nuclear energy **die Atomenergie, die Kernkraft**
nuclear power station **das Kernkraftwerk(e)**
oil **das Öl(e)**
oil production **die Ölherstellung**
oil-producing country **das Ölförderland(¨er)**
ozone layer **die Ozonschicht**

petroleum **das Petroleum, das Erdöl(e)**
propellant *(rocket fuel)* **der Raketentreibstoff(e)**
raw materials **der Rohstoff(e)**
solar cell **die Solarzelle(n)**
solar energy **die Solarenergie**
thermal energy **die Wärmeenergie**
wave power **die Wellenkraft**
tidal power station **das Gezeitenkraftwerk**
wind energy/power **die Windenergie**

Geology

carbon-dating **die Kohlenstoffdatierung**
I excavate **ich grabe aus***
geologist **der Geologe(n)** *(wk)*
gemstone **der Edelstein(e)**
layer **die Schicht(en)**
loam **der Lehm**
mine **das Bergwerk(e)**
I mine (for) **ich grabe (nach +dat)**
ore **das Erz(e)**
quarry **der Steinbruch(¨e)**
sand **der Sand(e)**
sediment **das Sediment(e), die Ablagerung(en)**
soil **das Erdreich**
stalactite **der Stalaktit(en)** *(wk)*
stalagmite **der Stalagmit(en)** *(wk)*

Space

asteroid **der Asteroid(en)**
eclipse **die Finsternis(se)**
it eclipses **es verfinstert**
galactic **galaktisch**
galaxy **das Sternsystem(e)**
light year **das Lichtjahr(e)**
meteorite **der Meteorit(en)** *(wk)*
moon **der Mond(e)**
full moon **der Vollmond**
new moon **der Neumond**

orbit   **der Orbit(s), die Planetenbahn(en)**
planet   **der Planet(en)**
shooting-star   **die Sternschnuppe(n)**
solar system   **das Sonnensystem(e)**
solstice   **die Sonnenwende(n)**
space   **der Raum, das Weltall**
star   **der Stern(e)**
sun   **die Sonne(n)**
sunspot   **der Sonnenfleck(en)**
the heavens   **der Himmel(-)**
universe   **das Universum (-en), das Weltall**

Space research & travel

antenna   **die Antenne(n)**
astrologer   **der Astrolog(en)** *(wk)*
astronomer   **der Astronom(en)** *(wk)*
astronaut   **der Astronaut(en)** *(wk)*
big-bang theory   **die Urknalltheorie**
cosmonaut   **der Kosmonaut(en)** *(wk)*
dish antenna   **die Parabolantenne(n)**
gravitational pull   **die Anziehungskraft**
launch   **der Raketenabschuß (ˉsse)**
launch pad   **die Abschußrampe(n)**
space module   **die Raumkapsel(n)**
moon-buggy   **das Mondfahrzeug(e)**

moon-landing   **die Mondlandung(en)**
observatory   **das Observatorium (-ien)**
orbit   **der Orbit(s)**
planetarium   **das Planetarium (-ien)**
it re-enters   **es tritt wieder ein***
relativity   **die Relativität**
rocket   **die Rakete(n)**
rocket fuel   **der Raketenkraftstoff(e)**
satellite   **der Satellit(en)** *(wk)*
   communications   **der Kommunikationssatellit(en)**
   spy   **der Spionagesatellit(en)**
   weather   **der Wettersatellit(en)**
sky lab   **das Observatorium (-ien)**
space   **der Weltraum**
space flight   **der Weltraumflug(ˉe)**
space probe   **die Weltraumsonde(n)**
space shuttle   **die Raumfähre(n)**
space walk   **der Weltraumspaziergang(ˉe)**
spacecraft   **das Raumschiff(e)**
spacesuit   **der Raumanzug(ˉe)**
stratosphere   **die Stratosphäre**
telescope   **das Teleskop(e)**
time-warp   **die Zeitverzerrung**
touchdow   **die Landung(en), das Aufsetzen**
zodiac   **der Tierkreis(e)**

By studying the light received from stars many millions of light years away, scientists hope to discover the origins of the universe.

Durch die Untersuchung des Lichtes, welches von Sternen empfangen wird, die viele Lichtjahre entfernt sind, hoffen Wissenschaftler, den Ursprung des Universums zu entdecken/ergründen.

The earth orbits the sun.

Die Erde umkreist die Sonne.

24 The environment: the natural world

24a Geography

area **das Gebiet(e), die Gegend(en)**
bottom **der Fuß(¨sse), der Grund(¨e)**
clean **sauber**
continent **der Kontinent(e)**
country **das Land(¨er), das Gelände(-)**
   in the country **auf dem Land(e)**
countryside **die Landschaft(en)**
dangerous **gefährlich**
deep **tief**
dirty **schmutzig**
earth tremor **die Erd- erschütterung(en)**
earthquake **das Erdbeben(-)**
equator **der Äquator**
equatorial **äquatorial**
eruption **der Ausbruch(¨e)**
it erupts **es bricht aus* (brechen)**
flat **flach, glatt**
it floods **es läuft über* (laufen), es überschwemmt**

it flows **es fließt**
friendly **freundlich, angenehm**
geographical **geographisch**
geography **die Geographie**
gradient/climb **die Steigung(en)**
hemisphere **die Hemisphäre(n), die Halbkugel(n)**
high **hoch**
incline **das Gefälle(-)**
it is situated **es ist gelegen, es liegt**
land **das Land(¨er)**
   land *(property/real estate)* **der Grund und Boden**
it is located **es ist gelegen, es liegt**
location **die Lage(n)**
map **die Karte(n)**
national park **der Nationalpark(s)**
nature **die Natur**
nature conservancy **der Naturschutz**
nature trail **der Naturlehrpfad(e)**
peaceful **ruhig, friedlich, still**

Germany extends from the mountains of the Alps to the North and Baltic Seas. There are no natural frontiers to the west and east.

Deutschland reicht vom Hochgebirge der Alpen bis zur Nord- und Ostsee. Es gibt keine natürliche Abgrenzung nach Westen und Osten.

The Zugspitze is the highest mountain in the Bavarian Alps.

Die Zugspitze ist der höchste Berg in den Bayerischen Alpen.

In the central mountain area one finds plateaux, hills, volcanic mountains and valleys.

In der Mittelgebirgszone findet man Hochflächen, Bergland- schaften, vulkanische Formen und Tallandschaften.

pleasant **angenehm**
pole **der Pol(e)**
province **die Provinz(en)**
region **die Region(en), das Gebiet(e)**
regional **regional**
sand **der Sand(e)**
scenery **die Landschaft(en)**
by the seaside **am Meer**
slope **der Abhang(⁻e)**
steep **steil**
tall **hoch**
territory **das Gebiet(e)**
top **die Spitze(n), der Gipfel(-)**
the tropics **die Tropen** *(pl)*
unfriendly **unfreundlich**
water **das Wasser(-)**
  fresh water **das Süßwasser**
  salt water **das Salzwasser**
zenith **der Zenit** *(no pl)*
zone **die Zone(n)**

Manmade features

aqueduct **das Aquädukt(e)**
bridge **die Brücke(n)**
canal **der Kanal(⁻e)**

capital (city) **die Hauptstadt(⁻e)**
city **die Großstadt(⁻e)**
country road **die Landstraße(n)**
dam **der Damm(⁻e), der Stausee(n)**
embankment **die Böschung(en)**
factory **die Fabrik(en), das Werk(e)**
farm **der Bauernhof(⁻e), das Gut(⁻er)**
farmland **der Acker(⁻), das Ackerland**
field **das Feld(er)**
hamlet **das kleine Dorf(⁻er)**
harbor **der Hafen(⁻)**
industry **die Industrie(n)**
marina **der Yachthafen(⁻)**
oasis **die Oase(n)**
reclaimed land **das gewonnene Land**
reservoir **das Reservoir(s), der Speicher(-)**
town **die Stadt(⁻e)**
track **der Feldweg(e)**
village **das Dorf(⁻er)**
well **der Brunnen(-)**

The surface of the North German plain was formed by the glaciers of the ice ages.

Die Oberfläche des Norddeutschen Tieflandes wurde von den Gletschern der Eiszeiten geformt.

The North Sea has very high and low tides. Many islands and low islands rise out of the shallow coastal waters.

Die Nordsee hat ausgeprägte Gezeiten (Ebbe - Flut). Vor der Küste erheben sich aus dem Wattenmeer viele Inseln und Halligen.

The bog was drained by ditches and reclaimed.

Das Moor wurde durch Kanäle entwässert und urbar gemacht.

24b The animal world

Animals

animal **das Tier(e)**
it barks **es bellt**
it bites **es beißt**
it bounds **es springt**
it breeds **es vermehrt sich**
burrow **der (Kaninchen)bau(e)**
cage **der Käfig(e)**
carnivore **der Fleischfresser(-)**
cat **die Katze(n)**
it crawls **es kriecht**
den **die Höhle(n), das Versteck(e)**
dog **der Hund(e)**
I feed **ich füttere**
it feeds **es frißt** *(fressen)*
food **das Futter**
gerbil **die Wüstenspringmaus(-̈e)**
goldfish **der Goldfisch(e)**
guinea pig **das Meerschweinchen(-)**
habitat **der Lebensraum(-̈e)**
hamster **der Hamster(-)**
herbivore **der Pflanzenfresser(-)**
it hibernates **es hält den Winterschlaf**
it howls **es heult**
hut/hutch **der Stall(-̈e)**
I keep a cat **ich halte eine Katze**
kitten **das Kätzchen(-)**
lair **das Lager(-), die Höhle(n)**
it leaps **es springt**
litter **der Wurf(-̈e)**
mammal **das Säugetier(e)**
it meows **es miaut**
omnivore **der Allesfresser(-)**
pack **das Rudel(-)**
pet **das Haustier(e)**
predator **das Raubtier(e)**
prey **die Beute, das Beutetier(e)**
puppy **das Hündchen(-)**
rabbit **das Kaninchen(-)**
rabies **die Tollwut**
reptile **das Reptil(ien)**
it roars **es brüllt**

safari park **der Safaripark(s)**
snail **die Schnecke(n)**
it squeaks **es piept, es quiekt**
I stroke **ich streich(e)le**
tortoise **die Schildkröte(n)**
I walk *(the dog)* **ich führe ... aus***
wildlife park **das Wildreservat(e), das Wildschutzgebiet(e)**
zoo **der Zoo(s), der Tiergarten(-̈)**

Birds

claw **die Klaue(n)**
it crows **es kräht**
it flies **es fliegt**
flock **die Schar(en), der Schwarm(-̈e)**
it hovers **es schwebt, es steht**
it migrates **es zieht nach Süden**
migratory bird **der Zugvogel(-̈)**
nest **das Nest(er)**
it nests **es nistet**
it pecks at **es pickt**
it sings **es singt**

Sealife/Waterlife

alligator **der Alligator(en)**
anemone **die Seeanemone(n)**
angling **das Angeln**
coral **die Koralle(n)**
crab **der Krebs(e)**
crocodile **das Krokodil(e)**
dolphin **der Delphin(e)**
fish **der Fisch(e)**
I fish **ich fische**
harpoon **die Harpune(n)**
hook **der Haken(-)**
marine **Meeres-, See-**
mollusc **die Molluske(n)**
net **das Netz(e)**
octopus **der Tintenfisch(e), der Krake(n)** *(wk)*
plankton **das Plankton** *(no pl)*
rod **die Rute(n)**
seal **der Seehund(e)**

shark **der Hai(e)**
shoal **der Schwarm(ᐨe)**
shrimp **die Krabbe(n)**
starfish **der Seestern(e)**
it swims **es schwimmt**
turtle **die Wasserschildkröte(n)**
whale **der Wal(e)**
whaling **der Walfang** *(no pl)*

Insects

ant **die Ameise(n)**
bee **die Biene(n)**
 queen bee **die Bienenkönigin(nen)**
 worker bee **die Arbeiterbiene(n)**
bedbug **die Wanze(n)**
beetle **der Käfer(-)**
bug **das Insekt(en)** *(wk)*, **der Käfer(-)**
butterfly **der Schmetterling(e)**
it buzzes **es summt**
caterpiller **die Raupe(n)**
cocoon **der Kokon(s)**
cockroach **die Kakerlake(n)**
cricket **die Grille(n)**
dragonfly **die Libelle(n)**

flea **der Floh(ᐨe)**
fly **die Fliege(n)**
hive **der Bienenkorb(ᐨe)**
insect **das Insekt(en)**
invertebrate **wirbellos**
ladybird/lady bug **der Marienkäfer(-)**
larva **die Larve(n)**
locust **die Heuschrecke(n)**
it metamorphoses **es verwandelt sich**
mosquito **die Stechmücke(n), der Moskito(s)**
moth **die Motte(n)**
scorpion **der Skorpion(e)**
silkworm **die Seidenraupe(n)**
slug **die Nacktschnecke(n)**
spider **die Spinne(n)**
it spins (a web) **es spinnt (ein Netz)**
it stings **es sticht**
termite **die Termite(n)**
tick **die Zecke(n)**
web **das Spinnengewebe(-)**
wasp **die Wespe(n)**
worm **der Wurm(ᐨer)**

The small low islands are important as a resting and migration area for northern birds of passage.

Die Halligen sind wichtig als Rast und Durchzugszone für nordische Zugvögel.

The state recognizes the value of the area for flora and fauna.

Der Wert des Gebietes für die Pflanzen- und Tierwelt wird staatlich anerkannt.

Many animals are threatened with extinction.

Viele Tiere sind vom Aussterben bedroht.

They are scattered, rare or endangered.

Sie sind zerstreut, selten oder gefährdet.

Seals get caught in the remains of nets.

Seehunde verfangen sich in Netzresten.

➤ BIRDS App.24b; FISH & SEA FOOD 10b, POULTRY 10c

THE ENVIRONMENT: THE NATURAL WORLD

24c Farming & gardening

Farm animals

bull **der Bulle(n)** *(wk)*
cattle **das Vieh** *(no pl)*, **die Rinder** *(pl)*
chicken **das Huhn(ِer)**
cock **der Hahn(ِe)**
cow **die Kuh(ِe)**
it crows **es kräht**
dairy *(adj)* **Milch-**
duck **die Ente(n)**
it eats **es frißt** *(fressen)*
feed **das Futter** *(no pl)*
it feeds **es frißt** *(fressen)*
foal **das Fohlen(-)**
fodder **das Futter**
food **die Nahrung**
it gallops **es gallopiert**
goat **die Ziege(n)**
goose **die Gans(ِe)**
it grazes **es grast, es weidet**
I groom **ich striegle, ich putze**
it grunts **es grunzt**
horse **das Pferd(e)**
horseshoe **das Hufeisen(-)**
it kicks **es tritt** *(treten)*
kid **das Zicklein(-)**
I milk **ich melke**
it moos **es muht**
it neighs **es wiehert**
ox **der Ochse(n)**
pasture **die Weide(n)**
it pecks **es pickt**

pig **das Schwein(e)**
pony **das Pony(s)**
poultry **das Geflügel** *(no pl)*
produce **das Produkt(e)**
it quacks **es quakt**
I ride (a horse) **ich reite (ein Pferd)**
rooster **der Hahn(ِe), das Hähnchen(-)**
I shear **ich schere**
sheep **das Schaf(e)**
sheep dog **der Schäferhund(e)**
I slaughter **ich schlachte**
stallion **der Zuchthengst(e)**
it trots **es trabt**

On the farm

agricultural **landwirtschaftlich**
agriculture **die Landwirtschaft**
arable land **das Ackerland** *(no pl)*
barn **die Scheune(n), der Scheuer(-)**
combine harvester **der Mähdrescher(-)**
crop **die Ernte(n)**
dairy **die Molkerei(en)**
farm **der Bauernhof(ِe)**
farmhouse **das Bauernhaus(ِer)**
farm labourer/laborer **der Landarbeiter(-)**
farmyard **der Hof(ِe)**
fence **der Zaun(ِe)**
harvest **die Ernte(n)**

The most important grain crops in Germany are wheat and rye. Besides grain, fruit, vegetables and wine are cultivated.

Die wichtigsten Getreidearten in Deutschland sind Weizen und Roggen. Neben Getreide werden Obst, Gemüse und Wein angebaut.

The common agricultural policy has as its aim to increase agricultural productivity and to stabilize the markets.

Die gemeinsame Agrarpolitik hat als Ziel, die Produktivität der Landwirtschaft zu steigern und die Märkte zu stabilisieren.

I harvest   **ich ernte**
hay   **das Heu**
haystack   **der Heuschober(-)**
irrigate   **ich bewässere**
milk churn   **die Milchkanne(n)**
milking machine   **die
Melkmaschine(n)**
orchard   **der Obstgarten(¨)**
pen   **der Pferch(e), die Hürde(n)**
pigsty   **der Schweinestall(¨e)**
silage   **die Silage** *(no pl)*
slaughterhouse   **der Schlachthof(¨e)**
stable   **der Stall(¨e)**
stud farm   **das Gestüt(e)**
tractor   **der Traktor(en)**

Agriculture & gardening

acorn   **die Eichel(n)**
allotment   **der Schrebergarten(¨)**
barley   **die Gerste**
it blooms   **es blüht**
bloom   **die Blüte(n)**
bouquet   **der Strauß(¨e)**
bud   **die Knospe(n)**
bulb   **die Zwiebel(n), die Knolle(n)**
bush   **der Busch(¨e), der
Strauch(¨e)**
compost   **der Kompost(e)**
corn   **das Getreide(-), das Korn(¨er)**
corn *(U.S.)*   **der Mais**
I cultivate   **ich kultiviere**
I dig   **ich grabe**
flower   **die Blume(n), die Blüte(n)**
it flowers   **es blüht**
flower bed   **das Blumenbeet(e)**
flower pot   **der Blumentopf(¨e)**
foliage   **das Laub, die Blätter**
forestry   **die Forstwirtschaft**
garden/yard *(U.S.)*   **der Garten(¨)**
I garden/work in the yard   **ich
arbeite im Garten**
gardening   **die Gartenarbeit(en)**
I gather   **ich ernte, ich sammle**
grain   **das Getreide(-), das
Korn(¨er)**
grass   **das Gras(¨er)**
I grow   **ich ziehe, ich baue ... an***

it grows   **es wächst** *(wachsen)*
hedge   **die Hecke(n), der Zaun(¨e)**
horticulture   **der Gartenbau**
house plant   **die Zimmerpflanze(n)**
lawn   **der Rasen(-)**
leaf   **das Blatt(¨er)**
maize   **der Mais**
market gardening   **der Gemüsebau**
I mow   **ich mähe**
oats   **der Hafer**
petal   **das Blütenblatt(¨er)**
I pick   **ich pflücke**
I plant   **ich pflanze**
plant   **die Pflanze(n)**
pollen   **der Pollen(-)**
I reap   **ich schneide, ich mähe**
ripe   **reif**
it ripens   **es reift**
rockery   **der Steingarten(¨)**
root   **die Wurzel(n)**
rotten   **faul, morsch, verdorben**
rye   **der Roggen**
sap   **der Saft(¨e)**
seed   **der Samen(-)**
species   **die Art(en)**
stem   **der Stiel(e), der Stamm(¨e)**
thorn   **der Dorn(en)/der
Dornenbusch(¨e)**
I trim *(hedge)*   **ich stutze**
I transplant   **ich verpflanze, ich
pflanze ... um***
tree   **der Baum(¨e)**
tuber   **die Knolle(n)**
undergrowth   **das Unterholz(¨er),
das Gebüsch, das Gestrüpp**
vegetable(s)   **das Gemüse** *(no pl)*
vegetable garden   **der
Gemüsegarten(¨)**
vegetation   **die Vegetation(en)**
vine   **die Weinrebe(n)**
vineyard   **der Weinberg(e)**
I water   **ich bewässere, ich gieße**
weed   **das Unkraut(¨er)**
I weed   **ich jäte**
wheat   **der Weizen**
it wilts   **es welkt**
wine cultivation   **der Wein(an)bau**

➤ FLOWERS & WEEDS, TREES App.24c; TOOLS App.8b

24d Weather

anticyclone **die Antizyklone(n)**
avalanche **die Lawine(n)**
average temperature **die Durchschnittstemperatur(en)**
bad weather **das Schlechtwetter**
bright **heiter**
bright period **die Aufheiterung(en)**
centigrade **das Grad Celsius**
changeable **veränderlich**
clear skies **der klare Himmel**
climate **das Klima(te/s)**
climatic **klimatisch**
cloud **die Wolke(n)**
clouded over **bewölkt**
cloudless **wolkenlos**
cloudy **wolkig**
cold **kalt**
it is cold **es ist kalt**
cold front **die Kaltfront(en)**
it is cool **es ist kühl/frisch**
cyclone **die Zyklone(n)**
damp **feucht**
day temperature **die Tagestemperatur(en)**
degree **das Grad(e)**
  above zero **über Null**
  below zero **unter Null**
depression **das Tiefdruckgebiet(e)**

drizzle **der Nieselregen(-), der Sprühregen(-)**
drought **die Dürre**
dry **trocken**
dull **trüb, grau, verhangen**
earth tremor **das Erdzittern, die Erschütterung(en)**
earthquake **das Erdbeben(-)**
it's fine **es ist schön**
flash/lightning **der Blitz(e)**
fog **der Nebel(-)**
it is foggy **es ist nebelig**
it's freezing **es ist eisig, es friert**
freezing fog **der gefrierende Nebel**
frost **der Frost(-̈e)**
frosty **frostig**
gale **der Sturm(-̈e)**
gale warning **die Sturmwarnung(en)**
it's hailing **es hagelt**
hailstone **das Hagelkorn(-̈er)**
  soft hail **die Graupel(n)**
heat **die Hitze**
heatwave **die Hitzewelle(n)**
high pressure **der Hochdruck**
highest temperature **die Höchsttemperatur(en)**
it's hot **es ist heiß/warm**

The forecast is for strong winds and icy polar air. Thick snow caused 90-kilometer-long traffic jams.

Die Vorhersage meldet starken Wind und eisige Polarluft. Dicker Schnee verursachte 90-km-lange Staus.

Further outlook: bright to start with, then overcast with thunder showers. Highest temperatures around nine degrees.

Weitere Aussichten: anfangs aufgeheitert, sonst stark bewölkt mit gewittrigen Schauern. Die Höchstwerte liegen um neun Grad.

A stormy low pressure trough is moving east.

Der Ausläufer eines Sturmtiefs zieht nach Osten.

hurricane **der Orkan(e)**
ice **das Eis**
Indian summer **der Altweibersommer**
low pressure **der Tiefdruck**
lowest temperature **die Tiefsttemperatur(en)**
mild **mild**
mist **der Dunst**
misty **dunstig**
meteorology **die Wetterkunde**
monsoon **der Monsun(e)**
moon **der Mond(e)**
overcast **bedeckt**
it pours **es gießt in Strömen**
rain **der Regen(-)**
it's raining **es regnet**
rainy **regnerisch**
shade **der Schatten(-)**
it shines **es scheint**
shower **der Schauer(-)**
snow **der Schnee**
snowball **der Schneeball(-e)**
snowdrift **die Schneewehe(n)**
snowfall **der Schneefall(-e)**
snowflake **die Schneeflocke(n)**
snowman **der Schneemann(-er)**
snow conditions **die Schneeverhältnisse** (pl)
it's snowing **es schneit**
snowstorm **der Schneesturm(-e)**

storm **der Sturm(-e)**
stormy **stürmig**
sultry **schwül**
sun/sunshine **der Sonnenschein**
sunny **sonnig**
thunder **der Donner(-)**
it's thunder and lightning **es blitzt und donnert**
thunderbolt **der Blitzeinschlag(-e)**
thunderstorm **das Gewitter(-)**
torrent **der Sturzbach(-e), die Flut(en)**
torrential **sintflutartig**
tropical **tropisch**
trough **der Ausläufer(-)**
typhoon **der Taifun(e)**
warm **warm**
warm front **die Warmfront(en)**
weather **das Wetter**
weather conditions **die Witterungsbedingungen**
weather forecast **die Wettervorhersage(n)**
weather report **der Wetterbericht(e)**
wet **nass**
wind **der Wind(e)**
windy **windig**
wonderful **wunderschön, wunderbar**

What foul weather! In this weather we stay home.

Was für ein Mistwetter! Bei diesem Wetter bleiben wir zu Hause.

Germany belongs to the temperate zone with rainfall at all seasons. The average temperature in summer is 17-21° centrigrade.

Deutschland gehört Zur gemäßigten Zone, mit Niederschlägen zu allen Jahreszeiten. Die durchschnittlichen Sommertemperaturen liegen bei 17° bis 20°C.

24e Pollution

balance of nature **das Gleichgewicht der Natur**
it becomes extinct **es stirbt aus* (sterben)**
conservation **der Umweltschutz**
conservationist **der Umweltschützer(-)**
I conserve **ich konserviere, ich erhalte**
I consume **ich verbrauche**
consumption **der Verbrauch** (no pl)
corrosion **die Korrosion**
I damage **ich beschädige**
damaging **schädlich**
danger (to) **die Gefahr** (+acc)
I destroy **ich zerstöre**
disaster **das Unglück(e)**
disposable **Einweg-, Wegwerf-**
disposal **die Beseitigung(en)**
I dispose of **ich beseitige**
I do without **ich komme ohne aus***
ecology **die Ökologie**
ecosystem **das Ökosystem(e)**
environment **die Umwelt**
environmentally friendly **umweltfreundlich**
harmful substance **der Schadstoff(e)**
I improve **ich verbessere**
I insulate **ich isoliere**
litter/garbage **die Abfälle** (pl), **der Müll** (no pl)
natural resources **die Bodenschätze** (pl)
nuclear reprocessing plant **die Atom(müll)wiederaufbereitungsanlage(n)**
nuclear waste **der Atommüll**
ozone **das Ozon**
poison **das Gift(e)**
I poison **ich vergifte**
pollutant **der Schadstoff(e)**
I pollute **ich verschmutze**
pollution **die (Umwelt)verschmutzung**
I predict **ich sage voraus***
I protect **ich beschütze**
recyclable **wiederverwertbar**
I recycle **ich verwerte wieder***
recycled paper **das Recyclingpapier**
recycling skip bin **der Recyclingcontainer(-)**
refuse **der Müll** (no pl)
residue **der Rückstand(¨e), der Rest(e)**
it runs out **es geht aus*, es wird verbraucht**
scrap metal **der Schrott**
solar power **der Solarstrom**
I throw away **ich werfe weg***
waste (domestic) **der Abfall(¨e), der Müll**
waste disposal **die Abfallbeseitigung(en)**

Chemical solvents can cause headaches and allergies.	**Chemische Lösemittel können Kopfschmerzen und Allergien verursachen.**
Artificial fertilizers and insecticides poison the soil and groundwater.	**Kunstdünger und Gifte gegen Schädlinge verseuchen Boden und Grundwasser.**
Young people are committed to environmental causes.	**Junge Leute engagieren sich für den Umwelt- und Naturschutz.**

waste disposal unit **der Müllschlucker**
waste product **das Abfallprodukt(e)**
wind power **die Windenergie**

On the earth

artificial fertilizer **der Künstdünger(-)**
biodegradable **biologisch abbaubar**
deforestation **die Abholzung(en)**
destruction of forests **die Zerstörung der Wälder**
nature reserve **das Naturschutzgebiet(e)**
nitrate **das Nitrat(e)**
pesticide **das Pestizid(e)**
radioactive **radioaktiv**
rain forest **der Regenwald(¨er)**
rubbish/garbage dump **die Abfalldeponie(n)**
soil erosion **die Bodenerosion**
weedkiller **das Unkrautvertilgungsmittel(-)**

In the atmosphere

acid rain **der saure Regen**
aerosol(system) **das Aerosol(e)**
aerosol can **die Spraydose(n)**
air pollution **die Luftverschmutzung(en)**
catalytic convertor **der Katalysator(en)** *(wk)*
CFCs **der FCKW**

emission (of gas) **die Emission(en), das Ausströmen**
it emits **es gibt ab*, es strahlt aus***
exhaust pipe **das Auspuffrohr(e)**
hole in the ozone layer **das Ozonloch(¨er)**
incinerator **der Verbrennungsofen(¨)**
lead-free/unleaded petrol/gasoline **das bleifreie Benzin**
skin cancer **der Hautkrebs**
I spray **ich spritze**
waste gases **die Abgase** *(pl)*

In rivers & seas

drainage **die Kanalisation, die Entwässerung**
drought **die Dürre(n)**
effluent/sewage **das Abwasser(¨)**
flooding **die Überschwemmung(en)**
ground water **das Grundwasser**
oil slick **der Ölteppich(e)**
phosphate **das Phosphat(e)**
sewage **das Abwasser(¨)**
sewage treatment **die Abwasserbehandlung(en)**
water consumption **der Wasserverbrauch**
water level **der Wasserstand**
water pollution **die Wasserverschmutzung**
water supply *(to town)* **die Wasserversorgung**

The development of harmful ozone must be prevented.

Die Entwicklung des schädlichen Ozons muß bekämpft werden.

People talk a lot about ecological farming, alternative energy sources and recycling.

Man spricht viel von ökologischem Landbau, alternativen Energien und Recycling.

Glass is recycled.

Glas wird wiederverwertet.

Government & politics

25a Political life

I abolish **ich schaffe ab***
act (of parliament) **das Gesetz(e)**
administration **die Administration(en)**
I appoint **ich berufe, ich ernenne**
appointment **die Berufung(en)**
asylum-seeker **der Asylbewerber(-)**
it becomes law **es wird (zum) Gesetz**
bill **der Gesetzentwurf(̈e)**
I bring down (government) **ich bringe zu Fall**
citizen **der Bürger(-) [-in]**
civil disobedience **der zivile Ungehorsam, die Unruhe(n)**
civil servant **der/die Beamte (adj/n) [-in]**
civil war **der Bürgerkrieg(e)**
coalition **die Koalition(en)**
it comes into effect **es tritt in Kraft**
common **gemeinsam**
constitution **das Grundgesetz(e), die Verfassung(en)**
cooperation **die Kooperation(en)**
corruption **die Korruption(en)**
county **der Bezirk(e), der Kreis(e)**
coup **der Staatsstreich(e)**
crisis **die Krise(n)**
debate **die Debatte(n)**
decree **der Erlaß (-sse)**
delegate **der/die Delegierte (adj/n)**
I demonstrate **ich demonstriere**
demonstration **die Demonstration(en)**
I discuss **ich diskutiere, ich bespreche**
discussion **die Diskussion(en)**
I dismiss **ich entlasse**
I dissolve **ich löse auf***
district **der Kreis(e), der Bezirk(e)**

I draw up (a bill) **ich setze auf*, ich entwerfe**
duty **die Pflicht(en)**
I emigrate **ich emigriere**
equality **die Gleichheit(en)**
executive **die Exekutive**
executive (government) **exekutiv**
foreign policy **die Auslandspolitik (no pl)**
I form a pact with **ich schließe einen Pakt mit jdm.**
freedom **die Freiheit(en)**
freedom of speech **die Redefreiheit(en)**
federal state **das Bundesland(̈er)**
I govern **ich regiere**
government **die Regierung(en)**
human right **das Menschenrecht(-)**
I introduce (a bill) **ich bringe ein***
judiciary **die Gerichtsbehörden (pl)**
law **das Gesetz(e)**
I lead **ich leite, ich führe**
legislation **die Gesetzgebung(en)**
legislature **die Legislative**
liberty **die Freiheit(en)**
local affairs/politics **die Kommunalpolitik**
local government **die Kreis-/ Stadtverwaltung(en)**
long-term **langfristig**
majority **die Mehrheit(en)**
meeting **dis Sitzung(en)**
middle-class **der Mittelstand (no pl)**
middle-class (person) **der Vertreter der Mittelklasse**
ministry/department **das Ministerium (-ien)**

minority   **die Minderheit(en)**
moderate   **der/die Gemäßigte**
   (adj/n)
   moderate *(adj)* **mäßig**
nation   **die Nation(en), das
   Volk(-̈er)**
national   **national**
national flag   **die
   Nationalflagge(en)**
I nationalize   **ich verstaatliche**
I oppose   **ich bekämpfe**
opposition   **die Opposition(en)**
I organize   **ich organisiere**
I overthrow   **ich stürze**
pact   **der Pakt(e)**
I pass (a bill)   **ich verabschiede
   (ein Gesetz)**
policy   **die Politik**
political   **politisch**
political group   **die Fraktion(en)**
politician   **der Politiker(-) [-in]**
politics   **die Politik**
power   **die Macht(-̈e)**
I privatize   **ich privatisiere**
I protest   **ich protestiere**
public   **die Öffentlichkeit**
   public *(adj)* **öffentlich**
public good   **das öffentliche
   Interesse, das Gemeinwohl**
public opinion   **die öffentliche
   Meinung(en)**
I ratify   **ich bestätige/ratifiziere**
reactionary   **reaktionär**
I reform   **ich reformiere**

reform   **die Reform(en)**
I reject   **ich lehne ab***
I repeal *(an act)* **ich hebe auf***
I represent   **ich vertrete**
I repress   **ich unterdrücke**
I resign   **ich trete zurück***
responsible   **verantwortlich**
responsiblity   **die
   Verantwortlichkeit(en)**
reunification   **die Wiederver-
   einigung(en), die Wende** *(fam)*
I rule   **ich herrsche**
sanction   **die Sanktion(en)**
seat   **der Sitz(e)**
solidarity   **die Solidarität**
speech   **die Rede(n)**
state   **der Staat(en)**
statesman   **der Staatsmann(-̈er)**
I support   **ich unterstütze**
I take power   **ich ergreife die
   Macht**
term of office   **die Wahlperiode(n)**
I throw out a bill   **ich lehne ein
   Gesetz ab***
unconstitutional
   verfassungswidrig
unilateral   **einseitig**
unity   **die Einheit**
veto   **das Veto(s)**
I veto   **ich lege ein Veto ein***
working class   **die
   Arbeiterklasse(n)**
working-class *(person)* **der
   Arbeiter(-) [-in]**

The wall between east and west
was opened in 1989. The
totalitarian communist regime was
removed.

**Die Mauer zwischen Ost und
West wurde 1989 geöffnet. Das
totalitäre, kommunistische
Regime wurde beseitigt.**

German unity was completed in
1990, when the first free elections
for the whole of Germany took
place.

**Die deutsche Einheit wurde 1990
vollendet, als die erste freie
gesamtdeutsche Wahl stattfand.**

➤ WAR 27a; SOCIAL ISSUES 12; THE ECONOMY 14e

25b Elections & political ideology

Elections

ballot   die Abstimmung(en)
ballot box   die Wahlurne(n)
ballot paper   der Wahlzettel(-)
by-election   die Nachwahl(en)
campaign   der Wahlkampf(-e)
candidate   der Kandidat(en) *(wk)*
constituency   der Wahlkreis(e)
I count   ich zähle
I elect   ich wähle
election   die Wahl(en)
electorate   die Wähler *(pl)*
enfranchised   wahlberechtigt
entitled to vote   wahlberechtigt
floating voter   der Wechselwähler(-)
general election   allgemeine
   Wahlen
I go to the polls   ich gehe zur
   Abstimmung/Wahl
I hold an election   ich halte eine
   Wahl ab*
opinion poll   die
   Meinungsumfrage(n)
poll   die Abstimmung(en)
I recount   ich zähle nach*
referendum   das Referendum (-en)
right to vote   das Wahlrecht(e)
I stand for election   ich stelle mich

zur Wahl
suffrage   das Stimmrecht(e)
swing   der
   Meinungsumschwung(-e)
term of office   die
   Regierungszeit(en)
universal suffrage   das allgemeine
   Wahlrecht
vote   die Stimme(n)
I vote (for X)   ich stimme (für X)
voter   der Wähler(-) [-in]

Political ideology

anarchist   der Anarchist(en) *(wk)* [-
   in]
anarchy   die Anarchie(n)
anti-Semitic   antisemistisch
anti-Semitism   der Antisemitismus
aristocracy   die Aristokratie
aristocrat   der Aristokrat(en) *(wk)*
   [-in]
aristocratic   aristokratisch
capitalism   der Kapitalismus
capitalist   der Kapitalist(en) *(wk)*
center   die Mitte
communism   der Kommunismus
communist   der Kommunist(en)
   (wk) [-in]

The members of parliament are elected for four years. The 5% clause means that a party must get 5% of votes before it gets a seat in parliament.

Die Mitglieder des Bundestages werden auf vier Jahre gewählt. Die "Fünf-Prozent-Klausel" bedeutet, daß eine Partei fünf Prozent der Stimmen bekommen muß, bevor sie einen Sitz im Parlament bekommt.

– How do you vote? – I have always voted Christian-Democrat.

– Wie wählst du? – Ich wähle seit jeher die Christdemokraten.

Since reunification we can freely visit the West.

Seit der Wende können wir den Westen uneingeschränkt besuchen.

conservatism **der Konservatismus**
conservative **konservativ**
democracy **die Demokratie(n)**
democrat **der Demokrat(en)** *(wk)* **[-in]**
democratic **demokratisch**
duke **der Herzog(-̈e) [-̈in]**
empire **das Reich(e)**
emperor/empress **der Kaiser(-) [-in]**
extremist **der Extremist(en)** *(wk)* **[-in]**
far left **linksradikal/-extrem**
far right **rechtsradikal/-extrem**
fascism **der Faschismus**
fascist **der Faschist(en) [-in]**
I gain independence **ich erlange die Unabhängigkeit**
ideology **die Ideologie(n)**
imperialism **der Imperialismus**
imperialist **der Imperialist(en)** *(wk)*
independence **die Unabhängigkeit**
independent **unabhängig**
king **der König(e)**
Labour party *(U.K.)* **die Labour Partei**
left **links**
left wing **der linke Flügel**
liberal **liberal**

Liberal Democrat **der Liberaldemokrat(en)** *(wk)* **[-in]**
liberalism **der Liberalismus**
Liberals **die Liberalen** *(pl)*
marxism **der Marxismus**
marxist **der Marxist(en)** *(wk)*
monarchy **die Monarchie(n)**
nationalism **der Nationalismus**
nationalist **der Nationalist(en)** *(wk)*
Nazi **der Nazi(s)**
patriotic **patriotisch**
patriotism **der Patriotismus**
prince **der Prinz(en)** *(wk)*
princess **die Prinzessin(nen)**
queen **die Königin(nen)**
radicalism **der Radikalismus**
radical **radikal**
republic **die Republik(en)**
republican **der Republikaner(-) [-in]**
republican *(adj)* **republikanisch**
republicanism **der Republikanismus**
revolutionary **revolutionär**
right **rechts**
right wing **der rechte Flügel**
royal **königlich**
royalist **royalistisch**
socialism **der Sozialismus**
Socialist **der Sozialist(en)**
socialist *(adj)* **sozialistisch**

Young Germans are not very interested in politics. Those who belong to the Green Party or to the extreme left parties are politically active.

Deutsche Jugendliche sind politisch nicht stark engagiert. Anhänger der Grünen oder der linksextremen Parteien sind politisch aktiv.

The chancellor is elected by Parliament. In the 12th Parliament the CDU/CSU/FDP coalition was in power.

Der Bundeskanzler wird vom Bundestag gewählt. Im 12. Deutschen Bundestag stand die CDU/CSU/FDP Koalition an der Macht.

➤ POLITICAL INSTITUTIONS, POLITICIANS App.25b

Crime & justice

26a Crime

accomplice **der Komplize(n)** *(wk)* **[-in]**

alias **der Deckname(n)** *(wk)*

armed **bewaffnet**

arson **die Brandstiftung**

assault **der Überfall(ˉe)**

assault and battery **die Körperverletzung**

attack **das Attentat(e)**

battered baby **das mißhandelte Baby**

bomb attack **der Bombenanschlag(ˉe)**

   fire bomb attack **der Brandanschlag(ˉe)**

bribery **die Bestechung**

burglar **der Einbrecher(-) [-in]**

burglary **der Einbruch(ˉe)**

I burgle/burglarize **ich breche ein***

car theft **der Autodiebstahl(ˉe)**

child abuse **die Kindesmißhandlung**

I come to blows **ich schlage mich (mit** +dat)

I commit **ich begehe**

crime **das Verbrechen(-)**

crime rate **die Kriminalitätsrate(n)**

crime wave **die Verbrechenswelle(n)**

criminal **der Verbrecher(-) [-in]**

I deceive **ich täusche**

delinquency **die Kriminalität**

drug abuse **der Drogenmißbrauch**

drug addict **der/die Drogenabhängige** *(adj/n)*

drug baron **der Drogenbaron(e)**

drug dealer **der Drogenhändler(-)**

drug pusher **der Dealer(-)**

drugs **die Drogen**

drug-trafficking **der Drogenhandel**

I embezzle **ich unterschlage**

embezzlement **die Unterschlagung(en)**

espionage **die Spionage**

extortion **die Erpressung(en)**

I fight **ich streite, ich kämpfe**

fight **der Streit(e), der Kampf(ˉe)**

firearm **die Schußwaffe(n)**

I forge **ich fälsche**

forged **gefälscht**

forgery **die Fälschung(en)**

fraud **der Betrug(ˉe)**

gang **die Bande(n)**

gang warfare **der Bandenkrieg(e)**

grievous bodily harm (GBH) **die schwere Körperverletzung(en)**

gun **die Schußwaffe(n)**

Carlos was captured in the Sudan. He was the internationally most wanted terrorist.

He had many aliases and he was on the run. He confessed to one bomb attack.

Carlos wurde im Sudan festgenommen. Er war der international meistgesuchte Terrorist.

Er trug viele Decknamen und war auf der Flucht. Er bekannte sich zu einem Bombenanschlag.

---

handbag snatching **der Taschendiebstahl(¨e)**
handcuffs **die Handschellen** *(pl)*
Help! **Hilfe!**
I hi-jack **ich entführe**
hi-jacker **der Entführer(-)**
hold-up **die Überfall(¨e)**
hooker **die Nutte(n)**
hostage **die Geisel(n)**
illegal **illegal**
I importune/harass **ich belästige**
I injure/wound **ich verletze**
I joy ride **ich joy-ride**
joy riding **das Joy-Riding**
I kidnap **ich entführe, ich kidnappe**
kidnapper **der Entführer(-), der Kidnapper(-)**
kidnapping **die Entführung, das Kidnapping**
I kill **ich töte, ich ermorde**
killer **der Mörder(-) [-in]**
knife **das Messer(-)**
I knife **ich ersteche**
knifing **die Messerstecherei(en)**
legal **legal**
living off immoral earnings **die Zuhälterei**
mafia **die Mafia**
I mug **ich raube ... aus*, ich überfalle**
mugger **der Straßenräuber(-)**
mugging **der Straßenraub** *(no pl)*
murder **der Mord(e)**
I murder **ich ermorde**
murderer **der Mörder(-)**
I offend **ich werde straffällig**

pickpocket **der Taschendieb(e)**
pickpocketing **der Taschendiebstahl(¨e)**
pimp **der Zuhälter(-)**
pimping **die Zuhälterei**
poison **das Gift(e)**
I poison **ich vergifte**
I procure **ich beschaffe**
prostitute **der/die Prostituierte** *(adj/n)*
prostitution **die Prostitution**
I rape **ich vergewaltige**
rape **die Vergewaltigung(en)**
receiver **der Hehler(-) [-in]**
reprisals **die Vergeltung(en)**
I shoot at **ich beschieße**
shop-lifting **der Ladendiebstahl(¨e)**
slander **die Verleumdung(en)**
I smuggle **ich schmuggle**
spy **der Spion(e) [-in]**
I steal **ich stehle**
stolen goods **das Diebesgut**
tax evasion **die Steuerhinterziehung(en)**
terrorist **der Terrorist(en)** *(wk)*
torture **die Folter(n)**
I torture **ich foltere**
theft **der Diebstahl(¨e)**
thief **der Dieb(e)**
traffic offence/violation **der Verkehrsverstoß (-e)**
I traffick **ich schiebe**
underworld **die Unterwelt(en)**
vandalism **der Vandalismus**
victim **das Opfer(-)**

Plutonium smugglers demand millions of dollars.
Plutonium-Schmuggler verlangen Millionen von Dollar.

They were caught red-handed.
Sie wurden auf frischer Tat ertappt.

We went to the police.
Wir sind zur Polizei gegangen.

▶ WEAPONS 27b; ADDICTION & VIOLENCE 12d

CRIME & JUSTICE

26b Trial

accusation **die Anklage(n)**
I accuse **ich klage ... an***
accused person **der/die Angeklagte** *(adj/n)*
I acquit **ich spreche jdn. frei***
appeal **der Einspruch(-e)**
I appeal **ich erhebe Einspruch**
I appear in court **ich erscheine vor Gericht**
case **der Fall(-e)**
compensation **die Entschädigung(en)**
confession **das Geständnis(se)**
I confess **ich gestehe**
I convince **ich überzeuge**
costs **die Kosten** *(pl)*
counsel for the defense **der Verteidiger(-) [-in]**
court **das Gericht(e)**
court of appeal **das Berufungsgericht(e)**
courtroom **der Gerichtssaal (-säle)**
I cross-question **ich verhöre**
I debate **ich debattiere**
defence/defense **die Verteidigung**
I defend (myself) **ich verteidige (mich)**
defendant **der/die Angeklagte** *(adj/n)*
diminished responsibility/insanity **verminderte Zurechnungsfähigkeit**
I disagree **ich stimme nicht überein***

I discuss **ich diskutiere**
dock **die Anklagebank(-e)**
I enquire/examine **ich untersuche**
evidence **die Aussage(n), der Beweis(e)**
examining magistrate **der Untersuchungsrichter(-)**
extenuating circumstances **mildernde Umstände** *(pl)*
I extradite **ich liefere aus***
eyewitness **der Augenzeuge(n)** *(wk)* **[-in]**
I find guilty **ich befinde für schuldig, ich spreche jdn. schuldig**
I give evidence **ich bezeuge**
I give evidence **ich sage für jdn. aus***
guilt **die Schuld**
guilty **schuldig**
high court of appeal **die höchste Berufungsinstanz(en)**
I impeach **ich klage an***
impeachment **die Anfechtung(en), die Anklage(n)**
indictment **die Anklageschrift(en)**
innocence **die Unschuld**
innocent **unschuldig**
judge **der Richter(-) [-in]**
juror **der/die Geschworene** *(adj/n)*
jury **die Geschworenen** *(pl)*
jury box **die Geschworenenbank(-e)**
justice **die Gerechtigkeit**
lawsuit **der Prozeß (-sse)**

What's the case for the prosecution?

Worauf stützt sich die Anklage?

We haven't enough evidence.

Wir haben nicht genug Beweise.

The police search was without result.

Die Polizeifahndung blieb ohne Erfolg.

lawyer **der Rechtsanwalt(-̈e)**
leniency **die Nachsichtigkeit(en)**
life imprisonment **die lebenslängliche Haft** *(no pl)*
litigation **der Prozeß (-sse)**
magistrate/Justice of Peace **der (Friedens)richter(-) [-in]**
magistrate's court/court **das Gericht(e)**
mercy **die Gnade**
minor offence **das leichte Vergehen(-)**
miscarriage of justice **das Fehlurteil(e)**
motive **das Motiv(e)**
not guilty **nicht schuldig**
oath **der Eid(e), der Schwur(-̈e)**
offence **die Straftat(en), das Vergehen(-)**
on remand/in detention **in Untersuchungshaft**
I pass judgement **ich fälle das Urteil**
perjury **der Meineid** *(no pl)*
plea **das Plädoyer(s)**
plea bargaining **die Verhandlung(en)**
I plead guilty/not guilty **ich bekenne mich schuldig/ unschuldig**
premeditation **der Vorsatz**
I prosecute **ich verfolge**
prosecution **die strafrechtliche Verfolgung**
public prosecutor **der Staatsanwalt(-̈e)**
district attorney **der Bezirksstaatsanwalt(-̈e)**

public prosecutor's office **die Staatsanwaltskanzlei**
I question **ich befrage**
I interrogate **ich verhöre**
retrial **die Wiederaufnahme des Verfahrens**
I rescue **ich rette**
I reward **ich belohne**
speech for the defence/defense **die Verteidigung**
I stand accused **ich stehe angeklagt**
I stand bail (for someone) **ich bürge (für jdn.)**
statement **die Aussage(n)**
I sue/I take to court **ich verklage, ich bringe vor Gericht**
I sue for divorce **ich reiche die Scheidung ein***
summons **die Vorladung(en)**
I suspect **ich verdächtige**
suspect **der/die Verdächtige** *(adj/n)*
Supreme Court **der Oberste Gerichtshof**
sustained! **stattgegeben!**
I swear **ich schwöre**
I take legal proceedings **ich bringe vor Gericht**
I take prisoner **ich nehme gefangen**
trial **das Verfahren(-)**
unanimous **einstimmig**
verdict **das Urteil(e)**
I witness **ich bezeuge**
witness **der Zeuge(n)** *(wk)* **[-in]**
witness box **der Zeugenstand**
writ **der Haftbefehl(e)**

– They've caught her. She pleaded guilty.
– What was the verdict?
– She went to prison. She got life.

– **Sie wurde erwischt/gefaßt. Sie hat sich schuldig bekannt.**
– **Wie lautete das Urteil?**
– **Sie kam ins Gefängnis. Sie hat lebenslänglich bekommen.**

26c Punishment & crime prevention

Punishment

confinement   **die Haft**
   in solitary confinement   **die Einzelhaft**
I convict   **ich erkläre jdn. für schuldig**
convict   **der Sträfling(e)**
death penalty   **die Todesstrafe(n)**
I deport   **ich weise aus***
I escape   **ich fliehe aus** +dat, **ich entkomme** +dat
fine   **die Geldstrafe(n)**
I fine   **ich belege mit einer Geldstrafe**
he was fined   **er mußte eine Strafe bezahlen**
I free   **ich spreche frei***
hard labour/labor   **die Zwangsarbeit**
I imprison   **ich inhaftiere**
jail sentence   **die Gefängnisstrafe(n)**
prison   **das Gefängnis(se)**
prisoner   **der/die Gefangene** *(adj/n)*
I punish   **ich bestrafe**
punishment   **die Bestrafung(en), die Strafe(n)**
I release on bail   **ich lasse jdn. gegen Kaution frei***
I reprieve   **ich begnadige**
I sentence to death   **ich verurteile zum Tode**
I serve a sentence   **ich sitze eine Strafe ab***

sentence   **die Strafe(n)**
severity   **die Strenge**
suspended sentence   **(zur Bewährung) ausgesetztes Urteil**

Crime prevention

alarm   **der Alarm(e), die Sicherung(en)**
   burglar alarm   **die Alarmanlage(n)**
   car alarm   **die Autosicherung(en)**
autopsy   **die Autopsie(n)**
arrest   **die Verhaftung(en)**
I arrest   **ich verhafte, ich stelle**
baton   **der Knüppel(-)**
(hearing) in camera   **hinter verschlossenen Türen**
I break the law   **ich breche das Gesetz**
I catch   **ich ertappe, ich fange**
chief of police   **der Polizeichef(s)**
civil law   **das Zivilrecht**
clue   **die Spur(en)**
crime prevention   **die Verbrechensverhütung**
criminal law   **das Strafgesetz(e)**
I have a criminal record   **ich bin vorbestraft**
customs   **der Zoll** *(no pl)*
customs officer   **der Zollbeamte(n)** *(adj/n)* **[-in]**
deportation   **die Abschiebung(en)**

The accused has no previous convictions. He was given a fine.

His friend is on probation.

Rainer has been inside.

Der Angelelagle ist nicht vorbestraft. Er wurde zu einer Geldstrafe verurteilt.

Sein Freund steht unter Bewährungsaufsicht.

Rainer hat gesessen.

---

detective   **der Detektiv(e) [-in]**
drugs raid   **die Drogenrazzia (-ien)**
drugs squad   **die Drogenfahndungsbehörde(n)**
enquiry   **die Untersuchung(en), die Nachforschung(en)**
error   **der Fehler(-)**
escape   **die Flucht(en)**
I escape (from)   **ich flüchte (vor +dat)**
examination/interrogation   **das Verhör(e)**
I examine   **ich verhöre**
extradition   **die Auslieferung(en)**
fingerprint   **der Fingerabdruck(-̈e)**
fugitive   **der Flüchtling(e)**
guard dog   **der Wachhund(e)**
handcuff   **die Handschelle(n)**
I handcuff   **ich lege die Handschellen an***
identikit/photofit picture   **das Phantombild(er)**
I inform the police   **ich verständige die Polizei**
informer   **der Informant** *(wk)* **[-in]**
interview   **die Befragung(en)**
I interview   **ich befrage**
I investigate   **ich untersuche**
investigation   **die Ermittlungen** *(pl)*
investigator   **der Ermittler**
   private investigator   **der Privatdetektiv(e)**
key   **der Schlüssel(-)**
law   **das Gesetz(e)**

law and order   **die öffentliche Ordnung**
lock   **das Schloß (-̈sser)**
I lock   **ich schließe ab***
padlock   **das Vorhängeschloß (-̈sser)**
plain-clothes police   **der Polizist** *(wk)* **in Zivil**
police   **die Polizei**
police headquarters   **das Polizeihauptquartier(e)**
police informer   **der Polizeispitzel(-)**
police station   **das Polizeirevier(e)**
policeman   **der Polizist(en)** *(wk)*
policewoman   **die Polizistin(nen)**
I question   **ich vernehme**
ransom   **das Lösegeld(er)**
reward   **die Belohnung(en)**
riot police   **das Überfallkommando(s)**
search   **die Fahndung(en)**
secret service   **der Geheimdienst(e)**
security   **die Sicherheit**
security firm   **der Sicherheitsdienst(e)**
speed trap   **die Radarfalle(n)**
station   **das Revier(e)**
traffic police   **die Verkehrspolizei**
traffic warden   **die Politesse(n)**
truncheon   **der Polizeiknüppel(-)**
warrant   **der Haftbefehl(e)**
   search warrant   **der Durchsuchungsbefehl(e)**

He was declared guilty and given a suspended sentence of two years.   **Er wurde schuldig gesprochen und zu zwei Jahren Gefängnis mit Bewährung verurteilt.**

The witness is under police protection.   **Der Zeuge steht unter Polizeischutz.**

There's a reward for the finder.   **Es gibt einen Finderlohn.**

27 War & peace

27a War

I abduct **ich entführe**
aggression **die Aggression(en)**
air force **die Luftwaffe(n)**
airlift **die Luftbrücke(n)**
air raid **der Luftangriff(e)**
air-raid shelter **der Luftschutzbunker(-)**
air-raid warning **der Luftschutzalarm(e)**
ambush **der Hinterhalt(e)**
antiaircraft **die Flugabwehr**
army **die Armee(n), das Heer(e)**
I assassinate **ich ermorde**
assault **der Angriff(e)**
atomic **Atom-**
I attack **ich greife an***
attack **der Angriff(e)**
barracks **die Kaserne(n)**
battle **die Schlacht(en)**
battlefield **das Schlachtfeld(er)**
blast **die Explosion(en)**
I blockade **ich blockiere**
blockade **die Blockade(n)**
I blow up **ich sprenge**
brave **mutig**
war breaks out **der Krieg bricht aus***
I call up **ich berufe ein***
camp **das Lager(-)**
campaign **der Feldzug(ẅe)**
I capture **ich nehme gefangen***
cause **die Ursache(n)**
I claim responsibility for **ich erkläre mich für verantwortlich**
I commit **ich begehe**
conflict **der Konflikt(e)**
confrontation **die Konfrontation(en)**
conquest **die Eroberung(en)**
I contaminate **ich verseuche**

conventional (weapon) **konventionell (Waffen)**
court-marshal **das Kriegsgericht(e)**
cowardly **feige**
the plane crashes **das Flugzeug stürzt ab***
I crush (opposition) **ich vernichte (den Gegner)**
I declare (war) **ich erkläre (den Krieg)**
defeat **die Niederlage(n)**
I defeat **ich schlage**
defence/defense **die Verteidigung(en)**
I defend **ich verteidige**
I destroy **ich zerstöre**
I detain **ich verhafte**
I detect **ich entdecke**
devastating **verheerend**
enemy **der Feind(e)**
espionage **die Spionage(n)**
ethnic cleansing **die ethnische Säuberung(en)**
I evacuate **ich evakuiere**
evacuation **die Evakuierung(en)**
I fight a battle **ich führe einen Kampf**
I fight off **ich wehre ab***
I flee (from) **ich fliehe (vor** +dat)
front **die Front(en)**
guerrilla warfare **der Guerrillakrieg(e)**
harmful **schädlich**
headquarters **das Hauptquartier(e)**
hostilities **die Feindseligkeiten** (pl)
I interrogate **ich verhöre**
interrogation **das Verhör(e)**
I intervene **ich schreite ein***

intervention **das Eingreifen**
intimidation **die Einschüchterung(en)**
I invade **ich überfalle**
invasion **die Invasion(en)**
I issue an ultimatum **ich stelle ein Ultimatum**
manoeuvres/maneuvers **das Manöver(-)**
massacre **das Massaker(-)**
missing in action **vermißt**
military service **der Kriegsdienst(e)**
mobilization **die Mobilmachung(en)**
I mobilize **ich mobilisiere**
morale **die Moral**
multilateral **multilateral**
navy **die Kriegsmarine(n)**
nuclear **Kern-**
occupation **die Besetzung(en)**
I occupy **ich besetzte**
offensive **die Offensive(n)**
I patrol **ich patrouilliere**
peace **der Frieden**
propaganda **die Propaganda**
I protect (from) **ich schütze (vor +dat)**
I provoke **ich provoziere**
it rages **es tobt**
raid **der Angriff(e)**
reinforcements **die Verstärkung(en)**
reprisals **die Repressalie(n)**
I resist **ich leiste Widerstand**

resistance **der Widerstand(¨e)**
retreat **der Rückzug(¨e)**
review **die Parade(n)**
I revolt **ich rebelliere**
revolution **die Revolution(en)**
riot **der Aufruhr(e)**
rubble **die Trümmer** *(pl)*
security check **die Sicherheitskontrolle(n)**
shelter **die Sicherheit**
siege **die Belagerung(en)**
skirmish **das Gefecht(e)**
I spy **ich spioniere**
I start a war **ich fange einen Krieg an***
strategy **die Strategie(n)**
strike power **die Schlagkraft(¨e)**
the vessel submerges/surfaces **das Schiff taucht unter*/auf***
survival **das Überleben**
tactics **die Taktik** *(no pl)*
terrorist attack **der Terroranschlag(¨e)**
I threaten **ich drohe** +dat
trench **der Schützengraben(¨)**
underground **die Untergrundbewegung(en)**
victory **der Sieg(e)**
war-mongering **die Kriegshetze**
I win **ich gewinne**
wound **die Wunde(n)**
I wound **ich verwunde, ich verletze**

The event which has most marked the twentieth century is the Second World War. Hitler invaded Poland on September 1, 1939.

Two days later, Britain and France declared war on Germany.

Der 2. Weltkrieg war das markierendste Ereignis des 20. Jahrhunderts. Hitler überfiel Polen am 1. September 1939.

Zwei Tage später erklärten Großbritannien und Frankreich Deutschland den Krieg.

➤ INTERNATIONAL RELATIONS 27c

27b Military personnel & weaponry

Military personnel

aggressor der Aggressor(en)
ally der/die Verbündete *(adj/n)*
Allies die Alliierten *(pl)*
archer der Bogenschütze(n) *(wk)*
assassin der Mörder(-) [-in]
casualty *(dead)* das Opfer(-)
cavalry die Kavallerie(n)
civilian der Zivilist(en) *(wk)*
commandos die Kommandos *(pl)*
conscientious objector der
  Kriegsdienstverweigerer(-)
conscript der/die Wehrpflichtige
  (adj/n)
convoy der Konvoi(s)
deserter der Deserteur(e)
division die Division(en)
foot soldier der Infanterist(en) *(wk)*
general der General(-̈e)
guard die Wache(n)
guerrilla der Guerrilla(s), der
  Freischärler(-)
hostage die Geisel(n)
infantry die Infanterie(n)
intelligence officer der
  Nachrichtenoffizier(e)
marine(s) die Marine(n)
NCO der Unteroffizier(e)
orderly der Sanitäter(-)
parachutist der
  Fallschirmspringer(-) [-in]
prisoner of war der/die
  Kriegsgefangene *(adj/n)*
rank der Rang(-̈e)
rebel der Rebell(en) *(wk)*
recruit der Rekrut(e) *(wk)*
regiment das Regiment(e)
seaman/sailor der Seemann
  (-leute)
Secretary of War der
  Kriegsminister(-)
secret agent der Geheimagent(en)
  (wk)
sentry der Wachposten(-)

sniper der Scharfschütze(n) *(wk)*
soldier der Soldat(en) *(wk)*
spy der Spion(e) [-in]
squadron das Schwadron(e)
staff das Personal, der Stab(-̈e)
terrorist der Terrorist(en) *(wk)*
traitor der Verräter(-) [-in]
troop die Truppe(n)
victor der Sieger(-)
War Minister der Kriegs-
  minister(-)

Weaponry

I aim (at) ich ziele (auf +acc)
aircraft carrier der
  Flugzeugträger(-)
ammunition die Munition(en)
armaments die Ausrüstung(en)
armored car der Panzerwagen(-)
arms die Waffen *(pl)*
arms trade der Waffenhandel
arms race das Wettrüsten
artillery die Artillerie(n)
bacteriological bakteriologisch
barbed wire der Stacheldraht(-̈e)
bayonet das Bajonett(e)
aerial bombing der Luftangriff(e)
I bomb(ard) ich bombardiere
bomb die Bombe(n)
bomb alert der Bombenalarm(e)
bombardment die
  Bombardierung(en)
bomber *(aircraft)* der Bomber(-)
bullet die Kugel(n)
car bomb die Autobombe(n)
chemical warfare die chemische
  Kriegsführung
chemical weapon die chemische
  Waffe(n)
crossbow die (Stand)armbrust(-̈e)
destroyer *(ship)* der Zerstörer(-)
I execute ich richte hin*
I explode a bomb ich bringe eine
  Bombe zur Explosion

explosive **der Sprengstoff(e)**
explosive *(adj)* **explosiv**
fallout **der Ausfall** *(no pl)*
fighter plane **das Jagdflugzeug(e)**
I fire (at) **ich feure (auf** +acc)**, ich**
verschieße
frigate **die Fregatte(n)**
gas **das Gas(e)**
gas attack **der Gasangriff(e)**
gun **die Schußwaffe(n)**
hand-grenade **die Handgranate(n)**
H-bomb **die Wasserstoffbombe(n)**
I hit **ich treffe**
jet *(plane)* **der Jet(s)**
I kill **ich töte, ich bringe ums**
Leben
knife **das Messer(-)**
laser **der Laser(-)**
letter bomb **die Briefbombe(n)**
machine gun **das**
Maschinengewehr(e)
minefield **das Minenfeld(er)**
mine sweeper **das**
Minensuchboot(e)
missile **die Rakete(n)**
missile launcher **der**
Raketenwerfer(-)
mortar **der Minenwerfer(-)**
neutron bomb **die**
Neutronenbombe(n)
nuclear warfare **der Atomkrieg(e)**
nuclear warhead **der**
Nuklearsprengkopf(̈e)
pistol **die Pistole(n)**

poison gas **das Giftgas(e)**
radar **der Radar** *(no pl)*
radar screen **der Radarschirm(e)**
radiation **die Strahlung(en)**
radiation sickness **die**
Strahlenkrankheit(en)
radioactive **radioaktiv**
revolver **der Revolver(-)**
rifle **das Gewehr(e)**
rocket **die Rakete(n)**
rocket attack **der Raketenangriff(e)**
I sabotage **ich sabotiere**
shell **die Granate(n)**
I shoot at **ich beschieße**
I shoot dead **ich erschieße**
shotgun **die Schrotflinte(n)**
shrapnel **das Schrapnell** *(no pl)*
I sink the ship **ich versenke das**
Schiff
the ship sinks **das Schiff sinkt**
I stockpile **ich lege Vorräte an***
submachine gun **die**
Maschinenpistole(n)
submarine **das U-Boot(e)**
tank **der Panzer(-)**
target **das Ziel(e)**
I test **ich prüfe, ich teste**
torpedo **der Torpedo(s)**
torpedo attack **der**
Torpedoangriff(e)
I torpedo **ich torpediere**
warship **das Kriegsschiff(e)**
weapon **die Waffe(n)**

War is waged on the civil
population.

**Der Krieg wird gegen die
Zivilbevölkerung geführt.**

Conventional weapons do not
deter.

**Konventionelle Waffen schrecken
nicht ab.**

Six people were wounded when a
shell landed in the old town.

**Sechs Leute wurden verwundet,
als eine Granate in die Altstadt
einschlug.**

➤ CRIME 26a

27c Peace & international relations

Peace

I ban   **ich verbiete**
cease-fire   **der Waffenstillstand(¨e)**
control   **die Kontrolle(n)**
I demobilize   **ich demobilisiere**
deterrent   **das Abschreckungsmittel(-)**
I diminish tension   **ich entspanne
  die Lage**
disarmament   **die Abrüstung(en)**
exchanges of information   **der
  Informationsaustausch(e)**
Federal Armed Forces service   **der
  Bundeswehrdienst**
free   **frei**
I free   **ich befreie**
freedom   **die Freiheit(en)**
human rights   **die Menschenrechte**
  (pl)
I make peace   **ich schließe den
  Frieden**
I mediate   **ich vermittle**
I negotiate   **ich verhandle**
negotiation   **die Verhandlung(en)**
neutral   **neutral**
neutrality   **die Neutralität**
pacifist   **der Pazifist(en)** (wk)
pacifism   **der Pazifismus**
peace plan   **der Friedensplan(¨e)**

peace protester   **der
  Friedensdemonstrant(en)** (wk)
peace talks   **die
  Friedensverhandlung(en)**
peace-keeping force   **die
  Friedenstruppen** (pl)
I ratify (treaty)   **ich ratifiziere**
surrender   **die Kapitulation(en)**
I surrender   **ich kapituliere**
test ban   **der Teststopp(s)**
treaty   **der Vertrag(¨e), das
  Abkommen(-)**
uncommitted   **nicht
  verpflichtet/ungebunden**
victory   **der Sieg(e)**

International relations

aid   **die (Entwicklungs)hilfe**
ambassador   **der Botschafter(-) [-in]**
arms limitation   **die
  Rüstungsbegrenzung**
attaché   **der Attaché(s)**
citizen   **der Staatsbürger(-) [-in]**
citizenship   **die Staatsbürgerschaft**
consul   **der Konsul(n) [-in]**
consulate   **das Konsulat(e)**
developing country   **das
  Entwicklungsland(¨er)**

We are looking for a compromise.

**Wir suchen nach einem
Kompromiß.**

Thc conditions in the ultimatum
must be respected.

**Die Bedingungen des
Ultimatums müssen beachtet
werden.**

The areas which had been
annexed had to be given back.

**Die Gebiete, die erobert worden
waren, mußten zurückgegeben
werden.**

The use of UN forces is
demanded.

**Man verlangt den Einsatz der
UN-Truppen.**

---

diplomacy   **die Diplomatie**
diplomat   **der Diplomat(en)** *(wk)*
diplomatic immunity   **die Immunität**
embassy   **die Botschaft(en)**
emergency aid   **die Nothilfe**
envoy   **der/die Gesandte** *(adj/n)*
famine   **die Hungersnot(-̈e)**
foreign affairs   **die Außenpolitik**
foreign aid   **die Auslandshilfe**
foreigner   **der Ausländer(-) [-in]**
I join *(organization)*   **ich trete** +dat
bei*
national security   **die Staatssicherheit**
non-aligned   **blockfrei**
overseas   **in Übersee**
relief organization   **die Hilfsorganisation(en)**
relief supplies   **die Hilfsgüter** *(pl)*
I represent   **ich vertrete**
sanctions   **die Sanktion(en)**
summit meeting   **die Gipfelkonferenz(en)**
Third World   **die Dritte Welt**

Trade

agricultural policy   **die Agrarpolitik**
balance of payments   **die Zahlungsbilanz(en)**

balance of trade   **die Handelsbilanz(en)**
Common market   **die EG, der Binnenmarkt(-̈e)**
currency   **die Währung(en)**
customs   **der Einfuhrzoll(-̈e)**
customs union   **die Zollunion(en)**
exchange rate   **der Wechselkurs(e)**
exports   **die Ausfuhr** *(no pl)*
floating currency   **die freigegebene Währung(en)**
it floats   **es schwebt, es variiert**
foreign exchange   **die Devisen** *(pl)*
foreign investment   **die ausländischen Investition(en)**
free-trade zone   **die Freie Handelszone(n)**
gap between rich and poor   **der Unterschied(e) zwischen Arm und Reich**
GNP (gross national product)   **das Bruttosozialprodukt(e)**
import control   **die Importkontrolle(n)**
import   **die Einfuhr** *(no pl)*
tariff barriers   **die Tarifschranken** *(pl)*
tariff   **der (Zoll)tarif(e)**
trade gap *(negative)*   **die Handelsspanne(n)**

An intervention by NATO could bring peace closer or extend the war.

Eine Intervention der Nato könnte den Frieden näher bringen oder den Krieg verlängern.

There is no foreign exchange to pay for German goods.

Die Devisen fehlen, um deutsche Lieferungen zu bezahlen.

Trade with the East is to be encouraged.

Der Osthandel soll gefördert werden.

GATT (General Agreement on Tariffs and Trade)

das Allgemeine Zoll- und Handelsabkommen

C
SUBJECT INDEX

Subject index

* Appendices are numbered by most relevant Vocabulary.

tangent   die Tangente(n)
trigonometry   die Trigonometrie
variable   die Variable(n)
vector   der Vektor(en)

5b Parts of the body

ankle   der Knöchel(-), das Fußgelenk(e)
appendix   der Blinddarm(¨e)
arm   der Arm(e)
artery   die Arterie(n)
back   der Rücken(-)
backbone   das Rückgrat(e)
bladder   die Blase(n)
blood   das Blut *(no pl)*
blood pressure   der Blutdruck(¨e)
body   der Körper(-)
bone   der Knochen(-)
bowel   der Darm(¨e)
brain   das Gehirn(e)
breast   die Brust(¨e)
buttocks   das Gesäß(e)
cheek   die Backe(n), die Wange(n)
chest   der Brustkorb(¨e)
chin   das Kinn(e)
ear   das Ohr(en)
elbow   der Ellbogen(¨/)
eye   das Auge(n)
eyeball   der Augapfel(¨)
eyebrow   die Augenbraue(n)
eyelash   die Augenwimper(n)
eyelid   das Augenlid(er)
face   das Gesicht(er)
finger   der Finger(-)
fingernail   der Fingernagel(¨)
foot   der Fuß(¨e)
forehead   die Stirn(en)
genitalia   die Genitalien *(pl)*
gland   die Drüse(n)
hair   das Haar(e)
hand   die Hand(¨e)
head   der Kopf(¨e)
heart   das Herz(en)
hip   die Hüfte(n)
hormone   das Hormon(e)
index finger   der Zeigefinger(-)
jaw   der Kiefer(-)
kidney   die Niere(n)

knee   das Knie(-)
knuckle   der (Finger)knöchel(-)
leg   das Bein(e)
lip   die Lippe(n)
liver   die Leber(n)
lung   die Lunge(n)
mouth   der Mund(¨er)
muscle   der Muskel(n)
nape of neck   der Nacken(-)
neck   der Hals(¨e)
nerve   der Nerv(en)
nervous system   das Nervensystem(e)
nose   die Nase(n)
nostril   das Nasenloch(¨er)
organ   das Organ(e)
penis   der Penis(se/Penes)
rib   die Rippe(n)
shoulder   die Schulter(n)
skin   die Haut(¨e)
stomach   der Magen(/ ¨)
thigh   der Schenkel(-)
throat   der Hals(¨e)
thumb   der Daumen(-)
toe   die Zehe(n)
tongue   die Zunge(n)
tonsil   die Mandel(n)
tooth   der Zahn(¨e)
vagina   die Scheide(n)
vein   die Vene(n)
waist   die Taille(n)
womb   die Gebärmutter(¨)
wrist   das Handgelenk(e)

6a Human characteristics*

absentminded(ness)   zerstreut, die
   Zerstreutheit
active   aktiv
adaptable   anpassungsfähig
adaptability   die Anpassungsfähigkeit
affectionate   liebevoll
aggression   die Aggression
aggressive   aggressiv
ambition   der Ehrgeiz, die
   Ambition(en)
ambitious   ehrgeizig
amusing   amüsant, lustig
anxious   ängstlich

---

* German negative forms are indicated where possible by **(in)** or **(un)**.

6a Human characteristics (cont.)

anxiety   **die Ängstlichkeit**

arrogance   **die Arroganz**

arrogant   **arrogant**

artistic   **künstlerisch**

attractive   **attraktiv**

boring   **langweilig**

brave   **mutig, tapfer**

careless(ness)   **unvorsichtig, die Unvorsichtigkeit**

caution   **die Vorsichtigkeit**

cautious   **vorsichtig**

charm   **der Charme** *(no pl)*

cheek   **die Unverschämtheit(en)**

cheeky   **frech**

cold   **kalt**

comic   **lustig**

confidence   **das Selbstvertrauen**

conscientious   **gewissenhaft**

courage   **der Mut**

courteous   **höflich**

courtesy   **die Höflichkeit**

cowardly   **feig, feige**

creative (-ity)   **kreativ, die Kreativität**

critical   **kritisch**

cruel(ty)   **grausam, die Grausamkeit**

cultured   **gebildet**

cunning   **schlau, die Schlauheit**

curious   **neugierig**

curiosity   **die Neugierde**

decisive (in-)   **(un)entschlossen**

demanding   **anspruchsvoll**

dependent (in-)   **(un)abhängig**

dependence (in-)   **die (Un)abhängigkeit**

diligence   **der Fleiß**

distrust   **das Mißtrauen**

distrustful   **mißtrauisch**

eccentric   **exzentrisch**

energetic   **energisch**

energy   **die Energie**

envy (-ious)   **der Neid, neidisch**

extroverted   **extravertiert**

extrovertion   **die Extravertiertheit**

faithful (un-)   **(un)treu**

faithfulness   **die Treue**

friendliness (un-)   **die (Un)freundlichkeit**

frivolous   **leichtsinnig**

generocity   **die Großzügigkeit**

gentle   **sanft(mütig)**

gentleness   **die Sanftmut**

greed(y)   **die Habgier, habgierig**

honesty (dis-)   **die (Un)ehrlichkeit**

honor   **die Ehre**

humane (in-)   **(in)human**

humble   **bescheiden**

hypocritical   **heuchlerisch**

idealistic   **idealistisch**

imagination   **die Phantasie(n)**

imaginative   **phantasievoll**

independent   **selbstständig**

individualistic   **individuell**

innocence   **die Unschuld**

inquisitive   **neugierig**

introverted   **introvertiert**

introvertion   **die Introvertiertheit**

ironic   **ironisch**

liberal   **liberal**

likeable   **sympathisch**

lonely (-iness)   **einsam, die Einsamkeit**

loveable   **liebenswürdig**

mad(ness)   **verrückt, die Verrücktheit**

malicious(ness)   **boshaft, die Boshaftigkeit**

mature (im-)   **(un)reif**

mean/stingy   **knauserig**

modest(y)   **bescheiden, die Bescheidenheit**

mood   **die Laune(n)**

moody   **launenhaft**

naive(ty)   **naiv, die Naivität**

natural   **natürlich**

nervousness   **die Ängstlichkeit**

niceness   **die Freundlichkeit**

obedience (dis-)   **der (Un)gehorsam**

obedient (dis-)   **(un)gehorsam**

open(ness)   **offen, die Offenheit**

original   **originell**

originality   **die Originalität**

patience (im-)   **die (Un)geduld**

politeness (im-)   **die (Un)höflichkeit**

possessive   **gebieterisch**

prejudiced (un-)   **(un)vorein-genommen gegen** +acc

pride   **der Stolz**

proud **stolz**
rebellious **rebellisch**
reserve **die Zurückhaltung**
reserved **zurückhaltend**
respectable **angesehen, anständig**
responsible (ir-) **(un)zuverlässig**
rudeness **die Unhöflichkeit(en)**
sad(ness) **traurig, die Traurigkeit**
sarcasm **der Sarkasmus (-en)**
sarcastic **sarkastisch**
scorn **der Spott**
scornful **spöttisch**
self-confident **selbstsicher,
    selbstbewußt**
self-confidence **die Selbstbewußtsein**
selfish **selbstsüchtig**
selfishness **der Egoismus**
self-sufficient **selbstständig**
self-sufficiency **die Selbstständigkeit**
sensible (not) **(un)vernünftig**
sensitive (in-) **(un)empfindlich**
sensitivity (in-) **die (Un)empfindlichkeit**
shyness **die Schüchternheit**
silent **schweigsam**
silly **dumm, doof, albern**
sincere **aufrichtig**
sincerity **die Aufrichtigkeit**
skill/skillfulness **die Geschicktheit, die
    Fertigkeit(en)**
sociability (un-) **die (Un)geselligkeit**
strange(ness) **eigenartig, fremd, die
    Fremdheit, Eigenartigkeit**
strict(ness) **streng, die Strenge**
stubborn(ness) **eigensinnig, die
    Eigensinnigkeit**
sweet **süß, lieb**
sympathetic (un-) **sympatisch,
    (un)verständnisvoll**
talkative **gesprächig**
thoughtful **rücksichtsvoll**
thoughtless **rücksichtslos**
tidy (un-) **(un)ordentlich**
tolerance (in-) **die (In)toleranz**
tolerant (in-) **(in)tolerant**
traditional **traditionell**
trust **das Vertrauen**
unselfish(ness) **selbstlos, die
    Selbstlosigkeit**
vain **eitel, eingebildet**
vanity **die Eitelkeit(en)**
violent (-ence) **brutal, die Brutalität**
virtuous **tugendhaft**
warm **warm, warmherzig**
well-adjusted **ausgeglichen**
well-behaved **wohlerzogen**
wisdom **die Klugheit**
wise **klug, weise**

7a Relatives

---

distant relative **der/die entfernte
    Verwandte** *(adj/n)*
distantly related **entfernt miteinander
    verwandt**
godchild **das Patenkind(er)**
goddaughter **die Patentochter(¨)**
godfather **der Pate(n)** *(wk)*
godson **der Patensohn(¨e)**
great-aunt **die Großtante(n)**
great grandchild **der Großenkel(-)**
great-grandfather **der Urgroßvater(¨)**
great-grandmother **die Urgroßmutter(¨)**
great-nephew **der Großneffe(n)** *(wk)*
great-niece **die Großnichte(n)**
great-uncle **der Großonkel(-)**

8b Tools

---

axe/ax **die Axt(¨e)**
bit **der Bohreinsatz(¨e)**
blade **die Klinge(n)**
bolt **der Bolzen(-)**
bucket **der Eimer(-)**
chisel **der Meißel(-), der Beitel(-)**
crowbar **das Brecheisen** *(no pl)*
drill **der Bohrer(-)**
file **die Feile(n)**
garden glove **der Gartenhandschuh(e)**
garden shears **die Heckenschere(n)**
hammer **der Hammer(¨)**
hedge clippers **die Heckenschere(n)**
hoe **die Hacke(n)**
hose **der Schlauch(¨e)**
ladder **die Leiter(n)**
lawn mower **der Rasenmäher(-)**
mallet **der Holzhammer(¨)**

219

nail   der Nagel(-)
nut   die (Schrauben)mutter(n)
paint   die Farbe(n), der Lack(e)
paint brush   der Pinsel(-)
pickaxe/ax   die Spitzhacke(n)
plane   der Hobel(-)
pliers   die (Kombi)zange(n)
rake   die Harke(n)
roller   die Walze(n)
   roller *(for paint)*   die Rolle(n)
sandpaper   das Schmirgelpapier *(no pl)*
saw   die Säge(n)
screw   die Schraube(n)
screwdriver   der Schraubenzieher(-)
shovel   die Schaufel(n), die Schippe(n)
spade   der Spaten(-)
spanner/wrench *(adjustable)*   der
   Schraubenschlüssel(-)
spirit level   die Wasserwaage(n)
step-ladder   die Stufenleiter(n)
tool   das Werkzeug(e)
   gardening tool   das (Garten)gerät(e)
toolbox   der Werkzeugkasten(-)
trowel   die Kelle(n)
varnish   der Lack(e)
vice/vise   der Schraubstock(-̈e)

9a Shops, stores, & services

antique shop/store   der
   Antiquitätenladen(-̈)
art shop/store   der Kunstladen(-̈)
baker's/bakery   die Bäckerei(en)
bank   die Bank(en)
betting shop/bookmaker's   das
   Wettbüro(s)
bookshop/store   die Bücherei(en)
boutique   die Boutique(n)
butcher's   die Metzgerei(en), die
   Fleischerei(en)
cakeshop/store   die Konditorei(en)
car accessory/spares shop/store   der
   Laden für Autozubehör
charity shop/store   der Karitasladen(-̈e)
chemist's/drugstore   die Apotheke(n),
   die Drogerie(n)
clothes shop/store   das
   Kleidergeschäft(e)

cobbler's/shoemaker   der
   Schuhmacher(-), der Sattler(-)
cosmetics shop/store   der
   Kosmetikladen(-̈)
covered market   der überdachte
   Markt(-̈e)
dairy   die Molkerei(en)
delicatessen   der Delikatessenladen(-̈)
department store   das Warenhaus(-̈er)
drugstore   die Drogerie(n)
dry-cleaners   die chemische
   Reinigung(en)
electrical shop/store   der Elektroladen(-̈)
fast-food shop/store   der
   Schnellimbiß(laden(-̈))
fishmonger's   der Fischladen(-̈)
fishstall   der Fischstand(-̈e)
florist's   das Blumengeschäft(e)
furniture shop/store   das
   Möbelgeschäft(e)
garden center   das Gartencenter(-), die
   Gärtnerei(en)
greengrocer's   der Obst- und
   Gemüseladen(-̈)
grocer's   der Lebensmittelladen(-̈)
hairdresser's   der Friseur(salon)
hardware shop/store   der
   Eisenwarenladen(-̈)
health-food shop/store   das
   Reformhaus(-̈er)
hypermarket   der Verbrauchermarkt(-̈e)
indoor market   der Hallenmarkt(-̈e)
jeweller/jeweler   der Juwelier(e)
jeweller's/jewelry store   das
   Schmuckwarengeschäft(e)
kiosk   der Kiosk(e)
launderette   der Waschsalon(s)
lottery kiosk   der Lotteriekiosk(e)
market   der Markt(-̈e)
menswear shop/store   das Geschäft für
   Männerbekleidung
music shop/store   der Musikladen(-̈)
newsagent's/newsstand   der
   Zeitungshändler/-stand(-̈e)
newspaper kiosk   der Zeitungskiosk(e)
open-air/outdoor market   der Markt(-̈e)
optician's   der Optiker(-) [-in]

petshop/pet store **die Tierhandlung(en)**
pharmacy **die Apotheke(n)**
photographic shop/store **der Fotoladen(¨)**
post-office **die Post** *(no pl)*, **das Postamt(¨er)**
pottery shop/store **das Töpferwarengeschäft(e)**
shoe repair shop/store **die Schuhreparatur(en), die Schusterei(en)**
shoeshop/store **das Schuhgeschäft(e)**
shop/store **das Geschäft(e), der Laden(¨)**
shopping arcade **die Einkaufspassage(n)**
shopping center/mall **das Einkaufszentrum (-en)**
souvenir shop/store **der Souvenirladen(¨)**
sports shop/store **das Sportgeschäft(e)**
stationer's/stationery store **das Schreibwarengeschäft(e)**
store **das Warenhaus(¨er)**
superstore **das Kaufhaus(¨er)**
supermarket **der Supermarkt(¨e)**
sweetshop/candy store **der Süßwarenladen(¨)**
take-out food shop/store **der Schnellimbiß (-bisse)**
tobacconist's/tobacco store **der Tabakwarenladen(¨)**
toyshop/store **das Spielwarengeschäft(e)**
travel agent's/store **das Reisebüro(s)**
vendor **der Verkäufer(-) [-in]**
vending machine **der Automat(en)**
video-shop/store **der Videoladen(¨)**

9a Currencies

Austrian shilling **der Schilling(e)**
dollar **der Dollar(s)**
franc **der Franc(s)**
guilder **der Gulden(-)**
lira **die Lira (-e)**
German mark **die D(eutsche)-Mark(en)**
peseta **die Peseta(s/-en)**

pound sterling **das Pfund(-)**
rouble **der Rubel(-)**
Swiss franc **der Schweizer Franken(-)**
yen **der Yen(s)**

9c Jeweler/Jewelry

---

bangle **der Armreif(e)**
chain bracelet **das Gliederarmband(¨er)**
brooch **die Brosche(n)**
carat **das Karat(e)**
chain **die Kette(n)**
charm **das Amulett(e)**
crown **die Krone(n)**
crown jewels **die Kronjuwelen** *(pl)*
cuff links **die Manschettenknöpfe** *(pl)*
earring **der Ohrring(e)**
engagement ring **der Verlobungsring(e)**
eternity ring **der Erinnerungsring(e)**
jewel **das Juwel(en), der Edelstein(e)**
jewel box **das Schmuckkästchen(-)**
jewelery/jewelry **der Schmuck** *(no pl)*
medal **die Medaille(n)**
medallion **das Medaillon(s)**
necklace **die Halskette(n)**
pendant **der Anhänger(-)**
precious stone/gem **der Edelstein(e)**
real **echt**
ring **der Ring(e)**
semi-precious stone **der Halbedelstein(e)**
signet ring **der Siegelring(e)**
tiara **das Diadem(e)**
tie pin **die Krawattennadel(n)**
wedding ring **der Ehering(e)**

9c Precious stones & metals

---

agate **der Achat(e)**
amber **der Bernstein** *(no pl)*
amethyst **der Amethyst(e)**
chrome **das Chrom** *(no pl)*
copper **das Kupfer** *(no pl)*
coral **die Koralle(n)**
crystal **das Kristall** *(no pl)*
diamond **der Diamant(en)**
emerald **der Smaragd(e)**

221

gold   das Gold *(no pl)*
gold plate   vergoldet
ivory   das Elfenbein(e)
jade   der/die Jade *(no pl)*
mother of pearl   das Perlmutt *(no pl)*
onyx   der Onyx(e)
pearl   die Perle(n)
pewter   das Zinn *(no pl)*
platinum   das Platin *(no pl)*
quartz   der Quarz(e)
ruby   der Rubin(e)
sapphire   der Saphir(e)
silver plate   versilbert
silver   das Silber *(no pl)*
topaz   der Topas(e)
turquoise   der Türkis(e)

10c Herbs & spices

aniseed   der Anis(e)
basil   das Basilikum *(no pl)*
bay leaf   das Lorbeerblatt(ër)
caraway   der Kümmel *(no pl)*
chives   der Schnittlauch *(no pl)*
cinnamon   der Zimt(e)
clove   die Nelke(n)
dill   der Dill(e)
garlic   der Knoblauch *(no pl)*
ginger   der Ingwer *(no pl)*
horseradish   der Meerrettich(e), der
   Kren *(no pl)*
juniper   der Wacholder *(no pl)*
marjoram   der Majoran(e)
mint   die Minz(e)
mixed herbs   die Kräuter *(pl)*
nutmeg   die Muskatnuß (ẅsse)
oregano   der Origano *(no pl)*
parsley   die Petersilie *(no pl)*
pepper   der Pfeffer(-)
rosemary   der Rosmarin *(no pl)*
saffron   der Safran(e)
sage   der Salbei *(no pl)*
tarragon   der Estragon *(no pl)*
thyme   der Thymian(e)

10d Cooking utensils

alumin(i)um foil   die Aluminiumfolie(n)
baking tray   das Kuchenblech(e)

cake tin   die Springform(en)
carving knife   das Tranchiermesser(-)
colander   der Seiher(-), das Sieb(e)
food processor   die Küchenmaschine(n)
fork   die Gabel(n)
frying pan/fry-pan   die Bratpfanne(n)
grater   die Reibe(n)
greaseproof/wax paper   das
   Pergamentpapier *(no pl)*
grill   der Grill(s)
kettle   der Kessel(-)
knife   das Messer(-)
lid   der Deckel(-)
pot   der Topf(ẅe)
rolling pin   das Nudelholz(ër)
saucepan/casserole dish   der
   Kochtopf(ẅe)
scales   die Waage(n)
sieve   das Sieb(e)
skewer   der Spieß(e)
spatula   der Teigschaber(-)
spoon   der Löffel(-)
tablespoon(ful)   der Eßlöffel(voll)
teaspoon(ful)   der Teelöffel(voll)
tenderizer   der Fleischklopfer(-)
tin/can-opener   der Büchsenöffner(-)

11c Illnesses & diseases

AIDS   AIDS
angina   die Angina
appendicitis   die
   Blinddarmentzündung(en)
arthritis   die Arthritis
asthma   das Asthma
bronchitis   die Bronchitis
bubonic plague   die Beulenpest
cancer   der Krebs
chickenpox   die Windpocken *(pl)*
cholera   die Cholera
colic   die Kolik
cold   die Erkältung(en), der
   Schnupfen(-)
constipation   die Verstopfung(en)
dermatitis   die Hautentzündung(en)
diabetes   die Diabetes, die
   Zuckerkrankheit

diarrhea **der Durchfall**
diphtheria **die Diphtherie(n)**
eczema **das Ekzem(e), der Hautausschlag(ˉe)**
epilepsy **die Epilepsie(n)**
fever **das Fieber(-)**
fit **der epileptische Anfall(ˉe)**
flu **die Grippe(n)**
food-poisoning **die Lebensmittelvergiftung(en)**
gall-stone **der Gallenstein(e)**
German measles **die Röteln** (pl)
gingivitis **die Zahnfleischentzündung(en)**
gonorrhoea **der Tripper**
haemorrhoid **die Hämorrhoide(n)**
heart attack **der Herzanfall(ˉe)**
hepatitis **die Hepatitis**
hernia **der Bruch(ˉe)**
HIV-positive **HIV-positiv, HIV-infiziert**
incontinence **die Inkontinenz**
influenza **die Grippe(n)**
jaundice **die Gelbsucht**
leukaemia **die Leukämie**
malaria **die Malaria**
measles **die Masern** (pl)
meningitis **die Hirnhautentzündung(en)**
mumps **der Mumps** (no pl)
pile **die Hämorrhoide(n)**
pneumonia **die Lungenentzündung(en)**
polio **die Kinderlähmung**
rabies **die Tollwut**
salmonella **die Salmonellen** (pl)
scabies **die Krätze**
seasickness **die Seekrankheit(en)**
sickness **die Übelkeit**
smallpox **die Pocken** (pl)
stroke **der Schlaganfall(ˉe)**
syphilis **die Syphilis**
temperature **das Fieber**
tetanus **der Tetanus, der Wundstarrkrampf**
thrombosis **die Thrombose(n)**
tonsillitis **die Mandelentzündung(en)**
tuberculosis **die Tuberkulose(n)**
ulcer **das Geschwür(e)**

urinary infection **die Harnwegsinfektion(en)**
venereal disease **die Geschlechtskrankheit(en)**
whooping cough **der Keuchhusten**
yellow fever **das Gelbfieber**

13b Holidays & religious festivals

All Saints (Nov 1) **das Allerheiligen**
All Souls (Nov 2) **das Allerseelen**
Ascension Day **der Himmelfahrtstag(e)**
Ash Wednesday **der Aschermittwoch(e)**
Assumption Day (Aug 15) **die Mariä Himmelfahrt**
Candlemas **das Mariä Lichtmeß**
Christmas **das Weihnachten**
Christmas Day **der erste Weihnachtstag**
Christmas Eve **der Heiligabend(e)**
Corpus Christi **der Fronleichnam**
Easter **das Osterfest(e)**
Easter Monday **der Ostermontag(e)**
Easter Sunday **der Ostersonntag(e)**
Good Friday **der Karfreitag(e)**
Labour/Labor Day **der Tag der Arbeit**
Lent **die Fastenzeit(en)**
New Year's Day **der Neujahrstag(e)**
New Year's Eve **das Silvester**
Palm Sunday **der Palmsonntag(e)**
Passover **das Passah**
Ramadan **der Ramadan**
Sabbath **der Sabbat**
Shrove Tuesday **der Faschingsdienstag(e)**
Whitsun **das Pfingstfest(e)**

14b Jobs & professions

The arts

---

actor/actress **der Schauspieler(-) [-in]**
announcer **der Ansager(-) [-in]**
architect **der Architekt(en)** (wk) **[-in]**
artist **der Künstler(-) [-in]**
book-seller **der Buchhändler(-) [-in]**
cameraman **der Kameramann(ˉer) [-frau]**

editor der Herausgeber(-) [-in]
film/movie director der Filmdirektor(en) (wk) [-in]
film/movie star der Filmstar(s)
journalist der Journalist(en) (wk) [-in]
musician der Musiker(-) [-in]
painter (artist) der Maler(-) [-in]
photographer der Fotograph(en) (wk) [-in]
poet der Dichter(-) [-in]
printer der Drucker(-) [-in]
producer (theatre/theater) der Regisseur(e) [-in]
publisher der Verleger(-) [-in]
reporter der Reporter(-) [-in]
sculptor der Bildhauer(-) [-in]
singer der Sänger(-) [-in]
TV announcer der Fernsehansager(-) [-in]
writer der Schriftsteller(-) [-in]

Education & research

headteacher/principal der Direktor(en) (wk) [-in], der Schulleiter(-) [-in]
lecturer der Dozent(en) (wk) [-in]
primary teacher der Grundschullehrer(-) [-in]
researcher der Forscher(-) [-in]
scientist der Wissenschaftler(-) [-in]
secondary teacher der Gymnasial/Realschullehrer(-) [-in]
student der Schüler(-), der Student(en) (wk) [-in]
technician der Techniker(-) [-in]

Food & retail

baker der Bäcker(-) [-in]
brewer der Brauer(-)
butcher der Fleischer(-) [-in], der Metzger(-) [-in], der Schlachter (-)[-in]
buyer der Käufer(-) [-in]
caterer (supplying meals) der Lieferant(en) (wk)
chemist/druggist der Apotheker(-) [-in], der Drogist(en) (wk) [-in]
cook der Koch(-e) [-in]

farmer der Bauer(n), die Bäuerin(nen)
fisherman der Fischer(-)
fishmonger der Fischhändler(-) [-in]
florist der Florist(en) (wk) [-in]
greengrocer der Obst- und Gemüsehändler(-) [-in]
grocer der Lebensmittelhändler(-) [-in]
jeweller/jeweler der Juwelier(e)
pharmacist der Apotheker(-)[-in]
representative der Vertreter(-) [-in]
shop assistant der Verkäufer(-) [-in]
shopkeeper/storekeeper der Ladenbesitzer(-) [-in]
tobacconist der Tabakhändler(-) [-in]
waiter der Kellner(-) [-in]
wine-grower der Weinbauer(n) [-bäuerin(nen)]

Government service

civil-servant der Beamte (adj/n), die Beamtin(nen)
clerk der Angestellte(n) (adj/n)
customs officer der Zollbeamte(n) (adj/n)
fireman der Feuerwehrmann(-er)
judge der Richter(-) [-in]
member of Parliament/senator der/die Abgeordnete (adj/n), der Senator(en) [-in]
minister der Minister(-) [-in]
officer der Offizier(e)
policeman/woman der Polizist(en) (wk) [-in]
politician der Politiker(-) [-in]
sailor der Matrose(n) (wk)
secret agent der Geheimagent(en) (wk) [-in]
serviceman der Soldat(en) (wk)
soldier der Soldat(en) (wk)

Health care

dentist der Zahnarzt(-e) [-in]
doctor (Dr) der Arzt(-e) [-in]
midwife die Hebamme(n)
nurse die Krankenschwester(n)
optician der Optiker(-) [-in]
psychiatrist der Psychiater(-) [-in]

psychologist **der Psychologe(n)** *(wk)*
[-in]
surgeon **der Chirurg(en)** *(wk)* **[-in]**
vet **der Tierarzt(-̈e)** **[-in]**

Manufacturing & construction

bricklayer **der Maurer(-)**
builder **der Bauunternehmer(-)**
carpenter **der Zimmermann**
(-leute)
engineer **der Ingenieur(e) [-in]**
foreman **der Vorarbeiter(-) [-in]**
glazier **der Glaser(-)**
industrialist **der/die Industrielle** *(adj/n)*
laborer **der Arbeiter(-) [-in]**
manufacturer **der Hersteller(-) [-in]**
mechanic **der Mechaniker(-) [-in]**
metalworker **der Metallarbeiter(-) [-in]**
miner **der Bergarbeiter(-) [-in]**
plasterer **der Gipser(-) [-in]**
stonemason **der Steinmetz(en)** *(wk)*

Services

accountant **der Buchhalter(-) [-in]**
actuary/sales agent **der Vertreter(-)**
[-in]
agent **der Agent(en)** *(wk)* **[-in]**
bank manager **der Bankmanager(-)**
[-in]
businessman **der Geschäftsmann**
(-leute)
businesswoman **die Geschäftsfrau(en)**
careers adviser **der Berufsberater(-)**
[-in]
caretaker **der Hausmeister(-) [-in]**
cleaner **die Putzfrau(en)**
computer programmer **der**
Computerprogrammierer(-) [-in]
counsellor **der Berater(-) [-in]**
drautsman/draftsman **der technische**
Zeichner(-) [-in]
dustman/garbageman **der**
Müllmann(-̈er/-leute)
electrician **der Elektriker(-) [-in]**
estate/real estate agent **der**
Grundstücksmakler(-) [-in]
furniture remover **der Spediteur(e)**

gardener **der Gärtner(-) [-in]**
gasman **der Gasmann(-̈er)**
guide **der (Stadt-/Reise)führer(-) [-in]**
hairdresser **der Friseur(e) [-euse]**
insurance agent/broker **der**
Versicherungsvertreter(-) [-in]
interpreter **der Dolmetscher(-) [-in]**
lawyer **der Anwalt(-̈e) [-in]**
librarian **der Bibliothekar(e) [-in]**
office worker **der Büroarbeiter(-) [-in]**
painter & decorator **der Anstreicher(-)**
[-in]
plumber **der Klempner(-) [-in]**
postman **der Briefträger(-) [-in]**
priest **der Priester(-) [-in]**
receptionist **der Empfangschef(s)**
[-dame(n)]
servant **der Diener(-) [-in]**
social worker **der Sozialarbeiter(-) [-in]**
solicitor **der Rechtsanwalt(-̈e) [-in]**
stockbroker **der Börsenmakler(-) [-in]**
surveyor **der Landvermesser(-) [-in]**
tax inspector **der Steuerbeamte** *(adj/n)*
[-beamtin]
trade-unionist **der Gewerkschafter(-)**
[-in]
translator **der Übersetzer(-) [-in]**
travel agent **der Reisebürokaufmann**
(-kaufleute)
typist **die Schreibkraft(-̈e)**
undertaker **der Leichenbestatter(-)**
[-in]

Transport

bus driver **der Busfahrer(-) [-in]**
driver **der Fahrer(-) [-in]**
driving instructor **der Fahrlehrer(-) [-in]**
flight attendant **der Flugbegleiter(-) [-in]**
lorry/truck driver **der LKW-Fahrer(-)**
[-in]
pilot **der Pilot(en)** *(wk)* **[-in]**
taxi driver **der Taxifahrer(-) [-in]**
ticket inspector **der**
Fahrkartenkontrolleur(e)

14b Places of work

blast furnace **der Hochofen(-̈)**

branch office   die Zweigstelle(n)
brewery   die Brauerei(en)
business park   der Industriepark(s)
construction site   die Baustelle(n)
distillery   die Schnapsbrennerei(en)
factory   die Fabrik(en)
farm   der Bauernhof(-e)
foundry   die Gießerei(en)
head office   die
   Hauptgeschäftsstelle(n)
hospital   das Krankenhaus(-er)
mill   die Mühle(n)
   paper mill   die Papierfabrik(en)
   rolling mill   das Walzwerk(e)
   sawmill   die Sägemühle(n)
   spinning mill   die Spinnerei(en)
   steel mill   das Stahlwerk(e)
   weaving mill   die Weberei(en)
mine   das Bergwerk(e)
office   das Büro(s)
plant   die Fabrik(en)
shop/store   der Laden(-e), das
   Kaufhaus(-er)
steelworks/steel plant   das
   Stahlwerk(e)
theme park   der Freizeitpark(s)
vineyard/winery   der Weinberg(e)
warehouse   das Lagerhaus(-er)
workshop   die Werkstatt(-en), die
   Werkstätte(n)

14b Company personnel & departments

accounts department   die
   Buchhaltung(en)
apprentice   der Lehrling(e)
assistant   der Assistent(en) (wk) [-in]
associate   der Kollege(n) (wk), die
   Kollegin(nen)
board of directors   der Vorstand(-e)
boss   der Chef(s) [-in]
colleague   der Kollege(n) (wk)
department   die Abteilung(en)
director   der Direktor(en) [-in]
division   die Abteilung(en)
employee   der/die Angestellte (adj/n)
employer   der Arbeitgeber(-) [-in]
executive   der Manager(-) [-in]

foreman   der Vorarbeiter(-) [-in]
labourer/laborer   der Arbeiter(-) [-in]
line manager   der/die Vorgesetzte
   (adj/n)
management   das Management(s)
manager/ess   der Manager(-) [-in]
managing director/CEO   der
   Geschäftsführer(-) [-in]
marketing department   die
   Marketingabteilung(en)
personal assistant   der persönliche
   Assistent(en) (wk) [-in]
president   der Präsident(en) (wk)
production department   die
   Produktionsabteilung(en)
sales department   die
   Verkaufsabteilung(en)
secretary   der Sekretär(e) [-in]
specialist   der Spezialist(en) (wk)
   [-in]
staff/personnel   das Personal
team   das Team(s)
trainee   der Praktikant(en) (wk)
   [-in]
vice president   der Vizepräsident(en)
   (wk) [-in]

15e Letter writing formulae

Dear Mr. & Mrs. ...   Sehr geehrter Herr
   ..., sehr geehrte Frau ...
Dear Hans   Lieber Hans
Dear Anja   Liebe Anja
Dear Anja and Hans   Liebe Anja, lieber
   Hans
Dear Sir   Sehr geehrter Herr
   Personalmanager!
Dear Madam   Sehr geehrte Frau
   Doktor ...
Dear Sirs   Sehr geehrte Herren, Sehr
   geehrte Damen und Herren
Dear colleague   Lieber Kollege, liebe
   Kollegin
My dear friends   Liebe Freunde
I am pleased   ich bin erfreut
I enclose   ich füge bei*
All the best   Alles Gute
Greetings from   Grüße aus/von

Love from **Viele liebe Grüße von** +dat,
alles Liebe
With best wishes **mit den besten**
Wünschen
With kind regards **mit freundlichen**
Grüßen
With greetings from **Es grüßt Sie ...,**
Herzliche Grüße von Deinem ...,
Yours faithfully **hochachtungsvoll**
Yours sincerely **mit freundlichen**
Grüßen

15f Computer hardware

---

adaptor **der Adapter(-)**
battery **die Batterie(n)**
brightness **die Helligkeit**
CD-ROM **die CD-ROM**
central processing unit **der zentrale**
Prozessor(en)
charger **das Ladegerät(e)**
chip **der Chip(s)**
compatibility **die Vereinbarkeit(en)**
compatible **vereinbar, kompatibel**
computer **der Computer(-)**
computer system **das**
Computersystem(e)
continuous paper **das Endlospapier**
cursor **der Cursor(s)**
daisy wheel **der Typenraddrucker(-)**
disc/disk drive **das Laufwerk(e)**
disc/disk **die Festplatte(n)**
diskette **die Diskette(n)**
display **die Anzeige(n)**
dot matrix **der Nadeldrucker(-)**
double density disc/disk **die DD**
Diskette (doppelte Dichte)
drive **das Laufwerk(e)**
floppy disc/disk **die Diskette(n)**
floppy drive **das Diskettenlaufwerk(e)**
function key **die Funktionstaste(n)**
hard copy **der Ausdruck(-e)**
hard disc/disk **die Festplatte(n)**
hardware **die Hardware**
high density disc/disk **die High-**
Density-Diskette(n)
IBM-compatible **IBM-kompatibel**
incompatible **inkompatibel**

ink cartridge **die Patrone(n)**
inkjet **der Tintenstrahldrucker(-)**
input **die Eingabe(n)**
integrated circuit **die integrierte**
Schaltung(en)
interface **die Schnittstelle(n)**
keyboard **die Tastatur(en)**
laptop **der Laptop(s)**
laser printer **der Laserdrucker(-)**
liquid crystal display **die**
Flüssigkristallanzeige(n)
low/high density **niedrige/hohe Dichte(n)**
mainframe computer **der**
Großrechner(-)
microprocessor **der**
Mikroprozessor(en) *(wk)*
mini computer **der Minicomputer(-)**
memory **der Arbeitsspeicher(-), die**
Speicherkapazität(en)
modem **das Modem(s)**
mouse **die Maus(-̈e)**
network **das Netz(werk)(e)**
note book **das Notebook(s)**
on line **angeschlossen, online**
package **das Paket(e)**
personal computer/PC **der**
Personalcomputer(-), der PC(s)
plug-in drive **das externe**
Diskettenlaufwerk(e)
port **der Anschluß (-̈sse), die**
Schnittstelle(n)
printer **der Drucker(-)**
processor **der Prozessor(en), der**
Rechner(-)
RAM **der RAM-Chip(s)**
ribbon **das Band(-̈er)**
screen **der Bildschirm(e)**
server **der Server(-)**
socket/port **der Anschluß (-̈sse)**
storage **die Speicherung(en)**
terminal **das Terminal(s)**
toner **der Toner(-)**
VDU **das VDU**
viewdata system **das Bfx-System(e)**
visual display unit **das**
Datensichtgerät(e)

SUBJECT INDEX

16c Photography

automatic **automatisch**
camera **die Kamera(s)**
camera case **die Fototasche(n)**
I develop **ich entwickle**
developing/processing **die Entwicklung**
I enlarge **ich vergrößere**
exposure counter **der Zähler(-)**
film **der Film(e)**
   black and white film **der Schwarzweißfilm(e)**
   colour/color film **der Farbfilm(e)**
filter **das/der Filter(-)**
flash **der Blitz(e)**
flash attachment **das Blitzlicht(er)**
home movie **das Heimvideo(s)**
I focus the camera **ich stelle ein***
   in focus **scharf (eingestellt)**
   out of focus **unscharf**
it is jammed **es klemmt**
lens **das Objektiv(e)**
   telephoto lens **das Teleobjektiv(e)**
   wide-angle lens **das Weitwinkelobjektiv(e)**
lens cap **die Schutzkappe(n)**
light **das Licht, die Beleuchtung**
   daylight **das Tageslicht**
light meter **der Belichtungsmesser(-)**
movie camera **die Filmcamera(s)**
negative **das Negativ(e)**
over-exposed **überbelichtet**
over-exposure **die Überbelichtung**
picture **das Bild(er)**
photogenic **fotogen**
photo(graph) **das Foto(s), die Fotografie(n)**
   holiday/vacation photo **die Aufnahme(n)**
   passport photo **das Paßfoto(s)**
photograph album **das Fotoalbum(s/-en)**
shutter **der Verschluß (¨-sse)**
slide **das Dia(s), das Diapositiv(e)**
snap **der Schnappschuß (¨-sse)**
I take (photos) **ich nehme auf***
video camera **die Videokamera(s)**

video cassette **die Videokassette(n)**
I wind on **ich spule weiter***

17a Artistic styles & periods

Art Nouveau **der Jugendstil**
Baroque **der Barock**
baroque **barock**
Bauhaus **das Bauhaus**
Byzantine **byzantinisch**
Celtic **keltisch**
classical **klassisch**
classical artist/writer **der Klassiker(-)**
Classical period **die Klassik**
Cubism **der Kubismus**
Dada **der Dadaismus**
Expressionism **der Expressionismus**
expressionist **der Expressionist(en)** *(wk)*
expressionistic **expressionistisch**
Flemish **flämisch**
Germanic **germanisch**
Gothic art **die Gotik**
Gothic **gotisch**
Greek **griechisch**
Impressionism **der Impressionismus**
Impressionist **der Impressionist(en)** *(wk)*
Impressionist **impressionistisch**
Naturalism **der Naturalismus**
naturalistic **naturalistisch**
Neo-classical **der Klassizismus**
Neo-gothic **die Neugotik**
New Objectivity **die Neue Sachlichkeit**
Norman **romanisch**
pop art **die Pop-Art**
Realism **der Realismus**
realist **der Realist(en)** *(wk)*
realistic **realistisch**
Renaissance **die Renaissance**
Rococo **das Rokoko**
Roman **römisch**
Romanesque **romanisch**
Romantic age **die Romantik**
Romantic **der Romantiker(-)**
romantic **romantisch**
Storm and Stress **der Sturm und Drang**

Surrealism   **der Surrealismus**
Surrealist   **der Surrealist(en)** *(wk)*
surrealistic   **surrealistisch**
Venetian   **venezianisch**

17b Architectural features

aisle   **das Seitenschiff(e)**
arch   **der Bogen(⁻)**
bas relief   **das Basrelief(s)**
battlement   **die Zinnen** *(pl)*
buttress   **der Strebepfeiler**
capital   **das Kapitell(e)**
choir   **der Chor(e/⁻e)**
colonnade   **der Säulengang(⁻e)**
column   **die Säule(n)**
   corinthian   **korinthisch**
   doric   **dorisch**
   ionic   **ionisch**
crossing   **die Vierung(en)**
crypt   **die Krypta (-en)**
cupola   **die Kuppel(n)**
drawbridge   **die Zugbrücke(n)**
eave   **der Dachvorsprung(⁻e)**
façade   **die Fassade(n)**
gable   **der Giebel(-)**
gargoyle   **der Wasserspeier(-)**
gothic arch   **der Spitzbogen(⁻)**
half-timbered   **das Holzfachwerk**
half-timbered house   **das Fachwerkhaus(⁻er)**
headstone   **der Grabstein(e)**
nave   **das Schiff(e)**
overhanging   **vorstehend**
pagoda   **die Pagode(n)**
pilaster   **der Halbpfeiler(-)**
porch   **die Vorhalle(n)**
portico   **der Portikus (-en)**
relief   **das Relief(s)**
roof   **das Dach(⁻er)**
sacristy   **die Sakristei(en)**
spire/steeple   **der Kirchturm(⁻e)**
stucco   **der Stuck**
transept   **das Querschiff(e)**
triumphal arch   **der Triumphbogen(⁻)**
vault   **das Gewölbe(-)**
vaulted   **gewölbt**

17c Publishing

abridged version   **die gekürzte Ausgabe(n)**
acknowledgments to   **mein/unser Dank gilt** +dat
appendix   **der Anhang(⁻e)**
author   **der Autor(en) [-in], der Verfasser(-) [-in]**
best seller   **der Bestseller(-)**
bibliography   **die Bibliographie(n)**
book fair   **die Buchmesse(n)**
catalogue/catalog   **der Katalog(e)**
chapter   **das Kapitel(-)**
contents   **der Inhalt(e)**
   table of contents   **das Inhaltsverzeichnis(se)**
contract   **der Vertrag(⁻e)**
copy   **das Exemplar(e)**
copyright   **das Copyright**
cover *(of book)*   **der Buchumschlag(⁻e)**
deadline   **der Fristablauf(⁻e)**
dedicated to   **gewidmet** +dat/**an** +acc
edition   **die Ausgabe(n)**
   first edition   **die Erstausgabe(n)**
   latest edition   **die neueste Ausgabe**
editor   **der Redakteur(e), der Herausgeber(-)**
   desk editor   **der Lektor(en) [-in]**
   general editor   **der Chefredakteur(e) [-in]**
footnotes   **die Fußnote(n)**
illustrations   **die Illustration(en)**
manuscript   **das Manuskript(e)**
out of print   **vergriffen**
paperback   **das Taschenbuch(⁻er)**
preface   **das Vorwort(e)**
I print   **ich drucke**
proofreading   **das Korrekturlesen**
publication date   **das Erscheinungsdatum (-en)**
I publish   **ich bringe heraus*, ich veröffentliche**
just published   **neu erschienen**
publisher   **der Verleger(-)**
publishing   **das Verlagswesen(-)**
publishing house   **das Verlagshaus(⁻er)**

translation   die Übersetzung(en), die Übertragung(en)

version   die Fassung(en)

with a forward by   mit einem Vorwort von +dat

17d Musicians & instruments

accompanist   der Begleiter(-) [-in]

accordion   das Akkordeon(s)

alto   der Alt(e), die Altstimme(n)

bagpipe   der Dudelsack(ẽe)

band leader   der Kapellmeister(-)

baritone   der Bariton

bass (singer)   der Bassist(en)

bassoon   das Fagott(e)

bells   die Glocke(n)

castanets   die Kastagnietten (pl)

cellist   der Cellist(en) [-in]

cello   das Cello(s/-i)

cembalo   das Cembalo(s)

chorister   der Chorknabe(n) (wk)

clarinet   die Klarinette(n)

classical guitar   die klassische Gitarre(n)

clavicord   das Klavichord(e)

conductor   der Dirigent(en) (wk) [-in]

contralto   der Alt(e), die Altstimme(n)

cymbal   das Becken(-)

double bass   der Kontrabaß (ẽsse)

drum   das Schlagzeug(e)

flautist   der Flötist(en) (wk) [-in]

flute   die Querflöte(n)

French horn   das Waldhorn(ẽer)

grand piano   der Flügel(-)

guitar   die Gitarre(n) (wk) [-in]

guitarist   der Gitarrist(en)

harmonium   das Harmonium (-ien)

harp   die Harfe(n)

harpist   der Harfenspieler(-) [-in]

harpsichord   das Cembalo(s)

horn   das Horn(ẽer)

hurdy-gurdy   der Leierkasten(ẽ)

jews' harp   die Maultrommel(n)

lyre   die Leier(n)

mandolin   die Mandoline(n)

mezzo-soprano   der Mezzosopran(e)

mouth-organ   die Mundharmonika(s)

oboe   die Oboe(n)

orchestra leader   der Konzertmeister(-) [-in]

orchestra player   das Orchestermitglied(er)

organ   die Orgel(n)

organist   der Organist(en) [-in]

percussion   das Schlagzeug (no pl)

percussionist   der Schlagzeuger(-) [-in]

pianist (professional)   der Pianist(en) [-in]

piano   das Klavier(e)

pipe   die Flöte(n)

recorder   die Blockflöte(n)

saxophone   das Saxophon(e)

soprano   der Sopran(e)

spinet   das Spinett(e)

squeeze-box   die Ziehharmonika(s)

steel drum   das (Stahl)schlagzeug (no pl)

street musician(s)   der Straßenmusikant(en) (wk) [-in]

synthesizer   der Synthesizer(-)

tenor   der Tenor(ẽe)

timpani   die Timpani (pl), die Kesselpauken

triangle   der/das Triangel(-)

trombone   die Posaune(n)

trumpet   die Trompete(n)

tuba   die Tuba(s)

viol   die Viola (-en)

viola   die Bratsche(n)

viola player   der Bratschenspieler(-) [-in]

violin   die Violine(n)

violinist   der Violinist(en) (wk) [-in]

violoncello   das Violoncello (-i)

vocalist   der Sänger(-) [-in]

xylophone   das Xylophon(e)

17d Musical forms

aria   die Arie(n)

ballad   die Ballade(n)

cantata   die Kantate(n)

canzonetta   die Kanzonette(n)

chamber music   die Kammermusik (no pl)

choral music   die Chormusik *(no pl)*
chorale   der Choral(¨e)
concerto   das Konzert(e), das
   Concerto (-i)
   piano concerto   das
      Klavierkonzert(e)
duet   das Duett(e)
fugue   die Fuge(n)
madrigal   das Madrigal(e)
march   die Marschmusik, der
   Marsch(¨e)
music drama   das Musikdrama (-en)
musical *(comedy)*   das Musical(s)
nocturne   die Nokturne(n)
octet   das Oktett(e)
opera   die Oper(n)
operetta   die Operette(n)
oratorio   das Oratorium (-ia/-ien)
overture   die Ouvertüre(n)
prelude   das Präludium (-ia/-ien)
quartet   das Quartett(e)
quintet   das Quintett(e)
recitative   das Rezitativ(e)
requiem Mass   die Totenmesse(n)
rondo   das Rondo(s)
sacred music   die geistliche Musik
septet   das Septett(e)
serenade   die Serenade(n)
sextet   das Sextett(e)
sonata   die Sonate(n)
song-cycle   der Liederzyklus (-en)
string quartet   das Streichquartett(e)
suite   die Suite(n)
symphonietta   die Sinfonietta (-en)
symphony   die Symphonie(n)
trio   das Trio(s)
   piano trio   das Klaviertrio(s)

17d Musical terms

accompaniment   die Begleitung(en)
arpeggio   die Arpeggio(s)
bar   der Takt(e)
beat   der Schlag(¨e)
bow   der Bogen(¨)
bowing   die Bogenführung
cadence   die Kadenz(en)
chord   der Akkord(e)

clef   der Notenschlüssel(-)
   bass   der F-Schlüssel
   treble   der Violinschlüssel
conductor   der Dirigent(en) *(wk)* [-in]
I conduct   ich dirigiere
discord   die Disharmonie(n)
first violin   die erste Geige(n)
harmony   die Harmonie(n)
improvisation   die Improvisation(en)
key   der Notenschlüssel(-), die
   Tonart(en)
   major   das Dur *(no pl)*
   minor   das Moll *(no pl)*
note   der Ton(¨e), die Note(n)
   breve   die ganze Note(n)
   minim/half note   die Halbe(n)
   crotchet/quarter note   das Viertel(-)
   quaver/eighth note   das Achtel(-)
   semibreve   die ganze Taktnote(n)
   semiquaver/sixteenth note   das
      Sechszehntel(-)
   semitone   der Halbton(¨e)
   tone   der Ton(¨e)
mute   der Dämpfer(-)
reed   das Rohrblattinstrument(e)
scale   die Tonleiter(n)
score   die Partitur(en)
sheet *(of music)*   das Notenblatt(¨er)
triplet   die Triole(n)

Notes & keys

C, C sharp, C flat   das C, Cis, Ces
D, D sharp, D flat   das D, Dis, Des
E, E sharp, E flat   das E, Eis, Es
F, F sharp, F flat   das F, Fis, Fes
G, G sharp, G flat   das G, Gis, Ges
A, A sharp, A flat   das A, Ais, As
B, B sharp   das H, His
B flat   B
B-minor   H-Moll
B flat minor   B-Moll
C double sharp, etc.   Cisis, usw.
C double flat, etc.   Ceses, usw.
B double flat, etc.   Bes, usw.
flat sign   das Be
sharp sign   das Kreuz(e)
natural sign   das Auflösungszeichen(-)

17e Film/Movie genres

adventure   **der Abenteuerfilm(e)**
animation   **der Trickfilm(e)**
black and white   **schwarz-weiß**
black comedy   **der schwarze
(Galgen)humor**
B-movie   **das B-Movie(s)**
cartoons   **der Trickfilm(e)**
comedy   **die Komödie(n)**
documentary   **der Dokumentarfilm(e)**
feature film/movie   **der Spielfilm(e)**
horror   **der Horrorfilm(e)**
low-budget   **der Film mit kleinem
Budget**
sci-fi   **Science-Fiction**
short film/movie   **der Kurzfilm(e)**
silent film/movie   **der Stummfilm(e)**
tear-jerker   **der Schmachtfetzen(-)**
thriller   **der Thriller(-), der Krimi(s)**
video-clip   **der Videoclip(s)**
war film/movie   **der Kriegsfilm(e)**
western   **der Western(-)**

19c Parts of the car

alternator   **die Lichtmaschine(n)**
automatic gear   **die Getriebeautomatik**
back wheel   **das Hinterrad(ᐨer)**
battery   **die Batterie(n)**
bodywork   **die Karosserie(n)**
bonnet/hood   **die Motorhaube(n)**
boot/trunk   **der Kofferraum(ᐨe)**
brake   **die Bremse(n)**
bumper   **die Stoßstange(n)**
carburettor   **der Vergaser(-)**
catalytic converter   **der Katalysator(-)**
choke   **der Choke(s)**
clutch   **die Kupplung(en)**
dashboard   **das Armaturenbrett(er)**
door   **die Tür(en)**
    front door   **die Vordertür(en)**
    passenger door   **die
    Beifahrertür(en)**
engine/motor   **der Motor(en)**
exhaust   **der Auspuff**
front seat   **der Vordersitz(e)**
front wheel   **das Vorderrad(ᐨer)**

gearbox   **das Getriebe(-)**
headlight   **der Scheinwerfer(-)**
horn   **die Hupe(n)**
hood   **die Haube(n)**
indicator   **der Blinker(-)**
license plate   **das Nummernschild(er)**
lights   **die Beleuchtung(en)**
passenger seat   **der Beifahrersitz(e)**
pedal   **das Pedal(e)**
    accelerator   **das Gaspedal(e)**
    brake   **das Bremspedal(e)**
    clutch   **das Kupplungspedal(e)**
plug   **die Zündkerze(n)**
rearview mirror   **der Rückspiegel(-)**
registration number   **die
    Registrationsnummer(n)**
roof   **das Dach(ᐨer)**
roof rack   **der Dachgepäckträger(-)**
safety belt   **der Sicherheitsgurt(e)**
spare   **Ersatz-**
    spare part   **das Ersatzteil(e)**
    spare wheel   **das Ersatzrad(ᐨer)**
speedometer   **der Tachometer(-)**
starter   **der Anlasser(-)**
steering wheel   **das Steuer(rad)(ᐨer)**
tank   **der Tank(s)**
tire   **der Reifen(-)**
    back tire   **der Hinterreifen(-)**
    front tire   **der Vorderreifen(-)**
    spare tire   **der Ersatzreifen(-)**
tire pressure   **der Reifendruck(ᐨe)**
wheel   **das Rad(ᐨer)**
windscreen/windshield   **die
    Windschutzscheibe(n)**
windscreen/windshield wiper   **der
    Scheibenwischer(-)**

19c Road signs

Danger!   **Gefahr!, Vorsicht!**
Diversion/Detour   **Umleitung**
End of diversion   **Ende der Umleitung**
Entry   **Einfahrt**
Exit   **Ausfahrt**
Expressway entrance   **die
    Autobahnauffahrt(en)**
Expressway junction   **das
    Autobahnkreuz**

Free parking **Parken gebührenfrei**
Keep clear **Halteverbot, Ausfahrt freihalten**
Maximum speed **die Höchstgeschwindigkeit(en)**
Men at work!/Road Construction **Achtung, Baustelle!**
No entry **Kein Zugang, Keine Zufahrt**
No parking **Parken verboten, Parkverbot**
No passing **Überholverbot**
One way **Einbahnstraße**
Pedestrians crossing **der Fußgängerübergang**
Pedestrian zone **die Fußgängerzone**
Residents only **Anlieger frei**
Road closed **Straße gesperrt**
Roadworks **Straßenbau**
Stop **Halt!, Stop!**
Toll **gebührenpflichtige Straße**

20a Tourist sights

abbey **die Abtei(en)**
amusement park **der Vergnügungspark(s)**
amphitheater **das Amphitheater(-)**
aquarium **das Aquarium (-ien)**
art gallery **die Kunstgalerie(n)**
battle field **das Schlachtfeld(er)**
battlements **die Zinnen** (pl)
boulevard **der Boulevard(s)**
casino **das (Spiel)kasino(s)**
castle **das Schloß (¨sser)**
catacombs **die Katakomben** (pl)
cathedral **die Kathedrale(n), der Dom(e)**
cave **die Höhle(n)**
cemetery **der Friedhof(¨e)**
circus **der Zirkus(se)**
city **der Stadt(¨e)**
city wall **die Stadtmauer(n)**
chapel **die Kapelle(n)**
church **die Kirche(n)**
concert hall **die Konzerthalle(n)**
convent **das Kloster(¨)**
exhibition **die Ausstellung(en)**
fortress **die Festung(en)**

fountain **der (Spring)brunnen(-)**
gardens **der Botanische Garten(¨)**
harbor **der Hafen(¨)**
library **die Bibliothek(en)**
mansion **das Herrenhaus(¨er)**
market **der Markt(¨e)**
monastery **das Kloster(¨)**
monument **das Denkmal(¨er)**
museum **das Museum (Museen)**
opera house **das Opernhaus(¨er)**
palace **der Palast(¨e), das Schloß (¨sser)**
parliament building **das Parlamentsgebäude(-)**
pier **der Anleger(-)**
planetarium **das Planetarium (-ien)**
ruin **die Ruine(n)**
shopping area **das Geschäftsviertel(-)**
square **der Platz(¨e)**
stadium **das Stadion (-ien)**
statue **die Statue(n)**
temple **der Tempel(-)**
theater **das Theater(-)**
tomb **das Grab(¨er)**
tower **der Turm(¨e)**
town centre/downtown **die Stadtmitte(n)**
town hall **das Rathaus(¨er)**
university **die Universität(en)**
wall **die Mauer(-)**
zoo **der Zoo(s)**

20a On the beach

bathing hut/cabana **die Badekabine(n)**
beach **der Strand(¨e)**
beach ball **der Wasserball(¨e)**
bucket and spade/pail and shovel **der Eimer(-) und die Schaufel(-)**
deck-chair **der Liegestuhl(¨e)**
I dive **ich springe, ich tauche**
diver **der Taucher(-) [-in]**
sand **der Sand** (no pl)
grain of sand **das Sandkorn(¨er)**
sandcastle **die Sandburg(en)**
sandy beach **der Sandstrand(¨e)**
scuba diving **das Sporttauchen**
sea **das Meer(e)**
sea shore **der Strand(¨e)**

snorkel das Schnorchel(-)
I go snorkelling ich gehe schnorcheln
suntan lotion das Sonnenöl(e)
sunshade der Sonnenschirm(e)
I surf ich surfe
surfboard das Surfbrett(er)
surfboarder der Surfer(-) [-in], der
  Wellenreiter(-) [-in]
surfing das Surfen, das Surfing
I swim ich schwimme
water skiing das Wasserskilaufen
windbreak der Windschutz *(no pl)*
windsurfing/sailboarding das
  Windsurfen
I go windsurfing ich windsurfe

**20a Countries/Regions
–adjectives–inhabitants**

All countries are neuter unless otherwise
shown. Where an article is shown, it should
always be used with the name of the country.

The adjective is normally used as a neuter
noun to form the language, e.g. **Englisch**
(sometimes **das Englische**). When used as an
adjective it always starts with a lower case letter, e,g. **englisch**.

The inhabitants are shown in the masculine
singular. They fall into the following groups:
– those ending in **-r** have no plural ending,
and form the feminine by adding **-in(nen)**;
– those ending in **-e** are weak masculine
nouns with an **-n** ending in every case except
the nominative; the feminine is formed by
dropping the **-e** and adding **-in(nen)**.
Note **der Franzose** fem. **die Französin**; **der
Schwabe** fem. **die Schwäbin**.
– **der Deutsche (ein Deutscher**, fem. **die/eine
Deutsche)** is an adjectival noun.

Africa **Afrika, afrikanisch, Afrikaner**
Alsace **Elsaß, elsässisch, Elsässer**
America **Amerika, amerikanisch,
  Amerikaner**
Arabia **Arabien, arabisch, Araber**
Argentina **Argentinien, argentinisch,
  Argentinier**

Asia **Asien, asiatisch, Asiat(en)** *(wk)*
Australia **Australien, australisch, der
  Australier**
Austria **Österreich, österreichisch, der
  Österreicher**
Bavaria **Bayern, bayrisch, Bayer**
Belgium **Belgien, belgisch, Belgier**
Bosnia **Bosnien, bosnisch, Bosnier**
Brazil **Brasilien, brasilianisch,
  Brasilianer**
Bulgaria **Bulgarien, bulgarisch,
  Bulgare**
Canada **Kanada, kanadisch, Kanadier**
China **China, chinesisch, Chinese**
Czech Republic **die Tschechische
  Republik, tschechisch, Tscheche**
Denmark **Dänemark, dänisch, Däne**
Egypt **Ägypten, ägyptisch, Ägypter**
England **England, englisch,
  Engländer**
Europe **Europa, europäisch, Europäer**
Finland **Finnland, finnisch, Finne**
France **Frankreich, französisch,
  Franzose**
Germany **Deutschland, deutsch,
  Deutsche** *(adj/n)*
Great Britain **Großbritannien, britisch,
  Brite**
Greece **Griechenland, griechisch,
  Grieche**
Holland **Holland, holländisch,
  Holländer**
Hungary **Ungarn, ungarisch, Ungar**
Iceland **Island, isländisch, Isländer**
India **Indien, indisch, Inder**
Iran **der Iran, iranisch, Iraner**
Iraq **der Iraq, irakisch, Iraker**
Ireland **Irland, irish, Ire**
Israel **Israel, hebräisch, Israeli(s)**
Italy **Italien, italienisch, Italiener**
Japan **Japan, japanisch, Japaner**
Lebanon **der Libanon, libanesisch,
  Libanese**
Lorraine **Lothringen, lothringisch,
  Lothringer**
Luxemburg **Luxemburg,
  luxemburgisch, Luxemburger**

SUBJECT INDEX

Morocco **Marokko, marokkanisch, Marokkaner**

Netherlands **die Niederlande, niederländisch, Niederländer**

New Zealand **Neuseeland, neuseeländisch, Neuseeländer**

Northern Ireland **Nordirland, nordirisch, Nordire**

Norway **Norwegen, norwegisch, Norweger**

Pakistan **Pakistan, pakistanisch, Pakistaner**

Palestine **Palästina, palästinensisch, Palästinenser**

Poland **Polen, polnisch, Pole**

Portugal **Portugal, portugiesisch, Portugiese**

Romania **Rumänien, rumänisch, Rumäne**

Russia **Rußland, russisch, Russe**

Saudi Arabia **Saudi-Arabien, saudiarabisch, Saudi(s)**

Scandinavia **Skandinavien, skandinavisch, Skandinavier**

Scotland **Schottland, schottisch, Schotte**

Slovakia **die Slowakei, slowakisch, Slowake**

South Africa **Südafrika, südafrikanisch, Südafrikaner**

South America **Südamerika, südamerikanisch, Südamerikaner**

Spain **Spanien, spanisch, Spanier**

Sudan **der Sudan, sudanesisch, Sudanese**

Swabia **Schwaben, schwäbisch, Schwabe**

Sweden **Schweden, schwedisch, Schwede**

Switzerland **die Schweiz, schweizerisch, Schweizer**

Turkey **die Türkei, türkisch, Türke**

Wales **Wales, walisisch, Waliser**

The East German states **die neuen Bundesländer**

European Community **die Europäische Gemeinschaft**

European Union **die Europäische Union**

The Far East **der Ferne Osten**

The Near East **der Nahe Osten**

United Kingdom **das Vereinigte Königreich**

United States **die Vereinigten Staaten, die USA** *(pl)*

Former countries

Czechoslovakia **die Tschechoslowakei**

East Germany **die DDR (Deutsche Demokratische Republik)**

Jugoslavia **Jugoslawien**

West Germany **die BRD (die Bundesrepublik Deutschland)**

Soviet Union **die Sowjetunion**

Soviet *(adj)* **sowjetisch**

USSR **die UdSSR** *(pl)*

20a Some towns

The adjectives are formed in most cases by adding **-er**. The capital letter is retained, e.g. **der Kölner Dom.**

Note: **Basler, hannoverisch, mailändisch, Münchner, römisch.**

The inhabitant ends in **-er**, fem. **-erin**. Note: **Hannoveraner, Mailänder, Münchner, Römer.**

Aix -la-Chapelle **Aachen**

Antwerp **Antwerpen**

Athens **Athen**

Basle **Basel**

Belgrade **Belgrad**

Bruges **Brügge**

Brussels **Brüssel**

Cairo **Kairo**

Cologne **Köln**

Dunkirk **Dünkirchen**

Edinburgh **Edinburg**

Geneva **Genf**

the Hague **Den Haag**

Hanover **Hannover**

Liege **Lüttich**

Lisbon **Lissabon**

Milan **Mailand**

Moscow **Moskau**
Mulhouse **Mülhausen**
Munich **München**
Naples **Neapel**
Nice **Nizza**
Nuremberg **Nürnberg**
Prague **Prag**
Rome **Rom**
Strasbourg **Straßburg**
Venice **Venedig**
Vienna **Wien**
Warsaw **Warschau**
Zurich **Zürich**

20a Rivers, lakes, mountains

Alps **die Alpen**
Antarctic **die Antarktis**
Antarctic Circle **der südliche Polarkreis**
Antartic Ocean **das Südpolarmeer**
Arctic **die Arktis**
Arctic Circle **der nördliche Polarkreis**
Arctic Ocean **das Nordpolarmeer**
Atlantic **der Atlantik**
Baltic **die Ostsee**
Caspian Sea **das Kaspische Meer**
Danube **die Donau**
Dead Sea **das Tote Meer**
Everest **der Mount Everest**
Himalayas **der Himalaja**
Lake Constance **der Bodensee**
Mediterranean **das Mittelmeer**
Moselle **die Mosel**
North Pole **der Nordpol**
North See **die Nordsee**
Pacific **der Pazifik, der Stille Ozean**
Pyrenees **die Pyrenäen**
Red Sea **das Rote Meer**
Rhine **der Rhein**
South Pole **der Südpol**
Thames **die Themse**
Vesuvius **der Vesuv**
Volga **die Wolga**

21a Languages*

Afrikaans **Afrikaans**
Basque **Baskisch**

Celtic *(adj)* **keltisch**
Flemish **Flämisch**
Gaelic **Gälisch**
Germanic *(adj)* **germanisch**
Hindi **Hindi**
Indo-European *(adj)* **indoeuropäisch**
Indo-Germanic *(adj)* **indogermanisch**
Latin **Latein, Lateinische**
Low German **Plattdeutsch**
Romance *(adj)* **romanisch**
Slavonic *(adj)* **slawisch**
Swiss German **Schweizerdeutsch**
Urdu **Urdu**

21b Grammar

accusative **der Akkusativ**
  accusative *(adj)* **Akkusativ-**
adjective **das Adjektiv(e)**
adverb **das Adverb(ien)**
agreement **die Übereinstimmung(en)**
it agrees with **es stimmt mit +dat überein***
article **der Artikel(-)**
case **der Fall(ˉe)**
case ending **die Endung(en)**
clause **der Satz(ˉe)**
comparative **der Komparativ**
conjunction **die Konjunktion(en)**
dative **der Dativ**
declension **die Deklination(en)**
definite **bestimmt**
demonstrative **Demonstrativ-**
direct object **das direkte Objekt(e)**
exception **die Ausnahme(n)**
feminine **weiblich**
gender **das Geschlecht(er)**
genitive **der Genitiv**
indefinite **unbestimmt**
indirect object **das indirekte Objekt(e)**
interrogative **der Interrogativ**
masculine **männlich**
negative **negativ**
neuter **sächlich**
nominative **der Nominativ**
noun **das Substantiv(e), das Nomen(-)**
object **das Objekt(e)**
phrase **die Phrase(n)**

* For other languages ➤App.20a Countries/Regions-adjectives-inhabitants

plural **der Plural, die Mehrzahl**
possessive **Possessiv-**
prefix **die Vorsilbe(n)**
preposition **die Präposition(en)**
pronoun **das Pronomen (-a)**
   interrogative **das Interrrogativpronomen**
   personal **das Personalpronomen**
   relative **das Relativpronomen**
reflexive **Reflexiv-**
rule **die Regel(n)**
sequence (of words) **die Wortfolge(n)**
singular **die Einzahl, der Singular**
suffix **die Nachsilbe(n)**
superlative **der Superlativ(e)**
subject **das Subjekt(e)**
syntax **die Syntax**
word order **die Wortstellung(en)**

Verbs

active voice **das Aktiv**
auxiliary **das Hilfsverb(en)**
compound **zusammengesetzt**
conditional **der Konditional**
formation **die Bildung(en)**
future **das Futur**
gerund **das Gerundium**
imperative **der Imperativ**
imperfect **das Imperfekt**
impersonal **unpersönlich**
infinitive **der Infinitiv**
intransitive **intransitiv**
irregular **unregelmäßig**
passive voice **das Passiv**
participle **das Partizip**
   past participle **das Partizip Perfekt**
past **die Vergangenheit**
   past *(adj)* **vergangen**
perfect **das Perfekt**
person **die Person(en)**
   first person singular **erste Person Singular**
present **das Präsens**
reflexive **das Reflexiv**
   reflexive *(adj)* **reflexiv**
regular **regelmäßig**

sequence (of verbs) **die Zeitenfolge(n)**
simple **einfach**
stem **der Stamm(-̈e)**
strong **stark**
subjunctive **der Konjunktiv**
system **das System(e)**
tense **die Zeitform(en)**
transitive **transitiv**
use **der Gebrauch**
verb **das Verb(en)**
weak **schwach**

21b Punctuation

apostrophe **der Apostroph(e)**
asterisk **das Sternchen(-)**
bracket **die Klammer(n)**
colon **der Doppelpunkt(e)**
comma **das Komma(s)**
dash **der Bindestrich(e)**
decimal point **das Komma(s)**
exclamation mark **das Ausrufezeichen(-)**
full stop/period **der Punkt(e)**
quotation mark **das Anführungszeichen(-)**
parentheses **die Klammer(n)**
question mark **das Fragezeichen(-)**
semicolon **das Semikolon(s), der Strichpunkt(e)**

22b The class in Germany

die Vorklasse(n) reception class
die Grundstufe(n) primary phase
die erste Klasse Class 1 (age 6/7)
die zweite Klasse Class 2 (age 7/8)
die dritte Klasse Class 3 (age 8/9)
die vierte Klasse Class 4 (age 9/10)
die Orientierungsstufe(n) transition phase
die fünfte Klasse Class 5 (age 10/11)
die sechste Klasse Class 6 (age 11/12)
die Sekundarstufe(n) secondary phase
die siebte Klasse Class 7 (age 12/13)
die achte Klasse Class 8 (age 13/14)
die neunte Klasse Class 9 (age 14/15
die zehnte Klasse Class 10 (age 15/16)

die Oberstufe(n) sixth form/final years
in der Oberstufe in the sixth form/final
  years
die Einführungsphase Class 11 (age
  16/17)
die elfte Klasse Class 11 (age 16/17)
die zwölfte Klasse (die Unterprima)
  Class 12 (age 17/18)
die dreizehnte Klasse (die Oberprima)
  Class 13 (age 18/19)

22b Stationery

adhesive tape **der Tesafilm**
ball-point **der Kugelschreiber(-)**
biro **der Kuli(s)**
boardrubber/eraser **der Schwamm(-̈e)**
carbon paper **das Kohlepapier**
card index **die Kartei(en)**
chalk **die Kreide(n)**
clip board **das Klemmbrett(er)**
compasses **der Zirkel(-)**
correction fluid **die
  Korrekkurflüssigkeit(en)**
diary/datebook **der Terminkalender(-)**
drawing pin **die Reißzwecke(n)**
envelope **der Briefumschlag(-̈e)**
exercise book **das Heft(e)**
felt-tip **der Filzstift(e)**
fiber/fiber-tip **der Faserschreiber(-)**
file **die Akte(n)**
filing cabinet **der Aktenschrank(-̈e)**
fountain pen **der Füllfederhalter(-)**
glue **der Klebstoff(e)**
highlighter **der Textmarker(-)**
hole punch **der Locher(-)**
ink **die Tinte(n)**
ink refill **die Nachfüllpatrone(n)**
in-tray/out-tray **die Ablage für
  Eingänge/Ausgänge**
label **das Etikett(e)**
marker **der Stift(e), der Marker(-)**
note book **das Notizbuch(-̈er)**
note paper **das Briefpapier(e)**
OHP **der Overheadprojector**
paper **das Papier(e)**
paper clip **die Büroklammer(n)**
paper cutter **die Schneidemaschine**

pen **der Stift(e)**
pencil **der Bleistift(e)**
photocopier **der Kopierer(-)**
pocket calculator **der Taschenrechner(-)**
protractor **der Winkelmesser(-)**
ring binder **der Ringordner(-)**
rubber band/elastic band **das
  Gummiband(-̈er)**
rubber/eraser **der Radiergummi(s)**
ruler **das Lineal(e)**
scissors **die Schere(n)**
screen **der Bildschirm(e)**
set square **das Zeichendreieck(e)**
sheet of paper **das Blatt(-̈er)**
shredder **der Papierwolf(-̈e)**
stamp **der Stempel(-)**
stapler **der Bürohefter(-)**
staple remover **der
  Heftklammerentferner(-)**
textbook **das Lehrbuch(-̈er)**
typewriter **die Schreibmaschine(n)**
typewriter ribbon **das Farbband(-̈er)**
transparency **das Transparent(e), die
  Folie(n)**
wastepaper basket **der Abfalleimer(-),
  der Papierkorb(-̈e)**
whiteboard **die Weißwand(-̈e)**

23a Scientific disciplines

applied sciences **die angewandten
  Wissenschaft(en)**
anthropology **die Anthropologie(n)**
astronomy **die Astronomie**
biochemistry **die Biochemie**
biology **die Biologie**
botany **die Botanik**
chemistry **die Chemie**
geology **die Geologie**
medicine **die Medizin**
microbiology **die Mikrobiologie**
physics **die Physik**
physical sciences **die
  Naturwissenschaft(en)**
physiology **die Physiologie**
psychology **die Psychologie**
social sciences **die
  Sozialwissenschaft(en)**

technology **die Technologie(n)**
zoology **die Zoologie**

23b Chemical elements

aluminium/aluminum **das Aluminium**
arsenic **das Arsenik**
calcium **das Kalzium**
carbon **der Kohlenstoff**
chlorine **das Chlor**
copper **das Kupfer**
gold **das Gold**
hydrogen **der Wasserstoff**
iodine **das Jod**
iron **das Eisen**
lead **das Blei**
magnesium **das Magnesium**
mercury **das Quecksilber**
nitrogen **der Stickstoff**
oxygen **der Sauerstoff**
phosphorus **der Phosphor**
platinum **das Platin**
plutonium **das Plutonium**
potassium **das Kalium**
silver **das Silber**
sodium **das Natrium**
sulphur **der Schwefel**
uranium **das Uran**
zinc **das Zink**

23b Minerals, compounds & alloys

acetic acid **die Essigsäure(n)**
alloy **die Metallegierung(en)**
ammonia **das Ammoniak**
asbestos **der Asbest**
bauxite **der Bauxit**
brass **das Messing**
carbon dioxide **das Kohlendioxid(e)**
carbon monoxide **das Kohlenmonoxid(e)**
chalk **die Kreide(n)**
chalky **kalkhaltig**
clay **der Lehm**
copper oxide **das Kupferoxid(e)**
diamond **der Diamant(en)** *(wk)*
granite **der Granit(e)**
graphite **der Graphit(e)**
hydrochloric acid **die Salzsäure(n)**

iron oxide **das Eisenoxid(e)**
lead oxide **das Bleioxid(e)**
lime **der Kalk(e)**
limestone **der Kalkstein(e)**
loam **der Lehm**
marble **der Marmor**
nickel **der Nickel**
nitric acid **die Salpetersäure(n)**
it oxidizes **es oxydiert**
ore **das Erz(e)**
ozone **das Ozon**
propane **das Propan**
quartz **der Quarz(e)**
sand **der Sand**
sandstone **der Sandstein(e)**
silica **die Kieselerde**
silver nitrate **das Silbernitrat(e)**
slate **der Schiefer**
sodium bicarbonate **das Natron**
sodium carbonate **das Natriumkarbonat(e)**
sodium chloride **das Natriumchlorid(e)**
sulphuric acid **die Schwefelsäure(n)**
tin **das Zinn**

23c The zodiac

Aries **der Widder(-)**
Taurus **der Stier(e)**
Gemini **die Zwillinge (pl)**
Cancer **der Krebs(e)**
Leo **der Löwe(n)**
Virgo **die Jungfrau(en)**
Libra **die Waage(n)**
Scorpio **der Skorpion(e)**
Sagittarius **der Schütze(n)**
Capricorn **der Steinbock(¨e)**
Aquarius **der Wassermann(¨-er)**
Pisces **die Fische** *(pl)*

23c Planets & stars

Earth **die Erde**
Venus **die Venus**
Mercury **der Merkur**
Pluto **der Pluto**
Mars **der Mars**
Jupiter **der Jupiter**
Saturn **der Saturn**

Uranus **der Uranus**
Neptune **der Neptun**
Pole star **der Polarstern**
Halley's comet **der Halleysche Komet**
Southern cross **das Kreuz des Südens**
Great Bear **der Große Bär** *(wk)*

24a Geographical features

archipelago **der Archipel(e)**
bank *(river)* **das Ufer(-)**
bay **die Bucht(en)**
beach **der Strand(̈-e)**
canyon **der Cañon(s)**
cliff **die Klippe(n)**
coast(line) **die Küste(n)**
creek **der Bach(̈-e)**
current **die Strömung(en), der Strom**
delta **das Delta(s)**
desert **die Wüste(n)**
escarpment **der Steilhang(̈-e), die Böschung(en)**
estuary **die Mündung(en)**
fjord **der Fjord(e)**
foothills **die Gebirgsausläufer** *(pl)*
forest **der Wald(̈-er)**
  coniferous forest **der Nadelwald(̈-er)**
  deciduous forest **der Laubwald(̈-er)**
geyser **der Geysir(e)**
heath **die Heide**
hill **der Hügel(-), der Berg(e)**
island **die Insel(n), die Hallig(en)**
jungle **der Dschungel(-), der Urwald(̈-er)**
lake **der See(n)**
marsh **der Sumpf(̈-e)**
meadow **die Wiese(n)**
moor **das Hochmoor(e)**
mountain **der Berg(e)**
  mountains **das Gebirge(-)**
  mountain range **die Bergkette(n), die Gebirgskette(n)**
mudflat **das Watt**
ocean **der Ozean(e), das Meer(e)**
ocean floor **der Meeresboden(̈-)**
peak **der Gipfel(-), die Bergspitze(n)**
peninsula **die Halbinsel(n)**

plateau **das Plateau(s), die Hochebene(n)**
reef **das Riff(e)**
ridge **der Rücken**
river **der Fluß (̈-sse)**
  river *(major)* **der Strom(̈-e)**
riverbed **das Flußbett(en)**
rockpool **die Vertiefung in einer Felsplatte**
sea **die See(n), das Meer(e)**
  shallow sea **das Wattenmeer**
by the seaside **am Meer**
shore **das Ufer(-), der Strand(̈-e)**
spring **die Quelle(n)**
steppe **die Steppe(n)**
stream **der Bach(̈-e), die Strömung(en)**
tundra **die Tundra (-en)**
valley **das Tal(̈-er)**
volcano **der Vulkan(e)**
waterfall **der Wasserfall(̈-e)**
woods **der Wald(̈-er)**
woodland **das Waldland(̈-er)**

24b Wild animals

badger **der Dachs(e)**
bear **der Bär(en)** *(wk)*
beaver **der Biber(-)**
bison/buffalo **der Büffel(-)**
coyote **der Kojote(n)** *(wk)*
deer **der Hirsch(e)**
elephant **der Elefant(en)** *(wk)*
elk **der Waldhirsch(e)**
fox **der Fuchs(̈-e)**
frog **der Frosch(̈-e)**
grizzly bear **der Grizzlybär(en)** *(wk)*
hare **der Hase(n)**
hedgehog **der Igel(-)**
lion **der Löwe(n)** *(wk)*
lizard **die Eidechse(n)**
mole **der Maulwurf(̈-e)**
monkey **der Affe(n)** *(wk)*
moose **der Elch(e)**
mouse **die Maus(̈-e)**
otter **der Otter(-)**
rat **die Ratte(n)**
reindeer **das Ren(e)**

snake die Schlange(n)
tiger der Tiger(-)
toad die Kröte(n)
whale der Wal(e)
wildcat die Wildkatze(n)
wolf der Wolf(ˉe)

24b Birds

albatross der Albatros(se)
blackbird die Amsel(n)
bluetit/chickadee die Blaumeise(n)
budgerigar der Wellensittich(e)
buzzard der Bussard(e)
chaffinch der Buchfink(en)
crow die Krähe(n)
dove die Taube(n)
eagle der Adler(-)
    golden eagle der Steinadler(-)
emu der Emu(s)
hawk/falcon der Falke(n) *(wk)*, der Habicht(e)
heron der Reiher(-)
hummingbird der Kolibri(s)
kingfisher der Eisvogel(ˉ)
magpie die Elster(n)
ostrich der Strauß(e)
owl die Eule(n)
parrot der Papagei(en)
peacock der Pfau(e)
pelican der Pelikan(e)
penguin der Pinguin(e)
robin das Rotkehlchen(-)
seagull die Möwe(n)
sparrow der Sperling(e), der Spatz(en)
starling der Star(e)
swallow die Schwalbe(n)
swan der Schwan(ˉe)
swift der Mauersegler(-)
thrush die Drossel(n)
woodpecker der Specht(e)
wren der Zaunkönig(e)

24b Animal body parts

beak der Schnabel(ˉ)
claw die Kralle(n)
comb der Kamm(ˉe)
feather die Feder(n)

fin die Flosse(n)
fleece das Schaffell(e)
fur der Pelz(e)
gills die Kieme(n)
hide das Fell(e)
hoof der Huf(e)
mane die Mähne(n)
paw die Pfote(n), die Tatze(n)
pelt der Pelz(e), das Fell(e)
scale die Schuppe(n)
shell die Schale(n)
tail der Schwanz(ˉe)
trunk der Rüssel(-)
tusk der Stoßzahn(ˉe)
udder das Euter(-)
wing der Flügel(-)

24c Trees

apple tree der Apfelbaum(ˉe)
ash die Esche(n)
beech die Buche(n)
cherry tree der Kirschbaum(ˉe)
chestnut der Kastanienbaum(ˉe)
cypress die Zypresse(n)
eucalyptus der Eukalyptusbaum(ˉe)
fig tree der Feigenbaum(ˉe)
fir tree die Tanne(n), die Fichte(n)
fruit tree der Obstbaum(ˉe)
holly die Stechpalme(n)
maple der Ahornbaum(ˉe)
oak die Eiche(n)
olive tree der Olivenbaum(ˉe)
palm die Palme(n)
peach tree der Pfirsichbaum(ˉe)
pear tree der Birnbaum(ˉe)
pine die Kiefer(n)
plum tree der Pflaumenbaum(ˉe)
poplar die Pappel(n)
rhododendron der Rhododendron (-en)
walnut tree der Walnußbaum(ˉe)
willow die Weide(n)
yew die Eibe(n)

24c Flowers & weeds

azalea die Azalee(n)
cactus der Kaktus (-een)

carnation **die Nelke(n)**
chrysanthemum **die Chrysantheme(n)**
clover **der Klee**
crocus **der Krokus(se)**
daffodil **die Osterglocke(n)**
dahlia **die Dahlie(n)**
daisy **das Gänseblümchen(-)**
dandelion **der Löwenzahn(-̈e)**
foxglove **der Fingerhut(-̈e)**
fern **der Farn(e), das Farnkraut(-̈er)**
geranium **die Geranie(n)**
hydrangea **die Hortensie(n)**
lily **die Seerose(n), die Lilie(n)**
lily of the valley **das Maiglöckchen(-)**
nettle (stinging) **die Nessel(n)**
orchid **die Orchidee(n)**
pansy **das Stiefmütterchen(-)**
poppy **der Mohn**
primrose **die Erdschlüsselblume(n)**
rose **die Rose(n)**
snowdrop **das Schneeglöckchen(-)**
sunflower **die Sonnenblume(n)**
thistle **die Distel(n)**
tulip **die Tulpe(n)**
violet **das Veilchen(-)**

25b Political institutions

assembly **die Versammlung(en)**
association **der Verein(e), der Verband(-̈e)**
cabinet **das Kabinett(e)**
  shadow cabinet *(UK)* **das Schattenkabinett**
confederation **der Bund(-̈e)**
congress **der Kongreß (-sse)**
council **der (Stadt)rat(-̈e)**
federal council **der Bundesrat(-̈e)**
federal government **der Bundestag(e)**
federation **der Staatenbund(-̈e)**
House of Representatives **das Repräsentantenhaus**
local authority **die Behörde(n)**
Lower Chamber/House **das Unterhaus(-̈er)**
parliament *(UK)* **das Parlament(e)**
party **die Partei(en), die Fraktion(en)**
Senate **der Senat(e)**

state parliament **der Landtag(e)**
town council **der Stadtrat(-̈e)**
town hall **das Rathaus(-̈er)**
Upper House/Chamber **das Oberhaus(-̈er)**

25b Representatives & politicians

Chancellor **der Kanzler(-) [-in]**
  federal chancellor **der Bundeskanzler(-)**
congressman/woman **der/die Kongreßabgeordnete** *(adj/n)*
Foreign Minister/Secretary of State **der Außenminister(-) [-in]**
head of state **das Staatsoberhaupt(-̈er)**
leader **der Fraktionschef(s) [-in]**
leader of the party/party leader **der/die Parteivorsitzende** *(adj/n)*
mayor **der Bürgermeister(-) [-in]**
member of parliament **der/die Abgeordnete** *(adj/n)*
minister **der Minister(-) [-in]**
Home Secretary/Minister of the Interior **der Innenminister(-) [-in]**
politician **der Politiker(-) [-in]**
President **der Präsident(en)** *(wk)* **[-in]**
  federal president **der Bundespräsident(en)** *(wk)* **[-in]**
Prime Minister **der Premierminister(-) [-in]**
representative **der/die Abgeordnete** *(adj/n)*
senator **der Senator(en)**
Speaker **der (Regierungs)sprecher(-) [-in], der/die Vorsitzende** *(adj/n)*

German political parties

BRD/Bundesrepublik Deutschland
  German Federal Republic
FDP/Freie Demokratische Partei Free Democratic party
die Grünen/Bündnis 90 Green parties
CDU/Christlich-Demokratische Union
  Christian Democratic Union
CSU/Christlich-Soziale Union
  Christian-Social Union

PDS/Partei des Demokratischen
  Sozialismus Democratic Socialism
  Party
KPD/Kommunistische Partei
  Deutschlands Communist Party
SPD Sozialdemokratische Partei
  Deutschlands Social Democratic
  Party

27b Military ranks

admiral **der Admiral(e/̈-e)**
air marshal **der Marschall(̈-e) der**
  Luftstreitkräfte
brigadier **der Brigadegeneral(e)**
captain **der Hauptmann(̈-er) (-leute)**
commodore **der Flotillenadmiral(e/̈-e)**
corporal **der Obergefreite** *(adj/n)*
field marshal **der Feldmarschall(̈-e)**
general **der General(e)**
lieutenant **der Leutnant(s)**
major **der Major(e)**
private **der einfache Soldat(en)** *(wk)*
rear-admiral **der Konteradmiral(e/̈-e)**

sergeant **der Feldwebel(-)**
sergeant-major **der Oberfeldwebel(-)**

27c International organizations

Council of Europe **der Europarat**
Council of Ministers **der Ministerrat**
EC/European Community **die**
  Europäische Gemeinschaft, EG
EU/European Union **die Europäische**
  Union, EU
NATO/North Atlantic Treaty Organization
  die Nato
OECD/Organization for Economic
  Cooperation and Development **die**
  OECD
Security Council **der Sicherheitsrat**
United Nations **die Vereinten**
  Nationen, die UN
WHO/World Health Organization **die**
  Weltgesundheitsorganisation, die
  WGO
World Bank **die Weltbank**

D
VOCABULARY INDEX

Vocabulary index

References are to Vocabulary Topics

VOCABULARY INDEX